THE RUSSIANS ARE COMING

THE POLITICS OF ANTI-SOVIETISM

BY THE SAME AUTHOR

Power in Trade Unions (Longmans, 1954)
Trade Union Leadership (Longmans, 1957)
Trade Unions and the Government (Longmans, 1960)
Militant Trade Unionism (Merlin Press, 1966)
International Bibliography of Trade Unionism (Merlin Press and Maspero, 1968)
The Sociology of Industrial Relations (Longman, 1971)
Social Analysis: A Marxist Critique and Alternative (Longman, 1975; The Moor Press, 1982)
The Militancy of British Miners (The Moor Press, 1981)

THE RUSSIANS ARE COMING

V. L. ALLEN

THE POLITICS OF ANTI-SOVIETISM

THE MOOR PRESS

Published by
The Moor Press
Bank House
Baildon Green,
Shipley, BD17 5JA

First published 1987

ISBN 0 907698 03 4 Cased
ISBN 0 907698 04 2 Paper

Printed in Great Britain by Fretwell & Cox Ltd.,
Goulbourne Street, Keighley, West Yorkshire

*To
Sheila,
Sophie
and
Lucy*

Contents

PART III

POWER IN THE USA

Charts

Tables

Introduction

There have been reasons for an analysis of anti-Sovietism ever since the Bolshevik Revolution almost 70 years ago. Since 1945, however, when the USA acquired the first atomic bomb, the need has become increasingly critical. My own reasons for attempting it lie in that crisis but were given clarity and urgency by two particular factors which stem from an invitation in 1982 from the All-Union Central Council of Trade Unions in Moscow to write about Soviet trade unions. I visited the Soviet Union to collect data and consulted all the available Western literature. I tried to place unions historically in the context of the development of Soviet society as a whole. This involved reading the extensive body of doctoral dissertations which have passed the scrutiny of external examiners and articles in learned journals which have been assessed by specialist referees.

It is generally recognized that the media, with the sole exception of the *Morning Star*, is hostile towards the Soviet Union. This phenomenon is common-place. We live with it and barely notice its existence. What is not generally recognized, however, is that virtually all literature about the Soviet Union contains a bias against it. It exaggerates the defects of Soviet society and either ignores or misrepresents its virtues. A Soviet admission of failure is perceived as a problem; the recognition of a problem constitutes a crisis. I found then that the academic literature was equally liable to misrepresent Soviet society as the mass media. In a sense it preceded it for much that was generally reported about the Soviet Union was legitimated by the finely bound volumes which emanated from universities and research institutes in Western capitalist societies. This bias was wrapped up in the jargon of academic disciplines and disguised by claims of impartiality and objectivity. But this made it more offensive for me. Eventually I became more concerned about the distortion of events in Soviet history than about the events themselves and felt impelled

xiii

to tackle the issue of prejudice against the Soviet Union before I could proceed with the analysis of trade unions.

I arrived in Moscow early in October 1982 and stayed for more than three months in order to collect data about trade unionism. The day following my arrival I sat in the office of the Vice-Rector of the Higher Trade Union School in Moscow, Professor Marat Baglai, to discuss my research plan. I wanted to cover as much of the Soviet Union as possible and to meet people at different institutional layers from unions, management and the Communist Party. So he laid a map of the country before me and through Moscow thus drew lines diagonally across it covering all the main areas. I visited each of those areas and saw something of all the regions of the Soviet Union except Eastern Siberia and the far eastern coast. I went to the institutions of my choice and talked with whomsoever I pleased.

1982 was a tense year in international relations. Both British and American governments were abrasive with the Soviet Union. NATO had decided three years previously to introduce Cruise and Pershing missiles into Europe and massive peace demonstrations had been held in protest. There were fast-growing Peace Movements in all the Western European countries chosen for the missiles. The spectre of a nuclear war began to haunt thinking people everywhere.

My concern in travelling around the Soviet Union was to ask questions about unions and their relationships with workers, the Communist Party and the government. Most people I met, however, also wanted to ask me questions and almost without exception these dealt with the issue of nuclear weapons, disarmament and the attitude of NATO countries towards the Soviet Union. Ordinary people everywhere, in the factories, farms, clinics and shops, showed a deep interest in international politics and were engaged in an intense and knowledgeable debate about it.

I was surprised, therefore, to read in the British press on my return the allegation that the Soviet government prohibited a free discussion of this vital issue and that there was no Peace Movement which represented the interests of ordinary people. It was argued that as the Peace Movement agreed with the policy of the Soviet government it must therefore be 'official' and controlled by it. I decided then to share my experiences of discussions in the Soviet Union with members of the Peace Movement in Britain. I visited many CND groups and became active in the leadership of national CND. I wrote letters and articles for the press about nuclear disarmament and the Soviet Union. I gave lectures on the topic, one of which, given to the J D Bernal Peace Library in 1983, was published as a pamphlet called *Images and Reality in the Soviet Union.*

These activities reinforced my belief that a thorough going examination of Western attitudes towards the Soviet Union was necessary. I encountered a disturbing degree of anti-Soviet bias amongst the national leadership of CND which was not present in the local groups. But more importantly I came to realize how the constant misrepresentation of Soviet life had given rise to a stereotype of the Soviet Union as the enemy of Western capitalist countries. This stereotype became the justification for the massive build-up of nuclear arms in the West. The Soviet Union had always been portrayed as an enemy but with the invention of nuclear weapons the portrayal was given a new sickening twist. Insofar as anti-Sovietism was used to justify the production of nuclear arms then it had become an issue of major international proportions. Indeed it is now the most important single issue in contemporary history. This factor added urgency to the task.

The story which unfolded is contained in the following chapters. Writing it was a constant learning process. I was surprised by the intensity of the hostility towards the Soviet Union and by the magnitude of the lies and distortions about it. Intellectually I knew, of course, that the conflict between the West and the Soviet Union was about power relations but what in practice did it entail? What was the meaning of anti-Sovietism? The West's attitude towards the Soviet Union had no historical antecedents. It did not contain the usual ingredients in national stereotyping such as familiarity, close proximity or competition. It was not about material matters such as access to markets or sources of raw materials.

The pre-eminent quality of the Soviet Union insofar as Western capitalist societies are concerned is that it is a land without capitalists. It stands as a model of an alternative form of society to all the exploited and aggrieved people in capitalist societies. It is, therefore, by its very existence and without taking any action, a continual threat to capitalism. Anti-Sovietism is an attempt to distort and exaggerate that threat by the constant drip of hostile propaganda, denigrating Soviet principles and practices of govern-ment, Soviet mannerisms and ideology, indeed all facets of Soviet life and re-constituting them as alien, hostile, frightening and threatening to everything good for which Western democracies are alleged to stand.

Those who defend capitalism by initiating and practising anti-Sovietism are really protecting their own access to wealth, privilege and authority but they are not doing it in a conscious, Machiavellian way. They can beat their breasts and protest their good intentions in all honesty because anti-Sovietism is a panoply of self-protective measures which arise out of the system itself. They do not have to be invented, organized and co-ordinated though doubtless there are people who think of new ways of denigration, who devise more effective means of destabilization and who collect finance to co-ordinate their application. Anti-Sovietism is an expression of one system of power struggling against another. As an abstraction it has occurred before. The transition from a feudal to a capitalist system of power relations was long and, for many people, painful but there was never a conscious on-going recognition of a clash of political systems as there is now. The present transition is distinguished too by the scale of international communications and the effectiveness of modern means of information technology. For this reason anti-Sovietism has internationally common features and appears as a planned, concerted and co-ordinated series of actions.

Put in this way anti-Sovietism is an historically inevitable and inexorable process. Come what may, the holders of power under capitalism use whatever means they have to retain it and anti-Sovietism is one such way. It is inconceivable that they would acquiesce in a workers' revolution or voluntarily accept a democratic verdict that they should move over for the poor and exploited. We are continually being made aware of this fact. The struggle between competing systems of power is occurring and cannot be glossed over. In this struggle the capitalists are prepared to take almost unbelievable risks. They are, however, almost always risks which are borne by others. Millions of poor people made poorer, millions killed in wars and lies also by the million published in praise of capitalism and in condemnation of communism. In its vendettas against humanity anti-Sovietism puts the Crusades in the shade. But there is now a risk which no-one can afford to take because there are no havens or off-shore islands for the refuge of besieged capitalists which would protect them. Everyone, regardless of class, would be a victim of a nuclear war in one way or another.

This raises two issues. First, in so far as a dispute between the

West and the USSR could lead to a nuclear conflict or, through the accumulation of nuclear weapons to a nuclear accident, then everyone should be concerned about anti-Sovietism. Indeed, even so long as nuclear weapons are simply being produced everyone is affected by anti-Sovietism. People everywhere are denied resources for social purposes because of arms production. Those with least in Third World countries suffer most. Anti-Sovietism, therefore, is not just the concern of political activists. It plays a vital role in the lives of all people.

Second, conflicts which arise out of the transformation of the capitalist system and the rise of socialist forms take on a new frightening dimension with the presence of nuclear weapons. Capitalists risk destroying what they seek to protect while socialism becomes possible only if peace is preserved. There have, therefore, to be rules governing the relationship between the two political systems which preclude the use of nuclear weapons. The most effective rule would be that which abolished nuclear weapons altogether for so long as they exist, even in small quantities, they can be used. Failing the complete abolition of nuclear weapons, means have to be devised to prevent the escalation of conflicts to nuclear ones. It must enter into everyone's consciousness that a new situation exists in international relations which precludes those old habits and practices which exacerbate conflicts and encourage wars. Anti-Sovietism is the most dangerous of them.

I encountered a number of problems in writing about the Soviet Union. Social research is often just a means of confirming obvious generalizations. My own investigations did that over the manner in which prejudice was generated against Soviet communism and the ways in which this led to enemy stereotyping. It provided me with a factual basis for believing what in general terms I already believed. In order, however, to test the accuracy of the enemy stereotyping it was necessary to examine the elements of Soviet reality which were used for the stereotype. Here research was truly informative. This can be seen in Part II, in particular the chapters dealing with Soviet Democracy and the Jewish Question.

There was a difficulty, however, concerning source material. Such is the bias against the Soviet Union that the use of Soviet data is prejudicial for a study for Western readers because they have been persuaded to be distrustful of it. The impression has been created that Soviet bureaucracy is continually at work, sifting and sorting through the mass of data about Soviet life to ensure that it makes a favourable public image abroad. The enemy, it is presumed, must be devious in all things; it can be trusted over nothing therefore even its data must be unreliable. On the other hand, Western data about the Soviet Union is so permeated with prejudice that to use it in an unadulterated form would simply perpetuate the prejudice. No concepts are immune to the influence of ideology. Those that concern the Soviet Union get their meaning, not from empirical evidence, but from the assumptions initially made about it. If the underlying premise is that the Soviet Union is "an evil empire" or "oppressively bureaucratic" or "intolerant of human rights" then everything subsequently written, every word, statement, conclusion will be as jaundiced as the initial assumption. What then can someone who wants to penetrate the reality of Soviet life do about this? Is the reality we perceive so enclosed in two impenetrable ideological cages that we have to choose one or the other?

It is a difficult problem which is made easier by being aware that it exists. There are no more prejudiced writers than the ones who believe that their work is value-free. I sought a way out of the dilemma by using information I had collected myself in the Soviet Union in combination with data from Western sources where the bias could be detected and isolated. I make no claim that what I have written in consequence is the truth or correct, only that it is nearer to reality than the works of those who have engaged in the business of distortion. In some instances I relied heavily on Western sources as in the case of Chapter Six 'The Jewish Question'. On that issue Western analysts have either ignored the implications of their information so that there is a dichotomy between their data and their conclusions or they have crammed the data into one end of their analytical boxes designed to pervert the Soviet Union, to come out at the other end as proof that it is a perversion.

Apart from this difficulty there is a general problem in writing about the Soviet Union. I am and always have been generally sympathetic towards its aims. This has not meant that I have endorsed all its methods or acquiesced in its mistakes. But I have tried to understand the reasons as a friend for whatever has happened. This book is a continued attempt at understanding. My political education began with a curiosity about the Bolshevik Revolution and was nurtured by the novels of Mikhael Sholokov and books such as *The Socialist Sixth of the World* by Hewlett

Johnson. I have never ceased to be curious. In so far as every book is in some ways a reflection of its author this reflects both my curiosity and my affinity with the Soviet Union. I do not believe that the Soviet Union is evil, imperialist or in any sense an enemy of the people in Western capitalist societies. This is not an act of faith but an analytical conclusion. When the bias is removed what remains is a country which is trying to create a society in which people can live without exploitation, discrimination, deprivation and instability. It has made mistakes and has suffered lapses but its motives remain commendable.

The problem arises because it is not legitimate within Western capitalist societies to praise communist practice, whatever form it takes. In the case of the Soviet Union the assumption is made that it is evil and repressive so that any comment which contradicts that is deemed to be either in justification of evil and repression or a cover-up. Praise of the Soviet Union is a form of heresy. The problem is then how to write objectively about the Soviet Union, presenting positive features with negative ones and combining praise with criticism, in a manner which will avoid an immediate spontaneous condemnation by the media and the public. How, in other words, to write so that the prose is read as seriously as it was intended to be read.

The most heretical assertion of all is to claim that there is a Soviet form of democracy. My understanding of the democratic character of the Soviet Union was influenced by the writings of Lenin and E H Carr. Lenin explained the essence of the new Soviet state in his polemics against Karl Kautsky. Carr, on the other hand, took issue only with Karl Popper, the philosopher, over the meaning of history. In his work on the Soviet Union he was and remains undoubtedly the greatest Western historian. A J P Taylor called him simply "the greatest historian of our age". His vast knowledge of Soviet history was synthesised in a brilliant series of lectures in February and March 1946 at Oxford when he analyzed the influence of the Soviet Union on Western capitalist countries. The lectures were published as *The Soviet Impact on the Western World* in 1946. In a brief chapter called "The Political Impact", Carr placed the Western and Soviet forms of democracy in their historical and structural contexts so that it was possible to contrast the qualities of one against the other. He believed that the Soviet Union was justified in describing its form of government as democratic and that it was not in any sense morally inferior to Western democracy.

Carr's comments were not then regarded as heretical. He wrote at a propitious time during the brief interregnum between when the USSR was a wartime ally and a 'Cold War' adversary. In any event, his opinions were always weighted by his enormous intellect and erudition. But even Carr might not have survived the pressures of the Cold War unscathed. His last book, a collection of essays called *From Napoleon to Stalin,* published in 1980 when he was 88 years old, contains a list of his publications with no reference to *The Soviet Impact on the Western World* which, unlike his many other publications, has not been reprinted since 1947.

I hold a view of Soviet democracy which is similar to that expressed by Carr though it has been put more aggressively and polemically than his. It is presented in some detail in Chapter Five. The gist of it, however, has been published in various forms since 1980 and on most occasions I have been accused of behaviour ranging from simplicity to duplicity; from white-washing "a brutal totalitarian regime" to wanting to take Britain into it. Correspondents in a letter to *The Times* on 10 July 1985 used a quotation about Soviet democracy from my pamphlet, *Images and Reality in the Soviet Union,* to endorse their contention that I wanted Britain to become "part of the Soviet empire". Later that year, on 22 September, *The Mail on Sunday* columnist, Alan Williams, made a similar point but under the heading "Proved: The KGB links with CND". Such assertions are a part of the "Go back to Moscow" syndrome which derives its logic from the international communist conspiracy theory. They are plainly silly but they have the effect of influencing people to dismiss the writings of anyone who displays friendship to the Soviet Union as cheap propaganda. The same derisive rhetoric is not used against non-conformist approaches to other subjects. Indeed in my own experience non-conformity has often been praised for its freshness and analytical clarity. Soviet communism clearly has special hatred inducing qualities for some.

The problem of how to penetrate the barriers of prejudice remains to be tackled. By definition those who challenge conventional wisdom are in a minority. In this case the minority has no access to the achievements of information technology. Its weapons in the struggle of ideas are still those of the Nineteenth Century advocates of democracy, namely, the public meeting and the tract. It has to rely on the force of argument and its political relevance. However, although the means of mass communications are in the hands of anti-Soviet forces the problem in Britain may not be quite as acute as appearances indicate. There is still much to be learned about the determinants of consciousness and the role played by the media. My impression is that that role is overplayed.

I have evidence to support this contention. In face to face discussions at the many public meetings I have addressed I have never met resistance to listening to arguments in favour of the Soviet Union. Many people were surprised to hear that there were plausible alternative democratic forms and that the much vaunted pluralistic parliamentary and presidential democracies might be morally inferior to the Soviet model. After each occasion on which my views about the Soviet Union have been published in *The Guardian* I have had letters from dozens of readers. None has ever been critical. Some have been moving in their responses. The most telling evidence, however, that the media stereotype has only superficially penetrated public consciousness comes from the examination of trade union attitudes in Chapter Twelve. There it is shown that since the October Revolution in 1917 British workers have possessed an underlying identity with Soviet workers. Whenever there was an international crisis such as over Hungary in 1956, Czechoslovakia in 1968 and Poland in 1980 public emotions were turned against the Soviet Union but only temporarily. Long before the incidents became history they were tucked into the recesses of trade union consciousness and normal friendly relations were resumed. The totality of my own evidence suggests that the problem of writers who wish to put the Soviet case is not overcoming a deepseated public prejudice but gaining access to the public to correct superficially held distorted notions about Soviet life. It is perhaps the recognition of this factor, which means, in effect, that the British workers are not properly convinced that the Soviet Union is the enemy, which feeds the desperation of the media defenders of capitalism.

I have tried to explain the reasons which prompted me to write this book and some problems encountered in the process of writing. But what is its purpose? It has two parts. The first is as a contribution towards lessening the tension between the nuclear powers by assisting people in the West to see the Soviet Union as a friendly but critical neighbour and not as an enemy. Only when this has happened will nuclear tensions dissipate and the world be safe for social change. The second aim is longer term and is dependent upon the fulfilment of the first. It is about social change. It is to encourage workers in Western capitalist countries to see the Soviet Union as a positive model for social change. The stereotype of Soviet communism is used to frustrate all but the most insipid social democratic changes. Any move which seriously departs from the ethics of capitalism is dubbed and denigrated as a Soviet inspired trap for the workers. Only when workers see Soviet communism as a genuine attempt to improve the material and emotional lives of people beyond anything which is possible under capitalism will they begin to break the chains of capitalist ideology.

Writing this book has been the most exciting and stimulating project I have ever engaged in. It was urgent and therefore had to be completed quickly. But it opened up so many issues which have been sources of great controversy in the British Labour Movement. Along with the issues came questions about communist practice which I had not answered previously, in particular those relating to Soviet democracy. I owe a debt to the hundreds of people in local CND groups, branches of the British Soviet Friendship Society and the Marxist Forum in Manchester who over the last 7 years have debated these issues and questions with me. Throughout the period of writing I have discussed them with Ken Gill and Michael Seifert and whatever clarity I have owes much to the Saturday evening debates over dinner we have had. In addition they read an early draft of the book and separately made the same suggestion, that much of it had to be scrapped. The book's present structure has been based on their advice. It now, I believe, has a coherence and relevance which it previously lacked. I hope they think so too when they see the completed book for the first time on publication. I wish to thank them both for the constant encouragement they gave me. Discussing is one part of the process; writing is another. But I write with pen and ink in a barely legible left-handed scrawl which sometimes I cannot read myself. The essential task of transcribing my writing so that others could read it was done by Sue Logan, always before time. I wish to thank her as well as Lucy Allen who read the proofs.

Finally, it has been possible, by coincidence rather than design, to publish this book on the 70th Anniversary of the Bolshevik Revolution. It is an opportune coincidence. Seventy years is a brief spell in the history of a society but it is long enough to create familiarity and to generate acceptance. There are few people in the West who can remember the Revolution and even less who can recall events in Czarist Russia. It is pertinent, therefore, to ask about the reasons for anti-Sovietism.

The Anniversary raises two factors against which the phenomenon of anti-Sovietism should be considered. First, the Soviet Union has survived as a consistent communist society for so long that, except in the Baltic Republics which became part of it in 1939, the vast majority of its population has been educated and socialized through communist values. For them capitalism belongs to history and other societies. They cannot be nostalgic about what they have never experienced nor are they likely to be envious of societies with characteristics, such as mass unemployment and poverty, of which they disapprove. The Soviet people are committed to the communist way of organizing their lives. It is dangerous nonsense to talk, as some politicians do, as if the Soviet people are waiting to be liberated. The history of the Second World War should have been evidence of that fact. There can be absolutely no possibility of rolling back the 70 years of developments in the Soviet Union.

Secondly, there is now ample empirical evidence to show that the changes which we define as Soviet communism are part of a universal process of social change. It is interesting to see this through the life of one person. My father was 16 years of age when the Bolshevik Revolution occurred. When he was born there was no Communist Party anywhere. The Soviet Union was the only communist state when he was 38 years at the outbreak of the Second World War. Yet when he died in 1981 there was a communist presence in virtually every country of the world and in an increasing and significant number there were governments which in various degrees practised communism. Put differently, until 1939 the Soviet Union was isolated without allies. Now it is a super-power with allies in all the hemispheres and their number is increasing. The 70th Anniversary is then a celebration of survival, of maturity and of expanding comradely friendships. It is in this context that anti-Sovietism must be analyzed.

V L Allen
1 October 1987

Baildon Green
Shipley.

PART I

The Prejudice of the West

Chapter One
The Enemy

Types of Enemy

The Soviet Union is regarded as the enemy of Western capitalist countries but in what ways and for what reasons? It is said that every country needs an enemy in order to project and preserve its own identity and unity. There is a long list of illustrations showing how those countries which have domestic difficulties divert attention to external forces. In doing so they generate chauvinistic, jingoistic attitudes which temporarily over-ride internal divisions. The USA, with its diverse geography, competitive economic interests and ethnic complexity, has a clear need for an over-riding interest to maintain its cohesion as a single, unified nation which defence against an enemy fulfils. When the US has entered wars, as in 1917 and 1942, it has done so with extreme, aggressive nationalistic fervour. Since 1917 it has always had an enemy of sorts, supplemented in the post Second World War period by a number of minor enemies such as Cuba, Vietnam, Grenada and Nicaragua. An enemy for the USA is therapeutic. This is not quite the case with Britain though the war against the Argentine over the Falklands in 1982 was a recent sad reminder of the use of an enemy to divert public attention from deep social and economic issues. It was, of course, war, national aggression, which created the shabby unity, not the enemy though an enemy was necessary to justify the war.

Enemies of this kind emerge in an ad hoc fashion. Their main qualities must be that they are not truly threatening, are geographically remote, and give rise to emotional rather than material consequences. In any event they must not pose the possibility of defeat and dispossession. In retrospect conflicts with them appear as a sort of game though this was not the appearance at the time. War of this kind, moreover must not be unduly destructive of property.

The Soviet Union is not perceived as an enemy necessary for nationalistic therapy though anti-Bolshevism and anti-Sovietism

3

have been used, not to achieve national unity, but to suppress internal dissent. The Soviet Union, and before that Czarist Russia, has never been a therapeutic enemy. Mr. Lloyd George aptly described the reason in his Guildhall speech on November 8th, 1919 after a decision had been made to withdraw British troops from the war of intervention in Bolshevik Russia.

> "Our troops are out of Russia", he said, "Frankly I am glad. Russia is a quicksand. Victories are easily won in Russia, but you sink in victories, and great armies and great Empires in the past have been overwhelmed in the sands of barren victories. Russia is a dangerous land to intervene in. We discounted it in the Crimea. But true to the instinct which has always saved us, we never went far from the sea, and we were able to extricate ourselves from there . . ."[1]

Hitler could have echoed Lloyd George's words in 1945, except that the German armies were far from the sea and sank in the Russian quicksands.

Nor is the Soviet Union a traditional enemy of Britain. The choice of enemies in the past has normally been determined by geo-political factors; by common frontiers and overlapping interests or competing ambitions. Wars between traditional enemies have moved frontiers, extended the hegemony of one country over another, provided labour supplies through enslavement, created outlets for overpopulation or ensured access to sources of raw materials or new markets. Many countries bordering each other have traditional hostile relations with each other. Such is the case with China and Vietnam, Greece and Turkey and France and Germany. Although many such countries still oppose each other militarily, guns have in some instances been replaced by jokes as a more innocuous means of expressing dislike. In Central Africa, previously warring tribes have developed joking relationships to express attitudes of superiority or inferiority. Maybe French jokes about the English perform this function. The English prefer to joke about ethnic minorities, the Welsh, Irish and Scots, whereas in Soviet Union ethnic jokes are often about Georgians and Armenians. The Russians and the English do not normally joke about each other. There was a ditty which was popular in Bolshevik Russia late in 1918 after the British, French, Italian, American and Japanese had intervened to help the White Russian armies topple Lenin's government but it was not a joke. It

4

went:

> "Uniforms British
> Epaulettes from France,
> Japanese tobacco
> Kolchak leads the dance"[2]

But by 1920 this was purely of historical interest. Since then the Russians and the British have had little need to communicate their feelings for each other through any medium, except for the episode of the Second World War when there was a deep sense of admiration in Britain for the Red Army.

Of course, in order for jokes to have any impact people need to have some acquaintance with each other. The British and the Soviet people do not meet except in trickles as tourists after long and relatively expensive journeys. Britain does not have a common frontier with Soviet Union at any point. Moscow is 1549 miles from London across many frontiers. It is the capital of a distant, mysterious country. Information about it comes either from the tales of travellers or through the media.

In war Britain and Russia have been on the same side more often than not. Russia has never invaded Britain though the horror of hordes of Russians arriving with snow on their boots is still conjured as a possibility as if at some time it had been a reality. Britain has, however, invaded Russia on two occasions. In 1854 British troops invaded the Crimea in an unprepared and futile act of aggression. In 1918 they entered Russia through Archangel and Vladivostock and fought with armies of 13 nations against the Bolsheviks. The British government told the Russian people on August 8th, 1918: "We are coming to help you save yourselves from dismemberment and destruction at the hands of Germany. We wish solemnly to assure you that we shall not retain one foot of your territory. The destinies of Russia are in the hands of the Russian people. It is for them, and them alone to decide their forms of Government, and to find a solution for their social problems." The British troops were still in Russia after the war with Germany had ended, not to protect Russians against Germans but, in the words of the Chief of the Imperial General Staff, "to create a ring of States all round Bolshevik Russia . . . to prevent Bolshevism from spreading (and) . . . with a view to crushing Bolshevism definitely at the earliest possible date."[4] They left at the instigation of the Russian people who decided for themselves that their destiny lay with the Bolsheviks.

5

In the great conflicts in the world since 1800, the Napoleonic Wars and the two World Wars, Britain and Russia have been allies and on each occasion the Russian people have suffered greatly in a cause which benefited us. By the time of the Bolshevik Revolution in October, 1917, the Russian Army had suffered more fatal casualties than Britain, France and Italy combined. About 2.8 million Russians were killed, 2.5 million were missing, presumed dead, and almost 5 million were wounded. Many Russian losses occurred in order to relieve pressure on the Western front. In the Second World War, 20 million Soviet citizens died, more than 50 times greater than the American losses in the war. 25 million people were made homeless.[5] This was the extent of Soviet sacrifices to win a war which enabled Britain to survive. There is no doubt that the outcome of the Second World War would have been different if the Soviet Union had not defeated the Nazis on their Eastern Front. 90 per cent of all German casualties in the war were caused by the Soviet armed forces. Mr. Winston Churchill was in no doubt about the Red Army's contribution when he told Parliament on August 2nd, 1944 "that the obvious fact . . . (is that) . . . it is the Russians who have done the main work in tearing the guts out of the German army." The Soviet Union was clearly not an ordinary ally in the Second World War.

On this reckoning the Russian have been traditional allies and not enemies. Yet today the Soviet Union is indicted as an enemy so evil, so potentially destructive of Western civilization that both Britain and the USA have refused to say that they will not engage in a pre-emptive strike with nuclear weapons to destroy it. They refuse even to accept a moratorium on nuclear tests. So far they have rejected the Soviet proposal to destroy the arsenal of nuclear missiles. What kind of society must it be to provoke such hatred and fear that Britain and the USA are prepared to risk genocide against themselves in order to protect themselves from it? What qualities caused the Soviet Union to be transformed from a heroic ally in 1945 to an implacable enemy in 1946? What is it that has generated such undiminished hatred from British governments, Labour and Conservative alike, since that time?

The intensity of Western opposition to the Soviet Union can be gauged from the scale of investment of resources in the American Strategic Defence Initiative or the Star Wars programme. The SDI is intended to be a three-layered defence shield against attack from the Soviet Union. Its effectiveness will depend upon the ability of the Americans to disable Soviet missiles near to their launching pads, maybe on their launching pads. The first and primary layer of the shield is therefore a military one over the Soviet Union and not a protective cover for the USA. In order to construct this nuclear-powered straight-jacket for the Soviet Union the American government is prepared to spend, at 1986 prices, up to $1.5 trillion. Such costs will jeopardize conventional defence expenditure, divert resources from social issues, including education, and will in general create serious destabilizing tendencies in the American economy. All of this damage, then, to protect itself from the enemy.

The reasons for ethnic enmity are important at all times but the advent of nuclear technology has transformed their importance. The character of war has been changed. War with nuclear weapons cannot be used as a release valve for a country in crisis by generating patriotism. A war which destroys all people makes frontiers irrelevant and market gains unnecessary. Even if the ghoulish consequences could be discounted a war technology which is so intensely capital intensive could not be utilized as a means of breaking out of an economic depression. It is said that there are American capitalists who would be prepared to countenance 20 to 40 million American deaths in order to maintain their control over world markets but as it is highly likely they would be included in the body count this seems a highly improbable suggestion. An enemy in the nuclear age is of more significance than any other enemy in history.

Enemy by Assumption

One would have thought that the question "who is the enemy and why?" would be uppermost in the minds of people in the West and at the centre of a continuous debate. After all, Western societies surely need to be absolutely certain of their ground before embarking on a course which could lead to the virtual destruction of human society. It does not require much world-wiseness to see the criminal futility of arming against a non-enemy, an enemy by assumption, without any empirical evidence to support the assumption.

One would have thought, too, that successive British governments, starting with the Labour government led by Clement Attlee in 1945, which have committed ordinary people to a nuclear war strategy, would have paused at every decision-making stage to say "are we really sure? Does the Soviet Union really pose such a threat as to risk a nuclear holocaust?" In addition, one would have thought, the same governments would have wanted to provide information about the Soviet Union in order to provoke an informed general discussion; in other words to inform and consult the electorate before embarking on, continuing, accelerating a build-up of nuclear arms. But for a seemingly unaccountable reason this has never happened.

Those governments, in fact, did the very opposite. Shabby deals contracted in high secrecy by cabals of favoured Cabinet Ministers have been the norm. Neither the British Parliament, nor even the Cabinet, has ever seriously and profoundly discussed the identity of Britain's enemy or how it should react to it. In the speedy and dramatic transition of the Soviet Union from wartime ally to 'Cold War' enemy, the Prime Minister did not consult the British people, or even his own party, but engaged in shady, humiliating diplomatic deals with President Truman.

This crazy, criminally bizarre situation has persisted ever since. The decision of the Labour government to replace Polaris in 1978, taken under the code-name Chevaline at a cost of more than £1 billion, was taken by a group of four Cabinet Ministers, without reference to the Cabinet, Government or Parliament. Tony Benn, who was a member of that Cabinet, complained that he only learned about the decision after the defeat of the Labour Government in 1979. He asked "why have successive governments . . . misled successive Parliaments about the development of Britain's nuclear weapons?" and added that "The British Parliament has never been told the whole truth, and even today, we do not know under what arrangements American nuclear missiles in this country are controlled." He said "It is the extra-Parliamentary powers of successive prime ministers and defence chiefs, and not the peace campaigners, which threaten parliamentary democracy.[6] When Mr Denis Healey, who was one of the four Ministers concerned, responded to Tony Benn's allegation he said that the decision had been "a mistake" which he regretted not having investigated more thoroughly.[7] The enormously costly replacement for Polaris was intended to match the Soviet ABM system which was never deployed.

The government then, and at other times, used the need to keep vital information out of the hands of the enemy as the reason for not informing Parliament or the electorate of its decisions. Sometimes it engaged in deceit to divert attention from its real motives. The post-war Churchill government planned the

8

announcement of its decision to build Britain's first nuclear reactor for civil purposes to deflect public opposition from its nuclear bomb programme. This became clear after Cabinet papers were released for public perusal under the 30 year rule. The decision to manufacture the H-bomb was taken by the Cabinet in July 1954. Six months later the Cabinet's defence committee decided "that the time has now arrived where a public announcement of this decision should be made." Both the Foreign Secretary, Anthony Eden and the Prime Minister, Mr Churchill were worried about the effect on the public of disclosure. Mr Churchill noted that "The Government would be embarrassed if there were any premature disclosure of this decision . . . there would be an advantage in publishing the Government's programme for civil development of atomic energy before announcing their decision to produce thermnuclear weapons."[8] The announcement about nuclear power preceded that concerning nuclear weapons by two days. The issue was duly clouded.

National security was given as the reason for secrecy at the end of 1982 when the decision to locate the US European Command War Headquarters in Britain was leaked to the public through a report in the *Guardian*. Mr Michael Meacher, MP, commenting on this, said "Life and death decisions are either kept secret from the British people . . . (as in the case of the Chevaline project) . . . or excluded from a parliamentary vote", as in the case of the decision to locate Cruise missiles in Britain.[9] Prime Ministers, who have carried the main responsibility for this insane behaviour, have acted as if battles were still fought only by professional soldiers with hand-weapons in field formations. They have behaved as if democratic decision-making was not only irrelevant for contemporary warfare, but was subversive. In consequence the British public has depended upon 'leaks' and gossip for its information. Politicians have talked to their constituents about defence through cliches, slogans, smears, innuendos, half-truths and downright lies.

It is essential that the whole question of nuclear defence is opened up for public discussion. Decisions which affect the survival of people should never be taken from their purview. Secret diplomacy and privileged decision-making are not simply inappropriate in the age of nuclear technology but confer impossible responsibilities on individuals which create their own grave dangers. All questions concerning war should be public property. There was a possibility of debating nuclear disarmament

9

in the elections of 1983 and 1987 but the issue was spoiled by the government's use of cliches. Political parties in the main have not wanted to explore their prejudices concerning international relations, to examine their assumptions in public, to publicize their real intentions. The chances are that if this were done the people would turn away in disgust. That is surely what would have happened in 1945 if Clement Attlee had informed the British public that his government was about to embark on a policy of acute anti-Sovietism.

So, forty-two years after the explosion of the first atomic bomb, after a continuous accumulation and refinement of nuclear weapons and after an extension of the arms race into space, the question still remains to be answered. What kind of enemy is it with which a country will engage in mutual genocidal conflict. What hideous qualities does it display? Can it possibly be inhabited by human beings?

FOOTNOTES

1. *History of Anglo-Soviet Relations* by W P and Zelda K Coates, 1943, p. 2.
2. *The Great Conspiracy Against Russia* by Michael Sayers and Albert E Kahn, 1946, p. 66.
3. ibid, pp. 62-3.
4. *Secrets from Whitehall and Downing Street,* by Fyodor Volkov, 1986, p. 69.
5. *Socialism and Capitalism: Score and Prospects* edited by Yuri Sdobnikov, Moscow, 1971, p. 44.
6. *The Guardian.* 18 December 1985.
7. *The Guardian.* 20 December 1985.
8. *The Guardian.* 2 January 1984.
9. *The Guardian.* 18 December 1985.

Chapter Two
The Stereotype

The Underlying Belief

The justification for treating the Soviet Union as an enemy lies in the stereotype which the West has created for that country. Attitudes towards other societies in general and the myths displayed about them are often embodied in the stereotypical terms used to describe their inhabitants. The stereotype of the Soviet Union does not arise from experience with its people, however, no matter how jaundiced, as in the case of the Germans, French, Italians and Japanese. It is portrayed as a system run by a bureaucracy. It has no heart and, because it is godless, no soul either. It has in consequence no sensitivities and no matter how it may be savaged it feels no pain and cannot weep. When Soviet mothers weep over the graves of the Second World War dead, they weep, it is claimed, only crocodile tears.[1] There is no need even for a flicker of conscience at the obliteration of this socialist sixth of the world.

The meaning of the Western contrived stereotype of the Soviet Union is expressed by President Reagan's description of the Soviet Union as an "evil empire" and Mrs Thatcher's comment that it is "brutal and tyrannical". Both statements are sloganized expressions of the deeply embedded, pervasive, historically determined and formally sanctioned views of the Soviet Union by Western capitalist countries. President Reagan's comment is an expression of the continuing official US Congress view that the Soviet Union is responsible for international communism which it equates with totalitarianism, terrorism and brutality. This is clearly expressed in the Congressional Preamble to US laws on Internal Security, published in 1976, which states:[2]

> "As a result of evidence adduced before various committees of the Senate and House of Representatives, the Congress finds that —
> (1) There exists a world Communist movement which, in its origins, its development, and its present practice, is

11

a world-wide revolutionary movement whose purpose it is, by treachery, deceit, infiltration into other groups (governmental and otherwise), espionage, sabotage, terrorism, and other means deemed necessary, to establish a Communist totalitarian dictatorship in the countries throughout the world through the medium of a world-wide Communist organization.

(2)   The establishment of a totalitarian dictatorship in any country results in the suppression of all opposition to the party in power, the subordination of the rights of individuals to the state, the denial of fundamental rights and liberties which are characteristic of a representative form of government, such as freedom of speech, of the press, of assembly, and of religious worship, and results in the maintenance of control over people through fear, terrorism and brutality.

(3)   The system of government known as a totalitarian dictatorship is characterized by the existence of a single political party, organized on a dictatorial basis, and by substantial identity between such party and its policies and the government and governmental policies of the country in which it exists.

(4)   The direction and control of the world Communist movement is vested in and exercised by the Communist dictatorship of a foreign country.

(5)   The Communist dictatorship of such foreign country, in exercising such direction and control and in furthering the purposes of the world Communist movement, established and causes the establishment of, and utilises, in various countries, action organizations which are not free and independent organizations, but are sections of a world-wide Communist organization and are controlled, directed, and subject to the discipline of the Communist dictatorship of such foreign country."

All-in-all there are 15 paragraphs in this section of the Code, expressing, emphasizing, repeating the conspiracy theory which locates the source of discontent in the USA, and elsewhere in the world, in Moscow. They are used to justify the internal repression of communist activities and to legitimize external military action to stop communist influence from spreading. President Reagan has said, for example, that action against the Sandinista government in Nicaragua is necessary to prevent the spread of Soviet influence. The same reason is given to justify American support of insurgents in Mozambique. Wherever indigenous conditions give rise to revolutionary activity the American governments sees the hidden hand of that "evil empire".

Inter-War Hostility

This paranoia about the Soviet Union is not new and is mild in comparison with what was said at other times. It began with the Bolshevik Revolution in October 1917 and has dominated Western thinking, education and even information about the Soviet Union since then. The images of Bolshevism, created when the Bolshevik government was struggling for its existence in a contracting segment of Russia, have become imprinted on people's minds through constant and sophisticated repetition.

For virtually the whole of its existence the Soviet Union has been regarded with anathema. There was some rejoicing in the West, especially in the USA, when the Russian Czar Nicholas II was deposed in February 1917 but this was replaced by apprehension when the Bolshevik Party assumed power in October of that year. The apprehension turned to fear when it seemed that Bolshevism would survive. From early in 1918 fear generated hostility and hostility legitimized the perversion of the truth.

From the time of the Bolshevik Revolution until the end of the First World War, the Bolsheviks were branded as agents of the German Kaiser and under his control. At that time, however, they were viewed as transient participants on the world stage. The American mind was concentrated on defeating the German enemy though occasionally the American press took time off to brand the Bolsheviks as even worse enemies than the Germans. Once they had entered the war in 1917, the Americans worked with amazing speed in establishing governmental, public and media agencies to foment anti-Germanism. But as soon as the war was over these agencies, namely the National Security League, the American Defence Society and the American Protection League, which had converted ordinary Americans into super-patriots and German spy-chasers set about transforming them into Bolshevik haters. Horror stories appeared in the press claiming that Bolshevik rule was a compound of slaughter, confiscation, anarchy and universal disorder and describing Bolshevik leaders as "assassins and madmen", "human scum", "crime mad" and "beasts". *The New York Times* had a headline in the spring of 1919 "Russia under Reds a Gigantic Bedlum" while the London *Daily Telegraph* reported a reign of terror in Odessa followed by a "free love week". It was alleged by the *Daily Telegraph* in 1920 that Russian women had been nationalized. Particular attention was given to lurid stories about the fate of bourgeois women and girls.

The political leaders of the great powers turned their attention to the Bolsheviks at the Paris Peace Conference in 1919. With revolutions erupting in Germany and Hungary and unrest manifesting itself in Britain and the USA, the conspiracy theory took form. The weak, struggling Bolshevik government, harassed by invading armies and Civil War, was identified as the nerve centre for social disorders throughout the world. The French Ambassador to Russia, M Noulens, told the Peace Conference that "the Bolshevik Government is definitely imperialistic. It means to conquer the world, and to make peace with no Government."[3] In Western minds it never ceased to act that part.

The hostility of the Western powers was expressed in various ways, apart from making military and economic threats. The media distortions continued, as did the periodic vitriolic denunciations by politicians. By the middle of the 1920s, the distortions had already become so commonplace that they were being passed off for truth without any attempt at verification. This subtle form of propaganda was illustrated by comments on Soviet Russia by John Maynard Keynes, the influential economist. Writing from the sanctuary of Kings College, Cambridge in 1925, he stated: "I am not ready for a creed which does not care how much it destroys the liberty and security of daily life, which uses deliberately the weapons of persecution, destruction, and international strife. How can I admire a policy which finds a characteristic expression in spending millions to suborn spies in every family and group at home, and to stir up trouble abroad?"[4] He provided no supporting evidence or references, an omission he would have regarded as intellectually dishonest in his own field of economics. His prejudice even interfered with his perception of people for when he spoke to Russian communists he could see "the full faith of fanaticism in their eyes".[5] At this stage the process of social conditioning was in full swing.

American trade unions were excessive in their condemnation of the Soviet Union for at the 1928 Convention of the American Federation of Labour, they branded it as "the most unscrupulous, most anti-social, most menacing institution in the world today", though they had no experience of Bolshevism. The US Government only recognized the Soviet Union in 1933 and was the last major power to do so. The minority British Labour Government recognized the Soviet Government in 1924 amidst much controversy, fuelled by the fraudulent "Zinoviev" letter in September 1924 which effectively caused the government to be defeated in the general election of the following month. Diplomatic relations between the two countries were ruptured in 1927 but resumed in 1929 when the second Labour Government was elected.

The diplomatic recognition of the Soviet Union by Western capitalist countries did not signify their acceptance of Bolshevism but merely altered the nature of diplomatic and trading relationships. Their basic hostility towards the Soviet system continued. Only their methods changed. The intervention of troops from 14 nations, but mainly from Britain, France, USA, Japan and Czechoslovakia, in support of the insurgent Czarist Generals, which started in February 1918 and lasted for 3 years, converted a virtually bloodless Revolution into a bloodbath. It caused a dislocation of transport and of food production on such a scale that in 1921–22 there was a famine in which an estimated 20 million Russians died. The cost to Soviet Russia of Western hostility was phenomenal in terms of destruction, chaos, human suffering and the organization of Soviet society in general.

Military intervention was superceded by economic sanctions. The economic war was particularly nasty as the details recounted by Andrew Rothstein indicate: "In 1930 they included a campaign in Great Britain and elsewhere against alleged religious persecution in the USSR and, later in the year, against alleged "dumping" of Soviet wheat and timber: both with the declared object of inducing business interests not to trade with the Soviet Government. Some success outside this country was won by these campaigns. In October, 1930, France instituted an economic blockade of Soviet goods, and early in 1931 Canada followed suit. The existence of the Labour Government in Britain, which signed a trade agreement with the USSR in April 1930, for a time interfered with the campaign in this country; but in February 1931, leading politicians and businessmen formed a "Trade Defence Union" for the express purpose of combating trade with the USSR and in November of the same year the British National Government . . . cut the duration of export credits on Soviet imports from two years to one. Throughout 1931–2 the Bureau of Research on Russian Economic Conditions of Birmingham University published eight memoranda proving the failure and collapse of Soviet economic efforts; and in 1932 a new campaign against Soviet goods was started in Great Britain, on the grounds that they were allegedly produced by "forced labour". When the campaign had been worked up to a considerable height the Anglo-Soviet trade agreement of 1930 was denounced by the British Government."[6]

The Western powers created a *cordon sanitaire* around the Soviet Union and treated it as a pariah amongst nations. Anti-Sovietism was spread through the media: films and radio were used to create images in the minds of people about the evils and degeneracy of communism. Lurid, distorted and exaggerated tales were told in the 1930s about the process of collectivisation, membership 'purges' in the Communist Party and the 'Great Trials' of 1936 and 1937. In a carefully prepared broadcast on 20 January 1940, Mr Winston Churchill was able to say, without serious contradiction, "Everyone can see how Communism rots the soul of a nation, how it makes it abject and hungry in peace and proves it base and abominable in war."[7] This was only 18 months before the Soviet Union became Britain's great and indispensible ally in war.

The Post-War Paranoia

The wartime experiences, which had such a profound effect upon the perceptions of ordinary people made not a dent in the anti-Soviet intentions of the Western political leaders, except those of Franklin D Roosevelt the US President who did not live to influence post-war events. Once the war was over the old rhetoric re-appeared as if there had been no interlude but this time the anti-Soviet pace was set by Americans. Averill Harriman, the US Ambassador to Moscow, warned the newly installed President Truman on 20 April, 1945, that the US was faced, in effect, with a "'barbaric invasion of Europe', that Soviet control over any foreign country did not mean merely influence on their foreign relations but the extension of the Soviet system with secret police, extinction of freedom of speech, etc . . . ."[8] The US foreign policy adviser, George F Kennan and US Ambassador in Moscow after Harriman, was a consistent advocate of containment of the Soviet Union during the war and after it. On 22 February 1946 he despatched a long telegram from the US embassy in Moscow to

16

Washington in which he explained: "At the bottom of the Kremlin's neurotic view of world affairs is traditional and instinctive Russian sense of insecurity . . . they have always feared foreign penetration, feared direct contact between Western world and their own, feared what would happen if Russians learned truth about world without or if foreigners learned truth about world within. And they have learned to seek security only in patient but deadly struggle for total destruction rival power, never in compacts and compromises with it . . ."[9] For this telegram Kennan achieved fame and influence for with it he set the post-war parameters of the US foreign policy. Soviet aggression, he stated, could not be allayed by concessions; it had to be contained by force. He modified the stereotype by rejecting the notion that there was a basic antagonism between the capitalist and socialist worlds and this enabled him to say "that the stress laid in Moscow on the menace confronting Soviet Society from the world outside its borders is founded not in the realities of foreign atagonism but in the necessity of explaining away the maintenance of dictatorial authority at home."[10] His intellectual argument legitimized the self-righteous approach to relations with the Soviet Union which the US and Britain have never deserted. Mr Winston Churchill took up the Kennan thesis in his speech in Fulton, USA on March 5th 1946. He talked of the "iron curtain" which had descended across Europe and spoke of the need for a partnership between Great Britain and the US to halt the Soviet colossus. There is nothing the Russians "admire so much as strength", he said, "and there is nothing for which they have less respect than military weakness". For that reason the old doctrine of a balance of power was unsound.[11] Much detail was added to the 1918 stereotype as a result of Soviet successes in the Second World War which portrayed the Soviet Union as an infinitely more dangerous and implacable enemy. The Cold War was underway.

The Stereotype and Internal Repression

The stereotype became an ogre when it was used to justify internal repression against radicals, trade unionists and communists. Paragraph (9) of "Title 50, War and National Defense in the US" stated "In the United States those individuals who knowingly and willfully participate in the world Communist movement, when they so participate in effect repudiate their allegiance to the United States, and in effect transfer their allegiance to the foreign

17

allegiance to the foreign country in which is vested the direction and control of the world Communist movement". Paragraph (11) added "The agents of communism have devised clever and ruthless espionage and sabotage tactics which are carried out in many instances in form or manner successfully evasive of existing law." These agents, the remaining paragraphs explained, enter the USA with diplomatic or semi-diplomatic status, or as deportable aliens. "One device for infiltration by Communists", paragraph (14) stated, "is by procuring naturalization for disloyal aliens who use their citizenship as a badge for admission into the fabric of our society." The sentiments underlying these paragraphs were a reality for many thousands of people during the Red Scare period from 1918 to 1924 and after the Second World War.

The image of a voracious Bolshevism sanctioned the wholesale oppression of political nonconformity in the USA in 1919. Police raids, arbitrary arrests, excessive prison sentences and physical violence were everyday risks for those who questioned the legitimacy or relevance of American capitalism. In May, 1918 a Federal Sedition Act was passed which made it a crime to utter, print, write or publish any "disloyal, profane, scurrilous or abusive language intended to cause contempt, scorn, contumely or disrepute as regards the form of government of the United States, or the Constitution, or the flag, or the uniform of the Army or Navy . . ." and so on.[12] By 1920 the majority of states had passed similar legislation directed at working class radicalism. Thirty-three states had passed legislation which even forbade the display of the red flag. It became illegal in many states to wear red ties or display buttons which were emblems of Bolshevism. There was a lengthy catalogue of convictions for displaying red flags, possessing radical literature, uttering comments critical of the state, belonging to revolutionary organizations. People with Russian sounding names and aliens in general who supported radical causes were particularly harassed and frequently deported.

Under the mantle of a crusade against Bolshevism in the USA Communist Party membership fell from 70,000 after being founded to about 12,000 in 1922; the Socialist Party membership fall was greater, from 110,000 in 1919 to 12,000 in 1922 while the militant Industrial Workers of the World was almost completely destroyed by systematic large scale arrests.[13] Coincident with the oppression of radicals was the rise of the right-wing paramilitary

18

groups, the American Legion and the Ku-Klux Klan.

There was not a comparable scare in Britain though the British government in 1919 was extremely apprehensive about revolutionary activity. Throughout, the British pursued the same aims as the Americans but more subtly. After the Second World War the pattern of the Red Scare was repeated in the USA and progressive politics, still suffering from the Red Scare, was virtually crushed by McCarthyism, as almost all types of political nonconformists were hounded out of their jobs and harassed in their social lives. The greatest sufferers were communists, many of whom were sent to Prison.[14] Again the policy of deportation of non-citizens was pursued. British communists suffered some discrimination after 1945. In general they survived but as a fringe group in politics.

The Revised Stereotype

Once the Soviet Union had tested its first nuclear weapon in 1949 anti-Sovietism was used for more sinister and macabre purposes. The military superiority which the USA believed the atomic bomb gave it from 1945 suddenly slipped away, never to be regained in the foreseeable future. The Americans, thereafter, could only reassure themselves of their superiority by producing bigger, more deadly, more elusive and more numerous bombs than the Soviet Union possessed. What began was an arms build-up not arms race for, except for the launching of the Sputnik satellite in 1957, the Soviet Union did not initiate any nuclear weapon development. It sought parity but this upset the balance as perceived by the US which went in further search of superiority. Military considerations, plus market ones for nuclear arms production became an extremely lucrative activity for the privately owned armaments manufacturing industry in the US, gave the manufacture of nuclear weapons a dynamic which became independent of external factors. The American military-industrial complex, in its single-minded pursuit of the twin objectives of military superiority and private profit, was largely insulated from world opinion, international pressure and Soviet overtures. Its main sensitivity was in response to American public opinion. It had to justify the colossal use of resources for such universally lethal purposes. And it did so by revising the stereotype of the enemy, adding new myths concerning military might and a reckless disregard for the fate of the world to the old

CHART 1 — NATO Medium-Range Nuclear Weapons Coverage Of The Soviet Union in 1983 [15]

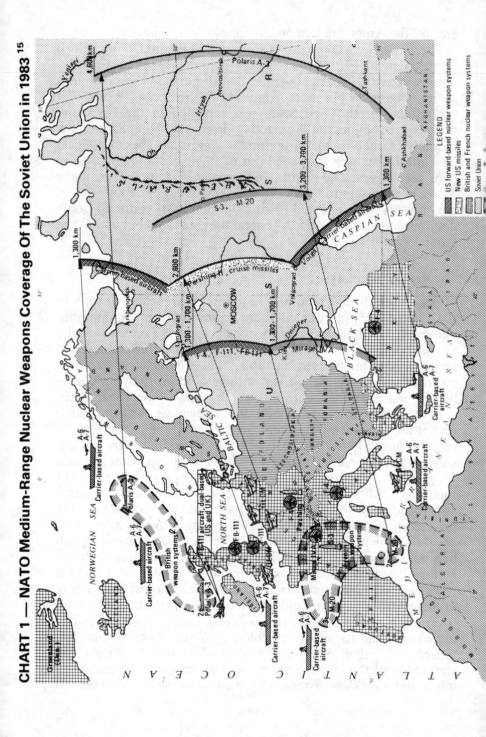

LEGEND

US forward-based nuclear weapon systems

New US missiles

British and French nuclear weapon systems

Soviet Union

ones about international political conspiracies. The new stereotype was not about world conquest but world destruction.

The makers of US foreign policy and their NATO cohorts redrew the image of the Soviet Union with a deft use of lies, half-lies, distortion and exaggerations into a rampaging international ogre. Dr Steve Smith put the issue and details of the myths more soberly but admirably in a powerfully argued article as follows:[16]

> "By myth, is meant a popular fictitious narrative. Thus, in talking of the myths surrounding the debate on the Soviet threat reference is made not to the fact that politicians or academics say things that are controversial—such is the essence of political debate—but that they make seemingly factual statements that are, in fact, incorrect. What are these myths? There are four which are, in increasing order of generality:
>
> − That the Soviet Union spends much more of its GNP on defence than do the leading powers of the West (thereby justifying vast increases in our defence expenditure).
> − That United States Inter-Continental Ballistic Missiles (ICBMs) are now or soon will be vulnerable to a Soviet first strike (thereby justifying M-X and the deployment of Cruise).
> − That the Soviet Union has a view of warfighting that "accepts" nuclear war as inevitable and potentially winnable (thereby requiring a move towards a nuclear war-fighting strategy in the West).
> − That the Soviet Union is embarked on a world-wide expansionist and aggressive foreign policy—as witnessed by Afghanistan (thereby justifying real increases in NATO defence expenditure and the development of a Rapid Deployment Force (RDF) for use outside the boundaries of NATO—specifically in the Gulf)."

The assumption underlying the entire Western defence strategy is that ultimately and inevitably the Soviet Union will wage nuclear war against NATO. It is this projected belief which is given as the public justification for the Star Wars Programme. Other distortions, however, have not been neglected. One in particular, concerning human rights in the Soviet Union, projecting it as a uniquely oppressive society, has been specially revived to undermine the efforts of the Western Peace Movements to change American and NATO military policies. In an important respect this is the most vital of the elements which make up the stereotype for it contorts the minds of ordinary people about the Soviet Union. "Evidence" is produced about the treatment of Soviet dissidents to confirm that conformity in the Soviet Union, acceptance of the communist system, only occurs through the physical suppression of individuals by the KGB, other state agencies and the Communist Party. The system of institutionalized pluralism which accommodates a diversity of views is contrasted with a Soviet monolith which behaves like Proscrustes, the robber of Attica, who fitted his victims to the length of his bed by stretching them or cutting off their legs or heads.

So long as people in general in the West perceive the Soviet Union as "brutal and tyrannical" they will tend to see sense in efforts to contain and resist it, no matter how extreme they might be. Only a "brutal and tyrannical" system would contemplate committing genocide with nuclear weapons; only such a system would resist reasonable efforts to spread democracy and bring peace to the world. But if this perception of the Soviet Union were altered and ordinary people began to see the Soviet system in an enviable, even positive light, then the whole ideological edifice of Western military policy would begin to collapse.

The Western stereotype of the Soviet Union, then, is pivotal in the defence of Capitalism, not simply against socialism but from its own contradictions. It is the justification for taking the world to the brink of a nuclear war. If the stereotype is a correct reflection of reality, however, there is no hope for the world anyway. The Soviet Union will strike and the West will retaliate and that will be the end. But if the stereotype is false, a reversal of the truth, yet the West causes a nuclear war because of it then it will have wreaked destruction on a largely innocent world because of a mistake—the most colossal, horrendous mistake in the history of the world. It is obviously important to know more about the stereotype. How is it constructed? Is it a correct reflection of Soviet society? How does it affect our lives?

FOOTNOTES

1. See for example comments about "weeping Soviet grandmothers" by E P Thompson in *The Guardian*, February 21, 1983.

2. United States Code, 1976 Edition. Title 50. War and National Defence, Chapter 23, Sec 781, p. 1894.
3. *The Great Conspiracy Against Russia* by Michael Sayers and Albert E Kahn, 1946, p. 78. See also *Memoirs of a British Agent* by R H Bruce Lockhart for details of Noulens' activity in Bolshevik Russia.
4. "A Short View of Russia (1925)", in *Essays in Persuasion* by John Maynard Keynes, 1931, pp. 299-300.
5. ibid, p. 305.
6. *Man and Plan in Soviet Economy* by Andrew Rothstein, 1948, pp. 24-25. See also *History of Anglo-Soviet Relations* by W P and Z Coates, Chapters XV to XVIII.
7. ibid, p. 90.
8. *The Origins of the Cold War* by Martin McCauley, 1983, p. 105.
9. ibid, p. 113.
10. *American Diplomacy* by George F Kennan, 1984, p. 113.
11. McCauley, *op cit*, p. 115.
12. *Human Rights in the Soviet Union* by Al Szymanski, pp. 164-5.
13. See Szymanski, *op cit;* also *Red Scare: A Study in National Hysteria* by Robert K Murray, 1955 and *We Shall Be All: A History of the Industrial Workers of the World* by Melvin Dubofsky, 1969.
14. See *The Great Fear* by David Caute, 1978: *Naming Names* by Victor S Navasky, 1980 and Szymanski, op cit, pp. 175-187.
15. Source: *Disarmament: Who's Against?* Military Publishing House, Moscow, 1983, pp. 32-33. Adapted for use here by the Graphics Department of the University of Leeds.
16. "The Myth of the Soviet Threat" by Steve Smith, in the *Journal of the Royal United Services Institute for Defence Studies,* June 1982, pp. 41-49.

Chapter Three
The Academics

The Dominant Paradigm

The stereotype of the Soviet Union as the implacable enemy interacts with the view which many ordinary people in the West have of the Soviet Union. That is, it both reflects that view and endorses and consolidates it. Indeed the government would not be able to sustain the contention that the Soviet Union were the enemy unless its constituents also believed that to be the case. The views of ordinary people, therefore, and how they are formed and sustained are an important part of the defence mechanism of the system. They are not left to chance.

The picture of the Soviet Union and of Soviet people which is conjured up in the minds of people in capitalist societies is formed by a continual presentation of interpretations about it, depicting its life, its institutions, its morality, its intentions. These interpretations enter the consciousness of people through the usual ways in which ideas are communicated, through the written and spoken word via newspapers and journals, radio and television, videos and films, novels and text books. Through these channels a picture is formed which becomes the basis for conversation about the Soviet Union and is communicated to children and kinsfolk in general. It enters into the educational system where it is reinforced by text books. Eventually the picture becomes folklore. Images of the pictures enter language and are reflected in words and concepts.

This ideological process works subtly on the mind until it enters the consciousness of each person. In doing this it becomes a part of the dominant paradigm. In other words it helps to form the linguistic terms of reference which act as the basis for their perception of events and in doing so both defines the questions people ask of Soviet situations and presents them with the answers. It is dominant in the sense that it has priority over all other views in all the channels of communication and this is because it reflects the attitudes of the dominant bourgeois class towards the Soviet Union. In some societies in some periods it has such absolute priority that no other views can be expressed except at the risk of punishment. But this is an extreme and tenuous situation for it indicates that the society can only survive if protected by physical coercion. A society is in its healthiest condition when its dominant protective ideas act on people's consciousness so that they think that the ideas are their own. It then so formulates the answers that when issues arise about, say, the Soviet Union, individuals have 'instant' explanations. They do not have to think a question out or delay a comment until some information has been collected. They draw on the image which has been created for them but which they now believe constitutes their own opinion. Opinion-forming is a very devious process for people can communicate ideas which they believe are their own but which reflect the interests of others. This is often the case in class dominated societies such as Britain and the USA.

An example of the lengths to which this opinion forming process can go was provided by Professor I Rabi of Columbia University, a Nobel Prize Winner in Physics in 1944 and a Presidential Adviser. He said "From the beginning we have coupled how terrible the weapons are with how terrible the Russian are. So the more you describe the horrors of nuclear war, the more you fear the Russians. One doesn't even think of them as human at all; the diabolical Russian . . . We have wasted our substance now for 30 years and more fighting some phantom Russian . . . There are people in this country who hate Russians more than they love America."[1] The former *New York Times* correspondent in Moscow, David K Shipley, described how media copywriters went about this task when he wrote that "Vicious and absurd caricatures of Russians have become standard fare in a current genre of commercials and films. Russians are made to look like the Nazis and even speak with German accents". [2] This process reached the level of absurdity in the USA in the 1980s with the production of such crudely anti-communist and anti-Soviet films as *Rambo* and *Amerika*.

Fortunately the authority of a dominant paradigm is never absolute. Where it does not reflect the actual experiences of people and appears to misrepresent them and, therefore, to mislead them, then it tends to become displaced and people look for alternative explanations. The displacement of inappropriate ideas is continually underway but it is a long process, proceeding unevenly and erratically. But it does mean that if the view of the

Soviet Union as the enemy does not reflect the reality of the position of the Soviet Union, it will have only a tenuous hold on the imaginations of people. The more it is shown to be false then the more people will discard it, not all at once, but by questioning its relevance in bits and pieces until it all falls apart.

In the meantime, however, the commonly held perception of the Soviet Union performs the dual function of reinforcing the stereotype and of acting as an obstacle to understanding it. If people want consciously to understand the Soviet Union what should they believe, who should they believe, to whom should they turn for the truth? How can they penetrate the propaganda which has been layered on for decades? Should they turn to the experts, the Sovietologists, the Kremlinologists, who have researched the Soviet Union in all of its facets and have produced libraries of footnoted texts? And if they do turn to them what will they find?

The Story of Collaboration

What they will find is a story of collaboration with the establishment. Academic studies in general do not escape the taint of political manipulation. But in Soviet studies it is obviously and grossly present. Soviet studies, virtually alone amongst academic disciplines, are pursued, in the main, by people in universities and research institutes who are hostile to the subject of their research. The function of the experts in Soviet studies has always been to give intellectual legitimation to the stereotype. Indeed it is more than that for without the credibility which the multiplicity of research monographs provide, the stereotype would collapse. Notoriously, many doctoral dissertations about the Soviet Union have contributed to the subversion of that country. Very few monographs adopt even a dispassionate view of the Soviet Union and even less have positive comments to make about it.[3]

In the USA the bulk of the funds to finance research institutions and research projects dealing with the Soviet Union comes from the Ford and Rockefeller Foundations and the US State Department, supplemented anonymously by the Central Intelligence Agency. British research is conducted mainly in three specially designated centres, namely the School of Slavonic Studies in the University of London, the Institute of Soviet and East European Studies at Glasgow University and the Centre for

Russian and East European Studies at Birmingham University. Of these three, the Birmingham Centre, since it was directed by Professor Alexander Baykov in the 1950s, has contributed most towards understanding the Soviet system. By comparison with that in the USA British research is poorly endowed but it too depends on the government and large foundations for its funding. The intention of the donors is to draw extra lines in the stereotype, to make it clearer and more easily recognizable and the researchers frequently oblige. The work is done in strict conformity with the practices of social science research except that it is started from a hypothesis about the Soviet Union which is merely confirmed. All the ritual of uncovering sources, collecting and collating data and laboriously drawing conclusions is followed. The final results appear in footnoted texts between neatly and often expensively bound covers. They look impressive.[4]

It is incredibly difficult to find scholarly works in the USA or Britain which portray the Soviet Union in a sympathetic light. The most impressive recent American writer is Albert Szymanski, a sociologist from the University of Oregon, who in the course of writing *Is the Red Flag Flying?* in the middle 1970s purged himself of prejudice about the Soviet Union. He went on to write a balanced account of human rights in the USA and the Soviet Union called *Human Rights in the Soviet Union*.[5] Szymanski risked the wrath of the US educational establishment with these works. Sadly he committed suicide early in 1985.

More names make up the British list but they tend to be concentrated in the generation which graduated well before the onset of the Cold War. The most notable of them have been Maurice Dobb[6], Andrew Rothstein[7], Sidney and Beatrice Webb[8], and E H Carr, pre-eminent as an historian of the Bolshevik Revolution but also the author of the most lucid analysis of the Soviet impact on the West.[9] The most recent example of a dispassionate analysis of Soviet affairs is the lengthy two-volumed study of the Soviet Union's war with Germany by John Erickson, *The Road to Stalingrad*, 1975, and *The Road to Berlin*, 1983. There is also a small group of British writers who contribute to our understanding of the Soviet Union but who in varying degrees fail to shake off the influences of bourgeois social science. The most prominent of these are Robert Davies, David Lane, and Mary McAuley.[10]

There are two other categories of academics who subscribe to the formulation of the stereotype. There are those who do so out of conformity with the capitalist system or its institutions such as Western democracy but without a perverse interest in the Soviet Union. This category has many members from the social sciences. And there are those who regard themselves as a part of the Labour Movement but who do not consider for different reasons the Soviet Union as a socialist society. These emphasize the areas where it is claimed the Soviet Union has deserted or distorted or maligned socialist principles. The details of the criticism in all cases are similar but they supplement each other even when they differ. They are not of equal importance, however. The main body of criticism arises from pressures for conformity within the system. It is this which has priority in the communications channels and becomes part of the dominant paradigm. It most neatly reflects the interests of private capital. The criticisms from within the Labour Movement confirm the stereotype created by the main group. They do not have a separate identity but they are important in that they are directed at people who, other things being equal, are most likely to be sympathetic to the Soviet Union. They reflect ideological divisions which have occured in socialist movements.

The Anti-Soviet Socialists

The primary ideological distinction within the Labour Movement is that between communism and social democracy. Its basis is analytical, involving different, contradictory perspectives of reality. It is not simply about attitudes towards the Soviet Union. Indeed these are by-products of profound theoretical differences about property relations in capitalist societies.

Communists recognize that capitalist property relations, namely the private ownership of the means of production, form the structure of capitalism and, therefore, have a causal significance for everything which happens in capitalist societies. The impact of private ownership is mediated through the class divisions which it creates. It is not possible to make analytical sense of anything under capitalism without first asking questions about class. It is not possible to solve any social, economic or political problems, therefore, without first removing their class causes and this involves changing the ownership of property from private to public. Historical experience has shown that this has not normally been achieved by evolutionary means through parliamentary democratic procedures.

Social democrats on the other hand, see capitalism as a composition of pluralistic interest groups. There is class conflict but also many other conflicts of equal causal value. Each of these conflicts can be treated without reference to the others. Thus the evils of capitalist societies can be remedied through a process of social engineering involving a series of short-run adaptations such as partial public ownership, protective legislation, social welfare schemes and Keynesian economic policies. Underlying this process is the belief that the changes can *only* be achieved through the normal political decision-making process. Social democratic societies have variable and vacillating mixtures of public and private enterprise but where private capital is dominant.

In a discussion between communists and social democrats it may be difficult to differentiate between their ends; they both want a transformed capitalist society. But they differ profoundly over the question of means and these differences are elevated to a matter of principle. Social democrats are committed to a gradual transformation through electoral means and cannot countenance the primary use of extra-parliamentary means. They reject out of hand the very idea of change through revolution.

It is through this principled commitment to electoral gradualism that the attitude of social democrats to the Soviet Union evolves. They are hostile to communism in general for it has a threatening status as an alternative option. In order to denounce communism they search for defects in its practice and condemn the means used to achieve it. Inevitably they concentrate their attention and criticism on the world's primary illustration of a communist society, namely the Soviet Union. They refuse to accept the Soviet Union as a proper expression of socialist principles and are thus obliged to denigrate it, to highlight its defects. They exploit the same issues as other critics of the Soviet system, perhaps with different emphases but with no less venom for as they adapt to capitalism, they accommodate to its main values and see communism as the main enemy. Social democrats in consequence pursue domestic communists and find no difficulty in joining capitalist alliances against communist countries. All social democratic parties, are anti-communist and, in the final analysis, anti-Soviet.

There has been relatively little theoretical legitimation of social democracy. In the USA there is no public discussion of roads to socialism whereas in Britain it is dominated by the mainstream Labour Party which is social democratic, pragmatic in its approach to politics and reflects the economism of British trade unions. The Labour Party, moreover, is not challenged domestically by parties advocating alternative roads to socialism so it is not compelled to justify itself in relation to the practice of communism. Its anti-Sovietism is a latent factor which emerges through its foreign policies supporting NATO, the 'special relationship' with the USA and, when in office, through continuing the essential parts of Conservative foreign policies. This assessment is reflected neatly in *The Future of Socialism* by C A R Crosland, written during the period of the Cold War. Crosland's book is most probably the most important post-war treatise on social democracy to be published in Britain. He considered it unnecessary to devote any time to a discussion of communism. He rejected Marxism as a body of analysis, in any case. "In my view", he wrote, "Marx has little or nothing to offer the contemporary socialist, either in respect of practical policy, or of the correct analysis of our society, or even of the right conceptual tools or framework. His problems have been almost without exception falsified . . . his teaching . . . holds little relevance today . . ."[11] He went on to illustrate from the experience of Britain in the late 1940s and early 1950s that capitalism had already been transformed through the process of social democracy in that capitalists had lost their commanding position to the state, the government was no longer the executive of the capitalist class, nationalization had transferred power to workers and that industry was largely managed by a non-capitalist managerial class. These ideas sound somewhat archaic in contemporary Britain but they are still how social democrats would explain the socialist transformation process. Crosland, moreover, did not question whether a socialist Britain should remain in NATO, under the tutelage of the USA. The implication of all his references to international relations was that Britain's alignment against the Soviet Union was correct. This has largely remained the position of the Labour Party.

The experiences of social democratic parties in West Germany, Scandinavia and the Netherlands confirm that of Britain. This is not the case in France and Italy, however, where social democrats have had to confront large communist parties and, have, therefore, had to be more explicit about their own identity. There is also a greater emphasis on comparative socialist theory on the continent of Europe than in Britain simply because European socialist movements have not been grounded in the economism of trade unions as in Britain. European socialist academics are called on, therefore, to play a greater part in articulating the virtues of social democracy than in Britain.

The second type of ideological division in socialist movements arises specifically out of anti-Sovietism and has been expressed through the rise of Trotskyist splinter groups and the break of Communist China with the Soviet Union in 1967 when the Chinese Communist Party argued that capitalism had been re-established in the Soviet Union. This division put many members of the radical left in capitalist countries in opposition to the Soviet Union. Some had joined Trotskyist groups in small numbers until 1956 when the events in Hungary and the revelations about Stalin at the CPSU 20th Congress in Moscow created dissension in Western communist parties. After that the anti-Soviet groups grew in size and in number, for their propensity to split continued. The Trotskyists, who were themselves conceptually divided, designated the Soviet Union as a degenerate workers' state, as Trotsky himself had done. Some of them described this degeneracy as 'state capitalism' while others condemned both the Soviet Union and China as bureaucratic.

The student unrest in the USA, France and West Germany in the 1960s introduced many new recruits to the radical left who admired the Chinese Revolution and followed the Chinese analysis of the Soviet Union. They joined the Maoist groups which believed that the Bolshevik leaders had "erected an out-and-out capitalist economic structure of a state monopoly type (which) conforms in all essential features to the classical analysis of imperialism given by Lenin."[12]

The Trotskyist and Maoist diversions attracted few workers but had a fascination for students at the undergraduate and post-graduate level as well as university teachers. In consequence it turned some academic Marxists to anti-Sovietism who were more perceptive and more persuasive than the conventional Sovietologists and Kremlinologists who attacked the Soviet Union. Such prominent Marxist writers as Paul Sweezy, the editor of *Monthly Review*, and Charles Bettelheim who had written extensively about class in the Soviet Union as well as about the Cultural revolution in China,[13] took up the Chinese position. Ernest Mandel rewrote Marxist economic theory to take account of his Trotskyist interpretation of the Soviet Union while Isaac Deutscher expressed his Trotskyist perception of the Soviet Union through his nonetheless scholarly biographies of Leon Trotsky and Joseph Stalin. There have, of course, been other intellectuals, especially from the "New Left" which tends not to dirty its fingers in practical politics, who have made their contributions to the stereotype, usually around the question of 'human rights'.[14]

The latest relevant ideological division within the Labour Movement is that caused by the rise of Eurocommunism within European Communist parties. As in the case of social democracy, the Eurocommunist attitude towards the Soviet Union is a consequence of the rejection of a class analysis of capitalism in general. The Italian Communist Party, which has been at the margin of electoral success for many of the post-war years, started the process by postulating that the transition to socialism had to be through existing capitalist institutions. It was followed by a number of European communist parties, including that in Britain. The main theoretical case for Eurocommunism was articulated by Santiago Carrillo, then general secretary of the Communist Party of Spain, in 1976 though he fairly quickly deserted it.[15]

The rejection of a consistent class analysis meant that the political categories which flowed from it, such as the leading role of the working class, the strategic importance of trade unions, the need for a dictatorship of the proletariat and the socialist basis of the Soviet Union, were also rejected. Although the Euro-communist approach to the Soviet Union was a consequence of an analytical position rather than a cause, the Soviet model was a specially important factor because Western European communist parties began to see an identification with it as an obstacle to electoral successes. This encouraged them to adopt a pragmatic approach towards the Soviet Union. They did not regard the Soviet Union with uniform suspicion and hostility as did social democratic parties and in the main continued to have a relationship with the Communist Party of the Soviet Union. They joined with social democratic parties, however, on selected issued such as the crisis in Czechoslovakia in 1968, the presence of Soviet troops in Afghanistan, the legitimacy of Solidarity in Poland and over the question of human rights in general. They became involved in anti-Soviet alliances within the Peace Movement. Thus in this way a new source of academic critics of the Soviet Union was uncovered which effectively endorsed the Western stereotype of that country. The occasional support of

Eurocommunists for Soviet policies was smothered by the establishments' acclaim for their criticism. Up till the present, however, Eurocommunist academics have not made a significant intellectual contribution one way or the other to the debate over the Soviet Union.

The Legitimizers of Capitalism

The reason why so few academics are willing to write favourably about the Soviet Union does not reflect well on their intellectual integrity. That is, it is not because the majority have analysed the Soviet Union and have made their preference for the Western way of life. Most academics either duck the issue or make their preference known simply by projecting Western institutions as ideal types, thus denigrating Soviet ones by implication. In their work, for example, whether it is about poverty, unemployment, crime or industrial unrest they locate the causes in the malfunctioning of the system and not in the structure of capitalism itself. In effect they are saying that there is nothing inherently wrong with capitalism, that nothing would be gained by changing it and, that, therefore, there is nothing to be learned or gained from differently structured societies such as the Soviet Union. Some go further than this and say that if only the malfunctioning could be cured everything would be perfect. These academics depict Western institutions as ideal types. Private ownership, the free market, the secret ballot, parliamentary democracy, the profit motive are all attributed with the virtue of perfection so long as they are allowed to function without interference, aggravation or modification. They state that economic resources can only be effectively distributed through the free market mechanism; that incentives to invest, to work, to innovate can only arise from the profit motive; that democracy can only exist where there are free elections with competing candidates in multiple parties. It follows that a society without a free market, with no profit motive and which is not governed through a parliamentary system must suffer from major economic and political defects which are expressed through inferior economic performances and a denial of political rights. Put differently, the inference is that private ownership is good in itself and that public ownership is bad; that individualism is good and that collectivism is bad; that the free market is good and that state planning is bad. By all or any of these scores the Soviet

33

Union is malformed.

This form of anti-Sovietism is a corollary of the need for capitalist societies to protect themselves with ideas which convince their populations that they live in the best of all possible worlds. Academics help fulfill this need with complex theories which do not necessarily refer to the Soviet Union but which analyze efficiency, freedom, democracy and equality solely in terms of Western capitalist values. Some of the most influential legitimizers of capitalism have, however, made direct references to the Soviet system and its form of organization. The most important contributors in this group are F A von Hayek and Milton Friedman, the principal theorists of monetarism, and Karl Popper, the most influential philosopher for capitalism in recent history. Both Hayek and Popper began to make their impact in the English speaking world with a frontal attack on marxism as a method and communism as a practice while the Second World War was in progress. They interacted with each other to provide formidable intellectual reinforcements for capitalism at a time when there was a widespread distrust of free market forces. Both wrote major works attacking the basis of communism whilst the Soviet Union was repelling the Nazi invaders. In fact, Hayek attempted to show in his book, *The Road to Serfdom*,[16] that communism was a totalitarian form of government which gave rise to fascism. Thus while the Russians and Germans were locked in bitter battle he tarred each with the same brush and posed them both as evil options to liberal capitalism. In order to do this he projected his own unique sequence of historical stages. Socialist societies, he claimed, arose because of the failure of political leaders to protect the conditions necessary for the operation of the free market. In other words they arose because free enterprise was not achieved rather than because of inherent defects in it. He emphasized totalitarian trends in socialism and compared them with fascism. To make this sequence credible Hayek defined the Weimar Republic as socialist, claimed that many of its leaders inevitably became fascists and that Nazism was a form, an outcrop of socialism. His arguments formed an intellectually devious case for free private enterprise but they were the soil in which the anti-state monetarist views of Milton Friedman were cultivated. Karl Popper, who was Professor of Logic and Scientific Method at the University of London, provided the philosophical arguments for Hayek and those economists, sociologists, political scientists and historians who supported the capitalist status quo. His book *The Open Society and Its Enemies* published in two volumes in 1945, was acclaimed by the classical economists of the time for its purported exposé of marxism. His work has continued to give encouragement to those academic social scientists who are busily legitimizing the capitalist system.

The Cost of Dissent

Just as societies encourage and facilitate ideas which support them so they disapprove of those which question their legitimacy. The effect is to reward academics whose work endorses capitalism and to penalize those whose work undermines it. The penalties vary but they can be severe. It would be misleading to show intellectual activity responding solely to rewards and penalties but there is undoubtedly some relationship. There are stereotypes about professions as well as about societies. That which portrays the academic profession shows it to be motivated by a search for truth above all else, and concerned with learning, developing and communicating knowledge. This image helps to protect a working environment in which free intellectual activity can take place. There are impediments in the environment, however, which are not easily recognized as such. Academics themselves are products of an intellectual milieu in which capitalist values predominate; they are as responsive as other persons to the pressures for conformity; they are involved in professional intellectual activity as a means of subsistence and are as concerned as managers or civil servants with their security of employment, promotion, status and rewards. In the same way, as with all other employees, the product of academic activity is not the object of that activity which is to subsist.[17] If ideological conformity produces stable and secure employment and intellectual enthusiasm for capitalist values results in promotion, and if promotion brings high status and material benefits then all of these factors will enter into the perception by academics of the character and purpose of their work. Moreover, in case there is a tendency to feel that the single-minded pursuit of subsistence is contrary to the single-minded pursuit of truth, then capitalist ethics equate high status and income with high quality intellectual activity. Those who make it in the profession need have no qualms about what they have done to get there.

So academics can conform to capitalist values in the righteous

35

belief that they are adhering to the highest intellectual values. But just in case they have doubts and might even be considering dissent, they learn that there are costs for non-compliance.

The costs of expressing dissenting views are often difficult to assess because, in many instances, they are hard to discern. But everyone in academic life knows they are present. They have always existed, as a survey of the history of science or of ideas in general would show. In academic circles, of course, dissent is not necessarily a political act. It refers to any disagreement with prevailing theories and can be as vituperous in the subjects of English Literature and Philosophy as in Economics or Politics as shown by the long saga surrounding Dr Leavis in the English Department of the University of Cambridge and the hostility shown by Oxford Philosophers to their critics in the post-war period. Life may be just as difficult for a dissenting specialist in mediaeval comedy as for one in contemporary social science.

Politically dissenting academics, however, confront not simply the hostility of an irascible professor backed by a university administration but the multifarious power of the state, exercised by the government and its security services, the press, television, publishers, editors of journals and their conforming peers. In this situation the costs of dissent are wide-ranging. Applicants for academic posts in the USA and Britain who have known dissenting views find it difficult to get them though rarely is the real reason for rejection exposed. Such candidates are usually told that they are under-qualified, over-qualified or wrongly-qualified. Where academics are employed on short-term contracts or where there is a tenure system as in the USA where all new entrants to university posts are compelled to seek tenure of employment after six years and in that period are judged by the scale of their published work, it is difficult for dissenters to survive.

There has been no serious study of the actual costs of political dissent in British universities as there has been in the USA. This may be because of the pretence that such things do not happen in Britain. But in a study which raises the issue in the field of adult education in the Cold War period it is quite clear that academics who disagreed with the Cold War hysteria were excluded from jobs, refused access to particular courses, put under scrutiny and, in isolated cases, dismissed.[18] Moreover, it is known that many activists in the student protest movement in the late 1960s, although academically highly qualified, failed to obtain university posts. This exclusion occurred even though at the time dissent was more permissible in part because the student revolt had made dissenting books commercially profitable.

The British government's concern about dissent has never been absent but it has vacillated in its intensity with the course of international relations. It was acute in the Cold War period; seemingly declined during the period of detente and re-emerged in the late 1970s with the frenetic growth of the Peace Movement. The state's attention was then focussed on the Soviet Union as the enemy. Anyone who questioned that perception was singled out for special attention.

The Repression of Academic Dissent in the US

The Cold War period spanned the administrations of Truman, Eisenhower and Kennedy, from 1946 until after the Cuba crisis. It was a conflict over communism in the USA and abroad, marked by red-baiting and witch-hunts at home and threats to depose socialist governments in Europe and the Soviet Union. Its essence was described succinctly at the time by Paul A Baran, an economics professor at Stanford University who himself became a victim of the red-baiting, in the following way:

"The Cold War is . . . by no means irrational from the point of view of the American ruling classes. Everything synthesizes beautifully in its general effects. It provides the political climate in which an agreement can be extracted from the American people to spend $20 billion annually for military purposes. It sets the stage for the complete destruction of an independent labor movement . . . It has reshuffled domestic political forces in such a way that openly fascist organizations and individuals, only a few years ago hiding in the underworld of American politics, are able to operate at the center of the political stage—witness the current McCarthy affair. And, last but not least, it provides the grand strategy for expanding and protecting American investment abroad . . . In one word: it furnishes the political formula for the concerted struggle for (the) preservation of capitalism abroad and for its strengthening and, if necessary, fascization at home."[19]

Internal repression was orchestrated by the US Congress

37

House Committee on Un-American Activities, the Senate Internal Security Sub-Committee and the Senate Permanent Sub-Committee on Investigations. This last Committee was chaired by Senator Joseph McCarthy who made the headlines through his assault on liberal opinion-formers in the US and in US agencies abroad. But, as Paul Baran indicated, political repression was an integral part of the period, interacting with the increase in armaments expenditure. There was already a barrage of anti-communist legislation on the American statute book. The Smith Act of 1940, introduced as a federal sedition act and intended for removing opposition to American involvement in the war against Germany, was used to ensnare communists who hitherto had been protected by the Constitution. In October, 1949, 12 of the 13 members of the national board of the Communist Party of the US were imprisoned under the Act for no less than 5 years. There was a clause in the Taft–Hartley Act of 1947 which prohibited communists from holding office in trade unions. The Internal Security Act of 1950 (the McCarron Act) established concentration camps for dissenters though they were never used. President Truman was active in filling up the loopholes through which dissent could be expressed. After the Congressional elections in 1946 in which the Republicans made substantial gains a loyalty programme became a shuttlecock between the parties and, in order to outdo the Republicans "Truman signed Executive Order 9835 which launched a purge on the federal civil service and inspired initiative purges at every level of American working life".[20]

Academics were a natural target for the red-baiters and a purge began of what David Caute called the "reducators".[21] The universities in many cases were willing participants thus exploding the self-generated myth of the university as a "free market-place of ideas". The President of the University of Washington defended the firing of six professors from the University for being members of the Communist Party on the grounds that "the characteristics of the Party were inimical to the future welfare of the institutions of freedom in the United States."[22] Numerous universities including Harvard, the Massachusetts Institute of Technology, and New York University, dismissed professors for communist affiliations or simply for refusing to reveal the names and activities of others. They were assisted by a formidable array of informers from the faculties. Secret FBI papers stolen by a radical group from Media University in Pennsylvania in 1971 revealed that campus police worked hand in hand with the FBI and that administrative and faculty personnel were high on the list of informants whom secret agents contacted regularly.[23] Sidney Hook, Professor of Philosophy at New York University, internationally known as a scholar of marxism, not only gained a reputation as an exposer of communist indoctrination techniques and the dangers of "Soviet fifth column" activities but established himself as a practitioner of red-baiting by informing against the celebrated specialist on China, Owen Lattimore, and Harry Slochower, a professor of German at Brooklyn College.[24] The details of Paul Baran's life at Stanford University add to the picture of academic establishments deserting academic freedom like the plague at the first whiff of a crisis. Baran was the only marxist economist with tenure at a leading American university during the Cold War. His death of a heart attack in 1964 was "hastened" it was alleged, "by the brutality of the University's hounding".[25] In a letter to Paul Sweezy in 1964 he wrote that if it were not for his small son "I would literally quit tomorrow . . . rather . . . than have to tolerate those bastards spitting in my face all the time."[26] When Stanford's confidential file on Baran was leaked to the press in 1971 it contained many letters and memos "from alumni insisting that the Administration . . . take action against Baran for treason and subversive statements . . ."[27]

The effect of the red-baiting was two-fold. The first was that many academics lost their jobs. David Caute has described the extent:

> "The political purges that hit American colleges and schools during the Truman–Eisenhower era cost at least six hundred and probably more, teachers and professors their jobs, about 380 of them in New York City. The scale of the intimidation was partly reflected in a survey conducted in 1955 of 2451 social science teachers, in 165 colleges and universities, who reported 386 incidents involving allegations of Communism, subversion or fellow-travelling, 10 per cent of which resulted in dismissal or forced resignation."[28]

By June, 1953 more than a half of over 100 professors who refused to reveal names under the protection of the Fifth Amendment had been dismissed or suspended. The University of California alone, had lost 110 scholars by March 1951—26 dismissed, 37 resignations in protest and 47 who had refused appointments. In one bitter year 55 regular courses had to be dropped.

The second effect was incalculable. This was the extent of the suppression of views critical of the USA and supportive of the Soviet Union. American liberalism of the New Deal era was shattered by the Cold War and a new creed, Cold War liberalism emerged "head and shoulders above its competitors to the Left and to the Right as the dominant ideology within government, the press and the world of learning. The linchpin of this creed was hostility toward the Soviet Union and American Communism . . ."[29] The Cold War liberals had an obsessive anti-Sovietism which blinded them to the excesses of those to their Right, like Richard Nixon and Joseph McCarthy, who were pressing for domestic purges but who shared their hostility to the Soviet Union. A consequence was not simply that academics became careful about what they said about the Soviet Union but that they tried to avoid the topic altogether. A study of the impact of the Cold War on social science teaching reported that "some teachers omitted certain topics which they believed, on professional grounds, ought to be discussed. Other respondents slanted their presentation away from their professional convictions, or balanced an intellectually preferred but controversial position with discussion of a more popular opposing viewpoint. All three ended up by giving students an altered version of what in their best judgement was the truth . . ."[30] It is hardly surprising, the Report added, that specific omissions occurred in connection with the study of communism, Soviet Russia and Red China and that where people had already published controversial views they engaged in toning them down or rewriting them altogether.

The repression of intellectuals in the USA during the Cold War period was unique only in its intensity. It arose again in the late 1960s following in the wake of the student protest movement and involved dismissals, censorship and police surveillance.[31] And it has re-emerged since the intensification of the arms race in the late 1970s. The features of the present international situation closely resemble those of the immediate post-war Cold War period. As Paul Baran commented on the First Cold War, everything synthesizes beautifully for the American ruling classes, particularly the domestic political forces where political authoritarianism and economic liberalism combine to create a consensus in favour of arms production. But there is a difference. Cold War liberalism has maintained an unbroken dominance over government, the media and the institutions of higher learning. The academics do not have to break with progressive habits as was the case with the New Deal liberals. They still have the memory of repression but have lost the habit of genuine ideological protest. Some joined together to protest at the Vietnam War, at US involvement in Nicaragua and at the US nuclear arms build-up, but there has not been any ideological basis to the protests. None of it has involved questioning the legitimacy of capitalism. There is no compulsion on academics to rethink their commitment to the American way of life. Even those who protest have a rhetoric which presents the American people with no options. The effect is that the methods of intellectual repression which were used under Truman and Eisenhower are no longer necessary. The academic milieu is dominated by a frightening consensus which has only shades of distinctions. It is the faithful servant, a compliant tool, of the capitalist system. The situation is different in Britain and more encouraging but until the contradictions in the USA have their own powerful ideological expressions British questioning of the stereotype of the Soviet Union will have little impact on international relations.

FOOTNOTES

1. *The New York Times*, Monday 18th November, 1985.
2. ibid.
3. This comment is based on my own recent experience involving research into Soviet trade unions, in the course of which I have consulted most British and American works dealing with the history of labour in general and trade unions in particular in the Soviet Union. Some contain usable information from which negative and derogatory conclusions are drawn; others are completely unusable. In the first category for example, is *The Origin of Forced Labour in the Soviet State, 1917-1921. Documents and Material*, by James Bunyan, California, 1967. This is an invaluable collection of documents about the problems of labour in revolution and civil war from which many lessons could have been drawn by capitalist nations in World War II. In the second category is *The Life and Death of Soviet Trade Unionism, 1917-1928* by Jay B Sorenson, New York, 1969. Sorenson, a faculty member of Smith College, Massachusetts drew on many original Soviet sources to create a sick fantasy which has no utility of any kind. There are many such works dealing with the history of the Communist Party in the 1930s, the life of Stalin and Soviet foreign policy. It would be tedious to repeat them.
4. See *The Russian Revolution of 1905. The Workers' Movement and the Formation of Bolshevism and Menshevism* by Solomon M Schwarz, University of Chicago Press, 1967. This book rewrites the history of the 1905 Revolution to favour the Mensheviks.

5. *Is the Red Flag Flying. The political economy of the Soviet Union today,* London, 1979, pp. 236 and *Human Rights in the Soviet Union. Including Comparison with the USA* London, 1984, pp. 338.

6. *Soviet Economic Development Since 1917,* 1948, pp. 474.

7. *A History of the USSR,* Pelican Books, 1950, pp. 384 and *Man and Plan in the Soviet Economy,* London, 1948, pp. 300.

8. Sidney and Beatrice Webb were authors of *Soviet Communism. A New Civilization?,* a lengthy and detailed study of the USSR in 1935.

9. Carr wrote prolifically from the 1930s until his death at the age of ninety in 1982. He was not a marxist but his 14 volume *History of Soviet Russia* is a classic, as is *The Soviet Impact on the Western World,* 1946, a brief, persuasive analysis of Soviet morality and institutions.

10. Robert Davies wrote 2 volumes in "The Industrialization of Soviet Russia" series which were, *The Collectivization of Soviet Agriculture, 1929-1930,* 1980, pp. 491 and *The Soviet Collective Farm 1929-1930,* 1980, pp. 216. David Lane wrote a number of books including *The Soviet Industrial Worker,* (with Felicity O'Dell), 1978, pp. 167, while Mary McAuley is the author of *Politics and the Soviet Union,* 1977, pp. 352.

11. *The Future of Socialism* by C A R Crosland, London, 1956, pp. 20-21.

12. *The Restoration of Capitalism in the USSR* by Martin Nicholas, Chicago, 1975, quoted by Szymanski in *Is the Red Flag Flying?* op cit, p. 5.

13. *Class Struggles in the USSR,* 2 volumes, 1976 and 1978. Sweezy and Bettelheim jointly wrote *On the Transition to Socialism,* New York, 1971, while Sweezy expressed his own thoughts about the Soviet Union in *Post-Revolutionary Society,* New York, 1980.

14. I have concerned myself here only with English speaking academics. All capitalist countries have experienced a similar academic legitimation of anti-Sovietism to that in Britain and the USA. There has been a plethora of academics in West Germany, France and Italy in all of the categories named here who have served the stereotype. There have also been some who have suffered for their non-conformity. West German academics suffered most for under the Berufsverbot decree introduced by Chancellor Willie Brandt's Social Democratic government in 1972, political dissent cost some of them their jobs. The decree was introduced allegedly to keep enemies of the West German Constitution out of civil service jobs. It was, however, used largely to get Communists and their allies dismissed from government employment. In West Germany university teachers are employees of the state. It covered a rather loose definition of acts considered detrimental to the Constitution but at its core was expressed sympathy with the Soviet Union. The decree's net was cast very wide, bringing in people who were neither communists nor marxists and who were simply protesting about specific issues such as women's rights.

15. *"Eurocommunism" and the State* by Santiago Carrillo, London, 1977.

16. *The Road to Serfdom* by F A Hayek, London, 1944.

17. See *Wage Labour and Capital,* by Karl Marx, p. 34.

18. *Adult Education and the Cold War* by Roger T Fieldhouse, Leeds, 1985.

19. *The Longer View,* by Paul A Baran, 1969, p. 206. This quotation was written in July 1950.

20. *The Great Fear* by David Caute, p. 27.

21. ibid, p. 403.

22. "Professionalism in the Social Sciences: Institutionalized Repression" by Marlene Dixon, in *Sociological Inquiry*, 1977, Vol 46, No 3-4. This article is a penetrating exposure of restrictions on academic freedom in the USA.
23. Caute, op cit, p. 428.
24. ibid, pages 319 and 444.
25. Marlene Dixon, op cit, p. 8-25.
26. ibid.
27. ibid, p. 8-20.
28. Caute, op cit, p. 406.
29. ibid, p. 51.
30. *The Academic Mind,* by Paul Lazarsfeld and Wagner Thielens, Jr, 1958, p. 197.
31. See *Human Rights in the Soviet Union* by Albert Szymanski, pp. 187-195.

PART II

Soviet Reality

Chapter Four
The Democratic Criteria[1]

Diversity

The reason for examining the reality of the Soviet Union is not simply to measure the extent to which the Western portrayal of it is a distortion but to try to understand why it is portrayed in such degrading terms. It is obviously not sufficient to establish that the Soviet Union is socially and culturally different from the Western nations. Differences between nations are commonplace. There are wide climatic, geographical, cultural and historical distinctions between Britain, Japan, the USA and West Germany yet they arouse no serious political interest nor do they currently form the basis for enmity between them. What then is so offensive about the Soviet Union?

There are two main difficulties in answering this question. The first is that the Soviet Union is so large and complex that it defies generalizations. Behind and in spite of the Western image, 265.5 million people interact with each other in kinship, neighbourhood and ethnic relations. They comprise 126 nationalities and ethnic groups and speak more than 100 different languages. Many of these people present greater contrasts than those which exist between the Western nations themselves. Neither Czarist Russia nor the Soviet Union has been a 'melting pot' for cultures, for national identities have always been jealously guarded throughout their histories. Russia was never a predator of the classic imperialist kind. Since the establishment of the Soviet Union the variety of languages and cultures has been preserved and developed so that in some ways there is greater diversity now than ever before. It combines the Ukranians, conscious of their heritage as the fountain of Russian culture; the Lithuanians proud of their role in European history and of the beauty of their language; the Innuits within the Arctic Circle who live semi-nomadic lives similar to the inhabitants of Greenland and Labrador, well inside the permafrost zone, and the inhabitants of Central Asia in the former colonies of Czarist Russia.

An indication of the complexity of the USSR can be gauged from the exceptional cultural and regional diversity of the 45.5 million Islamic peoples who live there. Soviet Muslims are found on the border of Poland, in Siberia, on the Chinese frontier, in Central Asia and in Transcaucasia. They have varied ethnic origins. There are the Turkic peoples such as the Tatars, Azerbaidzhanis, Uzbeks and Uighurs; the Iranians such as the Tadzhik, Ossetians, Kurds and Baluchis; the Caucasians, such as the Avars, Lezghis and Tabasarans; and a number of other groups such as the Arabs, the Armenian Khemshils, the Chinese Dunans, the Central Asian Gypsies and the Mongol Sart Kalmyks. The linguistic heritage of the Soviet Muslims includes 15 Turkic, 10 Iranian and thirty Caucasian languages as well as Chinese and Mongol. Their histories are equally varied. The Tadzhiks belong to an ancient urban tradition while the Kazakhs were nomadic until relatively recently; the Tatars arrived at the Volga in the Thirteenth Century while the Dungans entered Russian territory as refugees only a century ago; the Caucasians on the other hand, are descendants of the original aboriginal population. At the time of the Revolution the Azerbaidzhanis in the region of Baku were industrialized, the Volga Tatars were involved in commerce, the Turkmen were still plundering their neighbours and the Karakalpaks were primitive herders and farmers. This multiplicity of interests has produced contemporary diversity. In all areas of the Soviet Union, much of the education of Slav and Muslim is through the medium of their national languages. They maintain their own traditions and extol their own distinctive histories as well as their respective contributions to the general welfare of Soviet society.

The Soviet people live in an area of almost incomprehensible dimensions. They are distributed between continents. 71 per cent of them live in Europe yet 75 per cent of Soviet territory lies in Asia. The country covers 11 time zones ranging from Nachodka on the Korean border, facing Japan, to Minsk, the capital of Byelorussia, the most westerly Soviet Republic. The Soviet Union comprises one-sixth of the world's surface, an area fourteen times the combined size of Italy, France, Spain and Great Britain. Just one town in Western Siberia, Novosibirsk, with 1.3

CHART 2

The Principal Nationalities of the Soviet Union [2]

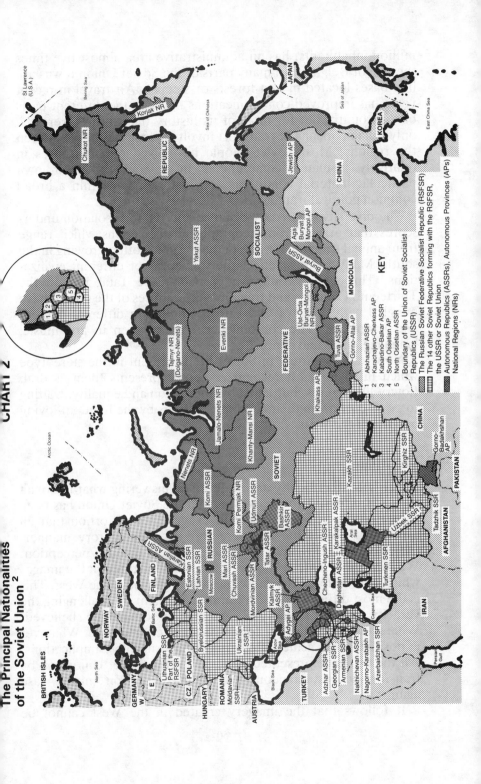

KEY

1 Abkhazian ASSR
2 Karachajevo-Cherkess AP
3 Kabardino-Balkar ASSR
4 South Ossetian AP
5 North Ossetian ASSR

Boundary of the Union of Soviet Socialist Republics (USSR)

The Russian Soviet Federative Socialist Republic (RSFSR)

The 14 other Soviet Republics forming with the RSFSR, the USSR or Soviet Union

Autonomous Republics (ASSRs), Autonomous Provinces (APs) National Regions (NRs)

million inhabitants, has an administrative area almost five times the size of Belgium. In many parts of the Soviet Union towns are like oases located in vast forests or steppes. Air travel in recent years has improved communications between the different parts of the country but for most of its history the railways were the only reliable means of transport involving long journeys between the regions. Most Soviet people have lived out their lives in relatively insulated communities in response to their own particular material conditions and histories but within a broad common political framework.

The diversity created by distance and relative isolation underscores that arising from geographical distinctions which range from animal trapping for furs in the north to cotton growing in the south. Many regions reflect the influences of different civilizations. Through invasions, in particular the Tatar one in the Thirteenth Century, and travellers the cultures of the Orient have mingled with those of Old Europe though in different degrees and intensities. The consequences can be seen in art, music, language, dress and dance.

None of this variety in Soviet life is present in the stereotype which in so far as it recognizes people presents them as drab Lowry-like figures, burdened by oppression and equality, waiting to be rescued from their communist jailors by the freedom-loving peoples of the West.

Distortion

The second difficulty encountered in answering what in Soviet reality is offensive to the West is that the Soviet Union has been subjected to such sustained and exaggerated distortion that all aspects of Soviet life are perceived in a derogatory manner. Objective qualities have no meaning except through perception. Whatever the Soviet Union is or does is seen through the images which have entered the consciousness of people in the West. This is the most difficult problem for anyone intent on challenging the veracity of the stereotype. An enemy cannot be believed. Whatever it does must be for a sinister ulterior motive. Whatever is positive in its achievements must have negative implications. All the evidence presented in favour of the Soviet Union can be transformed instantaneously through perception into a case against it.

It follows that the imagery created in the West cannot be

disproved by empirical investigations. All empirical data is subjected to perception and has no meaning apart from it. There is no point then, in starting with evidence about the living standards of Soviet workers, listing wage levels, price levels, the availability of consumer goods, the social wage and trade union benefits. Nor does it help simply to describe the legal rights of workers or their involvement in the political decision-making process. Not all data, of course, can be equally misconstrued. There is some information, for example, relating to the position of women in society, which cannot be so readily distorted. Nonetheless the assessment of all Soviet data has to commence with an analysis of the assumptions underlying Western perceptions. Only after that has been done can it be possible to question the meanings attributed to it.

Democracy

The Western view of Soviet society is based in the first instance on the premise that it is not democratic. Western political institutions, the multiparty system, contending candidates in elections, the periodic secret ballots and parliamentary or presidential government are seen as the essence of democracy. There is little in the Soviet system to resemble these elements. It does not govern itself according to the rules of the West. In the first place the Soviet Union condemns itself with its own words for it describes itself as a dictatorship of the proletariat. A dictatorship is regarded as the antithesis of democracy and historically has been associated with oppressive regimes in Fascist Italy, Nazi Germany, in Spain under Franco and Portugal under Salazar. Secondly, it has rejected multi-party politics and has enshrined the power and status of the Communist Party in the USSR Constitution. Thus the Soviet Union is governed by a party which cannot be voted out. This is presumed to have two consequences. Firstly, that a political party without competitors tends to become bureaucratic and authoritarian, succumbing to the 'iron law of oligarchy'. This particular oligarchy, moreover is perceived as a self-confessed dictatorship led by a succession of First Secretaries which all in varying degrees have been attributed with dictatorial powers though not all satisfying the classic role of dictators. The second consequence is that the controlling functionaries in a party which cannot be removed from power are presumed to be protected from public exposures and accountability and are free, therefore, to abuse their power in a corrupt fashion. In order to maintain a power position which is not accorded them by the free will of the people they have to resort to the use of state force, secret police and the organs of propaganda. The Soviet people are said in this situation to be oppressed, cowed and muted, waiting for freedom. As this is assumed anyway everything falls into place, thus completing the self-fulfilling prophesies of Winston Churchill that communism "rots the soul of the nation" and of F A von Hayek, that under communism the worst gets to the top.[3]

The manner in which Soviet politics is conducted has aided the Western image-builders. In the Soviet Union there is a recognized mechanism for political decision-making which is not constantly in the public eye as in the Western parliamentary democracies. It is not a point-scoring system, featuring public debate, influencing and responding to public opinion polls, enticed by a media searching for political sensations which, in dull periods creates its own. Major political decisions in the Soviet Union are made away from the public glare. People in general learn about them through communiques from the Political Bureau of the CPSU or from reports of the Central Committee of the CPSU. Soviet politics are not sensationalized through public clashes of personalities appealing to wider audiences and hoping to improve their poll ratings. There is, of course, gossip about personalities but it is not institutionalized as the substance of politics as it is in the West. The media has no part in the spread of Soviet gossip which circulates in spite of it.

The Soviet political system, then, lends itself to accusations that it is secretive and manipulative, that it is run by oligarchies in their own interests. Such assertions are re-inforced by Western media representatives in Moscow who, trying to meet their own standards of what is newsworthy, look for information about personalities and are forced to resort to gossip and 'informed' guesswork, thus emphasizing the secretive character of the Soviet system. This situation has been altered somewhat since Mr Gorbachev became the First Secretary of the CPSU in that he has used the media, particularly television, as a means of countering Western perceptions of the Soviet Union and he has reduced the scope for distortion. But all news from the Soviet Union, even visual information on television no matter how well presented, is still sifted through a perception which defines that country as undemocratic. The assumption underlying this perception, namely that only Western political institutions can be described as democratic, can be questioned on a number of counts.

Dissent in the West

The values which are considered to be so essential in the West for a democratic process, namely the protection of the rights of individuals in relation to the state and of dissenting minorities have resulted from the particular historical experiences of Britain and the USA and are not equally commonly held values in all Western capitalist countries. The countries in the West have evolved their political decision-making processes broadly along two types of historical routes.

The English speaking route came via the Renaissance, the Reformation, and the English Revolution. Along it the characteristic of individualism was acquired from the way in which British capitalism developed through individual traders and producers disentangling themselves from state commercial regulations, thus contrasting the rights of the individual with those of the state. The protection of the economic rights of individuals to acquire and accumulate capital and to dispense with it without hindrance from the state, became the focus of English and Scottish philosophy in the Eighteenth and Nineteenth Centuries. John Locke took up the question of individualism after the Civil War by posing the rights of individuals against the state and church but it was not articulated as economic doctrine until more than a century later when Adam Smith wrote about natural economic laws in the theory of *laissez-faire*. Smith was followed by David Ricardo[4] and between them they laid the basis for a theory which postulated that each person was the best judge of his or her own interests and who by pursuing those interests helped to maximize the utility of everyone. The best way of making people happy was, therefore, to reduce the restrictions on individual effort and initiative. This involved reducing government legislation to the minimum consistent with preserving individual freedom. Thus economic individualism, which reflected the aspirations of a nascent bourgeoisie in the Eighteenth Century, became the core of the ideology of the dominant class in the Nineteenth Century. And although it had a political purpose it eschewed making political comments by implying that there was no relationship between economic and political rights. It effectively, and successfully, separated economics and politics as distinct, unrelated subjects. The economic power of an owner of property was presumed to have no bearing on that person's political rights. This became the dominant feature of liberal political thought.

Along this English route political rights were achieved and extended through a series of confrontations ranging from revolution to political demonstrations between the state and dissenting groups seeking the right to dissent. The basic confrontation which gave character to the English political system was the Seventeenth Century Revolution. On that occasion the issue was religious dissent but because of the unity between church and state the results were profoundly political. The Revolution ended in a compromise between Anglicanism which was the state religion and the nonconformists but it endorsed the views of those who preached tolerance for religious dissent. After that time the right to dissent became established as nonconformist religious groups split and multiplied. At the same time groups of workers in the skilled trades struggled for the right to organize and to oppose both employers and the state. Throughout the Eighteenth Century trade unions were formed in a variety of trades in an uncoordinated ad hoc fashion with each group seeking its own right to dissent. The struggles became overtly political in the Nineteenth Century with the middle class in 1832 and the working class in 1867 obtaining the right to vote. It remained a patchwork, however, for coal miners, agricultural workers and women had to conduct their own struggles; women did not achieve limited political emancipation until 1918. It was in this peculiarly British way that the right to dissent from the state without institutional discrimination became synonymous with the democratic process. It enshrined compromise as the essence of political action.

The alternative route to contemporary Western democracy stemmed from the French revolution which, unlike the English one, did not diversify power but simply transferred it from one nominal ruler, 'the crown', to another, 'the people' without altering the autocratic character in which it was exercised. "The history of the revolution in France" E H Carr commented, "promoted the trend towards totalitarian democracy . . . (it) . . . did not issue in a balance or compromise: it was a victory not for political tolerance, or for the rights of the individual as against the state, but for a particular view of the authority of the state."[5] The French democratic system has retained its authoritarian character and, in consequence, its lack of concern for dissenting minorities. This characteristic is displayed, for example, in trade unions where different ideological interests have been incapable of associating within a single organization. In France there are three national centres representing Communist, non-Communist Socialist and Christian views.

Authoritarian, as against liberal, democracy is present in the many European countries which were influenced by the French during the Nineteenth Century. There the concerns about minorities have been over-ridden by the need for a strong, cohesive state which, in the manner suggested by Rousseau in the *Social Contract* in 1762, expressed the 'general will' of the society. Thus civil liberties have always been secondary to populist government thereby facilitating the transition from authoritarian to totalitarian government.

The USA had its own historical qualities which though visibly different from those in England had sufficient structural similarities to identify with the English democratic values. American society in the Nineteenth Century was forged from waves of immigrants escaping from various forms of authoritarianism. In the new society individualism was a precondition for economic survival whereas, due to the accumulation of immigrants from different cultures and religions, tolerance of dissent became a necessary condition for communal survival. By making virtue out of necessity, individualism and the right to dissent have emerged as essential but unrelated democratic values in the USA and are pursued with greater intent than in any other Western nation. Democracy clearly is a many-varied thing even amongst the Western capitalist countries.

Russia before 1917 had none of the societal qualities of England and the USA except that it was an emerging capitalist nation. Industrialization was nurtured by state intervention such as tariffs, subsidies and state orders rather than through market competition and took the form of large-scale, centralized production units. Thus economic growth in Czarist Russia had nothing to do with economic individualism. It was accompanied, moreover, by an oppressive, centralized state apparatus in which the secret police, arbitrary arrests and exile were common features. The notion of individual freedom had no part in Russian conditions. Liberal political thought, in consequence, had no relevance, right up to the Bolshevik Revolution. In so far as Russia developed democratic forms they were a version of French authoritarian democracy. No liberal traditions were on hand to influence the founders of the new Soviet state in 1917.

Tolerance and Intolerance of Dissent

The qualities which the Western democracies emphasize most when assessing the Soviet Union are tolerance of dissent and the freedom to escape from intolerable conditions by emigrating. No freedoms, however, are absolute in any country. Indeed there is a perpetual argument in most societies about the limits on dissent. Governments need to know the nature and extent of protest which is consistent with what they regard as the preservation of their societies. They continually scrutinize groups, movements, parties and individuals for their threats to the system. The definition of what constitutes a threat varies with circumstances. For example, when a country is under an external threat through war then restrictions on internal protests are intensified. This was the experience of Britain and the USA during both World Wars when those who were defined as potential sympathizers of the enemy because of their ethnicity or even because of the ethnic origins of their names were put under surveillance, socially harassed or interned. At the outbreak of the First World War for instance, The *Daily Mail* distributed posters urging the formation of Vigilance Committees "with the duty of examining the houses, gardens, outhouses etc, of all Germans and Austrians . . . It is better that every German, naturalized or not, in this country shall be safely put under lock and key than that one British soldier should die through the treachery of the enemy in our midst." In the Second World War German aliens in Britain were put into concentration camps irrespective of their loyalties.[6] The Japanese Americans who lived West of the Mississippi also suffered for, after the bombing of Pearl Harbour, they were forcibly relocated to camps in barren areas of the West and prevented from practising Japanese culture or language.

War, however, is simply an extreme example of a general sensitivity about dissent. Whenever the ruling class in Western societies has felt threatened it has reacted by imposing restrictions on those opposed to it. The facility to dissent, therefore, is a sort of barometer of the confidence of the ruling class. Since 1917 international communism has been perceived as the main threat to the stabililty of capitalism and on occasions, as in the USA after the two World Wars, it has been the justification for widespread repression. Domestic communists, regarded as the agents of international communism, have been the victims. But whatever the circumstances they have always been under some sort of surveillance by the state. This pre-occupation with communists, however, is a symptom of a much more general, pervasive and underlying intolerance in Western democratic societies, namely an inability to recognize and accept unregulated collective dissent.

In Western democratic societies legitimate dissent is that which conforms to the value of individualism and is, therefore, confined to individual protest. This is institutionalized in the electoral system based on the secret individual ballot vote. From the point of view of the ruling class this is a sensible recognition of protest because the greater the fragmentation the less it can endanger their power base. It results in pitting individuals against the institutions of capitalism, Parliament, the courts, the agents of government, multi-national companies and the like. There is no threat in such a grossly unequal struggle.

Dangers to the system only arise when individuals recognize their weakness and combine into collectives to rectify the power imbalance. It is for this reason that collective protest has never been fully legitimized in Western democracies, as the history of trade unionism in Britain and the USA testifies. US governments have consistently engaged in hostilities with trade unions, except for a brief interlude during the New Deal period, legislating to control them, taking administrative action to weaken them, siding invariably with employers and whenever necessary using state violence to suppress them. Trade unions have had similar experiences in all other capitalist societies. The state vendetta against trade unions in Britain has in general been less oppressive than in the USA mainly because British employers have at times attempted to control unions more by assimilation than confrontation. The rights of collective action in Britain, however, have always been fragile, likely to be whittled away or even demolished whenever the opportunity to do so has arisen. This fact has been illustrated by recent history. British trade unions after almost two centuries of struggle for the right to take collective action, and during which time it could have been presumed that they had established certain basic rights, have become weaker and more constrained by the law than at any time since before 1875. The intensity of the state's unease with collective protests was revealed firstly when unprecedented state force in both scale and intensity was used against the miners during their 1984-8 strike and then against the London printers in their dispute with News International in 1986-7.

The evidence about dissent clearly shows that its practice varies with circumstances within and between Western democratic societies irrespective of how strongly a belief in dissent is pronounced. There are of course marked differences between such societies for some, for historical and contemporary economic reasons, have wider margins of tolerance than others. In all situations, however, because of the imperative need of societies to sustain themselves, dissent is a phenomenon which can be afforded so long as it is not too dangerous.

The Question of Emigration

The ability of people to move freely within and between countries is similarly determined by material conditions rather than by an inherent belief in it as a right. The Western countries condemn the Soviet Union as a closed society because it restricts the right of its citizens to leave the country. For them emigration is described as an inalienable, incontrovertible right and campaigns are mounted to obtain exit visas for those Soviet citizens who are refused them. The elevation of emigration as a measure of democracy, however, is historically fortuitous in that it meets the needs of Western democracies at this moment.

States have always imposed restrictions on the movement of people between their borders in accordance with their assessment of the national interest.[7] There have been occasions where immigration has been encouraged as in Nineteenth Century USA and other occasions when it has been discouraged, as in contemporary USA. It has rarely been the case that restrictions on both exit and entry have been treated equally for usually economic conditions have favoured one or the other. The determining factor has been whether a society had surplus labour it wished to shed or whether it was short of labour.

In the Nineteenth Century many European countries encouraged emigration to remove labour surpluses caused by the movement of peasants to the towns. Britain was one of these but it also encouraged emigration because it was a necessary condition for colonial expansion. British citizens were needed to run the outposts of the British Empire as well as to settle in congenial conquered areas in Africa. In the post Second World War years Western democracies generally allowed free emigration because it matched their economic needs. Nonetheless some political restrictions on outward movement were imposed. The McCarran Act of 1950 gave the State Department the power to deny exit rights to anyone whose activities abroad might be detrimental to the interests of the USA, as well as forbidding the issue of passports to members of the Communist Party. There was the celebrated case of Paul Robeson, the singer and political activist, who was denied a passport in the 1950s and on whose behalf an international campaign was mounted. The USA has also imposed a blanket prohibition on travel to some countries, such as Cuba, China, Vietnam and Korea at different times since 1945. This still exists for Cuba and Vietnam.

While the freedom to emigrate has been elevated to the status of a right this has not been the case with the freedom to immigrate. Both the USA and Britain exercise strict controls over the right of entry. All persons wishing to visit the USA for any purpose, even for a day, have to complete long application forms with details of their political and social lives. The granting of a visa, moreover, is not permission to enter which is controlled by the immigration authorities on the spot. There have been many instances of British applicants being refused entry or subjected to time and place restrictions. The 1965 US immigration law insists that priority should be given to people with skills which would benefit the society with the consequence that preferential treatment has been given to educated professionals, such as medical doctors and university teachers. It has always been easy for refugees from socialist countries to obtain immigration rights though similar rights have not been conferred on refugees from oppressive regimes with which the US government has had friendly relations such as South Korea, El Salvador or Guatemala. In Britain, immigration is regulated by the British Nationality Act of 1981 under which it has become virtually impossible for black people to enter Britain. This too has been a response to changing labour market conditions.[8]

Types of Democracy

The Western democracies project themselves as the only form of democracy because to do otherwise would expose their claim to be democratic to be challenged. If alternative democratic forms were recognized or degrees of democracy admitted then the citizens of the Western capitalist countries might begin asking whether they possessed the most suitable form or whether they might not be able to improve on what they had by altering some of its conditions. But as democracy is about power-sharing it is inexcusably dogmatic to assert that there can be only one form of distribution of power.

Two main qualities are present in Western democracies. First, they are based on the premise that political decision-making is not related in any sense to economic power and that, therefore, it is possible to equalize the distribution of political power without similarly distributing economic power. Campaigns for universal suffrage were waged in Britain during the Nineteenth Century on the assumption that somehow the extension of the suffrage, secret ballots and periodic elections would produce a more equitable society but so complete has been the distinction between political and economic power that none of the anticipated changes occurred. "One man, one vote" was not an economic leveller.

This separation of political and economic power was not fortuitous but was the main protection of the capitalist system during the long process of political emancipation for workers. Political freedom was never volunteered in Britain by the mixed bag of landowners and the new bourgeoisie but so long as it had no effect on the ownership of the means of production it could safely be conceded in stages. In the USA political equality was granted from the outset for white Americans through the Constitution but this had not the slightest effect upon the distribution of income, of wealth, of property at large and, therefore, of economic power. Nor indeed when it was allowed to black Americans did it remove the causes of discrimination against them. There is not an automatic downward casual relationship between political decision-making and economic power. So long, therefore, as equality is confined to politics, ignoring economic inequalities, then the system is relatively safe.

It would be misleading to see the present system of political decision-making in Western capitalist countries as the result of some kind of Machiavellian plot to protect the private ownership of the means of production. It has been built on the structure of capitalism, at one and the same time expressing its contradictions as workers struggled for greater freedom yet always doing so in a manner which protected the essential structure of capitalism. It is a reflection of the uncanny ways in which societies practise the art of survival. The belief has been created that there is genuine majority rule when every member of the electorate has one vote from the poorest to the richest and can cast it in secret without any formal constraints. This, however, in no way disturbs minority control. The system would be perfect for the bourgeoisie if it did not involve pretence, propaganda and deception to prevent the working class from learning the truth about the nature of power.

The second quality is that Western democracy is formal and institutional; it is about the means of selecting governments and the procedures which regulate their practice. Western democracy passes no opinion about the results of government. To qualify as a democracy a society has to grant universal suffrage, hold secret elections and permit multiple parties to participate. It does not have to govern in the interests of the majority except that periodic elections may compel it to take those interests into account in order to gain re-election. It is not an infringement of Western democracy if a fascist government is elected. The accession of Hitler to power in Germany in 1933 was done in a perfectly constitutional way according to the democratic provisions of the Weimar Republic. After the Second World War, a major demand of the Western allies when effecting peace treaties was that former enemy nations, Germany, Rumania, Hungary and Bulgaria, should hold 'free' elections. It was of little concern that an authoritarian government might be returned, that the old land-owners might retain their power or that fascists might regain their influence. The Western allies actually used some of the Nazis and their collaborators, whom they had agreed at Yalta to remove from influence, in their endeavour to establish formal democratic forms. In Greece after 1945 the British government left former fascist collaborators in power and crushed the anti-fascist resistance in order to restore Western democratic procedures. It was a rather cruel paradox. In the British, American and French zones of defeated Germany the whole cloth of Western democracy was clearly exposed. German capitalists, including the industrial giants, Krupp and Thysson, which had financed the Nazi war and Jewish extermination machine, had their economic power restored through massive injections of American capital, thus ensuring the continued dominance of international capitalism; while a political edifice was constructed involving free elections and multiple parties with the participation of many who had exercised administrative and political power during the Nazi period. The qualification to be democratic did not involve Germans renouncing their fascist beliefs but simply accepting the British and American way of

61

making political choices. Fascism did not have to be eradicated. It was freshly packaged and given new labels to satisfy the conscience of the Western allies. The new German democrats learned quickly. In 1956 they outlawed the German Communist Party which on the eve of the Nazi takeover in 1933 had had nearly 400,000 members and both led the struggle against Nazism and suffered most from its impact.[9] The price for rejecting the Western perception of democracy has always been high. It is being paid in the 1980s by Nicaraguans and El Salvadorians.

The most serious consequence of defining democracy in terms of procedures for making political choices has been that there is no belief in the West in the substance of democracy. What happens in between elections is of little concern to the Western democrats. Western democracy is an area of contending opinions with not only no distinction between good and evil opinions but with no feeling for good and evil. Anything and everything is acceptable so long as the procedures are abided by. Because authoritarian or fascist or physically oppressive political practice could legitimately exist within the framework of democratic procedures it has been relatively easy to undermine and destroy them. Most of the Central and Eastern European countries, including Germany, which were forced to establish Western democratic procedures after 1918 as a condition for admission to the 'free' world as independent states had rejected them by the 1930s in favour of unadorned authoritarian governments. The Western conception of democracy was similarly forced on the newly independent states of tropical Africa but there it has had an even shorter existence. In other parts of the world, in Latin America and Asia, the Western inspired political institutions have crumbled through the firing of a few guns, the capture of a radio station or a proclamation from an army barracks. A system which is so frail that it cannot survive economic crises, which has to be suspended in times of war, which has no resistance to physical force, can surely claim no moral superiority over other forms.

FOOTNOTES

1. In this chapter I have drawn on two areas of my own work, namely the pamphlet "Images and Reality of the Soviet Union", 1983, and a forthcoming book *Trade Unionism in the Soviet Union.*
2. Detail for this map is taken from: *Islamic Peoples of the Soviet Union,* by Shirim Akiner, London, 1983, pp. 14-15. It has been adapted by the

Graphics Department of the University of Leeds. Akiner's book contains a comprehensive and detailed description of the Soviet Muslim population.

3. *The Road to Serfdom,* by F A von Hayek, 1944, ch. X.
4. See *The Wealth of Nations* by Adam Smith and *The Principles of Political Economy* by David Ricardo.
5. *The Soviet Impact on the Western World,* op cit, p. 7.
6. See *COLLAR the LOT. How Britain Interned and Expelled its Wartime Refugees,* by Peter and Leni Gillman, 1980.
7. See Szymanski, op cit, pp. 13-26 for an historical survey of the international movement of labour.
8. See *Immigration Control Procedures: Report of a Formal Investigation,* Commission for Racial Equality, London, 1985, for an examination of the restrictions on black immigrants.
9. See *Beating the Fascists?* by Eve Rosenhaft, 1983, for a penetrating historical analysis of the confrontation between communists and Nazis from 1929 till 1933.

Chapter Five
Soviet Democracy

When the Civil War in Russia was reaching its height and the new Bolshevik state was under threat from the intervention of the Western powers in the autumn of 1918, Lenin wrote a rebuttal of a pamphlet by Karl Kautsky called *The Dictatorship of the Proletariat* which had recently been published. Kautsky was a veteran and influential leader of the German Social-Democratic Party who had been involved in the historic debate about marxist revisionism with Edouard Bernstein and Rosa Luxemburg in 1899. His position changed during the First World War when, according to Lenin, he presented "a blend of loyalty to Marxism in word and subordination to opportunism in deed."[1] He was frequently and increasingly criticized by Lenin for turning "Marx into a common liberal". The offence, however, which spurred Lenin to action in 1918 was Kautsky's description of Bolshevism as dictatorial. Kautsky presented the Bolshevik and non-Bolshevik strands in the Socialist Movement as "the contrast between two radically different methods: the *dictatorial* and the *democratic.*" For Lenin, this raised a fundamental question which was the very essence of proletarian revolution and he was stung into staking the new Bolshevik state's claim to be democratic. "Proletarian democracy", he wrote, "of which Soviet government is one of the forms, has brought a development and expansion of democracy unprecedented in the world, for the vast majority of the population, for the exploited and working people . . . Proletarian democracy is a *million times* more democratic than any bourgeois democracy: Soviet power is a million times more democratic than the most democratic bourgeois republic. To fail to see this one must either deliberately serve the bourgeoisie, or be politically as dead as a doornail, unable to see real life from behind the dusty pages of bourgeois books . . ."[2] Stalin expressed similar sentiments when he described the new Soviet Constitution in 1936. These claims were in direct contrast with the Western stereotype of the Soviet Union and for that reason they were ridiculed. But, as E.

64

H. Carr warned, it "would be a mistake to dismiss such pronouncements as mere propaganda or humbug" and dangerous to regard them as having no relevance for the West by treating "Soviet democracy as primarily a Russian phenomenon without roots in the West or without application to western conditions."[3]

The basis for Lenin's claim was that economic and political power in Bolshevik Russia had been transferred from a minority bourgeois class to a majority working class. No matter what form of political representation was instituted to enable the working class to govern this was unquestionably an improvement. His argument was based on the assumption that it falsified the definition of power to separate economic from political power. How can there be political equality, he asked "between the exploited and the exploiters"?[4] Because he believed that democracy had an economic basis, there could never be a pure form. "Pure democracy", he stated, "is the mendacious phrase of a liberal who wants to fool the workers. History knows of bourgeois democracy which takes the place of feudalism, and of proletarian democracy which takes the place of bourgeois democracy."[5] In other words, democracy reflects the class basis of society and as that widens, giving economic power to the majority, then so must democracy be more extensive and real. "Bourgeois democracy", Lenin insisted, "although a great historical advance in comparison with medievalism, always remains, and under capitalism is bound to remain, restricted, truncated, false and hypocritical, a paradise for the rich and a snare and deception for the exploited, for the poor."[6]

(i) The Dictatorship of the Proletariat

The definition of democracy in terms of class rule gives meaning to the concept 'the dictatorship of the proletariat'. It simply means rule by the proletarian class in its own interests instead of 'the dictatorship of the bourgeoisie' for its own interests. There always has to be class rule, therefore there is always a dictatorship by one class or another. The concept has nothing to do with totalitarian government or indeed with any particular form of government. It is an analytical description of the basis of political decision-making in society and it is in this sense that it has been used in the Soviet Union. It is wrong, therefore, to conceptualize the Soviet form of dictatorship as being similar to that practised by Hitler, Mussolini, Franco or Pinochet.

Indeed, those dictators and bourgeois democracy had much in common for they served similar class interests. The concept of the 'dictatorship of the proletariat' has played a vital and continuous part in the history of the Soviet Union for it has been not merely a description of a form of democracy but an expression of the Revolution as something real, permanent and continuous. It is a key to understanding much of the behaviour of the Soviet Union both as a social organism and in its relations with other countries. When workers' and soldiers' soviets achieved power in 1917 it was a complete victory, not a step in a transitional process or a bourgeois revolution on the historical route to socialism. Any moves, therefore, to accommodate to hostile capitalist forces would have weakened the Revolution by eroding its base. Compromises with private capital such as concessions to attract international capital or political agreements to share power with contending political forces in the manner of pluralism would have been backward steps and admissions that the Revolution had been over hasty and too ambitious. The Bolsheviks, therefore, rejected such action in order to protect the working class as the suppository of state power. Where they did compromise, as when Lenin introduced the New Economic Policy in 1921, it was to avert economic collapse. As soon as that possibility was removed then the compromise was ended. There was no permanent middle way. The Bolshevik leaders had to choose their course. They decided to maintain the working class as the sole and absolute source of state power. The history of the Soviet Union has been dominated by the consequences of that choice.

The commitment of the Bolshevik leaders to working class power transformed the Bolshevik Revolution from being a single, isolated historical event, confined to the month of November in the year 1917, like the end of a war, the birth of a monarch or the assassination of a president, to an historical process without boundaries or time limitations. Therefore, the Revolution was always being waged in the sense that as both the symbol of the struggle for working class power and the source of that power it became mystified and sanctified in much the same way as property rights have been treated as the sacred source of bourgeois power in capitalist countries. The rights of private property have been written into constitutions, buttressed by laws and sanctified by ideology. In some countries they have become inviolate, protected by the laws of treason in a desperate attempt to facilitate the survival of their power structures.

A consequence of the dictatorship of the proletariat and, at the same time, its moral foundation is the absolute belief in proletarian democracy which pervades Soviet society. The rational basis for this belief is that unless the majority class holds power the workers cannot exercise it through economic and political decision-making processes. The preservation of unsullied working class power is then a necessary condition for democratic activity. This condition is not subject to modification in any way. Soviet democracy has never been prepared to countenance the possibility of its own destruction, whether or not a majority wished it, as is the case in Western democracies. There is no possibility of any individual or group being given the right to challenge the legitimacy of working class power. Indeed it is regarded as immoral to want to do so. This constraint is not generally seen as an infringement of individual liberty but as a means of protecting it by preserving the rights of workers as a class. Soviet people are as perturbed and puzzled by the Western tolerance of anti-democratic activities in the name of democracy as the West is critical of the Soviet lack of tolerance for such activities.

(ii)   *The One-Party State*

The second major consequence of the struggle to preserve the Revolution relates to the position of the Communist Party in Soviet society. A major criticism of the Soviet Union by the West is that it is a one-party state and is therefore undemocratic. The political dominance of the Communist Party, however, is a product of Soviet history. In the period between the Revolution and 1922 non-Bolshevik working class parties, the Mensheviks and the Right Social Revolutionaries operated freely. There was, at the same time, an intense debate conducted by factions within the Bolshevik Party. The major figues in the Revolution, Lenin, Trotsky, Zinoviev and Bukharin, belonged to different and changing groups. This situation altered through the exigencies of war and the attempts of parties and groups to undermine the Revolution for their own ends. The intervention of the Allies and the Civil War created many opportunities for counter-revolutionary activities. The Left Social Revolutionaries who had co-operated with the Bolsheviks on the Council of People's Commissars until July 1918 attempted an armed insurrection in that same month. At the end of August, Dora Kaplan, a Social Revolutionary, tried to assassinate Lenin, seriously wounding him with a bullet in the lung above the heart and another in his neck. An earlier attempt had been made on his life on 1st January 1918, as he was returning by car from a meeting with Fritz Platten, the secretary of the Swiss Social-Democratic Party. Lenin was unhurt but Platten was wounded. Some members of the government were assassinated; the lives of others were threatened. Both the Mensheviks and the Right Social Revolutionary Parties refused to support the Bolsheviks at the beginning of the Civil War then changed their minds. They were represented in the Soviets where they expressed their vacillating attitudes towards the Bolshevik regime. This all occurred at a most critical time for the Bolsheviks when they controlled only a rump in European Russia with Petrograd under threat and plans being laid for the evacuation of the government from Moscow. The Bolshevik Party responded by resolving on 2nd September, 1918 that "To the White terror of the enemies of the workers' and peasants' government, the workers and peasants will reply with mass 'Red terror' against the bourgeoisie and its agents."

The Civil War left its own legacy. The railway system, which was the lifeline of the economy, broke down through physical destruction and depreciation. Industry was starved of raw materials and incapacitated by military action. There were acute shortages of manufactured goods. The countryside too was disrupted. Frequently, even where the peasants had grain and foodstuffs, they refused to release them for the industrial workers, thus considerably worsening their plight and making the production of manufactured goods more hazardous. The various sections of the Soviet economy passed on the effects of the war to each other and thus compounded the problems each one faced. The economy was on a downward spiral.[7]

The most destructive effect was on the morale of the industrial workers, peasants, soldiers and sailors who had supported the Revolution in 1917 and had sustained it throughout the Civil War. Once the military pressures were removed in 1920 the participants were able to stand back and ask themselves what had been achieved. All they could see were controls, requisitioning, acute shortages and real starvation causing many deaths. The Revolutionary fervour which had brought military victory had to be sustained by some material gains and there were none available. Many people, ground down by the past and the present, became disillusioned with Bolshevism. Once the Allied military intervention had failed, the greatest threat to the Bolshevik system came in its aftermath, through its own contradictions. This was expressed by outbreaks of peasant unrest; by what Lenin called "banditism – where tens and hundreds of thousands of demobilized soldiers, who are accustomed to the toils of war and regard it almost as their only trade return, impoverished and ruined, and are unable to find work";[8] by strikes and demonstrations in Petrograd and Moscow and at the beginning of March 1921, by a mutiny at the Kronstadt naval base where the Baltic Fleet had its headquarters.

The Tenth Congress of the Russian Communist Party met while the Kronstadt mutiny was under way and Lenin's speech there dealt with it in relation to what he described as "crop failure, a crisis, ruin and demobilization". He saw evidence of a petty bourgeois counter-revolution which he regarded as more dangerous than all the White Russian Generals put together. Under such circumstances the Revolution could have disappeared like a whisp of smoke. Lenin's remedy was to try and heal the breach between workers and peasants and intensify the unity of the Communist Party. He said: "We must bear in mind that the bourgeoisie is trying to pit the peasants against the workers; that behind a facade of workers' slogans it is trying to incite the petty-bourgeois anarchist elements against the workers. This, if successful, will lead directly to the overthrow of the dictatorship of the proletariat and, consequently, to the restoration of capitalism and of the old landowner and capitalist regime. The political danger here is obvious. A number of revolutions have clearly gone that way; we have been mindful of this possibility and have warned against it. This undoubtedly demands of the ruling party of Communists, and of the leading revolutionary elements of the proletariat a different attitude to the one we have time and again displayed over the past year. It is a danger that undoubtedly calls for much greater unity and discipline."[9] The Tenth Congress agreed to proposals which led to the New Economic Policy and eased the tensions on peasants. It also banned organized factions in the Communist Party, called for their dissolution and reminded them that "Everyone who criticizes in public must keep in mind the situation of the Party in the midst of the enemies by which it is surrounded . . ." Other political parties were banned by 1921 so the Communist Party assumed its role as the sole political party and took its first official step towards eliminating dissent in its own ranks. It became the sole custodian of the Revolution in a political format which still operates.

The Bolshevik Party[10], though it shared government with the Left Social Revolutionaries until July 1918, always was the ruling party in Soviet Russia. It made the decision to wage an armed struggle and gave the Revolution its shape and direction. The Bolshevic state with its new superstructure was the creation of the Bolshevik leaders. So too was the state economic planning mechanism. The communist leaders took all the major decisions between 1917 and 1921. They dissolved the elected Constituent Assembly on 20 January 1918 when it conflicted with the All-Russian Congress of Soviets and framed the declaration made a week later which stated "Russia is declared a republic of workers". They drafted the first Constitution passed at the Fifth Congress of Soviets in July 1918 which guaranteed the dictatorship of the proletariat for the purposes of "suppressing the bourgeoisie, abolishing the exploitation of man by man, and establishing Socialism". The Bolsheviks formed the Extraordinary Commission to Combat Counter-Revolution and Sabotage (the CHEKA); they banned the Right Social Revolutionary and Menshevik Parties from participating in the Soviets in June 1918 and lifted the banning order later that year; they also made the decisions as to whether or not non-Bolshevik publications should be circulated. There was no question that from the moment a Bolshevik government was formed in November 1917, the Bolshevik Party monopolised political activity as a means of maintaining the dictatorship of the proletariat through intensifying crises and that without it the Revolution would have been reversed.[11] Thus the events in 1921 merely formalized and institutionalized an already existing power situtation.

The special conditions in the early life of Soviet Russia which led to the dominance of the Communist Party were present in varying degrees throughout most of its history. The country was continually subjected to threats, implicit or overt, during the inter-war years. Stalin talked in the late 1920s about the possibility of being invaded and then, in June 1941, the invasion occurred. Until that time the Soviet Union had lived as in a seige, surrounded by hostile nations, economically and militarily weak in comparison with its capitalist protagonists. It had become fearful to the point of being psychoneurotic about threats to its borders and counter-revolutionary tendencies within them. None of these threats was imaginery. Lenin spoke of the consequential behaviour of the Soviet government. "We were forced to use terror" he stated "in response to the terror employed by the

Entente, when the mighty powers of the world flung their hordes against us, stopping at nothing. We could not have lasted two days had we not replied to these attempts of officers and whiteguards in a merciless fashion. This meant the use of terror . . ."[12] The scale of the White Russian terror can be gauged from the fact that in Rostov alone the White Russian occupying forces shot about 25,000 workers.[13] For the government, survival entailed imposing extraordinary disciplinary-measures. Yet opposition groups within the Communist Party continued to operate openly until 1929. The prominent leaders of different groups, contended with each other on questions of trade unions, agriculture, industrialization and foreign policy. This tolerance ceased in 1928 when renewed domestic and international pressures produced a radical change both in the organization of Soviet society and its international perspectives. The leaders of the opposition in the Party, Leon Trotsky and Grigori Zinoviev were expelled from the Communist Party on 14 November, 1927 by the 15th Congress. Trotsky was sent into exile in Central Asia and, early in 1929, was forced to leave the country.

A different perception of the one-party state emerged after 1928 and was expressed by Stalin in 1936 when he introduced the revised Soviet Constitution which made provision for only one political party, namely the Communist Party. The programme of collectivization in agriculture and the First Five Year Plan from 1929 created a high degree of class homogeneity by destroying free markets, eliminated the profit-motive and dispossessing the rich peasants. The last remnants of capitalism were dismantled. Thereafter all Soviet citizens were either workers or peasants. There were no antagonistic class relations in the capitalist sense in the Soviet Union from that period. The question then was whether a multi-party system could operate in such a situation. Stalin answered it when he said:

"A party is a part of a class, its most advanced part. Several parties, and consequently freedom for parties, can exist only in a society in which there are antagonistic classes whose interests are mutually hostile and irreconcilable – in which there are, say, capitalists and workers, landlords and peasants, kulaks and poor peasants, etc. But in the USSR there are no longer such classes as the capitalists, the landlords, the kulaks etc.

71

In the USSR there are only two classes, workers and peasants, whose interests – far from being mutually hostile – are on the contrary friendly. Hence there is no ground in the USSR for the existence of several parties, and consequently for freedom for these parties . . . In the USSR only one party can exist – the Communist Party . . ."[14]

This analysis was essentially valid. There were undoubtedly contradictions along the Soviet road to socialism which created new social class formations. Even when Stalin was speaking in 1936 the Soviet leadership in Moscow was trying to solve the twin problems of inertia and repression by the middle levels of the state and party bureaucracy. Indeed in 1937 radicals in the Communist Party used the democratic provisions of the new Constitution as a weapon against the bureaucracy.[15] A closer analysis of the working class and the peasantry might have shown other divisions between town and country, industries and occupations. But none had permanent structural causes. Nor were the emerging relationships antagonistic in the sense of having permanently opposing interests which were irreconcilable and which, therefore, posed contrary courses for the development of the Soviet economy. There may have been individuals who believed that their own special needs could best be served by a return to capitalism but there were no groups or classes in that position. For this reason, there were no interests which were sufficiently clear and entrenched that they needed separate permanent institutional rights. No group's political rights therefore was harmed by the constitutional provision for a single political party. The Communist Party, in any event, was not a political monolith into which different interests were compressed but an organization which depended for its vitality on the extent to which it reflected the diverse interests of the society.

One further point which needs to be taken into account in connection with the Western aversion to a single party state is that the material conditions in the Soviet Union had given rise to political needs which could not have been met by a multiparty system of the West, where each party feeds on the discomforture, embarrassment and failures of the others. The persistent need in Soviet Russia and subsequently in the Soviet Union was for a politically unifying force which in the first instance could spread the virtues of socialism and then, by example, display the economic, social and political behaviour consistent with socialist values. Thus the Communist Party which had evolved in Czarist Russia as a cadre party retained the need to remain as a cadre party after the Revolution and to provide leadership in all aspects of the life of the society. Throughout its history the Communist Party members were the first to lead by example. This was so during the Civil War when the cadres volunteered for the Red Army; after the Civil War when they created the concept of free labour and devised what were called Subbotniks; during the early 1930s when they worked for the implementation of the collectivization programme; later in the 1930s when they led the drive for higher productivity with the Stakhanovite Movement; and during the Second World War when they maintained the socialist fabric of the society even in defeat and organized armed resistance to the German occupying forces. Thus the Communist Party's function has always been to reflect the society's needs and then tackle them through socialist action. It has had both a populist and mobilizing function which has not depended upon pandering to the vacillating tastes of people or on persuading the electorate through various and devious public relations techniques to give its endorsement. It has a legal as well as political responsibility to provide leadership. The 1977 Constitution of the USSR states this in Article 6: "The leading and guiding force of Soviet society and the nucleus of its political system, of all state organizations and public organizations, is the Communist Party of the Soviet Union . . ." A prominent feature of the life of the Communist Party has been its concern about its function as a cadre party. This concern lay behind much of the turbulence in the Party during the 1930s when there were purges and trials of members. It has resulted in much self-criticism and self-examination of the kind which would be anathema to Western political parties.

The dictatorship of the proletariat and the one-party state must be seen as part of one totality arising out of the same historical and material conditions. They both rest on the premise, in the first instance, that a society can only be democratic if the majority class, namely the working class, holds power. This is more than a necessary condition for effective democracy because, irrespective of forms of representation, workers exercise power through the ordinary day-to-day affairs involved in managing industry and the economy at large in much the same way as the bourgeoisie exercises power through its ownership and control of the means of production. Workers, therefore, take decisions concerning investment, what to produce, where and on what scale, which they are precluded from making where there is private industry. In other words they contribute substantially towards determining their own quality of life. Irrespective of other factors this must be much more democratic than when they are mere sellers of labour power.

Once the members of the working class hold power then the completion of their control over it depends upon the methods they devise for political representation. A defective or inadequate method of representation may have seriously adverse consequences but they will be reversible, for in a socialist society political representation is a matter for experimentation and is not an issue of princple. The most likely defect to occur is through the failure of the Communist Party to represent society's needs adequately. This has been the experience of the Soviet Union. And although some of the failings have resulted in setbacks they have never had permanent and fundamental consequences for the nature of the society. On a number of occasions deviations have been corrected and wrongs have been righted. This was the case after the death of Stalin and is being further illustrated by the democratic measures introduced by Mikhail Gorbachev. This is indicative of the strength of Soviet democracy. The working class in power always has the means at its disposal to return to the path of socialism.

Dissent

The summation of all the Western criticisms of Soviet democracy is that Soviet citizens are not free as individuals to criticize, oppose or change the political system. It is assumed that it is inconceivable that individuals would naturally refrain from making political criticisms or be disinterested in political opposition and that conformity had to be achieved, therefore, through physical restrictions on individual freedom. Thus the logic of Western thinking is that Soviet society is dominated by mechanisms of control such as the KGB, the Communist Party and various agencies of the state. An image of a Soviet monolith is constructed in which people are frightened, furtive, unsmiling, afraid to speak their minds, always anticipating the early morning police raid, reconciled to arbitrary arrests. Such a society could only be ruled by fear.

The societal contexts in which individuals obtain rights and exercise freedoms vary from one country to another depending upon the class structure and historical experience of each one. Even countries with similar class structures have taken different routes to individual freedom as was indicated in the previous chapter. The class structure of a society determines the substance of individual freedom. If that is changed then the conception of individuality changes too. The notion of an individual, the relationships between individuals and between individuals and society are qualitatively different in a socialist society compared with a capitalist one. When looking at the political rights of Soviet people, then, it has to be recognized first that they live in a wholly different structural context from people in the West and could never be like they are, enjoy similar liberties and suffer similar disabilities.

The Soviet Union is a collectivist society. The assumption underlying all activity there is that collective interests are prior to individual ones. This does not mean that individuals are neglected or subordinated for it is assumed that individuals fulfil themselves more through collectivism than in fragmented free markets. Indeed, the whole purpose of switching to common ownership is to obtain those benefits. Individuality, according to this view, is enriched by enhancing the interests of communities. It has two main consequences. First, most but not all decision-making is conducted through collectives. Second, individuals are not permitted the freedom to act contrary to the perceived interests of the collectives.

Under socialism the state itself is a collective. Individuals, therefore, are expected to subordinate themselves to it in order to enhance Soviet society at large. It would be immoral for any persons to project their own special interests in defiance of the wider community. A further constraint on individual action is created by the Soviet view that the 'dictatorship of the proletariat' is inviolate. No individual has the right to challenge the power which the Bolshevik Revolution brought the working class. No tolerance is extended to anyone who wants to undermine or subvert that power or to introduce other forms of power such as bourgeois democracy. These constraints are facts of life in the Soviet Union and permeate Soviet culture. The vast majority of Soviet people accept them as readily as the majority of Britons accept parliamentary democracy.

The Soviet treatment of dissidence, therefore, has not resulted

75

from the arbitrary use of authoritarianism but is derived from its conception of democracy. The detail of the treatment, however, has been determined by historical circumstances, varying both in method and intensity. Clara Kaplan and other would-be assassins of Lenin, the Social Revolutionaries who aimed for a coup d'etat and the class enemies of the Bolshevik state were countered by the Red Terror. Violence was countered by violence. After factions within the Communist Party were banned in 1921 their composition and policies changed but they remained in existence and argued about political directions until 1928. During that period there was a high level of political diversity with many private printing houses and non-party journals operating. The leaders of the opposition groups were sometimes penalized by being demoted, expelled from the Party or sent into exile but many were later rehabilitated, sometimes back into leadership positions. Many of Trotsky's supporters were released in 1928 and restored to Party positions. Some, Bukharin, Zinoviev, Kamenev, Rykov and Tomsky who had held senior Party positions were re-admitted back into the higher echelons of the Party. Bukharin who lost his membership of the Politburo, editorship of *Pravda* and the chairmanship of the Comintern in 1929 returned as editor of the government newspaper, *Izvestia,* in 1934; Tomsky, who had been dismissed from his chairmanship of the Central Trade Union Council in 1929 and lost his position on the Politburo at the same time, remained on the Central Committee of the Communist Party and was re-elected in 1930. Zinoviev and Kamenev were expelled from the Party in 1927, re-admitted the following year, expelled again in 1933 but readmitted again in 1934.[16] This period embraced the First Five Year Plan and the major part of the collectivization of agriculture involving the extension of the class struggle into the countryside, but it was described, even by critics of the Soviet Union, as a "liberal communist stage".[17]

The Purges

The period which has been used more than any other to discredit the Soviet Union followed the assassination of S M Kirov on 1st December 1934, a member of the Politburo, recently elected Secretary of the Central Committee and the First Secretary of the Leningrad Party Committee. It lasted until 1939. The events of those years attracted much adverse criticism at the

76

time in the West but it was not until the height of the Cold War that they featured as a major indictment of the Soviet Union.

Kirov was shot in his office by a young communist, Leonid Nikolaev. There was much speculation about Nikolaev's associates. He was linked with enemies of the state. Repressive counter-measures were introduced by the government such as summary trials of suspected terrorists, the suspension of the right of appeal and mandatory death penalties. In the period which followed there were a number of occasions on which, for different reasons, communist leaders and officials were arrested, tried and executed. Zinoviev and Kamenev were executed for treason and sabotage in 1936; Piatakov and Radek were executed in 1937 and the next year Bukharin and Rykov similarly lost their lives. At the end of September 1936, after a series of explosions at the Kemerovo Mines in Western Siberia in which a dozen miners were killed, N I Ezhov was appointed as head of the NKVD. During Ezhov's spell of office many amongst the leadership of the Communist Party and the army were arrested and executed. By the beginning of 1939, those who had suffered in this way included all the members of the Politburo during Lenin's time except Stalin and 98 of the 139 members and candidate members of the Central Committee of the CP elected at the 1934 Congress. 1,108 out of the 1,966 delegates to that Congress were arrested. The head of the Red Army, Marshal Tukhachevsky and other army leaders were arrested in June 1937 and then shot for treason. The regional leadership of the Party and the middle echelons of the army were virtually entirely displaced: many were arrested and an unknown number were executed. People talked of "the Ezhovshchina", which meant the time of Ezhov.

Western Sovietologists have fitted the events between 1933 and 1939 to match the stereotype of a totalitarian, dictator-led country which had no concern for the human rights of its citizens. For this purpose they made three assumptions about them. Firstly, they lumped everything in those years into a single totality and called it the "Great Purge" or the "Great Terror". Having done that they made a second assumption that the totality had a single cause, namely Stalin. To complete the picture they assumed, thirdly, that the "Purge" or "Terror" had been conducted on a mammoth scale, pervading the whole of Soviet society.

Until recently virtually all Western analysts of the Soviet Union made these three assumptions and set about producing figures of communists who were expelled from the Party, who were arrested, who were tried and executed, in order to confirm their validity. The Soviet government had published details of expulsions from the Communist Party but had provided no data about arrests and executions. The Western Sovietologists were only interested in those who were arrested and imprisoned. Offenders under the Soviet Penal Code in the 1930s could be sentenced to one of three types of punishment. Firstly, they could be compelled to engage in community work without confinement or to stay at their normal place of work and contribute up to 25 per cent of their pay to the state. Second, they could be exiled to remote parts of the Soviet Union without confinement but be compelled to engage in particular work projects. They were not allowed to leave their places of exile until their sentences had been served. Lastly, they could be sent to corrective labour camps administered from about 1929 by a central government department called the Gulag. The Sovietologists have concentrated on this last category and for much of the post-war period have been guessing the size of the forced labour camp population in the 1930s. This numbers game became the central issue for them.

The problem they all faced was that they had no statistical base with which to start so in order to present their case they engaged in an inventive, complex and ingenious deductive process. The first comprehensive study of the Soviet labour camp situation was *Forced Labour in Soviet Russia* by D J Dallin and B I Nicolaevsky, in 1948. The authors looked for evidence from every conceivable source: "estimates of former officials, former camp inmates, foreign visitors to the Soviet Union, figures based on the reports of former Polish prisoners, estimates based on the numbers and sizes of known camps and camp clusters and . . . estimates based on the reported numbers of newspapers received by places of detention and the reported number of inmates who shared a newspaper."[18] They also reviewed the available data on the scale of economic activities carried out by different parts of the labour camp network. They concluded that the population of Soviet labour camps rose from 2 million in 1932 to 10 million by 1941, when Germany invaded the Soviet Union. S G Wheatcroft has described in some detail how various subsequent calculations have been made in an article in *Soviet Studies* in April 1981. Some discovered new ways of calculating the penal population such as estimating the number of disenfranchised people and assuming that they would be in labour camps. But what is interesting is how the guesses of one became the statistical base for another until the assumptions underlying the original were lost from sight and mind. The most publicized description of Soviet labour camps was that by Alexander Solzhenitsyn in *The Gulag Archipeligo* published in 1973. Many in the West had their image of the Soviet Union reinforced by his partly anecdotal, partly fictionalized story. He asserted, without any empirical evidence, that there had been 12 million people in labour camps at the end of the 1930s, of which 6 million were political prisoners.[19] Solzhenitsyn's figures were sheer invention but were nonetheless used by others as indisputable facts. But the most influential accounts were the reputedly academic ones by Zbigniew Brzezinski who wrote *The Permanent Purge* in 1956, eight years after leaving Poland as an emigré, and Robert Conquest, whose book, *The Great Terror*, published in 1968, contains a statistical appendix under the heading of "Casualty Figures". The estimates of Brzezinski and Conquest entered into anti-Soviet folklore. Both contributed substantially to the grossly exaggerated and distorted picture of the 'purges'. Zbigniew Brzezinski, commenting on the crucial 18 month period of the Ezhovshchina, January 1937 to June 1938, claimed that during that time 850,000 members were expelled from the Communist Party and that most of them were arrested. This figure was 'worked on' and added to by subsequent writers. Brzezinski, however, had made the elementary but intellectually inexcusable mistake of getting his dates wrong. The number of expelled members he quoted referred to the 7 year period from 1932 till 1939 not the 18 month period as claimed by Brzezinski. Moreover there was no correlation between membership expulsions and arrests except in Brzezinski's mind. He had no data on which to base his correlation. He simply made an unverifiable assumption to provide himself with a statistic which then entered the records as a historical fact. Nonetheless, Robert Conquest referred to Brzezinski's figure as a "careful estimate" in his book, *The Great Terror*. He later admitted that Brzezinski had confused his dates but refused to amend his own estimate, based on Brzezinski's, that there were a million arrests of party members between 1936 and 1939. Conquest cited a claim by Andrei Sakharov, in support of his own estimate, that "in 1936 to 1939 alone more than 1.2 million party members, half of the total membership, were arrested."[20] But Sakharov's figure, like that of

79

Solzhenitsyn, was imaginery. Communist Party records show that between "October 1936 and the end of 1937 in the terrifying years of the Ezhovshchina only 108,000 party members were expelled and just under half this number, 46,000, were re-instated."[21] Taking the longer period from May, 1935 till January, 1939 between 200,000 and 240,000 party members were expelled and not re-instated. There is no data which shows how many of these were arrested. Thus this was the way in which the contorting lines of the stereotype were drawn.

Robert Conquest has remained as an authority in the numbers games. He claimed that 9 million people were in labour camps by 1939. To substantiate this figure he drew on the work of S Swianiewicz as well as Brzezinski. Swianiewicz, in his book *Forced Labour and Economic Development: an enquiry into the experience of Soviet Industrialization,* published in 1965, had estimated that there had been just under 7 million labour camp inmates in 1940. There was a process, it seems, of upward revision. Each analyst claimed to throw new light on the topic, took earlier calculations, refined them and produced a new and higher figure. Conquest added interpretation to Swianiewicz's "careful and conservative estimate"[22] which inflated the total by 2 million. Swianiewicz, however, had based his own estimate on the calculations made by N Jasny in an article called "Labour and Output in Soviet Concentration Camps", published in the *Journal of Political Economy,* No 59 in 1952. Jasny's figure had been a modest 3.5 million to which Swianiewicz had added some arbitrary estimates which doubled it. These calculations had no serious empirical basis and should never have been taken seriously by social scientists. In the pure and natural sciences they would have been ridiculed. Yet they have not ended.

The controversy about labour camp numbers in the 1930s was rekindled by an American, Steven Rosefielde, from the University of North Carolina, in 1981. He took Conquest's figure and added supplementary data from what he called new insights into the scale of the phenomenon.[23] The total figure crept up to between 9 million and 11.2 million.[24] Rosefielde, like Conquest, cited unsubstantiated claims to support his own. With some enthusiasm he referred to a statement by W. Averell Harriman, former US Ambassador in Moscow, to the effect that there were 12 million forced labourers in the Gulag in the early 1940s.[25] Harriman's figure was based, he claimed, on US Embassy data but though the Embassy files have been declassified the claim has never been substantiated. Rosefielde was keen to show that all the high figures produced out of hats by Solzhenitsyn, Sakharov and Harriman, were statistically reliable. His motive for doing this and for reviving the controversy was based purely in anti-Sovietism. He stated "one might have supposed that many scholars would have inferred that the success of the Soviet industrialization drive after 1929 was to some significant degree the result of Stalin's forced labour policies. This, however, has not been the case . . . This paper . . . makes it plain that Soviet economic development cannot be properly understood unless forced labour is endogenized into the growth process."[26] Rosefielde thus moved in the tradition of his predecessors. He united with Dallin and Nicolaevsky, the social democrats; Jasny the friend of Mensheviks; Brzezinski the emigré Pole and Conquest the middle-class English writer, all intensely anti-communist, who utilized their intellectual skills to subvert Soviet communism rather than to reveal and understand the real social forces which comprise the Soviet Union. This was surely an intellectually devious and dishonest process.

It was not necessary to guess about everything. Communist Party memberships, numbers and rates of expulsion, were regularly published and T H Rigby used this data for his book, *Communist Party Membership in the USSR 1917-1967*, published by the Russian Institute of Columbia University in 1968. The book is a valuable data bank which corrects important errors in the works of Brzezinski and Conquest. But Rigby was a conforming creature of his Cold War environment and he placed his own calculations within the same distorted analytical box as the others so that its outcome was pre-determined. He saw Stalin's lonely hand in all the 1930s events and believed, even, that he had planned them beforehand.[27]

Brzezinski, Conquest, Rigby and others obtained their data from a variety of sources, but most of it was anecdotal, obtained from emigrees and defectors invariably with limited knowledge and usually with the bias of disaffected people. This heavy reliance on unsubstantiated statements was accompanied by a dismissal of official Soviet sources. Conquest endeavoured to give intellectual credibility to this position, which he in particular adopted. "In a totalitarian country", he wrote, "the question of evidence assumes a special form. No particular credence can be attached to official pronouncements, many of which, indeed, are extravagant falsehoods. The truth can thus only percolate in the

81

form of hearsay . . . But of course not all hearsay and not all rumour is true. On political matters basically the best, though not infallible, source is rumour at a high political and police level".[28] On no other subject could rumour be elevated to the status of a source of research information. The data then on which many anti-Soviet works were founded came largely from the recollections of Mensheviks, Trotskyists, former Cadets, ex-army officers, intelligence agents, diplomats. The basis of Brzezinski's work was his analysis of the sample of 2,725 relatives of Soviet emigré's who had served sentences in prison camps during the 1930s. Anti-Sovietism is built into this source of information.

The same intellectual stricture can be levied against the work of Roy Medvedev, *Let History Judge,* published in the USA in 1971 but written in Moscow. Medvedev is a Soviet citizen but this was not a particular advantage, except that he was physically nearer source material than Western writers. The test of a writer's understanding of a situation does not depend on being there or necessarily being a part of it but on the method of analysis used. Medvedev was a child in the 1930s; his father suffered from the repression towards the end of the decade. Medvedev, however, was acutely critical of bourgeois historians who analyzed the Soviet Union from a "plainly anti-Soviet view". He accused foreign publications of mixing "invention and rumour, factual inaccuracies and distortions in their accounts . . ."[29] Yet his own work was intended to reveal Stalin's guilt for the events of the 1930s and to locate the cause in Stalin's criminal character. His work, in consequence, was largely biographical and was uninformative about social forces. It was as self-fulfilling as that of Conquest – like a trial in which the presumption of guilt is made before it begins its examination of the evidence. Its empirical base was as deficient as that of the Western Sovietologists for he too depended on recollections, anecdotes and interviews provided by surviving Party members after 1956. It all makes interesting reading but throws little light on the causes of the events with which it purports to deal.

The only substantial source of archival material in the West which relates directly to the events in the 1930s, and which would pass the test of the most intellectually scrupulous social scientist, is the Smolensk Archive. It is a unique collection. Merle Fainsod who first used it describes its history:

"In mid-July 1941, less than a month after Hitler

launched his invasion of the Soviet Union, German army units swept into the city of Smolensk. The local authorities were presumably under instructions to destroy or withdraw their records, but in the general confusion of the evacuation, arrangements went astray. At Party headquarters in Smolensk, where current files were kept, Party officials apparently managed to burn or remove all important documents; at least none of any real significance was found for the period 1939-1941. The back files, however, covering the period 1917-1938 were stored in another building far from Party headquarters and these remained largely intact. German intelligence officers, who discovered the collection, found it in a state of great disarray and made a rather random selection of more than 500 files containing approximately 200,000 pages of documents which were shipped back to Germany for examination. There at the end of the war they fell into American hands."[30]

The American authorities made no attempt to return the documents to their rightful owners after the war. Acting on the principle that "finding is keeping", the records became the property of the Departmental Records Branch, Office of the Adjutant General of the United States Army. This archive is a collection of Communist Party records from the Western Region in Byelorussia from before 1917 till 1939. It contains the files of the Party organizations from the local city cells to the regional committee. They include membership files, minutes of meetings, letters to and from Moscow, orders and documents from Moscow. Merle Fainsod had access to the Archive for the material for his book, *Smolensk Under Soviet Rule*. He was a product of the same Russian Research Centre at Harvard as Brzezinski and had already established a reputation in the field of Soviet studies with his work, *How Russia is Ruled,* in 1953. Unfortunately Fainsod ruined this opportunity to analyze the almost weekly workings of the Communist Party because he was unable to break out of the Cold War mould. In his introduction he described his conceptualization of the Communist Party to which the new data was added. "In the political sphere", he wrote, "Stalinism spelled the development of a full-blown totalitarian regime in which all the lines of control ultimately converged in the hands of the supreme dictator. The Party became a creature of Stalin's will . . . Its role was reduced to that of a transmission belt, which Stalin used to communicate his directives, to mobilize support for them by propaganda and agitation, and to check on their execution. As the purges of the mid-thirties approached their apogee, terror itself became a system of power, and the secret police flourished and multiplied. The fear which its agents inspired provided the foundation of Stalin's own security; through them he guarded the loyalty of the Party, the armed forces, the bureaucracy, the intellectuals, and the mass of the population generally."[31] It made a nonsense of the very notion of research to start from such a baseline. Not surprisingly Fainsod's work created the impression that the Smolensk Archive merely confirmed the widely publicized stereotype. Instead of consulting the Archive, Western Soviet-ologists since 1958 simply quoted from *Smolensk Under Soviet Rule.*

This pattern was altered by J Arch Getty. In 1979 Getty was awarded a doctorate for a dissertation at Boston College in the US on *The 'Great Purges' Reconsidered: The Soviet Communist Party 1933-1939.* The dissertation was published in 1985 under the title *Origins of the Great Purges. The Soviet Communist Party reconsidered, 1933-1938.* Getty's research was based on an analysis of the Smolensk Archive. Using the same data as Fainsod he contradicted him on every major point. In addition he produced evidence to challenge the presuppositions and conclu-sions of Brzezinski and Conquest about the scale and character of repression, the totalitarian nature of the Soviet state, the operation of the Communist Party and culpibility of Stalin as the prime architect. Getty entered the fray as a historian. He was not a marxist. Although he pointed to the need to examine the Soviet state, the Communist Party and Stalin in the context of social forces he did not do that himself but confined his analysis to the main variables which the Smolensk Archive revealed. He produced contentious conclusions such as that the Soviet adminis-tration was not totalitarian but chaotic, clumsy and inefficient, that democratic centralism in the Communist Party did not work so that the centre did not control the periphery of the Party and that within the leadership there were factions and arguments, with Stalin often playing a moderating role. But more important for subsequent researchers he clarified the periods, the issues and the events in a way which will encourage them to discard the predominant Western preconception about Stalinism.

Similar work of reappraisal has been undertaken in Britain at the Centre for Russian and East European Studies of the University of Birmingham. There S G Wheatcroft, as part of a research project concerning "Soviet economic balances and trends 1929-1941", has reassessed the statistics of the purges with the same kind of objectivity as Getty. He approached the issue by critically examining the assumptions underlying the calculations made by Conquest and others and found that they had little basis in reality. So distorted were the assumptions that the calculation of the pre-war penal population derived from them would have meant that nearly one-fifth of all Soviet adult males were imprisoned. Even the Bureau of Intelligence and Research in the US Department of State concluded that "So disastrous would have been the demographic and economic consequences of such a situation that its existence seems to have been highly improbable."[32] Wheatcroft's own conclusions, published in papers in the Journal *Soviet Studies,* volumes XXXIII and XXXV for 1981 and 1983, are that "the quantitative significance of the 1937-38 purge has generally been exaggerated" and that in particular Conquest's "estimates are erroneous or unreliable". These are rather generous comments about the work of earlier Sovietologists. The American sociologist, Albert Szymanski, who commented on the work of Brzezinski and Conquest came to the political conclusion that "Even though dealing with events of half a century ago, they serve to discredit future possibilities of socialist revolution in other countries, which is why the issue continues to receive such attention."[33] "The exaggerators", he added, "are rewarded with grants, publications, high positions and personal support in proportion to the outrageousness of the figures they generate".

The events between 1933 and 1939 comprised three distinct phenomena. There was, first, the "purging" of members from the Communist Party; second, an anti-bureaucratic campaign aimed particularly at the middle layers of the Party and government authority and third, a paranoia about attempts to destabilize the country and stage a military coup d'etat in alliance with Nazi Germany and Japan.[34] The three phenomena overlapped in time but they were never confused by Soviet people. Contemporary Western attention was concentrated mainly on the public trials of leading politicians and military officers accused of treason, with some embellishments from the anti-bureaucracy campaign.

The Communist Party of the Soviet Union periodically

screened its membership in order to eliminate undesirable elements and to maintain its integrity as a cadre party. After the Bolsheviks assumed power, membership of the Party held attractions for different reasons, some of which had nothing to do with socialism. Some people saw membership as a means to individual advancement. On some occasions the Party growth distorted its purpose in that it failed to reflect the occupational, ethnic or sex balance of the society at large. It had, for example, too few workers or women. Whatever the reasons the distortions in the Party were rectified through a *chistka,* translated into English as a purge but with a much softer meaning in Russian. *Chistka* is derived from chisteel, the verb to clean.

The first *chistka* was in 1921. The Communist Party had increased its membership twenty-seven fold between 1917 and 1921 with a half million "untested, unknown and potentially unreliable persons". *Pravda* warned against the "over-filling of the party" and expressed concern about careerism by the new members.[35] The Party's reaction was to weed out and expel between 10% and 15% of its members through a process of re-registration in 1919. In Russian this was called *pereregistratsiia.* It repeated the process in 1921 with both a *chistka* and a selective recruitment policy.[36] The main charges against the 25 per cent of the membership who were expelled were inactivity, careerism, failure to carry out Party instructions, drunkenness, corruption, practising religion and joining the Party with counter-revolutionary intentions. One-third of the white-collar workers were expelled, compared with one-sixth of the manual workers and two-fifths of the peasants. Although there were important political divisions in the Party in 1921 no recognizable opposition-ists were expelled.

As well as *pereregistratsiia* and *chistka* the Communist Party carried out *proverka* which involved the verification of member-ship cards and also resulted in expulsions. In 1928 the member-ship was "screened" in seven Party regions resulting in 13 per cent of their members being expelled. The following year there was a *chistka* with an expulsion rate of 11 per cent, amounting to 170,000 members. On each occasion expelled members had the right of appeal. In 1929, 37,000 people were re-instated, reducing the expulsion rate to 8 per cent.[37] Each time the membership was reviewed in response to special circumstances. Following the introduction of the First Five Year Plan and the collectivization of agriculture in 1929 there was strong pressure on workers to join the Party, identify with the new policies and supervise their application. Almost one million new members were enrolled in 1931. Recruitment was eased off in 1932 and halted at the beginning of 1933. But by then the membership of the Party had increased by 131.6 per cent since 1929. This fact alone gave rise to concern about the state of the Party. At the same time as recruitment was suspended the Central Committee decided to conduct another *chistka*. A special Central Purge Commission was formed at the head of a hierarchy of ad hoc commissions at all levels of the Party. At the point where the credentials of the members were actually examined were the regional committees, comprised of communists of at least 10 years' standing. Eighteen per cent of the membership was expelled for moral corruption, careerism, violating party discipline, passivity, for hiding their social background and for acting as bureaucrats.[38]

These Soviet purges were not aimed at political dissent. When, for instance, a verification of Communist Party cards was held in 1935 the Smolensk City Communist Party Committee warned, in line with the Regional Committee, "That secretaries of the raion committees and leaders of party organizations must not transform the work of verifying party documents into a campaign of unmasking, but rather must ensure, by conducting the necessary organizational measures and by improving methods of party work, a constant increase in party awareness, a raising of integrity in the struggle to strengthen the ranks of party organizations . . . ."[39] This was a far cry from the manner in which the purges were interpreted in the West where the expulsion of members was deemed to be part of a pattern of violence, arrests, prosecutions, trials and executions. Purges were such a systematic organizational practice in the Soviet Union that books and articles were published on the theme advising how to conduct one in such a way as to strengthen rather than weaken the Party.

The second phenomenon which Western sovietologists lumped with the *chistka* to discredit the Soviet Union was the anti-bureaucratic campaign which eventually decimated the lower and middle levels of the Party. This was unrelated to the *chistka* except that in the process of checking Party members an awareness of the obstructiveness and inefficiency of the regional party organizations began to spread. Criticisms of the Party were made both formally within the Party and publicly in the media. In November, 1933 the Central Committee ordered local organizations to be more efficient in keeping membership records. Then at the seventeenth Party Congress early in 1934 a member of the Central Purge Commission, Ian Rudzutak, spoke of chaos in membership accounting. No one, he and others claimed, knew who was in the Party and who was not.[40] The outcome was a Central Committee decision in October 1934 to conduct a general registration of membership, known as the *proverka* or Verification of Party Documents, the following year.

A variety of factors concerning the character of the Soviet Communist Party began to coalesce from 1935 in a manner no-one could have predicted and with wholly unexpected consequences. The *proverka*, a serious matter from the point of view of the Central Committee, was bungled by the inertia of regional secretaries to whom the task had been entrusted. Where they did not ignore the *proverka* they passed on the job of interviewing each of their members to their subordinates who in turn gave it little attention. The Central Committee became dissatisfied with the bureaucratic manner in which the operation was handled though it also had misgivings about disorders in the membership accounting system. It was stated, for example that: "Leaders did not know their members; glaring discrepancies existed between records and real membership; party cards had been given out wholesale; genuine members did not have cards at all; and expelled persons had kept their membership cards . . . Party cards of dead persons were being used by relations, spies, White Guard, Trotskyists, and various alien elements."[41]

A twist was given to the *proverka* by the reaction to Kirov's assassination in December, 1934. The Central Committee, believing that it was the work of Trotskyist groups, ordered local Party organizations to search out their Trotskyist members. The task of "unmasking" became appended to the *proverka* though by coincidence rather than design. This did not visibly affect the results but introduced an air of scepticism, suspicion and criticism which affected the relations between party organs and members and between members themselves.

Through its dissatisfaction with the *proverka* the Central Committee ordered a second Verification of Party Documents from July, 1935. This time it publicized its criticisms, named some of the officials involved and called on the rank and file to participation through a series of local meetings. Communists were encouraged to engage in open criticisms of each other and of the local Party functionaries. In effect the central leadership appealed to the ordinary members to tackle the deficiencies at regional and local level. The attention of the Party was directed more and more to its bureaucratic middle. The expelled members during the *chistka* had been mainly rank and filers without any formal positions but during 1935 lower-level office-bearers were expelled. As each stage unfolded the locus of the criticisms moved closer to the middle and upper level power-holders.

Altogether, nine per cent of the membership was expelled during the *proverka*. Thus between the beginning of the 1933 *chistka* and the end of the first *proverka* in May 1935, about 613,000 members were expelled. There were three grades of membership: full member, candidate member and sympathiser. During that period, however, 1.3 million people left the Party which meant that 469,000 simply failed to appear before the Party organizations to account for their membership and, therefore, voluntarily left the Party. The most important single reasons for the fall in Party membership were clearly apathy amongst members and incompetence on the party organs to keep track of their members.[42]

The *proverka* was followed by an Exchange of Party Documents in 1936 and this completed the analysis of the Party membership. This last stage was necessary, it was stated, because many Party cards needed to be replaced in order to reconsider questionable cases of Party membership and to provide those expelled or censured with the possibility of reinstatement. The instructions for conducting the Exchange were meticulous and based on "sound accounting procedures and careful regulation of membership cards"[43] The Central Committee added that "in the exchange, they must turn their principal attention toward freeing themselves of passive party members not deserving the high title of member of the party; of people who accidently find themselves in the VKP(b)"[44] In the period between May, 1935 and September 1936 about 261,000 Party members were expelled by their local committees but more than 167,000 of these were reinstated on appeal.

The anti-bureaucratic pressures came to a head in 1937. They received increasing encouragement from the central leadership. As the Exchange of Party Documents was nearing its end, *Pravda* reported that there had been too many hasty, wrongful expulsions on insufficient grounds; that lower party organizations had been far too free in their censures, reprimands and expulsions; that too much had been decided in closed meetings of Party committees; that the rules on appeals procedures were not being followed. Expelled members complained to the Central Committee of wrongful expulsion. Local Party secretaries were criticized for being too formal, bureaucratic and mechanical. There was increasing comment about heartless bureaucrats. A circular letter from the Central Committee on 24 June 1936, stated: "Many regional party organizations have acted in an intolerably arbitrary manner with respect to expelled persons. For concealing their social origins and for passivity, and not because of hostile activity against the party and the Soviet power, they have been automatically fired from their jobs, deprived of their apartments, etc."[45]

The momentum to condemn bureaucratic officials was heightened by events outside the Party. As a reflection of the success of the First Five Year Plan and the confident feeling that Soviet society was maturing, the Seventh Congress of Soviets decided in February, 1935 to bring the 1924 Soviet Constitution up to date. A Constitutional Commission under the chairmanship of Stalin was established in July 1935, and, eleven months later, submitted a new draft Constitution for discussion. 60 million copies of the Constitution were distributed throughout the country. Public discussion was widespread and intense. An estimated 527,000 meetings were held, attended by over 36 million people, to discuss its terms and suggest amendments. Much of the discussion was about the rights and duties of Soviet citizens for the draft proposed direct elections for all organs of state power. There was to be a single franchise for all citizens at 18 years of age, a secret ballot, candidates were to be nominated by the branches of working class and peasant organizations, they were required to have a 50 per cent majority in at least a 50 per cent poll to be elected, and successful candidates were liable to recall by their constituents.[46] Altogether 150,000 amendments were submitted to the Constitutional Commission. The Constitution came into force in December 1936 and much of 1937 was spent by organizations in every part of the Soviet Union in preparing for the elections for which it provided.

A single candidate was nominated for each constituency but before this happened there was a selection procedure which was conducted in a variety of ways such as primaries or election conferences and through which encumbents were criticized and sometimes rejected. One third of the local and national successful candidates were elected for the first time in 1937.

A similar process of criticism and selection took place in the

Communist Party after the Central Committee had launched its "democracy/anti-bureaucracy" campaign in February 1937 to mobilise rank and file opposition to bureaucratic inertia. The Communist Party leadership responded to the mismanagement revealed by the *chistka* and *proverka*. At other levels dissatisfaction about the conduct of the party was expressed by the new generation of political activists who had been completely educated under socialist conditions. These came from working class and peasant backgrounds but belonged to a new socialist intelligentsia. They were impatient with the older, less-educated body of leaders who had remained relatively unchallenged for most of the time since the Revolution, who had become fixed in their ways and, as *Pravda* commented, thought of their positions as fiefs.

At the February plenum of the Central Committee in 1937 Andrei Zhdanov who had succeeded Kirov as the Leningrad First Secretary and member of the Politburo, spoke strongly against bureaucratic methods of leadership and in favour of increased participation of rank and file members. He proposed direct elections by secret ballot for the Communist Party. Based on his speech the Central Committee ordered the immediate abolition of cooption to committees, voting by lists instead of individuals and insisted that secret ballot elections should be held for all Party organizations up to the level of *oblat* or region by 20 May 1937. At the plenum Zhdanov was generally supported by Stalin.[47]

The elections were held in the Spring accompanied by a widespread press campaign with articles headed "Under the banner of self-criticism and connection to the masses" and dealing with the issues of self-criticism, democracy, learning from the rank and file and verifying the leaders. At some meetings of *raion* or district committees the denunciations of the officials were so intense that they were voted out of office before the elections were held. There was a widespread protest vote. Altogether, 55 per cent of the committees were voted out of office throughout the country. In the Leningrad region 48 per cent of the raion committees were new. In most of the large towns about 20 per cent of the Secretaries and party organizers were elected for the first time. Many of the officials were young worker-Stakhanovites or technical workers.[48] The elections, however, did not remove the regional leaderships, even where they had been strongly criticized. For that to happen the anti-bureaucratic campaign had to be taken further by the Central Committee.

The secretariat of the *obkom,* the regional committee, was elected from that committee with the endorsement of the Central Committee. It was difficult for rank and file protests to maintain their momentum through to that level. The First Secretary of an *obkom* was a powerful person in his own right, usually surrounded by supporters through patronage and cooption. Take the position of First Secretary Ivan Petrovitch Runyantsev of the Western *oblat,* centred on Smolensk in Byelorussia at that time. His region had a population of 6.5 million, bigger than some countries. It encompassed 110 districts each with between 50,000 and 75,000 inhabitants. It included 3 substantial cities. Runyantsev, moreover, was from 1934, a member of the Central Committee. It needed more than encouragement to depose him and others like him. Indeed only four regional secretaries out of the twenty-five whose regional conferences were reported in the press were removed by conference decisions in 1937.[49]

It was at this point that the anti-bureaucratic campaign merged at the edges with the third phenomenon, the Ezhovshchina, the period of mass arrests. Soviet society felt increasingly vulnerable to attack following the rise of fascism in Italy and Germany and the widespread preparations for war. It expressed its nervousness after the Kirov assassination when accusations were made against the opposition groups led by Trotsky and Zinoviev and a wave of arrests was initiated. This resulted, however, in relatively few expulsions from the Party. Zinoviev, Kamenev and thirteen of their associates were arrested and tried for the assassination but were found guilty only of moral complicity. The reaction from the assassination had dissipated by the middle of 1935 and for a year there was no evidence of any political arrests. There was a renewal of the unease from the middle of 1936 when extra-ordinary powers were given to the political police to counter 'enemies of the people'. The NKVD was authorized to arrest and sentence non-Party members suspected of counter-revolutionary activities without trial or right of appeal. This was a recipe for oppression because people, in their jumpiness, began accusing each other. The first of the renown "Moscow trials" occurred in August 1936 when Zinoviev, Kamenev and fourteen others were charged again with the Kirov assassination and on this occasion found guilty.

The second major trial was held when Radek, Piatakov and 15 others were found guilty of 'wrecking' and economic sabotage in January 1937. They were alleged to have acted in complicity with

92

German and Japanese intelligence forces. Trotsky was implicated. There was an understandable fear of war in the Soviet Union. A classical war set piece was being tried out in Spain by Germany and Italy following the beginning of the Spanish Civil War in July, 1936 with the Soviet Union in opposition on the side of the Republicans. Hitler had spoken of the attractions to Germany of the fertile plains of the Ukraine and the raw materials of the Urals. [50] Then at the end of 1936 Germany and Japan concluded an 'Anti-Commintern Pact'. The view that an invasion was imminent spread throughout the country. The search for 'enemies of the people' began to assume a new and desperate dimension at all levels of Soviet society.

The trial of the military leaders in 1937 activated the convergence of many factors which created the period in Soviet history described as Ezhovshchina. It stemmed from allegations which came from Germany via Czechoslovakia that the Soviet military leaders were planning a coup d'etat to coincide with a German-Japanese invasion. Documents were leaked which linked two Deputy People's Commissars for Defence, Tukhachevsky and Gamarnik and a number of generals with the Germans. Marshall Tukhachevsky, the leading Soviet military expert, and army commanders covering various regions of the Soviet Union were arrested in May and tried and executed in June. The regional army commanders had close links with the Regional Communist Party Secretaries so suspicion fell on them too. Evidence about the complicity of the Regional Secretaries is contradictory[51] but there was another reason for indicting them. They had survived the anti-bureaucratic campaign from the rank and file members. Extra-ordinary meetings of the Regional Committees were convened at which members of the Politburo were present. In Smolensk, for example, L M Kaganovitch attended an extra-ordinary plenum of the Western Obkum when the Regional Secretary and his secretariat were removed from office. G Malenkov went first to Byelorussia and then with A Mikoyan to Armenia; L Beria went to Georgia while Molotov, Ezhov and Khrushchev went to the Ukraine. The removal of the Regional Secretaries was unpopular only with those who had received patronage from them. The ordinary members welcomed the opportunity to unleash their criticisms on those who had been insulated from them before.

The decision to implicate the Regional Secretaries was clearly made by Stalin and the Politburo but the consequences which flowed from it were not the result of a disciplined and co-ordinated approach to repress dissent. Concern about spies, a fear of war, the attack on bureaucracy and the eagerness of Soviet workers to criticize generated a paranoia within the Communist Party at all levels. Members informed against each other for being enemies of the people and were then informed against themselves. Some used the occasion to settle old scores. Others cleared out adversaries or those they mistrusted. The political police were the weapon of repression. Party members had always been protected from the arbitrary acts of the NKVD but late in 1937 the NKVD acquired the authority to arrest those in the Party who had not been subject to Party discipline or expelled. The NKVD, however, was also the subject of repression. The Commissar of Internal Relations, G G Iagoda, was removed from his post in September, 1936, allegedly for laxity in exposing the Trotksy and Zinoviev group. Later he and many leading officials of the NKVD were arrested. Iagoda was tried with Bukharin and Rykov in March 1938, found guilty and executed. The regional and local officials of the NKVD were caught up in the maelstrom of political violence and put under pressure to uncover spies, saboteurs and wreckers. Arrests followed arrests as threads linked the exposures and confessions. Officials who did not respond to accusations put themselves under suspicion for complicity. They arrested many innocent people out of sheer inefficiency and by the same standard allowed others to get away. Getty reports that "a person who felt that his arrest was imminent could go to another town and, as a rule, avoid being seized."[52] Yet the NKVD was not seen in the public eye as an oppressor but as a saviour. There was an Ezhov – NKVD cult in the press. Many NKVD officials received honours from the state. It was a complex period, containing many contradictions.

The Ezhovshchina in Perspective

In so far as it is possible to identify the main characteristics of the Ezhovshchina from the evidence available they have little in common with the widely projected Western view. There is general agreement that the repression was extensive and painful, resulting in many personal tragedies and leaving scars on Soviet society which are still present. But there the agreement ends. The repression, in the first instance, did not extend through the years from 1933 to 1939 but was concentrated into a period of about 7 months, from the trial of Marshall Tukhachevsky in June 1937 to the early part of 1938. There was, of course, a building up stage and a trailing off period but the Ezhovshchina as described by Brzezinski and Conquest was of short duration. Secondly it was neither planned nor in any sense intended. There was in 1937 a coincidence of circumstances which interacted with and on each other to produce a collective hysteria about enemies within and without. The arrest of military leaders arose from allegations of treason which were never proved or disproved; the anti-bureaucratic campaign led the central leadership to attack the middle levels of the Party, some sections of which were associated with the military leaders; ordinary communists exploited their new-found freedom to criticize officials and played a pivotal role in removing and punishing them. The deteriorating international situation led many people at all levels to believe that the Soviet Union was going to be invaded with the complicity of Britain and the USA and generated a nervousness about 'spies' and 'wreckers'. All of these forces coalesced to produce a national paranoia through which, Medvedev stated, "Hundreds of thousands of Communists voted for the expulsion of 'enemies of the people' (and) millions of ordinary people took part in meetings and demonstrations demanding severe reprisals against 'enemies'."[53]

The repression had both irrational and rational qualities. It was irrational in that many unsuspecting and innocent people were caught up in it. Agents provocateurs were active; old scores were settled; false accusations were made; conspiracies were imagined; accidents became sabotage. "The smallest error of a manager, miscalculation of an engineer, misprint overlooked by an editor or proofreader, publication of a bad book, was taken to be deliberate wrecking and cause for arrest. People looked every-where for secret signs or fascist symbols, and found them in drawings in books, in note-books, in scout badges. Even such difficulties as the low pay of teachers, shortages of funds, high drop-out rates from high school, the wearing out of equipment, were demagogically attributed to sabotage."[54]

At the same time there was an element of rationality about it. For many people the Ezhovshchina had a definite and legitimate purpose. The rank and file members of the Party defined their adversaries as those with authority over them and these suffered the greatest toll. The main casualties were the elite of Soviet society, the administrative and managerial personnel, army officers, party functionaries and intellectuals. Ordinary Party members were relatively untouched by the Ezhovshchina.[55] Many, indeed, benefited from its consequences. Numberless vacancies were created in every field of public activity. "In the five years from 1933 to 1938", Isaac Deutscher commented, "about half a million administrators, technicians, economists, and men of other professions had graduated from the high schools . . . This was the new intelligentsia whose ranks filled the purged and emptied offices. Its members . . . were either hostile to the men of the old guard or indifferent to their fate. They threw themselves into their work with a zeal and enthusiasm undimmed by recent events . . ."[56] Hundreds of thousands of skilled men and women whose paths had been blocked by the rigid bureaucracy of the middle layers suddenly found welcoming avenues opening for them. Stakhanovite workers became factory directors; rank and file scientists took over research institutes while ordinary soldiers moved rapidly up the military hierarchy. Ironically, the repression which created so many gaps in the decision-making processes generated a sense of solidarity which was reflected in the commitment with which the new cadres approached their tasks. It created a mobility within the Communist Party which had rejuvinating effects and served it well during the critical years of the war.

An examination of the membership changes in the Communist Party during 1937 confirms that the Ezhovshchina was not directed at ordinary members. There was not a mass expulsion of members. Indeed the rate of expulsions fell after the 1933 *chistka* and reached its lowest level in 1937. The number of members expelled during the whole of 1937 was less than 100,000, amounting to about 5 per cent of the total membership.[57] This was little more than half of those expelled in the 1935 *proverka* and one eighth of the number expelled in the 1933 *chistka*. The statistics for the Moscow Party which suffered inordinately from the repression show a similar picture. There, 33,000 members were expelled in 1937 compared with 45,500 in 1935 and 133,000 in 1933.[58] Moreover, although Party members suffered most during the Ezhovshchina, the Party itself was not tarnished by it. Recruitment to the Party was suspended in January, 1933 for almost 4 years. It was the longest moratorium on recruitment in the history of the Party. The moratorium was eased at the end of 1936 and gradually lifted during 1937. Recruitment took place on an increasing scale during the Ezhovshchina. There was little sign of any reluctance by people to join the Party though local branches proceeded cautiously by carefully vetting applicants. The "number of new candidates rose from 12,000 in the eight months November 1936 to June 1937, to 28,000 in the second half of 1937, to 109,000 in the first half of 1938, and in the second half of that year apparently totalled over 400,000. This acceleration continued after the Eighteenth Congress in March 1939, and the party grew by the record number of 1,100,000 in that year".[59] If mass arrests and executions had been associated with Communist Party membership as Brzezinski and Conquest assert, then the eagerness of the young non-members to belong to the Party would be inexplicable except as a desire for self-destruction.

In conclusion, the Ezhovshchina was not by itself or in conjunction with the expulsions from the Communist Party during the previous four years, including the 'Great Trials', either Stalin's Purge or a reign of terror imposed by a totalitarian system to stamp out dissent and annihilate all possible contenders for Stalin's leadership position. What happened resulted from social forces and not evil machinations of individuals or, as Medvedev contends, of one individual. Many 'Old Bolsheviks' who had served with Stalin during the Revolution suffered from the repression. But they as persons were not the targets of the repression. They suffered because the targets of the anti-bureaucratic bias during the Ezhovshchina were office-holders, many of whom were communists who had joined the Party before 1917. "Old Bolsheviks fell", Getty maintained "because of their leadership positions in 1937, not because of their age or past experience."[60] He believed that "It is not inconsistent with the evidence to argue that the Ezhovshchina was rather a radical, even hysterical, reaction to bureaucracy. The entrenched office holders were destroyed from above and below in a chaotic wave of voluntarism and revolutionary puritanism".[61]

Stalin's part in this process was undoubtedly important though it was by no means as crucial as the Western obsession with the cult of the personality suggests. He worked within social forces which he did not and could not control but even at the institutional level of activity he moved between alternative courses of action advocated by other members of the Politburo, between Molotov who urged rapid industrialization and Serge Ordzhonikidze who believed in cautious development, between Ezhov who acted through repression and Andrei Zhdanov who saw the solution to the Communist Party's problems in terms of political education and propaganda. During the course of the

1930s he moved from a moderate to a radical stance but he frequently had to find a balance between competing forces. It is a malevolent distortion to portray the Politburo as his plaything as did Adam Ulam, yet another product of the Russian Research Centre at Harvard University. Ulam wrote that from 1936 "the Politburo's function even as an advisory organ was challenged",[62] in support of his contention that Stalin masterminded "an incredible plan of repression and terror", had "a thirst for blood", pushed his scheme "to the border of madness"[63] The Politburo, Ulam insisted, was comprised of "half-men, who even in their criminality were pale imitations of their leader."[64] But as Getty observed, Stalin could not control everything that happened in the Party and country. "The number of hours in the day, divided by the number of things for which he was responsible, suggests that his role in many areas could have been little more than occasional intervention, prodding, threatening, or correcting. In the course of a day, Stalin made decisions on everything from hog breeding to subways to national defense. He met with scores of experts, heard dozens of reports, and settled various disputes between contending factions for budgetary or personnel allocations. He was an executive, and reality forced him to delegate most authority to his subordinates, each of whom had his own opinions, client groups, and interests."[65] His political subordinates were powerful in their own right, representing interests and reflecting social forces.

Stalin, the Politburo and the Central Committee of the Communist Party were responsible for the Ezhovshchina in that the state agencies through which it was mediated and applied were under their direction. Through this they were guilty of failing to identify and reverse negative forces. They were, in fact, carried along by those forces and, in this sense were guilty of complicity at least. There is no doubt that their responses both facilitated and legitimized the repression. The Politburo, including Stalin, however, took a hard line over the alleged treachery of the military and favoured both the trial and the sentences it produced. Both he and members of the Politburo regarded the extension of the anti-bureaucratic campaign to Regional Secretariats as prophylactic and assisted in their removal. Stalin presumably endorsed making the link between regional military commanders and Regional Party Secretaries which resulted in the arrest of many of them. But what neither he nor members of the Politburo did was to plan the interaction of the various elements which resulted in the Ezhovshchina. Indeed as no one could have foreseen the outcome of that interaction such a plan was inconceivable. Getty, giving a more cautious estimate, stated that his study "more than once failed to conclude that the events were part of a coherent plan . . . Careful analysis of archival, documentary, press, creditable memoir sources neither supports nor disproves the existence of a plan . . . the evidence indicates that a master Stalin plan must remain an a priori assumption, an intuitive guess, or a hypothesis."[66]

The precise policies which Stalin supported in the Politburo are not known. The main indicators of his views are his public statements. Speeches by the General Secretary of the Communist Party were an important means for communicating policies. They were not instruments for persuasion in order to raise the poll ratings. They usually simply informed people about Politburo and Central Committee deliberations. Insofar as they dealt with controversial issues they reflected Stalin's approach to them. It is significant then that mostly in public Stalin sided with Andrei Zhdanov's view that only political measures could solve the Party's problems. He quickly became concerned about the turn Ezhovshchina had taken. In little over six months after the June trial of Marshall Tukhachevsky there were signs that the Ezhovshchina was beginning to end. The Central Committee in January 1938 roundly turned on Party officials who had abused their power through their heartless and bureaucratic attitude towards communists accused of being enemies of the people. It did not criticize the political police though the rate of arrests fell sharply. In the Party the number of expulsions declined, expelled members began to be rehabilitated and the new recruitment campaign was set in motion. The trial of Bukharin, Rykov and Iagod was held in March, 1938 but the defendants had been in custody for just over a year and the trial attracted little publicity. Some arrests continued to be made during 1938 but at the end of the year Ezhovshchina ended completely. Ezhov was relieved of his duties on 8 December at his own request, disappeared from the public eye and was executed. The convictions of former enemies of the people began to be reversed. The NKVD came under attack and a number of its officials were dismissed and arrested for criminal actions. When the Party Congress met in March 1939 the events of the past 3 years were strongly criticized both by Stalin and Zhdanov. The Party rules were changed to strengthen a member's right of appeal against expulsion and to ban the practice of purging the membership. Many thousands of expelled numbers returned to the Party and their jobs. Amongst them were army officers who on the eve of the war, and in its early stages, took up their commands again.

The Dissidents

In the 1950s and 1960s the events of the 1930s were at the centre of the Western debate about the Soviet Union but now they are the backcloth for other criticisms of the communist system. The focus of Western attention nowadays has been turned to the question of human rights, by which is meant the right to engage in political criticism of the Soviet system and to organize opposition to it, on the one hand, and the right as an individual to emigrate, on the other hand. Two distinct issues are involved here and they are treated separately. The right to emigrate was raised in Chapter Four and is examined in the following chapter "The Jewish Question". In some circumstances there is overlap where Soviet Jews, in order to further their own specific aims, engage in dissenting action. The dissidents, however, can be examined without the complications of Zionism and anti-Semitism which the Jewish issue raises.

In the Soviet Union citizens are protected from arbitrary arrest by Article 3 of the 1960 Code which provides that no persons can be punished unless they have committed a crime provided for by law. Dissenters, however, can be punished by infringing Articles 70, 190-1 and 190-3 of the Criminal Code, which are designed to protect the Soviet social system from subversion. Article 70 penalizes "agitation or propaganda carried on for the purpose of subverting or weakening the Soviet regime or of committing particular, especially dangerous crimes against the state, or the circulation, for the same purpose, of slanderous fabrication which defame the Soviet state and social system or the circulation or preparation or keeping, for the same purposes, of literature of such content"[67] Article 190-1 covers acts which constitute a slander of the Soviet state but which do not involve a subversive intent. Article 190-3 introduced in 1966, is directed against group demonstrations and makes punishable "organization of, and likewise, action participation in, group actions which violate public order in a coarse manner", or "clear disobedience of the legal demands of representatives of authority."

The scope of the Articles is wide, enabling almost any form of objectionable political activity to fall within their terms. Their application, however, has been strongly influenced by the constant attempts by capitalist countries to isolate and undermine the Soviet Union with the intention of destroying its basis. In this process the experience of the German invasion in 1941 with its devastating effect upon the lives and property of Soviet people has had an indelible effect. Nothing can be understood about Soviet reactions to criticisms and threats, no matter how insignificant they might seem from the outside, without taking their war experiences into account. It is unlikely that they will ever be erased from the collective Soviet memory. Whilst the wounds from the war were healing and the damage to property was being repaired the Cold War began which, with variations in intensity, has never ceased. It would be surprising under the circumstances if the Soviet Union were not sensitive to criticisms.

In terms of their actual operation, the Articles differ little from the catch-all Public Order Acts in Western countries. If the law enforcement authorities in Britain want to suppress dissent there is legislation on hand suitable for all occasions. The British authorities could cover all the contingencies in the Soviet Articles without introducing new legislation. The British police had no difficulty in arresting 10,000 coal miners during the 1984-5 Miners' Strike for simple public order offences even though many of them were engaged in a variety of acts of political dissent. Legislation does not have to be specifically directed at dissent, as in the Soviet Union, in order to curb it.

Those who are arrested under the Soviet Articles 70, 190-1 and 190-3 are described in the West as political offenders and those who are in consequence imprisoned are termed political prisoners. The status of dissidents, however, is controversial. Those same people have broken the law and are regarded by the Soviet authorities as criminal offenders. The dilemma is common to many countries. Every terrorist is someone's freedom fighter. In Northern Ireland, Republican supporters regard those Republicans arrested for terrorist offences as political offenders and there has been a long struggle there to obtain the status of political prisoners for the ones who are imprisoned. From the 1972 hunger strike by the Republican prisoner, Billy McKee, a classification of political prisoners, called Special Category prisoners, was recognized in Northern Ireland. These prisoners were identified by the special concessions they received. There were approximately 2000 Republican and 800 Loyalist or Protestant Special Category prisoners by 1976, out of a population in Northern Ireland of 1½ million. The British government abolished the Category in March, 1976 so that it was no longer possible to identify political prisoners. But they remained and started the 'blanket protest' from September, 1976, for the restoration of their political status. As many as 300 Republican prisoners, by 1978, were refusing to wear prison clothes and do prison work on the grounds that they were not criminals. Many Irish Catholics also regard the British Prevention of Terrorism Act as a means of political repression and define the 6,155 people who have been detained under it during the last 12 years as its victims and not as criminals. Yet the British government literally describes those who have been convicted as terrorists, murderers and criminals. Many British coal miners regard those who were imprisoned during the Strike as victims of political repression just as the dismissed printers from News International in London regarded the imprisonment of one of their leaders, Mike Hicks, for alleged assault on a picket line in 1986 as a political act. Quite clearly the Western pre-occupation with Soviet dissidents as victims of political repression contains an element of hypocracy.

Although the Western media was always willing to publish details of what it considered to be Soviet violations of human rights its interest was stimulated by the trial of Andrei Sinyavsky and Yury Daniel in February, 1966 and a new emphasis began. The two authors were accused under Article 70 of maligning and slandering the Soviet state in works published abroad. Before their trial, on 5 December, 1965, a group of intellectuals demonstrated in Pushkin Square, Moscow with slogans which stated: "Respect the Constitution, the Basic Law of the U.S.S.R." and "We demand that the Sinyavsky – Daniel Trial be Public". Sinyavsky and Daniel were found guilty and sent to labour camps for seven and five years respectively. There was a chain reaction. The demonstrations led to further arrests and trials which then led to more demonstations and so it went on. The writer Alexander Ginzburg wrote a "White Book" account of the Sinyavsky – Daniel trial in a self-published or samizdat form. For this he was arrested on 23 January, 1967. So too was Yuri Galenskov for producing a samizdat almanac *Phoenix 1966*. The day before Ginzberg's arrest a group of about 30 people demonstrated in Moscow against the arrest of Galenskov. Two of the demonstrators, Victor Khaustov and Vladimir Bukovsky, a writer, were arrested and sent to labour camps. The trial of the demonstrators was recorded in another "White Book" by a physicist, Pavel Litvinov, who was exiled in south-east Siberia. Samizdat material began to multiply in 1968 and a *Chronicle of Current Events* was published in samizdat form from April of that year which provided a catalogue of the activities of the dissenting intellectuals and the reactions of the authorities. The events in Czechoslovakia in 1968 both acted as a stimulus to dissent and provoked a stern official response. It was as if dissenters and authorities were both on a treadmill. It moved remorselessly through the 1970s taking with it people, like Vladimir Bukovsky, who had been on it more than once.

The samizdat, typed by the author or a friend, handed around informally, usually reached the West where it was published in an emigré publishing house in Russian or in translation, and often broadcast back to the Soviet Union by Western radio stations. Radio Liberty in Munich, West Germany, which is financed by the US government, has a research staff which specializes in samizdat material and collects and stores it in a Samizdat Archive. It began its collection in the late 1960s but since 1972 the processed contents of the Archive have been available at four American and four European repository libraries, including the Library of Congress in Washington, D.C. and the British Museum in London. One Western compiler of samizdat estimated that between 1967 and 1971 about 700 documents, articles, stories, plays and books had reached the West.[68] Books about Soviet dissent and containing samizdat articles began to appear on Western library shelves. In effect Soviet dissidence became a highly organized business in the West. It had its specialists, regular channels of communication and sources of finance. Doubtless, given the priorities of capitalism, it generated profits too. Some dissidents, in consequence, became household names and very rich at the same time. Many in the West who have never heard of a protesting British or American intellectual know the names of Solzhenitsyn, Medvedev, Shcharansky, Bukovsky and Sakharov. A letter from Solzhenistyn to the fourth Soviet Congress of Writers in 1967 protesting against censorship became an international document. The same treatment was accorded to almost any letter written by the physicist, Andrei Sakharov, but in particular to his open letters to the Supreme Soviet in 1971 and to the US Congress in 1973.

The issue of Soviet dissidents was heightened by the Israeli campaign to gain exit for Soviet Jews after the Six Day War in

1967. Those Jews who organized protests or who wrote samizdat documents were arrested and brought to trial under Article 70 in the same way as non-Jews. The process of arrest followed by demonstration followed by arrest was repeated for the Jewish advocats of free emigration. A group of Soviet Jews tried to hijack a plane and fly it to Sweden in 1970. They were accused of treason. Two were sentenced to death but their sentences were later commuted to fifteen years' imprisonment. After the sentences were announced, a group of British Jews protested outside the Soviet Embassy in London. In this way Western Jewry became involved in the campaign about Soviet dissidents though their concern was always primarily with the right of Soviet Jews to emigrate. In February 1971 a trial of protesting Jews was held in Leningrad; then in May, a third one took place in Riga, the capital of Latvia. The trials, and the demonstrations, fed on each other.

Western organizations, in the main, did not differentiate between dissenting Jews and non-Jews. The International Pen Club, the American Academy of Arts and Science and Amnesty International generated an interest in the West of dissidents in general. Amnesty International, in particular, systematically collected and disseminated data about imprisoned dissidents as "prisoners of conscience". It published a report in 1975 on *Prisoners of Conscience in the USSR: Their Treatment and Conditions*, which it updated in 1980. It also published an English translation of the journal, *A Chronicle of Current Events*, up to 1975.

Until the election of Jimmy Carter as President of the USA, the American government was not directly involved in the issue concerning Soviet dissidents. Richard Nixon and Henry Kissinger adopted what Zbigniew Brzezinski called a "stance of moral indifference" towards dissidents which, Brzezinski claimed, was reflected in Kissinger's advice to Nixon not to receive the exiled Soviet writer Solzhenitsyn.[69] Given the consequences of US involvement in Vietnam, Cambodia and Chile it would indeed have been highly hypocritical if President Nixon had chastized the Soviet Union. There were pressures in Congress on Nixon, however, to take up the cause of Soviet Jewish dissidents. In 1972 a United States Trade Reform Act was passed which embodied the Soviet/American Trade Agreement and opened up the possibility of greatly increased trade between the USA and the Soviet Union. The National Conference on Soviet Jewry had opened a Washington office late in 1972 through which it lobbied

American Senators and Congressmen to insert a human rights clause in the Act. The result of the lobbying was the Jackson Amendment which made trade concessions subject to the Soviet "respect for the right to emigrate". This was followed by the Arms Control Export Act of 1976 and the Harkin Amendment which placed significant restrictions on military and economic assistance to countries which displayed a "consistent pattern of gross violations of internationally recognized human rights." This was the period of detente when the relationship between the USA and the Soviet Union was closer than at any time since the war. The influence of the American Jewish lobby, however, carried the dissident question into the realm of American government. In 1975 the US government had signed the Final Act of the Conference on Security and Co-operation in Europe, along with the Soviet Union and 33 European nations, which focussed international attention on the issues raised by Soviet Jewish dissidents. Thus when Jimmy Carter became President in January 1977 the American political mood was ready to respond to his 'human rights' appeals.

The Conference on Security and Co-operation in Europe which had been convened in Helsinki on 3 July 1973, continued in Geneva and was concluded at Helsinki on 1 August, 1975. It was signed by President Ford, who had taken over from the impeached Richard Nixon, President Brezhnev and Harold Wilson along with other Heads of State. The Agreement had much to say about human rights and freedoms.[70] The context was a recognition of sovereignty. It was accepted by the signatories that they "will . . . respect each other's right to freely choose and develop its political, social, economic and cultural systems as well as its right to determine its laws and regulations."
Principle VII then stated:

"The Participating States will respect human rights and fundamental freedoms, including the freedom of thought, conscience, religion or belief, for all without distinction as to race, sex, language or religion. They will promote and encourage the effective exercise of civil, political, economic, social, cultural and other rights and freedoms all of which derive from the inherent dignity of the human person and are essential for his free and full development.
Within this famework the participating States will

recognize and respect the freedom of the individual to profess and practise, alone or in community with others, religion or belief acting in accordance with the dictates of his own conscience.

The participating States on whose territory national minorities exist will respect the right of persons belonging to such minorities to equality before the law, will afford them the full opportunity for the actual enjoyment of human rights and fundamental freedoms and will, in this manner, protect their legitimate interests in this sphere.

The participatory States recognize the univeral significance of human rights and fundamental freedoms, respect for which is an essential factor for the peace, justice and well-being necessary to ensure the development of friendly relations and co-operation among themselves as among all States.

They will constantly respect these rights and freedoms in their mutual relations and will endeavour jointly and separately, including in co-operation with the United Nations, to promote universal and effective respect for them.

They confirm the right of the individual to know and act upon his rights and duties in this field . . ."

The Declaration enumerated ways in which co-operation between the States could be facilitated and, under the heading of *Human Contacts*, stated

"(a) *Contacts and Regular Meetings on the basis of Family Ties*

In order to promote further development of contacts on the basis of family ties the participating States will favourably consider applications for travel with the purpose of allowing persons to enter or leave their territory temporarily, and on a regular basis if desired, in order to visit members of their families . . ."

"(b) *Re-unification of Families*

The participating States will deal in a positive and humanitarian spirit with the applications of persons who wish to be reunited with members of their family,

106

with special attention being given to requests of an urgent character – such as requests submitted by persons who are ill or old . . ."

It was possible for the various countries to sign the Helsinki Declaration in good faith because each attached its own meaning to the words. In the case of socialist and capitalist countries this meant using contrasting values so that even the very words democracy, individual, freedom and human rights were essentially interpreted differently. There was, then, bound to be conflicting evidence when the achievements of the Declaration were assessed. Nonetheless the immediate consequence in the Soviet Union was an acceleration of the rate of emigration of Jews. The number of Soviet Jews who emigrated rose from 13,363 in 1975 to 51,320 in 1979. From May, 1976, five unofficial groups were formed in Moscow, the Ukraine, Lithuania, Georgia and Armenia to monitor the application of the Helsinki Final Act. They had a total of about 50 members by 1979,[71] some of whom were harassed by the authorities and then arrested as dissidents. Among the members of the Moscow Helsinki Monitoring Group who were arrested were Yury Orlov and Anatoly Shcharansky. From the point of view of bourgeois liberal opinion in the West this situation was unsatisfactory and the agitation against the Soviet Union intensified. Orlov and Shcharansky became widely known in Britain and the USA. By this time, 1978, President Carter was at the front of the human rights campaign.

There is no question that President Carter became a leading protagonist of human rights all over the world because of his own strongly held humanitarian views. His administration, however, elevated the issue of human rights as a prime goal of American policy in order to cleanse America's tarnished image after Vietnam and the Nixon affair and not for humanitarian reasons. This was made clear by Zbigniew Brzezinski, Carter's anti-communist, anti-Soviet Assistant for National Security Affairs. Brzezinski wrote in his autobiographical account of his work with Carter that:

"Jimmy Carter took office sensing clearly a pressing need to re-invigorate the moral content of American foreign policy. After an almost unending series of revelations about the abuse of governmental power at home and abroad, the American people were dissatisfied with their government. In international affairs, there seemed to be a moral vacuum. The Carter Administration resolved to make a break with the recent past, to bring the conduct of foreign affairs into line with the nation's political values and ideals, and to revitalize an American image which had been tarnished by the Vietnam experience.

I had long been convinced that the idea of basic human right had powerful appeal in the emerging world of emancipated but usually non-democratic nation-states and that the previous Administration's lack of attention to this issue had undermined international support for the United States . . . I felt strongly that a major emphasis on human rights as a component of US foreign policy would advance America's global interests by demonstrating to the emerging nations of the Third World of the reality of our democratic system, in sharp contrast to the political system and practices of our adversaries. The best way to answer the Soviets' ideological challenge would be to commit the United States to a concept which most reflected America's very essence."[72]

The question of human rights was raised in Jimmy Carter's speeches both when he was a candidate and President. His inaugural speech, in words written by Brzezinski, stated "because we are free we can never be indifferent to the fate of freedom elsewhere . . . our commitment to human rights must be absolute". Then, with Carter's approval, Brzezinski established what was called a "Global Issues Cluster" on the National Security Staff to deal with human rights issues and thus institutionalized their projection by the US government. This ensured that memoranda on human rights would be produced and that Carter would continually receive policy suggestions. An Inter-Agency Group on Human Rights was formed "to examine bilateral/multilateral aid decisions from the standpoint of human rights, and to provide guidance on loan support and coordinate policy".[73] This Group gave advice to the Administration to support, abstain from, postpone or oppose the granting of loans to a variety of countries depending on their human rights record. In the first two years the US Administration opposed more than 60 loans to 15 countries. Brzezinski, in his account, emphasized America's world-wide concern, listing the release of political prisoners in

Peru, Chile, Indonesia, and the decline in "disappearances" in Argentina. But there was no question that the US Administration's primary concern was to isolate the Soviet Union for violations of human rights in contrast to the USA. This reflected Brzezinski's hawkish attitude to the Soviet Union. He wrote: "By the mid-1970s it became increasingly evident that detente was not the panacea many thought it would be. Mounting public and congressional pressures forced the Executive Branch to make further movement in relations with Moscow contingent on the Soviets' allowing greater freedom to emigrate and easing their treatment of dissidents."[74] He stated: "I felt strongly that in the US–Soviet competition the appeal of America as a free society could become an important asset, and I saw in human rights an opportunity to put the Soviet Union ideologically on the defensive . . . I suggested that by actively pursuing this commitment we could mobilize for greater global support and focus global attention on the glaring internal weaknesses of the Soviet system".[75] In a memorandum to Carter, Brzezinski advised: "(i) Scrupulous fulfillment of the Helsinki agreement. Hence it is important that the fulfillment or non-fulfillment of the agreement be closely monitored, especially in regard to human rights. Making it unmistakably clear to the Soviet Union that detente requires responsible behaviour from them on fundamental issues of global order . . ."[76]

In this way 'human rights' became first a bargaining counter in arms negotiations with the Soviet Union and then, in the hands of President Reagan, an obstruction. The formula was taken up by other Western governments with great enthusiasm and without the slightest sign of hypocracy. Although Brzezinski was not a social democrat, his approach to the Soviet Union appealed to them for it enabled them to pursue anti-Sovietism whilst disclaiming it, saying that their only concern was human rights. It became fashionable for political leaders in the West to carry dossiers about Soviet dissidents with them to meetings with Soviet leaders. The practice was taken up by sections of the European Peace Movement. The Campaign for Nuclear Disarmament in Britain, as is shown in a later chapter, gave high prominence to the human rights issue and made satisfactory relations with socialist Peace Movements conditional upon its resolution. The Green Party in West Germany and Codene in France adopted a similar posture. Immense publicity was given when dissidents were released. Anatoly Shcharansky, for instance, was received by the British Prime Minister and the US President after his dramatic release over the Glienicke Bridge, spanning East and West Berlin, on 11 February 1986.

The size of the dissident movement was always relatively small. Peter Reddaway stated in 1974 that only about 2000 names were known from all sources.[77] During 1977, Roy Medvedev, one of the best known dissidents remaining in the Soviet Union, stated that the "dissidents do constitute a relatively small circle, usually alienated from the masses . . ."[78] Some estimates include nationalists and Jews with other dissidents while others do not. When Dr Theodore Friedgut, Director of the Soviet and East European Research Centre at the Hebrew University of Jerusalem, attempted to assess the size of the dissident movement in 1974 he found that it was a matter of conjecture rather than measurement, that it included people who had registered no more protest than putting their signatures on a petition and that, in any event, it constituted "at best a tiny percentage of the intelligentsia".[79] The estimates of the number of people who had signed petitions or contributed to samizdat documents ranged from a few hundred to 3,000. The most common estimate was in the region of 1,000 which is the figure Friedgut's Institute arrived at after examining samizdat sources in Russian.[80] Friedgut found that there were regions and institutions in the Soviet Union with no known dissenters. In other regions where there was some dissent it was not indigenous, as in Riga the capital of the Latvian Republic, where the participants "were Russians or Jews, with very few Latvians." In general Soviet students were disinterested. Friedgut's view was that dissidents comprised a "small and dwindling band" centred in Moscow.[81]

It is generally recognized that the dissidents came overwhelmingly from the intelligentsia. "On the whole", Medvedev stated, "they are intellectuals".[82] "Socially", Reddaway added, "the movement is overwhelmingly middle-class. Among its informal leaders are a high percentage of people from research institutes, including a disproportionately high number of mathematicians and physicists. Other leaders and supporters are engineers, teachers, lawyers, writers, artists, journalists and students, with a very small number of workers and military men."[83] For a brief period from 1978, the Western media claimed, there were rumblings of dissent in the Soviet trade union movement. A group of workers, describing themselves as unemployed, held two press conferences in Moscow in January,

110

1978, announcing the formation of a Free Trade Union Association. It claimed to have 110 candidate members but that 200 altogether were ready to join. The organizers made little effort to spread their views among Soviet workers but concentrated on influencing international opinion. They sent an appeal through Amnesty International to the International Labour Organization and trade union centres in Western countries for recognition as a trade union. Amnesty forwarded the appeal with a copy of the Association's statutes to the ILO. It was taken up by the British TUC, the European Trades Union Congress and the International Confederation of Free Trade Unions. The principal organizer, Vladimir Klebanov, was a mining engineer so the appeal was discussed by the National Executive Committee of the National Union of Mineworkers at its meeting on 9 March 1978. The NUM decided to raise the matter with the Soviet authorities and the Soviet Miners' Union. The TUC used its own channels, including the Soviet AUCCTU, to seek clarification. The European TUC had doubts about the objectives of the Association and held judgement until the ILO had stated its opinion. This came in April, 1978 when the ILO concluded that the documents received did not constitute a complaint which it could take up through its constitutional procedures. The issue did not rest there for the Executive Board of the ICFTU in May submitted a formal complaint to the ILO alleging a contravention of the ILO Convention on Freedom of Association. The National Executive Committee of the Labour Party also had the matter on its agenda and wrote to the TUC for information. Given the extensive interest in Britain in the intentions of the group of seven people who held the press conference on 20 January, 1978, it is probable that a similar reaction was occurring in the USA and other capitalist countries.

The British TUC doubted whether the Association could be described as a trade union. It stated that "the material available (indicated) that the members primarily sought to secure redress within the Soviet system for grievances which they maintained had been mishandled or ignored by the Soviet authorities, who harassed them in various ways. Neither the constitution nor the supporting material indicated that the Association was intended to act as a union in an industrial sense . . ."[84] Then the TUC received a reply to its letter to the Soviet All-Union Central Council of Trade Unions which outlined "the Soviet system for dealing with labour disputes and dismissals, mentioned the recent revision of legal provisions affecting labour inspection and dismissals, acknowledged by implication that complaints arose to be dealt with, and stated that a number of trade unions had been formed in the Soviet Union in recent years". It added that the concept of a trade union implied an association of people of the same occupation or employed in the same enterprise and that the group comprising the complainants claiming to be a trade union could not pretend to pursue trade union objectives.[85] These comments, the TUC concluded, were directed at the substance of the matter and settled it.[86]

The organizers of the press conference which launched the Free Trade Union Association were harassed by the police and arrested, whereupon the International Confederation of Free Trade Unions complained to the Soviet Government of repression and the violation of trade union rights. The Soviet government's reply stated that the allegations were unfounded because the right to organize collectively was guaranteed by the Constitution, trade unions had extensive rights to defend workers' interests and the complainants had nothing to do with trade unions or the occupational interests of workers whom they did not represent. This did not satisfy the ICFTU which wanted the Soviet government to detail why Soviet workers could not form trade unions of the Western kind. In Britain, however, there was satisfaction over the case in point, though at the 1978 Trades Union Congress a motion calling for a charter for basic human rights in all countries, but aimed at the Soviet Union, was carried without a debate.

With neither internal nor external support the Free Trade Union Association disappeared from sight. Nothing happened subsequently to change the social character of the dissidents. There was no sign that the Soviet workers felt the need to emulate the Polish workers who had rebelled against the Communist Party and the government by forming Solidarity in 1980 and 1981.[87] The dissident movement remained the "small and dwindling band" of intellectuals including some Jews wanting to emigrate, some religious objectors and a few conscientious objectors. Amnesty International which monitored the arrest of Soviet citizens for taking part in non-violent protests had listed the names of 580 individuals in 1986 "whom it knew or suspected to be prisoners of conscience . . ."[88] Early in February, 1987, the number had fallen to 530, of whom about 20 were Jewish protesters and 11 were conscientious objectors. Then Andrei

Sakharov and his wife Elena Bonner were unconditionally released from internal exile. During the second week of February a further 43 dissidents were released. The number who had received pardons rose to between 140 and 150 before the end of February. As all the cases of dissidents imprisoned under Article 70 were under review Amnesty's total was likely to fall further. A Soviet Commission was established to examine, amongst other things, the implications of Article 70. It was becoming difficult for the West to continue using the issue of dissidents for anti-Soviet purposes.

There are questions, however, which nonetheless need to be raised about dissidence in the Soviet Union. The first one concerns the reasons for dissent and the second the explanation for the Soviet response to it.

There is no sense in which dissidents constitute an opposition in the Soviet Union. They have no unity and the causes of their dissent have no structural basis. There are Jews who wish to emigrate, nationalists who wish to sever from the Soviet Union, religious protestors who desire greater religious freedom, individuals who object to military service and intellectuals with mixed motives. There is very little overlapping between the groups. The physicist, Andrei Sakharov, who in the autumn of 1970 had been a founder member of the Soviet Committee on Human Rights, appealed in May the following year for the right of Jews to emigrate. His identification with the Jewish campaign was epitomized through his relationship with Elena Bonner, who is Jewish and whom he met at a demonstration and subsequently married. Sakharov's attitude, however, was unusual. Mostly the various groups were divided by antagonisms. There were nationalists in the Ukraine and the Baltic Republics who were both anti-Semitic and suspicious of Moscow based intellectuals. In the main, each group was afraid that identification with any of the others would spoil its case.

But why should only intellectuals be dissidents? Roy Medvedev believed that intellectuals in most countries became the dissidents[89] but that is clearly not the case in British history where working-class trade unionists have been most prominent. His explanation as to why others in the Soviet Union did not protest was that they were afraid. This was the view of most Sovietologists, expressed graphically by Theodore Friedgut who described Soviet society as one atomized by fear and suspicion through a system of "active networks of informers, both paid and

113

volunteer."[90] This favourite Western explanation fits the stereotype neatly but it bears no relation either to the history of the Soviet people or people elsewhere. History shows that protest derived from social forces cannot be permanently repressed, though it may be temporarily defeated. Time and time again ordinary people have risen against the most repressive regimes. Russian workers rose against a cruelly oppressive system in 1905 and 1917; it was they who defeated the Western armies which intervened in 1918. In the Second World War no people resisted an invading army as determinedly as Soviet people. It was generally believed until 1976 that physical protest was impossible in South Africa and that, in any event, the black people had neither the will nor the ability to engage in it. Then school children in Soweto showed that the regime was vulnerable to protest. Since 1976 ordinary black South Africans, without facilities and often without organization, have continued and intensified their struggles. Nicaraguan peasants and Chilean workers have taken extreme risks in their struggle for freedom. It is obvious that protest cannot be permanently muted by fear.

Soviet trade unionists do not engage in collective protest against the system because there is no structural reason for it. The intelligentsia, in the main, does not protest either. So what activates the minority that does protest? Firstly there is a close identification between the aspirations of the disaffected segments of Soviet society and Western democratic values.[91] In other words some Soviet intellectuals are envious of the lifestyle and individual freedom of Western intellectuals. They derive their impressions of life under capitalism from international conference centres and communications with Western academics who are a privileged élite. Envy, however, is a sandy base for protest because by its very nature it is individualistic.

The fragmented character of dissent is shown by the mixed bag of motives given by dissidents for their actions. Roy Medvedev commented about this in an interview with an Italian journalist in 1977.[92] Some writers, artists and film and stage directors, he stated, became dissidents because they resented the restraints which working within collectives imposed on what they described as their natural creativity. Other intellectuals, such as Andrei Sakharov and Valentin Turchin, both theoretical physicists, began to protest because of events unconnected with their working conditions. Sakharov, for instance, criticized attempts to rehabilitate Stalin whom he believed was personally responsible

114

for the purges in the 1930s. Others joined in for selfish, personal reasons. "Unfortunately", Medvedev stated, "Soviet dissidents don't always represent only the best elements of the intelligentsia; a lot of people dissent because they're unhappy with their private or social lives. Many join the ranks out of sheer egocentricity, urging foreign correspondents to broadcast to the whole world their crude proclamations, appeals, and horror stories, full of ferocity."[93] He quoted the story of the Soviet poet Urin who resigned from the Writers' Union and made statements which were broadcast in Russian from a foreign radio station because the Union refused to celebrate his fiftieth birthday.

The dissidents were politically divided. They ranged from Solzhenitsyn who demanded the moral regeneration of the Russian nation, meaning the restoration of the hegemony of the Russian Orthodox Church, and whose politics were so reactionary that he offended his American hosts, to Roy Medvedev who wanted a purer version of Leninism. In between were social democrats, liberals, apolitical humanitarians, nationalists, Christian Socialists and Zionists. Their political postures were fluid. Sakharov, for example, moved from neo-marxism in the mid-1960s to liberal socialism and then liberalism, much to the disquiet of Medvedev who believed that many of Sakharov's statements and political actions had not been either well thought out or rational.[94] Once having taken the initial step of opposing Soviet communism and, by implication, identifying with Western values, they reflected the politically diffused character of Western pluralism. But whereas in the West pluralism is grounded in the capitalist mode of production, in the Soviet Union it has no material basis. The dissidents with their own specific recipes for a backwards political transformation are, therefore, anachronisms and misfits. They represent no problem to Soviet society except insofar as they are used by the West to discredit communism and to justify aggression against its practice. Soviet society undoubtedly possesses its own contradictions with consequential social class formations, but these push it forward to a progressive transformation of communism. The democratization of Soviet society means releasing the social forces which will expedite this transformation. It does not mean espousing bourgeois liberal values for these belong to the Soviet past, not its future.

The Soviet Union has experienced great difficulty in coping with dissent. Because the possession of power by the working class was the pre-requisite for socialist democracy, its preservation became the Soviet Union's primary consideration. Indeed the preservation of working class power has become the dominant value in the Soviet system and is reflected in Soviet law, the operation of Soviet courts and the forces of law and order in general. In a world environment which posed no threats to the Soviet Union there would have been there an unparalleled extension of workers' rights. The world environment, however, was implacably hostile. Until the Second World War the Soviet Union was enclosed within an ideological cordon sanitaire, perpetually threatened by subversive and economic destabilization. The Bolshevik Revolution was consistently in danger of being reversed. This situation generated a genuine fear of counter-revolution and provoked a suspicion of dissent. The grievous experiences of the German invasion in 1941 and the subsequent Nazi attempts to eradicate communism from Soviet society confirmed the fears and suspicion. The Soviet state developed, therefore, explicit, complex and inflexible protective mechanisms. A state apparatus was created to uncover, identify, expose and arraign those who threatened the system. But in the style of bureaucracies the apparatus lacked the facility to operate with discernment and discrimination. It was incapable of identifying degrees of dissent and of differentiating, therefore, between that which involved opposition to the system, that which was ineffective and irrelevant and that which was positive for the society. It became sensitive to all kinds of dissent and tended to repress it even when it was cosmetic, the figment of Western imagination and hopes.

An additional complication was created by the fact that the dissidents were primarily intellectuals for throughout Soviet history and beyond into that of Czarist Russia, intellectuals have been regarded with mixtures of suspicion, circumspection and respect. The repressive Czarist state prevented the development in the nineteenth century of a critical philosophy and social science through which Russian society could be analyzed, leaving literature, both prose and poetry, as the only effective means of communicating intellectual criticisms of society. Thus novelists and poets assumed a political significance in the eyes of both the state and the general population. From Pushkin and Lermontov to Tolstoy and Gorky, they were harassed by the police, arrested, exiled. They became national heroes in their own time. Through their works the written word assumed an almost mystical significance as the vehicle for forbidden ideas. It was searched out, avidly read and distilled for its hidden meanings.

The importance of the written word continued during and after the Bolshevik Revolution. All of the principal Bolsheviks were writers of high calibre. Lenin used the written word almost to the limits of its capacity as a means of arguing his case and of politicising others. Revolutionary feelings were expressed by writers such as Mayakovsky whose poems succinctly expressed the substance of the time. Artists too galvanised their talents to symbolize revolutionary aims in posters. As illiteracy was eliminated the Soviet people became avid readers and enhanced the importance of literature, and, thereby, the significance of writers. Literature continued to be a source of analysis, of criticism and of praise.

People who are treated seriously by society must expect to carry responsibilities and obligations. Where there are rewards there are usually costs. A number of Soviet writers have discovered this through their own experiences. Only where intellectuals in general and writers in particular play no serious critical analytical role, as in Britain, or where the system absorbs their criticism like a sponge, as in the USA, is a general freedom of expression permitted. In other words, where intellectuals are harmless because they are ignored or in other ways disarmed, they are free. But it is a spurious freedom.

Political Opposition

Yet despite the institutional restrictions on dissent there have frequently been oppositional factions within the Communist Party, while outside of it criticisms of the administration of communism have been facilitated and encouraged. This reality is in sharp contrast to the Western stereotype which portrays an inherently and totally repressive Soviet society. For this reason and because people find great difficulty in conceptualizing beyond their own experiences, there is a general failure in the West to understand the character and extent of criticism in the Soviet Union.

There have always been different, contending approaches within the Soviet Communist Party to the country's social and economic problems. Just as there are sharp differences about priorities within capitalist societies so there are arguments within communist societies about the allocation of scarce resources. Indeed the significance and complexity of policy options are

117

greater in the Soviet Union because there, decisions, which are determined by the hidden hand of the market mechanism in capitalist countries, are made consciously through the planning mechanism after a process of analysis and debate. The course taken by a capitalist country results largely from the interaction of market forces whereas whether the Soviet Union industrialises or not, the rate of its development, the allocation of resources between investment and consumption, the development of agriculture are all issues over which there are different views, representing different political positions and reflecting social forces which constitute interest groups in Soviet society.

The history of the Soviet Union is replete with illustrations of intensely contested arguments about policy issues within the Communist Party. During the 1920s the differences were institutionalized in factions. This led Stalin to describe the Sixteenth Congress of the Party in 1930 as "one of the few Congresses in the history of our Party at which there is no opposition of any crystallised kind, able to lay down its line and to counterpose it to that of the Party".[95] For a decade there had been organized but erudite debates about the role of trade unions in Soviet society. This issue was overtaken in 1927, however, by proposals for the First Five Year Plan and the collectivization of agriculture, both of which were opposed by the Right Opposition. There were two contrasting policies of industrialization. The opposition, namely N I Bukharin, Mikhael Tomsky and A I Rykov, wanted to pursue a path of industrialization within the framework of the New Economic Policy which had operated since 1921. Stalin's proposals, on the other hand, were for accelerated industrialization involving the complete rejection of the NEP. Stalin won the argument within the Party and by the time of the Sixteenth Congress there was no serious criticism of the Party policy. The leaders of the opposition were present but were quiet. Stalin taunted them, though in a good-humoured manner. They were, he said, "afflicted with the same disease as that of Chekhov's well-known character Belikov, teacher of Greek, "the man wrapped in padding". That character, Stalin elaborated, "always went about in galoshes and a padded coat, carrying an umbrella in hot and cold weather. 'Excuse me, but why do you wear galoshes and padded coat in July, in such hot weather?' Belikov used to be asked. 'You never can tell', Belikov would reply, 'Something untoward might happen; a sudden frost might set in, what then?' Everything new, everything that was outside the

118

daily routine of his drab philistine life, he feared like the plague . . . The same thing must be said about the former leaders of the Right opposition . . . As soon as any difficulty or hitch occurs anywhere in our country they become alarmed, fearing that something untoward might happen . . . they begin to howl about a catastrophe, about the downfall of the Soviet regime".[96]

Subsequent policy differences in the Party were not always dealt with in such a polemical fashion. But there was always opposition to the policy of the Party, even during its most difficult years. The Party was never monolithic. The question of how fast the rate of industrialization should be continued to arouse deep feelings though other issues arose and new personalities appeared around Stalin to propagate them. In the mid-1930s no one argued against the notion of centralized planning and collectivization but there were sharp divisions about the rate of development with G K Ordzhonikidze, the Minister for Heavy Industry, favouring caution and V M Molotov arguing for speed.[97] From about 1934 the state of the Communist Party became the issue which overrode all others. Andrei Zhdanov wanted to cleanse and rejuvenate the Party through raising the consciousness of its members, using education and propaganda while N I Ezhov argued for its expurgation. There were always Right and Left or Moderate and Radical factions over each important issue.

With the fall of Ezhov from power in 1938, Zhdanov assumed responsibility for the press, agitation and educational departments of the Central Committee. This put him in an advantageous position to argue his case. From the Eighteenth Party Congress in March, 1939, however, the argument was not over the condition but the role of the Party and Zhdanov had a new adversary in the Politburo. At that Congress he was partnered as a Secretary of the Central Committee by Georgi Malenkov who believed that the Party should have direct control over production in contrast to Zhdanov who stressed the ideological work of the Party and insisted that if the communists who manned the state organizations worked consciously as communists there would be no need for direct intervention by the Party. Malenkov's view was that the Secretariat of the Party should supervise the Council of People's Commissars (Sovnarkom) which was responsible for the country's industrial administration rather than concern itself with achieving theoretical clarity. He believed that 'political leadership' was too nebulous when separated from direct involvement in running the economy.

The role of the Party had been an important issue from the outset in 1917 but it took on a new emphasis with the introduction of centralized planning and complete state ownership in 1929. It was present during the 1930s but submerged by the concern about the Party membership. When that issue was settled the question about how to run the economy became paramount. The different perspectives were reflected in the main Central Committee journals and in the editorials of *Pravda*. It was, however, a matter which affected the whole Party apparatus for it determined the relationship between the local Party secretaries and managers of every enterprise in manufacturing industry and agriculture. It was of particular concern to the new generation of low and middle level functionaries who had taken office in the wake of the purges and the Ezhovshchina. By the same token the level of consciousness of those officials was the reason for Zhdanov's concern.[98]

The dispute between Zhdanov and Malenkov continued for a decade, until Zhdanov's death in 1948. Its outcome changed with circumstances. In times of crisis, as during war, when there was uncertainty about the country's political direction or when, in confusion, the political direction became threatened, then the Politburo came down on the side of Malenkov. When circumstances eased or when the needs of the situation demanded that production should be given priority over everything else and that Sovnarkom should be allowed to get on with its job unimpeded by Party supervision, as in the immediate post-war years, then Zhdanov got his way and the Party production branches were run down. After Zhdanov's death Malenkov restored the influence of the Party in production but that did not end the matter. Malenkov himself became a casualty of the dispute but, ironically, for protecting the state apparatus and over-riding the authority of the Communist Party. When Stalin died, Georgi Malenkov became the Chairman of the Council of Ministers, or Prime Minister, and was responsible, therefore, for the economic administrative apparatus of the state. At first Malenkov held both this post and that of First Secretary of the Party but he soon relinquished the Party post.[99] Nikita Khrushchev succeeded him as First Secretary and advocated the views which Malenkov had held in the arguments with Zhdanov. Khrushchev, from the outset, attempted to extend the Party's managerial role – "to give the lead to the 'managerial' rather than 'ideological' elements within the party, to its cadre of working executives rather than its political-ideological overseers, to the territorial party machines and not the central apparatus".[100] Thus Khrushchev wanted to increase the authority of the Party at the regional and local levels and in this matter too he was opposed by Malenkov who sought to improve the efficiency of industry through further centralization.

The principal policy issues in the Politburo after 1953, apart from the role of the party, were about whether to give priority to consumption or industry and in what ways to develop argiculture. Malenkov was in the minority on both issues. He favoured increased investment in the light industries and in developing the established agricultural regions. As he had been responsible for Soviet agriculture during Stalin's last years and the harvest yields in 1954 were low, his agricultural policy had been tested and failed. He took the blame for the failure and resigned from his position as Chairman of Council of Ministers in 1955 to be demoted to that of Minister of Electric Power Stations, though until 1957 he remained a member of the Politburo. Khrushchev took a different view about agriculture and advocated opening up 'virgin lands' in northern Kazakhstan, western Siberia and south east European Russia as the primary means of increasing production. This policy was applied and, at first, showed signs of success. In 1956 there was a record harvest. Khrushchev's political position was strengthened but opposition in the Politburo grew because of other policies he pursued.

There was, first, the policy of 'De-Stalinization' introduced at the Twentieth Congress of the Party in 1956. In practice this involved the rehabilitation of many people who had been arrested and sentenced from the mid-1930s onwards. The process inevitably cast suspicion on a number of existing Communist officials, including 3 or 4 members of the Politburo, including Molotov, Kaganovitch and the veteran Civil War commander Voroshilov, who opposed the policy. Others disliked it because they did not accept the condemnation of Stalin made by Khrushchev. "It was no secret to Khrushchev", Roy Medvedev wrote, "that he had opponents in the Presidium, but they were not united: the intrigues and feuds of the Stalin period still divided them. Yet discontent with his activities mounted at all levels of the Party and state apparatus as a result of his political and economic initiatives in the first half of 1957."[101] The opposition was united by Khrushchev's proposal to decentralize the management structure of the economy. From the beginning of 1957 he rushed through plans to abolish a number of central Ministries and substitute them with territorial Economic Councils. The opposition in the

Politburo coalesced in June 1957 and a motion to dismiss Khrushchev was passed. The attempt was foiled, however, by the Central Committee of the Party which comprised many Regional Party Secretaries who had benefited from the decentralization. The Politburo members who led the opposition, Molotov, Kaganovitch and Malenkov, were described as the anti-Party group. They lost their seats on the Politburo and were dismissed from their posts. They were each given other jobs. Molotov became the Ambassador to Mongolia, Malenkov was made the director of a large electric power station in Siberia while Kaganovitch worked as a manager of a factory. But their removal did not resolve the issues which were the basis of their opposition. Agricultural policy was a running sore. The 'virgin lands' policy had both encountered problems and created others. Nearly half of the area of the 'virgin lands' was damaged by soil erosion by 1964 due to the hurried efforts to get results. The maize harvest failed and livestock production fell. There were food shortages and the Soviet Union was compelled to import grain for the first time. Khrushchev was assessed by his own predictions. In 1957 he had declared that in about five years the Soviet Union would catch up with the USA in her production of meat, milk and butter per head of the population. Khrushchev had been popular with most of the population in 1957 when the first attempt to unseat him was made but by 1964 he was unpopular both with the general public and with Party leaders. There was much dissatisfaction with the methods and results of his leadership amongst a majority of Regional Party Secretaries and state functionaries on the Central Committee who had supported him in 1957. The Central Committee confirmed his dismissal as First Secretary of the Party in October 1964 after hearing 15 charges levied against him.[102] Leonid Brezhnev, a secretary of the Central Committee, succeeded Khrushchev as First Secretary and remained in that position until his death in 1982.

The changes in the Soviet leadership which have been described so far in this section have usually been attributed by Western observers to "bitter manouvres . . . for influence and power" between contenders. This, for instance, was how Brzezinski described the dispute between Zhdanov and Malenkov.[103] This conclusion stemmed from the assumption made about the Soviet Union that it is a monolithic totalitarian society. It is perceived as being led by a dictator who imposes his own personal style of stability. Thus any movement in the government of the society is assumed to be derived from the actions of the leader. Policy is deemed to be the consequence of decrees from above rather than social forces from below. Struggles amongst the leaders is for the succession and not about policies. The leader imposes stability by the use of his dictatorial powers. Merle Fainsod typified this approach in his work on the Soviet Union. In his comments about Khrushchev he stated: "Khrushchev, like Stalin before him, tolerates no derogation of his own authority, permits no opposition to raise its head within the Party, and insists that the Party function as a unit in executing his will."[104] He added that "Like Stalin before him, Khrushchev monopolizes control of the media of mass communications, saturating the channels of public opinion with party propaganda and permitting no outlet for political programs which challenge his own". Thus political opposition in the Party becomes simply a means for the First Secretary to channel his changing whims. It exists purely at his discretion. He treats the Politburo and Central Committee as if they were puppets at the end of string he was holding. By the same token the First Secretary is attributed with the responsibility for all events which flow from the political centre. In this setting there can be no seriously sustained political opposition. When factions are identified then they are tolerated only in so far as they serve the interests of the First Secretary, to enable him to play one against the other.

This functionalist interpretation of Soviet politics held away during Stalin's spell as Soviet leader after the war. When Khrushchev took office it was amended to take account of the obvious factional struggles in the Party. The focus was still on power rather than policy but it was not just power for power's sake. Some consideration was given to the issues behind it. The work of Robert Conquest typified this new approach. It was, however, only an amendment of the static totalitarian view of Soviet society to bring it more into line with observed reality. There was no recognition in it of the causal importance of the contradictory forces which made up society's structure. The amended approach was analogous to structural functionalism in the field of sociology which emerged to take account of the conflict in society which was seen to exist but which was not recognized by functionalist sociological theory. The revised theory was more plausible than the old one but retained its conceptual inadequacies. It focussed on people who were seen as individuals; it was concerned with personalities as the determinants of behaviour; in its analysis of Soviet politics, therefore, it was unable to escape from the Politburo and the formal Soviet political structure. There is no doubt that the formal decision-making framework of the Communist Party is an important influence on Soviet politics and that within it the position of the First Secretary is pivotal. But the communist leader interacts with the forces within the Communist Party and responds to its contradictions. The Communist Party is in a similar context in the wider society. The contradictions in Soviet life permeate all levels of political activity and are reflected in contrasting political attitudes. It is impossible for any Soviet leader to fail to respond to them.

The two decades which followed the dismissal of Nikita Khrushchev were marked by relative internal stability. There was an increase in dissent and the emergence of the Jewish Question but there were no serious political challenges to the leadership. For much of the time there was a collective leadership within the Politburo comprising Leonid Brezhnev as First Secretary of the CPSU, A.N. Kosygin, Chairman of the Council of Ministers and N.V. Podgorny, President of the Supreme Soviet USSR. The Politburo itself became more widely representative of interests within Soviet society rather than a collective of individuals who had emerged through the party apparatus. In other words, its members tended to be there because of the positions they held rather than for their personal qualities. For this reason there was a high degree of stability in the membership of the Politburo after 1965. Changes became dependent upon ill-health or deaths. The institutions of government, involving the Party and the state organs, became more integrated and bureaucratized. Thus from the mid-1960s the Soviet Union possessed a complex but unified system of government which did not depend on individual traits and which, in consequence, provided little scope for political factions.[105]

The integration of the political decision-making process narrowed the perspectives of the individual decision-makers and lessened their impact. There were fewer political leaders with the grand visions of the future of communism than there had been in the inter-war years. And those who were concerned about the future rather than just the day to day events were circumscribed by the bureaucratized system of policy-making. Quite clearly Yuri Andropov, the Chairman of the K.G.B. and long-standing member of the Politburo was in this position, as he revealed during his brief tenure as First Secretary of the C.P.S.U. on the death of Brezhnev in 1982. The general effect was that politics became much less flamboyant after Khrushchev.

But there were other more profound reasons for the absence of political discord during the Brezhnev period. The main issues before the society were no longer the great dividing ones of choosing the correct path to communism and resource allocation between investment and consumption or manufacturing industry and agriculture. They were instead a variety of non-divisive tasks such as quality control, distribution, new technology and work incentives which had administrative and technological solutions. The primary aim was to make Soviet society work under the prevailing structures along a pre-determined path. There was no political disagreement about this.

The world environment facilitated for the first time non-spectacular decision-making in the Soviet Union. Detente may in retrospect have been illusory but at the time it afforded the Soviet Union time and opportunity to get on with menial but important tasks such as replacing the housing stock, constructing kinder-gartens and improving educational facilities. The questions were not whether to build homes or tractors but how big the homes should be; not whether to build cars or tanks but how many cars to build. World events, of course, had an effect upon Soviet behaviour but none was seriously divisive. The Soviet intervention in Czecho-Slovakia in 1968, the international campaign to get Soviet Jews the right to leave and the increasing activities of Soviet dissidents generated political arguments but not political divisions.

Underlying these issues was a need by Soviet society for a spell of political quiescence as a part of the healing process after a series of traumatic events culminating in the war. Just to do familiar things in the ordinary course of events, no matter how inefficient or how politically circumscribed they were, was therapeutic for the society as a whole. In psychological terms it was a re-charging process through which communism in all of its apparel became quietly and completely accepted as a way of life. There is no doubt that the Brezhnev period of mundane politics was as necessary for the progress of the Soviet Union as the events which have followed. Unfortunately it carried with it a number of characteristics which have had negative effects upon the development of the Soviet economy. The attempt to correct those effects has aroused political opposition again.

Mr Mikhael Gorbachev, the First Secretary of the C.P.S.U since 1985, has described the negative features of the Brezhnev period in detail and has pronounced the policies to counter them. The features were inertia, an unwillingness to come to grips with the socio-economic issues, the emergence of an ossified concept of socialist relations, the treatment of reality as if it were static, a weakening of the economic tools of government, defects in the planning mechanism and the emergence of an ideology and mentality of stagnation which affected the operation of the Communist Party, the organs of government, the work ethic, culture, literature and the arts. The list was long and the criticisms were uncompromising.[106] Bureaucratic inertia, which lay at the base, led to corruption and crime. Some Party officials, Gorbachev stated "abused their authority, suppressed criticism, sought gain, and some of whom even became accomplices in, if not organisers of, criminal activities."

The solution submitted by Gorbachev on behalf of the Politburo lay in democratizing Soviet society. This has two aspects, namely 'perestroika' meaning restructuring, and 'glasnost' or openness. He outlined the implications of the policy. "The main purport of our strategy is to combine the achievements of the scientific and technological revolution with a plan-based economy and set the entire potential of socialism going. Re-organisation is reliance on the creative endeavour of the masses, all-round extension of democracy and socialist self-government, encouragement of initiative and self-organised activities, better discipline and order, greater openness, criticism and self-criticism in all fields of public life, and high respect for the value and dignity of the individual . . . Re-organisation means vigorously ridding society of any deviations from socialist morals, consistent enforcement of the principles of social justice, harmony between words and deeds, indivisibility of rights and duties, promotion of conscientious, high quality work, and overcoming of pay-levelling and consumerism . . . The final aim . . . is to effect thorough-going change in all aspects of public life, to give socialism the most advanced forms of social organization, and bring out the humane nature of our system . . ."[107] These aims, in short, involve the restructuring of economic mechanisms, the alteration of established administrative practices, the widening of the sphere of decision-making to include ordinary people and the election of senior management. They amount to a radical change in established institutional practices. 'Glasnost' reinforces 'perestroika' by encouraging the discussion of issues and the criticism of both institutional practices and officials who execute them. The strategies thus threaten the positions of middle-level Party functionaries, senior managers of enterprises and government officials with a pincer-like movement which compels them either to accommodate to the idea of institutional innovation or risk being removed from their posts. Many of them, particularly at regional level, are resisting what in effect is a 'cultural revolution' but there is opposition to the strategies at all levels from people who either believe that they are wrong for the Soviet Union or are simply suspicious and apprehensive of change like Chekhov's character, Belikov.

The new democratizing policies are generating a widespread, intense and open debate, with opinions ranging from enthusiastic support to scepticism and outright condemnation. They have emerged through the formal policy-making procedures of the Communist Party. Their first formal presentation was at the 27th Congress of the CPSU in February 1986. The broad political strategies to achieve them were formulated at the Plenum of the Central Committee of the CPSU which followed the Congress in April. As the implications of the policies emerged so the opposition to them became more overt and obstructive. The next Plenum of the Central Committee, at which it was intended to outline the strategies further, had to be postponed on three occasions because of the opposition to democratization. In the interim there was an extensive reshuffling of the personnel in Moscow concerned with policy formulation. Following the April Plenum, Mikhael Gorbachev stated, "a large part of the Secretariat and heads of department in the CPSU Central Committee have been replaced, practically the entire composition of the Presidium of the USSR Council of Ministers has been renewed."[108] At the Plenum of the Central Committee, eventually held in January 1987 to discuss "Re-Organization and the Party's Personnel Policy", Mr Gorbachev stated that he and "other Politburo members and Central Committee Secretaries had many meetings and conversations with Members of the Central Committee, public figures, workers, collective farmers, intellectuals, veterans and young people" in order to assess opinion about the policy. He spoke of the opposition but described it in structural terms. "We see", he said, "that change for the better is taking place slowly, that the cause of re-organization is more difficult and the problems which have accumulated in society more deep-rooted than we first thought. The further we go with our re-organization work, the clearer its scope and significance become: more and more unresolved problems inherited from the past come out."[109]

The way in which 'glasnost' is being exercised by Mikhael Gorbachev highlights that kind of Soviet criticism which is largely incomprehensible to the West. The speech which he made to the Plenum of the Central Committee in January, 1987, was in Western eyes, a devastating critique of the Soviet system. "No accomplishments", he said, "even the most impressive ones, should obscure either contradictions in societal development or our mistakes and failings . . . at some point the country began to lose momentum, difficulties and unresolved problems started to pile up, and there appeared elements of stagnation and other phenomena alien to socialism. All that badly affected the economy and social, cultural and intellectual life . . . The main cause – and the Politburo considers it necessary to say so with the utmost frankness at the Plenary Meeting – was that the CPSU Central Committee and the leadership of the country failed, primarily for subjective reasons, to see in time and in full the need for change and the danger of the intensification of crisis phenomena in society . . . Comrades it is the leading bodies of the Party and the state that bear responsibility for all this." He listed some problems which they faced such as the use of socialist property to obtain unearned income, the corruption of officials, the spread of alcohol and drug abuse, the rise in crime, defective planning and negative attitudes towards work. His language was trenchant. "Disregard for laws, report-padding, bribe-taking and encouragement of toadyism and adulation had a deleterious influence on the moral atmosphere in society. Real care for people, for the conditions of their life and work and for social well-being were often replaced with political flirtation – the mass distribution of awards, titles and prizes . . ."[110]

This blistering criticism was not a form of flagellation which carries no lessons and brings no changes, as is the case with the Senate and Congressional Hearings in the USA. Nor was it a statement that Soviet society is in danger of collapse. It was, on the contrary, the use of self-criticism as therapy. It exposed some elements but did not condemn the society. It was a special kind of exhortation which other Soviet leaders have practised. Lenin consistently used speeches to explain and exhort which were models of analytical rigour. They acknowledged mistakes, defects, defeats and setbacks without embellishment in the belief that understanding reality was a necessary condition for action to change it. This correlation implies that if the analysis is deliberately distorted in order to hide unpalatable facts then the policies derived from it will be defective. Objective analysis is inevitably critical. When practised by political leaders it becomes self-criticism. It was such analysis which led Lenin to the New Economic Policy in 1921 and then convinced Stalin to institute the First Five Year Plan and collectivization. It has, in the main, featured in the Central Committee Reports to Congresses of the CPSU though on occasions in the 1970s the analysis was fudged. Gorbachev thus is following the policy of 'glasnost' practised by Lenin.

Political self-criticism in the Soviet Union is an activity with some risk but only to the individual leaders. When in 1921 Lenin described the catastrophic food situation which was causing widespread starvation his only motivation was to devise policies to resolve it.[111] It was not an admission of failure but a recognition of a particular constellation of forces. He did not fear that his Party would be displaced as a consequence though he himself might have been a casualty as Khruschev was in 1964. He did not have to gloss over problems in competition with other Parties or seduce voters with false promises. Nor did he have to defend his own class interests against another. None of the political forces which compel Western political leaders to disguise failure, to project it on to the shoulders of others, to find scapegoats, is present in the Soviet Union. It is this difference of experience which makes the Soviet use of self-criticism largely incomprehensible to people in the West.

Forums for Criticism

The Communist Party is the only legitimate forum for organized political opposition in the Soviet Union. This follows from the fact that it is the only political party and that, therefore, only through it can government policy be changed. Any other kind of opposition must, to be successful, act on the forces within the Communist Party. Although the Party with about 17 million members is large in absolute terms it remains a cadre Party, comprising 15 per cent of the population. It operates therefore in a milieux which is predominantly non-Party. In order to fulfil its primary task of providing political leadership it has to understand that milieux and respond to its pressures. It can only maintain its position in the long-run by having credibility with the broad population. It has, therefore, to produce the political decisions which serve the whole of Soviet society. This does not mean that the Party has to pursue a populist line. It is a leading Party and has to initiate and experiment and, in consequence, on occasions to take unpopular decisions. But unpopular, as well as popular policies must relate closely to the needs of the society. There is no sense in which the Party can lead without being a political sensor and in order to be this there have to be mechanisms whereby criticisms, needs and aspirations of ordinary people can be communicated to the Party.

The milieux of the Communist Party is a collectivist one. The ethos of the system is collectivism. All persons act through collectivities at work and in their leisure. The society resolves its economic and social problems, ranging from the anti-social behaviour of an individual in a block of flats to the macro-social issues, such as the character of the education system, through discussion. There are facilities for meetings everywhere, in Palaces of Culture, trade union offices, at work where every factory or shop has a 'Red Corner' where workers meet before or after work to debate issues and air their grievances. No major changes in legislation are made without wide-ranging debates. As was stated earlier, the alterations to the Soviet Constitution were preceded by wide-ranging discussion throughout the country. The new 1936 Constitution stipulated that the USSR Supreme Soviet should establish a Labour Code to introduce uniformity between the various Republics. This was not done until 1970 when the draft of the 'Fundamental Labour Legislation' was published in the press for a nationwide discussion. Workers in factories and offices, teachers and scientists, trade unionists and management, engaged in discussions and submitted amendments to the Draft Bill Commission. The 1936 process of nationwide consultation was repeated when the Constitution was revised for the second time in 1977. "The Constitutional Commission of the USSR Supreme Soviet consisted of experienced Party and Government officials and representatives of the working class, the collective farm peasantry and the people's intelligentsia. Prominent scientists, specialists and representatives of state bodies and public organizations took part in drafting the Constitution. The draft was considered twice at Plenary Meetings of the Central Committee of the Communist Party of the Soviet Union. The draft Constitution was put up for nationwide discussion which lasted nearly four months at about a million and a half meetings at factories, collective farms, in units of the armed forces and in residential neighbourhoods. It was discussed at trade union plenary, actif and general meetings, the Young Communist League, co-operative societies and organizations of creative workers. All the Soviet Union's Communists participated in the discussion. There were more than 450,000 open Party meetings at which over 3,000,000 people took the floor. The draft was examined at sessions of all the Soviets, from rural Soviets to the Supreme Soviets of constituent republics, that is, by more than 2,000,000 deputies representing the entire Soviet people. The Constitutional Commission, the press received an endless stream of letters from all parts of the Soviet Union . . . Upwards of 140,000,000 people, that is, more than four-fifth of the country's· adult population, took part in discussing the Draft Constitution . . . About 400,000 proposals clarifying and amplifying the wording of articles of the Constitution were put forwards . . ."[112] Not a single law on education is adopted without a preliminary nation-wide discussion. The 1973 Draft Fundamental Legislation on Public Education was published in the press and discussed for four months. 120 million people participated in the discussion of the 1984 Draft Reform of General and Vocational Schools, a particularly contentious proposal of which was that to lower the age at which children start primary school from 7 to 6 years.

The means used to enable ordinary people to submit their views about major changes in the law are, on the one hand, collective organizations such as trade unions, the Young Communist League and Cooperative Societies, where collective opinions are expressed and, on the other hand, letter writing to the Communist Party, government departments, trade unions and the press through which both collective and individual views are communicated. The means, however, are constantly available and are continually used as forums for criticism. Trade unions are the most influential means for they are mass organizations with close relations with the Communist Party, access to government ministries and, under the 1977 Constitution, the right to make direct proposals for legislation. More than 99 per cent of the labour force belong to trade unions, giving them, in 1987, a membership of nearly 140 million. The rate of membership participation is high. Indeed the quorum for local union meetings is two-thirds of the total member-ship. The topics discussed at the meetings cover all facets of union activity and range from work situation problems to kindergarten facilities, education, housing, tourism, industrial health provisions, social security and foreign policy. Workers, however, have other opportunities to discuss their work situations and to criticize management. They meet in Work Collectives to discuss the problems at their immediate respective points of production and in Standing Production Conferences for matters at the enter-prise level. Through these various means workers raise issues of bureaucracy, managerial inefficiency, corruption and defective planning. Many managers have been dismissed as a result of complaints lodged by individual workers backed by collective support.

The extensive and persuasive character of group discussion should be a clue to the character of Soviet society. It is not possible to combine a high level of universal education with a system of decision-making and consultation based on collectives and, at the same time, prevent debates which will lead to criticism. This was learned early on by totalitarian states. Fascist Italy, Nazi Germany, Franco Spain, South Africa and other contemporary totalitarian regimes in Asia and South America have all been compelled to ban every kind of public gathering, even conversation by more than 2 or 3 people in the streets, in order to preserve their totalitarianism. If people are allowed to meet then surely they will talk and criticize. It does then seem perverse of the Soviet Union, if it is trying to muzzle criticism, to encourage group discussions.

A long-standing formal means for communicating individual complaints are the Committees of People's Control. These were started as Complaints Bureaus in April 1919 under the People's Commissariat of State Control, to receive, investigate and check complaints and statements by workers and peasants. In 1932 Stalin described the Bureaus as a means of countering bureaucracy and red-tape. Since 1932 they have changed their designation but not their purpose. They have become particularly active under the 'glasnost' policy of Mr Gorbachev.

Letter writing to the press, trade unions, the Communist Party and governmental departments is a particularly important forum for enabling Soviet people to express their opinions. It has always been regarded as a serious channel of communication both by ordinary people and the government and has become protected by law. At the Ninth All-Russian Conference of the Russian Communist Party in September, 1920, a Special Control Commission was formed on Lenin's initiative to deal with written complaints sent to the Party. The resolution stated that "not a single complaint should be left unanswered . . ." In 1921 non-Party people were advised to criticize the Party if necessary. The Special Control Commission was told in 1923 to handle complaints "in a Party spirit" with no arrests or searches. From 1924 the Central Committee of the Russian Communist Party began to concern itself with letters to newspapers. For instance, in 1926 it ruled that "letters sent to the press by workers and peasants should be treated as serious sources of information about complaints by information departments of Party Committees"; while the following year those who handled the complaints were warned not to be "guilty of a condescending, patronizing attitude to the complainants" for if they were they would be taken to court and prosecuted. Readers Conferences were set up to discuss complaints. Newspapers were given guide-lines for handling letters expeditiously and were admonished if they failed. For instance in 1936 the editors of two newspapers, the *Northern Caucasian Bolshevik* and *The Star,* were dismissed for handling letters incompetently, humiliating writers and forgetting that "there is a living person behind every letter". The Supreme Soviet in 1981 stipulated that all complaints and letters to State, Public Bodies, Enterprises, Establishments and Offices should be replied to within one month and those which could be answered without a follow-up should have a reply within 15 days. In consequence, trade unions, the Communist Party and newspapers have established departments to deal with letters. Each letter is filed; every letter gets an answer. Many are collective ones. In 1983, 6,000 collective letters were sent to the All-Union Central Council of Trade Unions. The newspapers *Trud, Pravda* and *Izvestia* receive in the region of one million letters each year.

Comparisons:

There is a similarity between democracy in the Western capitalist countries and the Soviet Union in that, at bottom, it is about ordinary people running their own lives. After that there are profound differences. The Soviet Union starts off with a structure which has no major class or power divisions. The working class is the only class and the problem is finding ways in which it can permeate the decision-making process directly and through representatives. The extent to which that is done is the measure of Soviet democracy.

Soviet society is a collectivist one so that its democracy cannot be gauged by the degree of individual freedom to criticize, oppose and subvert. Individuals achieve their freedom through that of the collectives to which they belong. Their interests, therefore, are subordinate to collective ones. But this subordination does not mean that individuals play no part. On the contrary, they constitute the collectives and the quality of their deliberations and interactions determines the level of collective achievement. Thus democracy in the Soviet Union has a positive connotation. It is not simply about the right to attack and discard but also about the task of building and improving.

The manner in which the Soviet Union has tackled this task has been significantly influenced by its own environmental conditions. Throughout most of its history it has been compelled to act as if it were under siege, guarding against external attacks and internal subversion. This situation generated a climate of suspicion, the visible signs of which were restrictions on the right of expression and punishment in corrective labour camps or internal exile for those who violated them. The Soviet Union's own democratic processes were an inevitable casualty. The country went through phases of fluctuating intensity about its security. Its concern was high during the Civil War, during the period leading up to the Second World War, during the War itself and its immediate, Cold War, aftermath. Restrictions on the freedom of expression varied as the concern about internal security changed. But they were never absolute and during some periods were insignificant. The need to be alert about threats to the system, however, gave rise to institutions whose task it was to regulate dissent, thus bureaucratizing repression. Bureaucracies have the tendency to respond automatically to signs without sensitivity about the nature of the issues. In the Soviet context this meant that dissent was sometimes repressed even when it was marginal and in no sense a threat. This has happened during the last two decades when dissidents have been neither numerous nor united in intent.

The question which arises is whether the action which has been taken against dissidents has given character to the whole of Soviet society as commentators in the West suggest. Is a society repressive because it harasses a marginal group of protesting intellectuals? Quite clearly repression is repression whatever the numbers or special positions of those affected. The circumstances of repression, however, cannot be ignored. Nor, in relation to those circumstances can the marginal character of repression be disregarded.

In other words, the combined effects of the transformation from capitalism to socialism and the intense resistance of international capitalism to the transformation made it impossible for Soviet society to develop logically on the premise of socialism. There were bound to be distortions, even mutations, in the practice of administering society. None of these consequences, however, have been shown to be endemic to Soviet society for they have changed in quality and eased in intensity. In this respect the marginal character of dissidents does have a relevance. The historical experience of the Soviet Union indicates that its treatment of dissidents has not been a function of internal structural conflicts but mainly of international circumstances. Given a propitious international environment the Soviet Union would have practised a tolerance of dissent consistent with socialist values.

A wholly different picture of the character of Soviet society emerges if human rights are viewed in their wider and more appropriate sense, as is described below in chapter seven. Then the right to dissent is put alongside other rights such as the right to live, to work, to be educated and to be healthy. If poverty is regarded as tyranny and unemployment is treated as a denial of human rights, then the Soviet Union scores against all capitalist countries. But, it can be argued, making comparisons between the defects of different societies is invidious. It does not correct a wrong because others have committed it too; even if they have committed it doubly. But by comparing the records of the accusers it may help to understand their motives and their priorities. The major Western capitalist countries would be lowly placed on a league table of broadly based human rights. The USA has a record of consistent discrimination against its black population and a systematic denial of even basic human necessities to the Native Americans. Its intervention in Vietnam caused approximately 4 million casualties while in Chile the democratic system as well as many lives were the casualties of American interference. No American can accuse the Soviet Union of human rights violations without applying double standards. Then what of US allies? What penance is required of West Germany for its genocidal treatment of its Jewish inhabitants and the Jews in Europe in general? Moreover, through the policy of Berufsverbote it denies employment to people because of their political beliefs. Turkey, a member of NATO, applies a particularly brutal form of political discrimination involving torture and long prison sentences. The complete leadership of the Confederation of Progressive Trade

Union (DISK) was arrested in 1981 for engaging in normal trade union activities. The government demanded death sentences for all 51 members of the union executive. By 1986 as many as 1,477 trade unionists were standing trial. South Africa, America's close political ally has an indescribable record of violence against black people. Britain, of course, has a colonial history which reaches into the present through discrimination against black immigrants and its own black citizens. Its contemporary treatment of Irish Catholics in Northern Ireland through the operation of jury-less Diplock Courts and on the English mainland through the Prevention of Terrorism Act seriously stains its own record. The selection of the Soviet Union for special denunciation by such countries seems rather suspicious. But, perhaps, before a conclusive judgement can be made the Soviet Jewish question and the wider human rights issue should be examined.

FOOTNOTES

1. *Lenin Collected Works,* vol. 28, p. 230.
2. ibid, p. 246 and p. 248.
3. *The Soviet Impact on the Western World,* op cit, p. 5.
4. *Lenin Collected Works,* vol. 28, p. 249.
5. ibid, p. 242.
6. ibid, p. 243.
7. See *The Bolshevik Revolution, 1917-1923,* by E H Carr, Penguin Books, vol. 2.
8. *Lenin Collected Works,* vol. 32, p. 172. Speech to the Tenth Congress of the Russian Communist Party (Bolshevik) March, 1921.
9. ibid, pp. 185-6.
10. The Russian Social-Democratic Labour Party of Bolsheviks was renamed the Russian Communist Party (Bolshevik) in March 1918 in order, Lenin stated, to conform to the terminology formulated by Marx and Engels in the *Communist Manifesto.*
11. This was recognised by Soviet critics of the Communist Party such as Roy Medvedev. See his work *Let History Judge.*
12. *Lenin Collected Works,* vol. 30, p. 327. A speech made on 2 February 1920.
13. *A History of the USSR* by Andrew Rothstein, p. 106.
14. ibid, p. 245.
15. See *Origins of the Purges* by J Arch Getty, p. 112.
16. Szymanski, op cit, pp. 228-229.
17. *Soviet Jewish Affairs,* Vol. 12, No. 3, November, 1982, p. 46.
18. "On Assessing the Size of Forced Concentration Camp Labour in the Soviet Union, 1929-56" by S G Wheatcroft, *Soviet Studies,* vol. XXXIII, No. 2, April, 1981, p. 266.
19. *Gulag Archipeligo, 1973, (Fontana edition) p. 595.*
20. *The Great Terror,* p. 713.
21. "Analysis of Forced Labour Statistics" by S G Wheatcroft, *Soviet Studies,* April, 1982, p. 227.

22. *The Great Terror*, p. 706.
23. "An Assessment of the Sources and Uses of Gulag Forced Labour, 1929-56", *Soviet Studies*, Vol. 33, January, 1981. A polemic developed between Wheatcroft and Rosefielde over the question of Soviet labour camps. They differed over the role of forced labour in the industrialization of the Soviet Union and over the size of the camp populations from 1929 until Stalin's death. Wheatcroft consistently accused Rosefielde of exaggerating the significance of forced labour and the size of the camps. The *Slavic Review*, The American Quarterly Journal of Soviet and East European Studies, took up the questions in its autumn issue, No. 3, in 1985. It allowed Wheatcroft and Rosefielde to make comments on each other's position and then invited two specialists in Soviet demography, Barbara A Anderson and Brian D Silver, to review the debate in an article called "Demographic Analysis and Population Catastrophes in the USSR". The issue by that time had become a straight-forward demographic one, namely, 'what was the loss of Soviet population due to forced labour camps and collectivization?' This led to a further question about the amount of excess mortality between 1929 and 1963. The authors covered Conquest's intervention in the debate and reviewed the main analysts of Soviet population statistics. In a closely argued article they concluded with a gentle reprimand for those who made unwarranted assumptions about the data and supported Wheatcroft's approach. The main goal of the article, Anderson and Silver stated had "been to demonstrate the sensitivity of estimates of excess mortality to assumptions about the "normal" trends in fertility and mortality. If one were able to make defensible assumptions about these trends, one might reduce the range of uncertainty about the extent of excess mortality. But a considerably greater effort to defend assumptions, to verify the quality of extant demographic data, and to determine what the actual demographic trends were is needed before more precise estimates of excess mortality during the 1930s can be made. Stephen Wheatcroft's work has been very helpful in moving scholarship in that direction. We hope that increased awareness of the sensitivity of any estimates to the assumptions will help scholars to avoid making or tolerating unwarranted interpretations of the data." (Slavic Review, No 3, Vol. 44, pp. 535-6).
24. ibid, p. 65.
25. ibid, p. 60.
26. ibid, p. 51.
27. *Communist Party Membership in the USSR 1917-1967*, by T H Rigby, Princeton, New Jersey, 1968, p. 214.
28. *The Great Terror*, p. 754.
29. *Let History Judge*, p. xxxii.
30. *Smolensk Under Soviet Rule* by Merle Fainsod, 1958, p. 3.
31. ibid, p. 12.
32. Quoted by Wheatcroft in *Soviet Studies*, Vol. XXXV, 1983, p. 232.
33. Szymanski, op cit, p. 247.
34. ibid, p. 229.
35. Getty, op cit, p. 40.
36. The most detailed Western source for Communist Party membership changes is Rigby, op cit.
37. ibid, pp. 178-179.

38. Getty, op cit, p. 54.
39. Quoted in Getty, op cit, pp. 67-68.
40. ibid, p. 55.
41. ibid, p. 66.
42. "Towards a Thorough Analysis of Soviet Forced Labour Statistics" by S G Wheatcroft, *Soviet Studies*, Vol. XXXV, No. 2, April 1983, p. 227.
43. Getty, op cit, p. 88.
44. ibid, p. 89.
45. ibid, p. 110.
46. Up to 1936 only the city and village soviets were elected by direct election. Other levels comprised of delegates elected from the body at the next level down. See *A History of the USSR*, by Andrew Rothstein, pp. 238-248.
47. Getty, op cit, pp. 137-149.
48. ibid, p. 158.
49. ibid, p. 164.
50. Rothstein, op cit, p. 252.
51. See Getty, op cit, p. 168 for details of the situation in the Western Region.
52. ibid, p. 178.
53. *Let History Judge*, p. 365.
54. ibid, p. 351.
55. Rigby, op cit, p. 211.
56. *Stalin: A Political Biography*, 1949, p. 384.
57. ibid, p. 212. Similar figures are found in "Analysis of Forced Labour Statistics" by S G Wheatcroft, *Soviet Studies*, Vol. XXXV, No. 2, 1983, pp. 226-7.
58. Szymanski, op cit, p. 241.
59. Rigby, op cit, pp. 217-219.
60. Getty, op cit, p. 175.
61. ibid, p. 206.
62. *Stalin: The Man and his Era*, 1973, p. 419.
63. ibid, pp. 418, 420 and 421.
64. ibid, p. 422.
65. Getty, op cit, p. 203.
66. ibid, p. 203.
67. *Dissent in the USSR*, ed. by Rudolf L Tökés, 1975, p. 60.
68. *Uncensored Russia* by Peter Reddaway, 1972, p. 20.
69. *Power and Principle. Memoirs of the National Security Adviser 1977-1981* by Zbigniew Brzezinski, 1983, p. 150.
70. See *How to Secure Peace in Europe* by Denis and Cynthia Roberts 1985, for the full text of the Helsinki Declaration and an informative interpretation of it.
71. *Prisoners of Conscience In the USSR: Their Treatment and Conditions*. An Amnesty International Report, 1980, p. 20.
72. Brzezinski, op cit, p. 124.
73. ibid, p. 126.
74. ibid, p. 124.
75. ibid, p. 149.
76. ibid, p. 150.
77. *The Soviet Union Since the Fall of Khrushchev*, edited by Archie Brown and Michael Kaser, 1975, p. 128.

78. *On Soviet Dissent* by Roy Medvedev, 1980, p. 2.
79. Tökés, op cit, p. 123.
80. ibid, p. 124.
81. ibid, pp. 126-127.
82. Medvedev, op cit, p. 2.
83. Reddaway in *The Soviet Union Since the Fall of Khrushchev,* op cit, p. 128.
84. *TUC Report,* 1978, p. 259.
85. ibid, p. 60.
86. Documents relating to the case including biographical details of some of those involved were published in *Workers Against the Gulag,* edited by Viktor Haynes and Olga Semyonova, Pluto Press, London, 1979.
87. I travelled extensively throughout the Soviet Union in 1982 talking with trade unionists and found no sign of the unrest which was manifest in Poland.
88. *Amnesty International Report,* 1986, p. 310.
89. *On Soviet Dissent,* op cit, p. 6.
90. Tökés, op cit, p. 128.
91. Reddaway, *The Soviet Union Since the Fall of Khrushchev,* op cit, p. 131.
92. *On Soviet Dissent,* pp. 2-7.
93. ibid, p. 5.
94. ibid, p. 4.
95. *J Stalin Works,* Vol. 13, p. 1.
96. ibid, pp. 13-14.
97. Getty, op cit, pp. 14-17.
98. See "The Origins of the Conflict Between Malenkov and Zhdanov: 1939-1941" by Jonathan Harris, *Slavic Review,* vol. 35, No. 2, 1976, pp. 287-303.
99. *Khrushchev, The Years in Power* by Roy A Medvedev and Zhores A Medvedev, 1977, pp. 2-7.
100. *Khrushchev and the Soviet Leadership* by Carl A Linden, USA, 1966, p. 30.
101. *Khrushchev* by Roy Medvedev, Oxford, 1982, p.112.
102. ibid, pp. 235-245.
103. *The Permanent Purge,* op cit, p. 23.
104. *How Russia is Ruled* by Merle Fainsod, Harvard, USA, 1963, p. 583
105. For an interesting examination of the structure of the Soviet Government see *Politics and the Soviet Union* by Mary McAuley, Penguin Books, 1977.
106. See Mr Gorbachev's speech to the Plenum of the Central Committee of the CPSU, January 27th 1987, *Moscow News,* Supplement to issue No. 6, (3254), 1987.
107. ibid.
108. ibid.
109. ibid.
110. ibid.
111. *Lenin Collected Works,* Vol. 32, pp. 441-449.
112. *Constitution of the Socialist State of the Whole People* by Alexander Kositsin, Moscow, 1979, pp. 11-12.

Chapter Six
The Jewish Question

It is not possible to discuss the issue of human rights in the Soviet Union without examining the position of Soviet Jews for there have been repeated accusations in the West that the Soviet authorities practise anti-Semitism. The allegations have been based on claims that Soviet Jews face discrimination in education, employment and in the refusal of the government to allow them an unrestricted right to emigrate. But the Western case is more complex than this for it involves the Soviet attitude to dissent in general. As was seen in the previous chapter, a number of Jews have been arrested and imprisoned for dissident activities but this was in no sense related to their Jewishness. The core of the case concerning Soviet Jews is not about dissent but arises from the fact that on the one hand the West has elevated the right to emigrate as a principal human right and on the other hand the Soviet Union controls emigration and, therefore, regulates the distribution of exit visas to Jews. Claims that Soviet Jews are discriminated against in other ways are made to support that grievance.

Jews and the Revolution

The Jews are a recognized ethnic group in the Soviet Union but, unlike the others, without a natural homeland. They have been concentrated however, in European Russia—in the Soviet Republics of the Ukraine, Byelorussia and Lithuania—in areas annexed initially by Czarist Russia from Poland early in the nineteenth century and described as the Pale of Settlement. There, indeed, they were confined by the Czarist authorities in ghettos, repressed and subjected to frequent pogroms. As they always lived under restrictions their activities were channelled into a narrow occupational range. In 1818, for instance, over 85 per cent of gainfully occupied Jews in Russian controlled territories were merchants of different kinds—traders, estate managers, tax collectors and money lenders. Most of the remainder were artisans.[1] As Russia industrialized during the course of the nineteenth century non-Jews competed for the traditional Jewish occupations. The position of the Jewish middleman was undermined. The "state came to monopolise the collection of taxes and the production of liquor . . . intensified domestic production of many goods aided by tariff barriers, ruined the livelihood of many exporters and importers. Capital, credit and jobs formerly generated by the wealthiest elements of the Jewish community dried up as they mobilised funds for external investment in banks, railway construction, sugar-beet and oil production. Modern financial institutions obviated the need for so many petty money-lenders. Aside from the few who became wealthy businessman or highly educated professionals, the members of the Jewish community were thus turned into peddlers, hawkers and small shopkeepers; owners of small, undercapitalised enterprises engaged in the production of clothing or footwear; or artisans employed in those workshops."[2] In the early twentieth century even these activities began to be squeezed by the growth of large-scale capitalist enterprises. Jews became increasingly impoverished, oppressed by a series of government regulations aimed at creating assimilation but which in effect exacerbated already existing prejudices and constantly subjected them to social and physical hostility from the non-Jewish population.

The Jews in Russia, then, had good reason to oppose the Czarist regime and to welcome its overthrow in March 1917. They became free in an instant. "With a strike of the pen the Provisional Government abolished the whole complicated network of laws directed against the Jews. Suddenly their chains fell off. Disabilities and discriminations were cast on the refuse heap . . ."[3] But they were not so pleased when the Bolshevik Party seized power in November of that year. There were a number of Jews in leading positions in the Bolshevik Party but by and large they disliked the communist policies aimed at eliminating profit-making and usury from economic activities. The Bolshevik Revolution destroyed the traditional occupations of Jews but placed them in the same position as all other citizens of the new state. There was some reversal to profit-making during the period of the New Economic Policy from 1921 to 1929 but it came to a dramatic and painful halt when the First Five Year Plan in 1929 extended state planning to every sphere of economic activity. The last vestiges of profit-making were removed when agriculture was collectivized in the early 1930s and the property of the kulaks, the rich peasant class, was confiscated. The Jews were forced to adjust to the life expectancies of the majority of ordinary Russians. By 1935 there were three times as many Jewish manual workers as there had been in 1926.[4]

Many Jews suffered in the upheavals following the Revolution. Pogroms broke out in the Ukraine and Byelorussia during the Civil War, mainly facilitated by the White Russians. "As a result, Jewish attitudes began to shift in a pro-Bolshevik direction from late 1918 onwards: anti-Soviet sympathies came more and more to be associated with pillage and death, Bolshevism with the suppression of anti-Jewish violence."[5] But their businesses were destroyed nonetheless and their way of life was upset. Once the Soviet government was established there was no further physical violence against the Jews. The social and economic problems they faced had no ethnic causes. As Sidney and Beatrice Webb wrote in 1935 after an intensive study of the Soviet Union: "The condition of thousands of Jewish families in White Russia and the Ukraine is still one of poverty relieved only by the alms of their co-religionists . . . But they suffer, not as Jews but as shopkeepers and moneylenders whose occupation has become unlawful. They are protected from violence as never before. They retain their synagogues and their vernacular speech. Their sons and daughters find all branches of education, and all careers, open to them. Many thousands of families have been assisted to settlement on the land. Wherever there is a group of Jewish families together they have their own local government and their cultural autonomy. They are not prevented from maintaining their racial customs and ceremonies . . ."[6]

But there were ethnic difficulties, nonetheless, though they did not always arise from the Soviet society. "It cannot be denied" the Webbs added "that all the blessings of security from pogroms and freedom to enter professions that the USSR accords to the Jews involve, in practice, their acceptance of the Soviet regime; and make, on the whole, for assimilation. The policy of the Soviet Union accordingly meets with persistent opposition, and even denigration, from the world-wide organization of the Zionists, among whom the building up of the "national home" in Palestine brooks no rival."[7] The problem posed by Zionism for Soviet Jews simmered until well after the formation of Israel and then, following the Six Day War in 1967, it began to boil.

The Soviet government tried to cope with the influence of Zionism by allocating a piece of virgin territory at Birobidzhan in 1928 as the basis for a Jewish homeland. This land in Eastern Siberia, with no indigenous inhabitants, was half as large as England and was well equipped with resources for agricultural settlements with a climate similar to a Canadian wheat province. It was formally established as a Jewish Autonomous Region in 1934. But it failed to attract an adequate number of Jewish settlers. It had a total population of about 50,000 in 1934, most of whom were Jews. But the Jewish element in the Region declined as Jews became assimiliated into Soviet life. About 90 per cent of Soviet Jews chose to live in towns and most of those who worked in agriculture preferred the warmer climate of the Ukraine and the Crimea. Their interest in Yiddish education in general dropped off. There were more than 1000 Yiddish language schools in the early 1930s and at least two dozen Yiddish language newspapers. Between 1928 and 1935 about 3650 books were published in Yiddish.[8] All of these activities declined as the pace of industrialization increased and as Jews were drawn into it. Then, with the Second World War most such activities were brought to an abrupt end. But by that time the picture had emerged of Jews becoming preponderantly professional people, experiencing what would be described in the West as 'upward social mobility'. They worked in all major Soviet institutions. They held positions, for example, in the NKVD and had a marked presence in all ranks of the Red Army. During the Second World War, 500,000 Jews served in the armed Services and more than 300 of them were Generals.[9]

Soviet Jewry in War

The population of approximately 3 million Jews in the Soviet Union in 1939 was largely concentrated in the Ukraine and Byelorussia in the areas bordering Eastern Europe. Another 2 million Jews came under Soviet jurisdiction through the Soviet occupation of Eastern Poland and the addition of Lithuania. Four million of these people lived in areas over-run by the German army after June 1941. The Nazi government, while planning the invasion of the USSR, decided to annihilate the Jews in the territories occupied. Special mobile death units called *Einsatzgruppe* were to follow directly behind the frontline troops and round up Jews to be killed. These units were given the special facility to operate "not only in army group rear areas but also in the corps areas right on the front line. This concession was of great importance to the *Einsatzgruppe*, for the Jews were to be caught as quickly as possible. They were to be given no warning and no chance to escape."[10] An agreement to this effect was signed by Reinhardt Heydrich, the chief of the Reich Security Main Office, at the end of May, 1941. It was generally understood to sanction the killing of Jews, Communists and insane people on the spot. There were four units, totalling about 3,000 men, and led almost without exception by professional men such as a lawyer, a physician, a church pastor and a professional opera singer.

The units were expert killers. In the first wave between June and December, 1941 they murdered half a million Jews mainly through mass shootings at large grave sites. A second wave of killings initiated to take account of those accidentally missed on the first occasion resulted in almost 1 million deaths. The Soviet authorities evacuated many Jews to safe areas. Hilberg reported that "the *Einsatzgruppe* which operated in the central and eastern Ukrainian territories found that many Jewish communities were reduced by 70-90 per cent and some by 100 per cent. In Melitopol an original Jewish population of 11,000 had dwindled to 2000 before *Einsatzgruppe* D arrived. Dnepropetrovsk had a pre-war Jewish community of 100,000; about 30,000 remained. In Chernigov, with a pre-war Jewish population of 10,000, Sonder-kommando 4a found only 309 Jews. In Mariupol and Taranrog *Einsatsgruppe* D encountered no Jews at all. On the road from Smolensk to Moscow *Einsatzgruppe* B reported that in many towns the Soviets had evacuated the entire Jewish population."[11] Altogether about 1,500,000 Jews succeeded in eluding the killing units. These evacuation measures were taken when virtually the whole of Soviet industry was on wheels, being relocated in and beyond the Urals. It was German practice as they entered Soviet territories to encourage the local populace to engage in pogroms against the Jews as a first stage in their genocidal policy. They had some success in those areas which had become part of the Soviet Union since 1939 but in the Soviet Union proper there was no evidence of spontaneous anti-Semitism. A Jewish historian commentated that "In Byelorussia, a conspicuous difference is evidenced between the old Soviet part of the region and the area which had previously belonged to Poland and was under Soviet rule from September 1939 to June 1941. Nazi and anti-Jewish propaganda drew a weak response in the former Soviet Byelorussia: we encounter complaints in Nazi documents that, 'it is extremely hard to incite the local populace to pogroms because of the backwardness of the Byelorussian peasants with regard to racial consciousness.'"[12] Another view of the cause of the racial attitudes in Byelorussia was given in a secret memorandum by a collaborator to the chief of the German army in August 1942. He wrote: "There is no Jewish problem for the Byelorussian people. For them, this is purely a German matter. This derives from Soviet education which has negated racial difference . . . The Byelorussians sympathize with, and have compassion for the Jews, and regard the Germans as barbarians and the hangman of the Jew, whom they consider human beings equal to themselves . . . "[13]

There is much evidence provided by survivors themselves to support this view of the Soviet attitude to the Jews.[14] Contrary to the general opinion of Jewish docility in the face of Nazi violence there was large-scale Jewish participation in the partisan movement in the German occupied part of Soviet Union. Indeed the German army blamed the Jews for starting guerrilla activity. The German generals had rationalized their co-operation with the killer units "through the pretence that the Jewish population was a group of Bolshevist diehards who instigated, encouraged, and abetted the partisan war behind the German lines. The army thus had to protect itself against the partisan menace by striking at its presumable source – the Jews."[15] This, of course, fitted in with the Nazi inspired belief that there was an international Jewish and Bolshevik conspiracy aimed at undermining Western civilization. The army's attitude was based on a half-truth for many Jewish families and survivors did take to the forests and fight back. They fought in the same way and for the same purpose as hundreds of thousands of other Soviet citizens. They also suffered and survived in the same way. Jews, Russians and Communists were spoken of in the same breath by the German invaders. The general instruction was that they were to be shot on the spot.

Western Attitudes to Jewish Refugees

While Soviet Jewry was being slaughtered the Germans built six extermination centres in Poland to annihilate the rest of the European Jews. Almost 3 million Jews from most parts of European went to their death in those camps throughout 1942,

1943 and 1944. At first the perpetrators of extermination tried to keep their actions secret. They engaged in secret communications and used code words like *final solution* for systematic extermination and *special treatment* for gassing. Nonetheless the news percolated out to the West. News reports were published from July 1941, following the invasion of the Soviet Union, listing and describing massacres. *The New York Times* carried articles about them. The BBC broadcast news items referring to the numbers killed.[16] It was clear in the West by mid 1942 that the Germans were engaged in a mass extermination programme and that all European Jews were at risk. Two million Jews had already been killed. No other evidence should have been needed.

This situation presented a test both of the capacity of Britain and the USA for humanity and of the presence of anti-Semitism. It concerned human rights on a mammoth scale and should be indelibly printed on the memory of history. No nation who failed the test should have ever been able, without hypocrisy, to accuse another of anti-Semitism or of infringing human rights. It left scars on all the nations who could have helped, as well as on Germany the perpetrator.

It was a test because there were real opportunities to rescue European Jews. It was not until the end of 1941, just before the 'Final Solution' was agreed at the Wansee Conference, that the Jews were finally stopped from leaving Europe. By then almost a million Jewish lives had probably been lost. But there were at least 4½ million Jews alive then who subsequently died. Some of those millions might have lived.

The question then is, while the Soviet people in all the Republics west of the Urals were struggling for their lives and taking special precautions to evacuate Jews, what were the only two countries which were in a position to help them, namely Britain and the USA, doing? Both countries exercised strict immigration regulations under the influence of anti-Semitic establishment attitudes. Jews began to seek asylum away from Germany as soon as the Nazis came to power in 1933. The British Cabinet expressed its view then for it agreed to "try and secure for this country prominent Jews who were being expelled from Germany and who had achieved distinction whether in pure science, applied sciences, such as medicine or technical industry, music or art. This would not only obtain for this country the advantage of their knowledge and experience, but would create a very favourable impression in the world, particularly if our hospitality were offered with warmth."[17] This hypocritical approach to the vicissitudes of German Jews persisted until the war started. The official British attitude to Jewish immigrants in general was that Britain was a country of transit and not of settlement. Moreover, in so far as Britain accepted Jewish refugees, the government had extracted an understanding from Jewish organizations that the refugees would provide them with financial support so that they would not be a charge on the state.[18] In consequence, most Jewish immigrants came through individual and professional contacts. Then from 1939 German and Austrian Jews were treated as enemy aliens so that any admission to Britain had to be on a negotiated basis with the government.

The United States operated a rigidly restrictive immigration quota system which was underpinned by the fear created by the Great Depression that refugees would damage the job prospects of unemployed Americans and by widespread and intense anti-Semitic feelings. The quota system limited the number of immigrants from any particular country in any one year irrespective of circumstances. Germany had a fixed quota and that was that. The Jewish question had no bearing on it. The anti-immigration pressure groups, however, succeeded in keeping the actual numbers admitted to about only 10 per cent of the quota which could have been admitted.[19] The US immigration laws, more-over, imposed particular restrictions on Jewish refugees because they contained a prohibition on those 'likely to become a public charge'.[20] From October, 1934, the Nazi government allowed each emigrant to take out only about four dollars. Under Section 7(c) of the 1924 Immigration Act applicants for visas had to produce a police certificate of good character for the previous five years, a record of military service and other data, an almost impossible task for fleeing Jews. The immigration laws reflected public feelings. In 1938 just as the persecution of the Jews was intensified "four separate polls indicated that from 71 to 85 per cent of the American public opposed increasing the quotas to help refugees. And 67 per cent wanted refugees kept out altogether. In a survey taken in early 1939, 66 per cent even objected to a one-time exception to allow 10,000 refugee children to enter outside the quota limits"[21] Not surprisingly the USA admitted only slightly more refugees than Britain in the years leading to the war. Altogether between 1933 and 1939, about 370,000 Jews left the German Reich. Of these 57,000 went to the

USA and 50,000 to Britain. The remainder went mainly to Palestine, France, Belgium and Switzerland.

The news of the holocaust percolated into Britain and the United States slowly and in an abridged form, often in short articles on the inside pages of newspapers or, as in the case of the BBC on 2 June 1942 with the facts of extermination but without emphasizing that they were part of a programme. It aroused neither governments nor public to action. When, for instance, the Nazis offered to allow 2000 Jews to leave Luxembourg in 1940 the British government refused to admit them into the British Commonwealth: nor in 1942 would it allow 1000 Jewish children to enter Vichy France.[23] Britain, of course, controlled the admission of refugees to its then vast Empire and to Palestine. Yet it virtually sealed the refugee outlets from Europe and refused to admit Jews to those countries where it exercised power over entry. As one government official remarked, the British Empire had an absorption capacity of nil when it came to Jewish refugees.[24] The British policy on Palestine for the duration of the war was set by a 1939 White Paper which specified that Palestine was not to become a Jewish State, that the sale of land from Arabs to Jews was to be restricted and that even though "His Majesty's Government are conscious of the present unhappy plight of large numbers of Jews who seek a refuge from certain European countries',[25] a quota of 10,000 immigrants a year for the next five years was to be imposed, though "as a contribution towards the solution of the Jewish refugee problems, 25,000 refugees will be admitted as soon as the High Commissioner is satisfied that adequate provision for their maintenance is ensured . . ."[26] The constant flow of illegal immigrants into Palestine during the 1930s was intensified after the Nazis moved into Poland and the Soviet Union. This law-breaking activity offended the British official mind so that during the war the British authorities were pre-occupied with preventing the rescue of Jews. Coastal patrol vessels intercepted refugee ships approaching Palestine, diverted them, sent them back, even fired on them. The ships, packed with fleeing people under inhuman, insanitary conditions, were left without food and provisions, sometimes for months.[27] The British with a perverted sense of fairness, after putting the illegal immigrants in internment camps, subtracted their number from the official quotas.

Both Britain and the USA refused to bomb Auschwitz as a means of stopping the extermination process there.[28] Auschwitz operated as a killing centre for 32 months. The average rate of killings for the whole period was about 4,100 per day. About half of those were Jews while the majority of the remainder were Soviet prisoners of war. When the proposals to bomb it were made the camp was operating at its maximum which could have been as high as 6000 killings each day.

The American record on refugees was no better than that of the British. The British public showed more understanding of the Jewish tragedy towards the end of the war than did its government for in the USA the public remained implacably opposed to allowing Jewish refugees into their country. After the appalling facts of genocide were known, 78 per cent of a sample asked whether "it would be a good idea or a bad idea to let more immigrants come into this country after the war" thought it was a bad idea. And at the end of 1945, with news of millions of displaced persons in Europe, only 5 per cent in the poll thought the USA should admit more immigrants than before the war.[29] Government practice was consistent with public opinion. It is best described by David S Wyman in his detailed study of the American responses to the holocaust. He concluded that:

> "1. The American State Department and the British Foreign Office had no intention of rescuing large numbers of European Jews. On the contrary, they continually feared that Germany or other Axis nations might release tens of thousands of Jews into Allied hands. Any such exodus would have placed intense pressure on Britain to open Palestine and on the United States to take in more Jewish refugees, a situation the two great powers did not want to face. Consequently, their policies aimed at obstructing rescue possibilities and dampening public pressures for government action.
> 2. Authenticated information that the Nazis were systematically exterminating European Jewry was made public in the United States in November 1942. President Roosevelt did nothing about the mass murder for fourteen months, then moved only because he was confronted with political pressures he could not avoid and because his administration stood on the brink of a nasty scandal over its rescue policies.
> 3. The War Refugee Board, which the President then established to save Jews and other victims of the Nazis,

received little power, almost no co-operation from Roosevelt or his administration, and grossly inadequate government funding. (Contributions from Jewish organizations, which were necessarily limited, covered 90 per cent of the WRB's costs). Through dedicated work by a relatively small number of people, the WRB managed to help save approximately 200,000 Jews and at least 20,000 non-Jews.

4. Because of State department administrative policies, only 21,000 refugees were allowed to enter the United States during the three and one half years the nation was at war with Germany. That amounted to 10 per cent of the number who could have been legally admitted under the immigration quotas during that period.

5. Strong popular pressure for action would have brought a much fuller government commitment to rescue and would have produced it sooner. Several factors hampered the growth of public pressure. Among them were anti-Semitism and anti-immigration attitudes, both widespread in American society in that era and both entrenched in Congress; the mass media's failure to publicize Holocaust news, even though the wire services and other news sources made most of the information available to them; the near silence of the Christian churches and almost all of their leadership; the indifference of most of the nation's political and intellectual leaders; and the President's failure to speak out on the issue.[30]

There was no mention in the West during the almost indescribably harrowing years for European Jews from 1933 until 1945 of the hallowed right to emigrate. There was much sanctimonious rhetoric about human rights but no action. One statistic encapsulates the sense of the period: *for the whole year* of 1944, 5,606 refugees, mostly Jews, were allowed into the United States.[31] This was less than the *daily* rate of killing at one killing centre, Auschwitz, in the same year. When the whole macabre picture of mass extermination had been unfolded, eight days after the end of the war with Germany, Mr Herbert Morrison, the Labour leader who was the British wartime Home Secretary, made his views about Jewish refugees known to the Cabinet:

"as regards such persons [refugees] in the United Kingdom he was clear that we ought to act on the assumption that those who had come here had done so temporarily, and that they should eventually go back whence they came. It was often said that the Jewish refugees in this country were terrified of returning to Germany. We should not be influenced by this attitude. It was possible that post-war Germany would abandon anti-Semitism altogether. If the Jews were allowed to remain here they might be an explosive element in the country, especially if the economic situation deteriorated."[32]

The question of resettling refugees, many of whom were Jews, after the war continued to be a sensitive human rights issue but it ceased to be focussed only on Britain and the USA. Jews were able to travel to a multiplicity of countries. The creation of Israel as an independent Jewish state in 1948 provided displaced Jews with a homeland. From 1948 until the Yom Kippur War in 1973 it was the rise of Israel in a hostile Arab environment which dominated the attention of the West towards Jews. Israel, based primarily on American capital, became a Middle-East outpost for US imperialism and, therefore, a strategic participant in the Cold War. It became the sensitizer for anti-Semitism and played its part by focussing on the treatment of Soviet Jewry. In doing so, Israel provided the West with a powerful ideological weapon in its campaign of anti-Sovietism. Its litmus test was simple: opposition to Zionism in general and Israel in particular constituted anti-Semitism. The Soviet Union, as Sidney and Beatrice Webb learned, was highly critical of Zionism in the inter-war years. Yet ironically, it was support from the Soviet Union, against ambivalence by the USA, which ensured the *de jure* creation of Israel in 1948. The Soviet view was put succinctly by Mr Andrei Gromyko, then the Soviet Deputy Minister of Foreign Affairs, in a speech before the General Assembly of the United Nations on 14 May 1947. He said: "The aspirations of a considerable part of the Jewish people are linked with the problems of Palestine . . . During the last World War indescribable pain and suffering were experienced by the Jews . . . This fact . . . explains the Jews' aspirations to extablish their own State. It would be unjust to ignore or to deny the right of the Jewish people to realize this aspiration."[33] The USSR was amongst the first countries to give

Israel diplomatic recognition. This initial enthusiasm became a casualty of Israel's commitment to the USA during the Cold War. It was reported in *Colliers*, a widely circulated American magazine, in October 1951, that Israel had agreed to act as a bombing base for the USA in the event of a nuclear war with the USSR.[34] The Soviet leader, Mr Nikita Khrushchev, stated the Soviet attitude in May 1957 when he said: "Our position towards Israel is determined by the Cold War, and we hope that this is a passing phenomenon."[35] The Soviet Union supported the Arab states in their successive wars against Israel and has backed the Palestinian Arabs in their struggle for independence. After the 1967 Six Day War in which Israel was victorious, the Soviet Union broke off diplomatic relations with Israel and they have not yet been restored.

The Process of Assimilation

Israel's role in the Cold War, combined with a vision of Zionism as an international capitalist conspiracy, created a paranoia in the leadership of the Soviet Communist Party after 1948 about the intentions of some leading Soviet Jewish intellectuals. There was no real evidence that the Jewish intellectuals were disloyal but from 1948 until after Stalin's death in 1953 there was no tolerance for those whose loyalty appeared to be to Zionism rather than the Soviet Union. In 1948 the entire system of Yiddish language teaching was suppressed. Twenty-five Soviet Jewish leaders, many of them Communists, were arrested, tried and executed. For five or more years Jewish intellectuals were intimidated. There was a frame-up of Jewish doctors in which they were accused of planning to use medical means to kill off Soviet leaders. About 430 members of the Jewish intelligentsia were sent to concentration camps where many of them died. This blot on the record of Soviet ethnic relations has left stains which are difficult to erase. Yiddish language teaching has been resumed and Yiddish publications are appearing again. But affirmative action cannot eradicate fear quickly or easily.

Although many Soviet Jews were undoubtedly affected by the purge of their intellectual elite the vast majority of Jews were not materially threatened. Those, ranging from L M Kaganovich, a Bolshevik since 1911, Politburo member since 1930 and the wartime head of the Soviet railways, to Jewish generals, managers, scientists, doctors, teachers and workers in collective farms and state farms as well as mines and factories, lived as before and continued the process of occupational development which had been interrupted by the war. Soviet society at large had not been afflicted by anti-Semitism. There had been no measures to discredit Jewishness. Yiddish continued to be spoken in Jewish homes though a declining proportion described it as their native language. In 1959 this proportion was 21.5 whereas in 1979 it had fallen to 14.24. In 1926 it had been 72.6. This recent decline was partly the result of the emigration of Yiddish speaking Jews in the 1970s and partly because of an increasing tendency of Soviet Jews, like those in all other countries, to speak the language of the country to which they belonged.

The population of Soviet Jews declined from 2.3 million in 1959 to 1.8 million in 1979, representing only 0.7 per cent of the total population. This decline resulted mainly from a low fertility rate among Jewish women, a high percentage of mixed marriages, the children of whom were not registered as Jews, and emigration.[36] Almost 74 per cent of Soviet Jewry is now concentrated in the Russian and Ukranian Republics but, as the following table shows, in no Republic do Jews constitute more than 2.03 per cent of its total population. The vast majority are second generation urban dwellers; indeed in the 1970 census only 2.1 per cent were classified as rural. 26 per cent lived in Moscow, Leningrad and Kiev. The rest were scattered in relatively small cities.

Soviet Jewry is not a homogeneous group. It consists of different types and degrees of Jewishness. The main distinction is between the 'heartland' and the 'periphery'. About three-quarters of Soviet Jewry live in the 'heartland' which comprises these areas which have been part of the Soviet Union for two generations. These people have experienced the greatest degree of assimilation in Soviet society. They tend not to be religious. They generally live where there are no centres of Jewish social or religious activity. They are highly educated. Many of them belong to mixed families. These factors have been both a consequence and a cause of assimiliation. They have reinforced the assimilia-tion process. It "is generally agreed", Zaslavsky and Brym commented, "that degree of Jewish identity varies inversely with level of education and rate of out-marriage, and proportionately with use of Jewish language".[39]

The periphery consists largely of the Baltic Republics which have had only a post-Second World War experience of belonging to the Soviet Union and where, in consequence, the assimiliation

TABLE I

THE DISTRIBUTION OF JEWS IN THE USSR ACCORDING TO THE 1979 CENSUS[37]

REPUBLIC	NUMBER OF (000's)	% OF TOTAL POPULATION	% OF SOVIET JEWS	% URBAN IN[38] 1970
RSFSR	701	0.51	38.7	97.4
Ukraine	634	1.27	35.0	98.3
Byelorussia	135	1.41	7.5	98.3
Uzbekistan	100	0.65	5.5	97.0
Moldavia	80	2.03	4.4	97.8
Georgia	28	0.56	1.6	98.3
Azerbaidzhan	35	0.58	1.9	98.8
Latvia	28	1.11	1.6	99.1
Lithuania	15	0.44	0.8	99.1
Tadzhikistan	15	0.40	0.8	98.7
Estonia	5	0.34	0.3	97.7
Kazakhstan				95.3
Kirkiziya				95.6
Turkmenia				98.5
Armenia	35	0.15	1.93	97.1
TOTAL	1,881	0.69	100.00	97.9

process has been relatively brief, anti-Semitic forces have not been entirely eradicated and Jewish traditions have tended to survive. The periphery also includes Georgia, Uzbekistan, Azerbaidzhan and the mountain regions of the Caucasus. There, many Jews are non-Ashkenazi Jews whose origins lie in Persia rather than Germany and for whom religion is still a vital component of their lives. They are Messianic and regard the creation of Israel as the ultimate Jewish objective. They live in small, traditionally based communities where their activities have changed little since the Revolution. For these reasons the non-Ashkenazi Jews have possessed the highest level of Jewishness amongst all Soviet Jews. But they were a minority, numbering only between 50,000 and 60,000 during the post-war years till 1970.

The socio-economic position of Jews was transformed after the revolution "from a destitute community engaged in occupations with no future into an exceedingly highly educated group placed well up in the Soviet system of social stratification . . . In less than two generations the majority had undergone a series of metamorphoses from peddler to physician, shop-keeper to research scientist, artisan to engineer . . ."[40] A critical commentator added that "A remarkably upward social mobility, based on the acquisition of higher education, transformed the Soviet Jews in just two generations. Instead of being a community dislocated by war and concentrated mainly in the starving market towns of the former Pale of Settlement, as they were in the first years of the advent of Soviet rule, they are now a cultural, technical and scientific elite . . . This is a success story which rivals, and perhaps overshadows the economic and social achievements of North American Jewry . . ."[41] A similar point was made by Zaslavsky and Brym when they stated that "it is an entirely open question whether the Jews' rate of upward mobility in the USA – 'the land of golden opportunities' – has been at all higher".[42]

The evidence of the prominence of Soviet Jewry in Soviet intellectual life is compelling. Jews are by far the most highly educated ethnic group. The number with a university education is four times the national average. Their position in graduate education is even more pronounced. In 1973 there were more Jewish doctors of science in absolute terms than from any other ethnic group except the Russians. For example, although there were 41 million Ukrainians, the Jews, with a population of just over 2 million, had twice as many doctors of science. In 1973, Jews represented 0.9 per cent of the total Soviet population but 1.9 per cent of all university students, 6.1 per cent of scientific workers, 8.8 per cent of all scientists and 14.0 per cent of all doctors of science.[43] This disparity was greater in the main urban centres. In Moscow, for instance, where Jews were 3 per cent of the population in 1970 they comprised 13.6 per cent of all scientists and 17.4 per cent of doctors of science, the equivalent in Britain of university professorships. In that same year the number of people from the top six different ethnic groups who had completed higher education, for every 10,000 persons over the age of 10 years were as follows:[44] Jewish, 239; Georgian, 155; Armenian, 76; Estonian, 66; Russian, 60; Ukrainian, 58.

This picture was part of a changing process in which educational opportunitites were being equalized by affirmative state action. Jews were early beneficiaries of affirmative action and, as a result, developed both the expectation that their children should reach at least equivalent educational standards and the environmental facilities to make that possible. If there had been no contemporary administrative intervention in regulating access to higher education then Jews as an ethnic group would have become an established educational elite at the expense of other ethnic groups whose cultural and environmental characteristics had disadvantaged them. The consequence for Jews is that they constitute a declining proportion of the Soviet student body. In 1960 they made up 3.2 per cent of the student body but only 2.3 per cent in 1970. This decline has continued.[45] They were 15.5 per cent of all scientific workers in 1950 but only 6.9 per cent in 1970. The declining Jewish involvement in higher education is in part the negative side of afffirmative action favouring other ethnic groups. They are not alone, however. The number of Estonian graduates fell by 20 per cent between 1970 and 1973 while the number of Armenian and Georgian graduates fell by 10 per cent. There are other factors. Official Soviet policy is to preserve a certain proportion of available university places for the children of workers and peasants. In the Law Faculty of Moscow University, for example, such people are given 20 per cent of first year places. The children of the intelligentsia could easily fill all the places. Because Jews figure prominantly in the intelligentsia some Jewish applicants are bound to be unsuccessful. Within the Republics university selection procedures favour local ethnic majorities and this operates against Russians, Ukrainians and others as well as Jews who may be local minorities in all Republics. Irrespective of all other factors which influence the entrance of ethnic groups to higher education, there was a rapid and tremendous expansion in higher education in general and scientific training in particular from the 1950s which was bound to upset the ethnic balance at the time by creating its own influences. From the early 1970s Jewish emigration raised the age structure of Soviet Jewry. Between 1971 and 1976 it is estimated that about half of the emigrants were under the age of thirty thus diminishing the volume of Jewish applicants to universities for a number of years.[46]

Given the number and variety of pressures shaping the ethnic character of higher education in the Soviet Union since the end of the Second World War it is virtually impossible to identify 'official anti-Semitism' as a dominant influence. Even where discrimination against Jews can be identified this is more likely to be part of the equalizing process than a racist act. Jews, very much like other ethnic groups, have to compete in the increasingly intense competition for university places; they may have to search for places amongst the non-prestigious institutions in outlying Republics where the minority quotas have not been filled; they may be compelled to enrol as factory or agricultural workers either permanently or until they can gain access to higher education. In each of these situations the sensation of exclusion may feel like discrimination but it is a widely-shared experience without any racial basis.

One other factor relating to the assimilation of Jews into Soviet society is their membership of the Communist Party. Jews have figured prominently as communists. Zinoviev, Kamenev, Radek, Trotsky and Sverdlov were Bolshevik leaders during the Revolution. Jacob Sverdlov was President of Bolshevik Russia during Lenin's time. Since then Jews have played a prominent though changing role in the Communist Party. A quarter of the membership of the Central Committee was Jewish in the 1920s while they comprised almost 5 per cent of the total Party membership. Their involvement in the leadership declined from the 1930s. L M Kaganovitch in Stalin's administration was the last Jewish member of the Politburo. It was to be expected, that as the Communist Party grew and a large non-Jewish urban intelligentsia emerged, the Jewish involvement in it would diminish. It did so but not in proportion to its position in the total population. In 1976, 294,774 out of the 16 million Party members were Jews, representing 1.9 per cent. This meant that one out of every six or seven Jews eligible to join the Party had applied and been accepted into it. The actual rate of application was most probably higher because most Jewish applicants would have been intellectuals who had a restricted access to the Party compared with workers. Nonetheless Jews had the highest rate of Party affiliation of any ethnic group at 137 per thousand compared with the next highest, the Georgians, with 80 per thousand. Put differently, at least 13.7 per cent of the total Jewish population from 1970 were members of the Communist Party. They were the most "Party-saturated" Soviet nationality,[47] despite intensified anti-Sovietism by Jewish groups in the West.

The generalized picture of Soviet Jewry then is that it is highly urbanized with at least 80 per cent living in cities, mostly without Jewish communities or access to Jewish religious or cultural activities. It is highly educated and forms a significant segment of Soviet scientific and technological intelligentsia. Many Jews occupy leading positions in Soviet institutions. They have a social status which is commensurate with their educational attainments. Their material well-being is high by Soviet standards partly because of their occupations, partly because they have small families and partly because they are urbanized. Their commitment to the communist system is expressed through their disproportionate presence in the Communist Party. In the main, the relative position of the Jews is deteriorating but this is largely because previously disadvantaged ethnic and occupational groups are encroaching on them.

Igor Birman, an economist who emigrated from the USSR in 1974 assessed the position of Soviet Jews as follows: "Zionist-oriented Jews . . . are a distinct minority. The great mass of Soviet Jewry has been thoroughly assimilated. Few know Yiddish and almost no one knows Hebrew . . . Even the most casual observer must admit that the number of believing and practising Jews is extremely small . . . Thorough assimilation and anti-religious feeling are in large measure . . . a result of education. From this also springs a lively interest in cultural values, and the over-whelming majority of Soviet Jews have become people of Russian culture in the broadest sense of the word, not solely in terms of language. For all practical purposes little remains in the country of the Jewish cultural tradition; thus, the majority of Jews have embraced Russian culture, literature and even history as their own."[48] The exceptions to this picture were mainly to be found amongst the half a million Ashkenazi Jews in the regions of the 'periphery' and the non-Ashkenazi Jews who resided mainly in Georgia. The social position of many of those Jews was similiar to that of Jews in the 'heartland' but there were factors in their environment which obstructed assimilation. This, then, was the situation when large-scale Jewish emigration from the Soviet Union began in 1971.

The Soviet Attitude to Jewish Emigration

The general description of Soviet Jewry, then, is of a relatively privileged minority which is distinguishable from the rest of Soviet intelligentsia only by the nationality entries in their internal passports. They generally live dispersed with other Soviet citizens in urban communities, revealing their Jewishness either in their inner family relationships or even, perhaps, concealing it in their own minds. In all objective respects most of

158

them are as other Soviet citizens except that they derive more social benefits from Soviet society than the rest.

Why then is there such an outcry in the West about the condition of Soviet Jewry? Why is the Soviet Union abused as an oppressive society for its attitude to Jews and described as anti-Semitic? And why, more particularly, should about 256,450 Jews have emigrated to Israel and the USA in the decade following 1971? What contradictions in their lives caused so many to leave Soviet society?

Many people have offered answers. Peter Ustinov, for instance, wrote: "If today there are demonstrations in the United States and elsewhere in support of Soviet Jewry, it is largely because of the creation of the State of Israel, and the reluctance of the Soviet Government to allow an exodus in the direction of a National Home to the creation of which it was amongst the first to subscribe."[49] A different perspective was expressed by William Mandel who wrote that "The interest in Soviet Jews in the United States and Canada is a consequence of their numbers, not in the USSR, but here in the United States. Of all the Americans with roots in what is now Soviet territory, Jews are the most numerous, actually outnumbering the Ukrainians, Lithuanians, Armenians and all the others combined."[50] Most explanations, however, published in the popular press and those learned journals which have arisen to analyze Soviet Jewry point the finger at the Soviet Union and accuse it of totalitarianism because it refuses to grant the primary and elementary freedom to emigrate. They state that anti-Semitism is the cause of the exodus.

The Soviet Union has an attitude to emigration which is contrary to that currently prevalent in the West. There are two aspects to it. One concerns the rational use of resources while the other stems from socialist morality. The Soviet Union has experienced full employment since the beginning of the Second Five Year Plan in 1934. In effect it has been short of labour, a situation seriously worsened by the casualties of the Second World War. Thus the labour situation imposed on the Soviet Government a dire need to conserve labour power by preventing wastages to other countries as well as by controlling its domestic utilization. Both types of measures would, in any event, have resulted from the government's use of centralized planning measures. It would have been illogical and self-defeating to plan the use of all resources except labour power. The planned use of

159

labour, however, involved restricting the right of individuals to take their skills to another country.

There is a moral argument against free emigration. If, for instance, the emigration of a physician prevents a community from having adequate health care whose right should be given priority? Should the doctor's right to leave the society be protected or should the community's right to health care be upheld? The issue has been crudely expressed through the experience of India where the unrestricted emigration of skilled medical practitioners to Western countries has been allowed while in India itself there have been less than 3 doctors for every 10,000 population compared with more than 15 doctors in Britain and more than 20 doctors in the USA for every 10,000 population. The problem is resolved in a socialist society through the predominance of collectivist values over individualistic ones so that the interests of individuals are not allowed to have priority over those of a community. There is, therefore, no moral dilemma for the Soviet Union when presented with requests from skilled personnel to emigrate. It simply asks whose interests would be affected and in what ways and then takes the side of the community.

There are then strong material reasons to account for the Soviet Union's reluctance to agree to emigration. But it has in no sense been a closed society. It has received people, mainly political refugees who would have been unwelcome in the West or who were actually fleeing from the West. And it has permitted controlled emigration in order to repatriate people to their homelands and to re-unify families which were broken up by the Second World War.

Groups of Koreans moved into Siberia after 1917 in order to escape Japanese oppression. They have maintained their language and culture though they are now permanent residents in the Soviet Union. One such group formed the "Politotdel" collective farm in 1925, 15 kilometres from Tashkent in Uzbekistan and they still it as one of the most successful farm units in the Soviet Union. Spaniards fled to the Soviet Union during the Civil War as did many Greeks after their Civil War in 1949. A large number of Poles fled to the Soviet Union to escape from the invading German army in 1939. Repatriation agreements were concluded between the Soviet government and the governments of Spain, Greece and Poland. The Spanish agreement was concluded after 1977 because between 1939 and 1977 there were no diplomatic ties between Spain and the Soviet Union. The Greek repatriation began in 1965 and within about 2 years between 4,000 and 6,000 Greeks returned to their homeland. The first agreement covering Poles in the Soviet Union was concluded in September 1944. This gave individuals of Polish and Jewish nationality who were Polish citizens on 17 September 1939, the day the Soviet armies occupied Eastern Poland, the right to evacuate to Poland. This agreement was implemented during the first year after the war. A second agreement was signed in March 1957 to assist the voluntary repatriation of those Poles who had not been able to take advantage of the earlier agreement because of circumstances beyond their control. A special clause enabled Jews who had been Polish citizens to return to Poland with their families and it has been estimated that 25,000 actually left the USSR for Poland at the time. Altogether about 1½ million Poles, including about 175,000 Jews, were repatriated in this way.[51]

About 14,000 Armenians who had moved to the Soviet Republic of Armenia in the years following the Second World War from the middle East, including Palestine, were allowed to emigrate to the USA between 1976 and 1980. In most cases this emigration was to re-unify families. This principle, plus the right to return to the homeland were at the basis of an agreement between the governments of the Soviet Union and the Federal Republic of Germany in 1958 to repatriate the million or so Germans who for one reason or another resided in the Soviet Union.

All of this emigration was voluntary but none of it was individual. No person had the right to emigrate outside the terms of the agreements or without the permission of the Soviet government which regulated entry into and exit from the Soviet Union with Statutes passed by the USSR Council of Ministers. These Statutes made no mention of any nationalities. They were loosely worded and allowed some scope for administrative discretion in their application. Those Jews who were not covered by bilateral agreements had to seek exist visas through the normal, difficult channels. There was no agreement with Israel.

The Impact of Aggressive Zionism

Israel created a special situation for Jews who wished to emigrate for it granted them automatic immigration rights. It had no immigration quotas, no visa formalities for them. Indeed the state was based on the right of every Jew to emigrate to it. When the first statute on immigration, the Law of Return, was being introduced into the Israeli Parliament in 1950 by the Prime Minister, David Ben Gurion, he said:

> "This law does not provide for the State to bestow the right to settle in Israel upon the Jew living abroad; it affirms that this right is inherent in him, from the very fact of his being a Jew. The State does not grant the right of return to the Jews of the diaspora. This right preceded the State; this right built the State; its source is to be found in the historic and never broken connection between the Jewish people and the homeland."[52]

The first legislative act of the Israeli Provisional Council of State abolished the mandatory restrictions on Jewish immigration which the British had imposed. The second was the Law of Return which spelled out the details behind Ben Gurion's statement. This asserted the right of every Jew to immigrate and declared that every Jew who expressed the desire to settle in Israel should receive an immigrant's visa. In practice this meant that Jews could become Israeli citizens simply by landing in Israel. The Nationality Amendment Law of 1971 extended this right to Jews who merely expressed a desire to emigrate to Israel but were unable to leave their existing countries. It was expressly intended for Soviet Jews who were being refused permission to emigrate to Israel. Thus the Ministry of the Interior in Israel could grant a Jew Israeli nationality before immigrating. The law created dual nationality by unilateral action and in the face of Soviet opposition.

With the creation of Israel, Jewish nationalism turned on all forces which hampered its growth, in particular those countries which refused to give Jews the freedom to emigrate as they wished. It turned, therefore, on the Soviet Union. During Stalin's time there was no officially endorsed Jewish emigration. Some Jews left the Soviet Union in the chaos of the post-Second World War. Indeed one of the charges against Jewish intellectuals in 1952 was they had aided and abetted the smuggling of Jews to Palestine. After 1953 there was a trickle of emigrants wholly for family re-unification purposes and largely comprising old people. The rate was about 18 per month from 1955 to 1964. It rose to a monthly average of 150 in the 2½ years prior to the Six Day War in 1967. Jewish emigration was stopped entirely at the end of the

162

Six Day War and did not really start again until 1971.

The Six Day War in 1967, in which Israel defeated the Egyptians and the Syrians, was a catalyst for Jewish emigration. It had two main consequences. The Soviet Union had supported the Arab states. Israel, through its victory, was seen more clearly than hitherto as an instrument of American capitalism, as America's armed camp in the Middle East. The Soviet Union saw Zionism as an instrument of the Cold War, a 'fifth column' operating within its own frontiers, undermining communism. It turned, in consequence, against any manifestation of Zionism, no matter how innocent it might have been. Since the brief, transient endorsement of a Jewish state in 1947, the Soviet Union had become increasingly aware of Israel's role in international capitalism. 1967, therefore, was not qualitatively different. It simply produced a clearer picture.

The second consequence was more dramatic for it was the resurgence of a confident aggressive Zionism which regarded the Soviet Union as its main target. There was a revival of Zionist sentiment among Soviet Jews. There was a more pronounced expression of what was described as the "infrastructure of Jewish unofficial spiritual life in the USSR". Study circles for learning Hebrew, Jewish literature, music and history, were formed.[53] In some areas of the Soviet Union the process of Jewish assimilation into Soviet life was halted and put in reverse. There were undoubtedly contradictions in the lives of Soviet Jews which were sensitive to external pressures. The victory in the Six Day War touched chords which some Soviet Jews did not know existed. The Zionist campaign throughout the Western world about the treatment of Soviet Jewry ensured that they would not be allowed to forget they were there.

Organizing Emigration

The basic work of providing the media with its copy about Soviet Jewry was done by Western Jewish intellectuals who analyzed and re-analyzed every facet of the emigration process, starting invariably from the assumption that Soviet Jews were persecuted and, in spite of the evidence, concluding by confirming the assumption. In the Jewish euphoria following the Six Day War the Institute of Jewish Affairs in London, in association with the World Jewish Congress, published the *Bulletin on Soviet and East European Jewish Affairs*. This was replaced by *Soviet Jewish*

Affairs in June 1971 to cover "the entire range of knowledge directly or indirectly relevant to an understanding of the position and prospect of Jews in the USSR and the Communist-governed countries of Eastern Europe including historical and contextual aspects." This Journal, published twice yearly, has dealt with "the Jewish question" ever since. Its first article was "The 'Right to Leave'"; later ones were "Soviet Jews and Israeli Citizenship", "New Soviet Laws on Emigration"; "Emigration from the USSR"; "Freedom of Emigration of Soviet Jewry". The theme of each issue has remained the same through to 1987. The February 1985 issue was devoted to the proceedings of the "Experts' Conference on Soviet Jewry" which dealt with "The Jewish Question in the USSR", "The Emigration of Soviet Jews" and "Anti-Jewish Discrimination in Education and Employment". In September, 1986, a new Journal appeared in Britain called the *Journal of the Academic Proceedings of Soviet Jewry* with an academically impressive editorial board. Its pre-publication publicity stated that its authors should be "Jews resident within the Soviet Union; or authors of works presented to such persons; or Jews who, while no longer resident, have undertaken the work, which is the subject of the contribution, while resident in the Soviet Union." Its purpose is self-evident. It stated that it would "chart the circumstances of a highly developed population, many of whom are constrained against their will . . ." All in all no facets of the lives of Soviet Jewry are nowadays left unexplored.

Propaganda was intense and highly effective. Small sounds left the Soviet Union and returned as resonant echoes.[54] Soviet Jewish protagonists of emigration became household names in the West as Western governments took up their cases with the Soviet government. They made the relaxation of restrictions on Jewish emigration a condition for progress in negotiations over trade and over arms reduction. The most publicized of the Jewish emigrants were courted by the President of the USA and the Prime Minister of Britain. The question of Jewish emigration from the Soviet Union was converted into a major human rights issue.

The campaign was not simply to convince the world that Soviet Jews suffered from discrimination but to persuade Soviet Jews to emigrate and for this reason it was taken into the Soviet Union. Western radio stations, for example the BBC and the Voice of America, conveyed Western perceptions about Israeli and Soviet affairs to Soviet listeners. Radio Liberty in West Germany specialized in broadcasting material critical of the Soviet Union. The most important part, however, was played by the Voice of Israel whose contribution was described as follows:

> "While the Israelis were absent from the Soviet Union after 1967, the Voice of Israel was instrumental in helping Soviet Jews affirm their positive identification with Israel. The impact of the Voice of Israel . . . was certainly important . . . It was perhaps the only radio station outside the USSR that contributed to an important socio-political movement within the Soviet Union. The Voice of Israel was widely heard by diverse groups of Soviet Jews."[55]

Zionist dissident groups were formed both to communicate with the West and to translate its propaganda into internal political action. They linked with other dissident groups and used similar methods to publicize their case, such as letters of protest to leading members of the government and the Communist Party and for publication in the West. In the autumn of 1969 when the Israeli government began its widely publicized campaign for the free emigration of Soviet Jews to Israel, Mrs Golda Meir, the Prime Minister of Israel, publicized one such letter signed by 18 Jews in Georgia while Israel's Permanent Representative at the United Nations presented it to a press conference in New York. The Zionist groups organized the transition from individual to collective protest. They distributed clandestinely produced political journals which Russian, Lithuanian and Ukrainian emigré publishing houses, daily newspapers, literary and political journals then published in the West. The US government financed Radio Liberty in Munich employed a research staff to collect every scrap of this "Samizdat" or self-published material and collate it in a "Samizdat Archive". Since 1972 the processed contents of the Archive have been available in four American and four European Libraries, including the Library of Congress in Washington and the British Museum in London. Radio Liberty has published its own research papers and has become a major source of critical data. Thus, whatever the motives of the writers of the "Samizdat" material, it has been used in the West for anti-Soviet purposes.

Propaganda was one arm of the Zionist campaign. The other was a network of institutional support for the actual emigration of Soviet Jews. A number of Western Jewish organizations such as the American Jewish Committee, the American Jewish Congress, the World Jewish Congress and the National Council for Soviet Jewry, provided material assistance. In Israel, the Ministry of Immigrant Absorption and the Jewish Agency, with its own network of international representatives, performed major co-ordinating functions. The main link between the source of immigrants and Israel has been provided by the Hebrew Immigrant Aid Society (HIAS). This body has dealt only with those who were registered as Jews in their internal passports. Other Jews and non-Jews who wished to emigrate with Israeli visas have been assisted by the International Rescue Committee and the Tolstoy Foundation. At the diplomatic level in Moscow the question of Jewish exit visas has been handled since 1967 by the Dutch Embassy which represents Israeli interests in the Soviet Union in the absence of normal diplomatic relations. The final say was had by the Department for Visas and Registrations of the Ministry of Interior of the USSR (OVIR), which distributes emigration visas.

The Soviet Union has remained consistent in its approach to emigration by being opposed to emigration as such but in favour of repatriation to a homeland and the re-unification of families. As Israel was not recognized as a homeland for Soviet citizens the only recourse Soviet Jews had was to seek re-unification with families in Israel. For this purpose, they were required to supply an affidavit, received by post from a relative in Israel, which was an invitation confirming the family ralationship. This *vyzov* was supplied by the Jewish Agency on request. Many Jewish families had been scattered by the war and Nazi occupation and some, in its aftermath, were distributed between the USSR and Eastern Europe on the one hand and Israel and the USA on the other. There were genuine reasons for re-unification.

Family re-unification was not a clear-cut issue for most of those who wished to emigrate to join families were leaving families behind. The Soviet authorities, conscious of the situation, stated their attitude as follows:

> "We are in favour of families being re-united, but not infrequently we are faced with a situation in which the wish of some persons to leave the country in order to be "re-united with relatives" actually leads to the disintegra-tion of existing families and relations between relatives: children leave parents, parents leave children, husbands

divorce wives and vice-versa. How should we act in such cases? Naturally, we protect in the first place, the interests of Soviet citizens who are remaining in the country. It is not easy to find the right criterion of objectivity and justice in settling such complicated and delicated questions . . ."[56]

In an attempt to ensure family unity, applicants for emigration visas were compelled, wherever possible, to get parental permission. But matters did not always work out to everyone's benefit. In the early rush for visas after 1969 OVIR officials bent the rules and showed the recipients of *vyzovs* how to explain the relationship between themselves and the Israeli names on their invitations.[57] Until 1978 the closeness of the kinship relationship was not important. Then OVIR officials were instructed to insist that the relationship should be close. Yet despite the various precautions husbands left wives and children, wives left husbands and parents and went with children alone. Many thousands of families were divided.

The Soviet Union responded to the Western pressures for the emigration of Soviet Jews in two ways. It counter-attacked with extensive and detailed criticisms of Zionism in the Soviet media and it permitted an increasing number of Soviet Jews to emigrate with Israeli visas. Anti-Zionist comments in the Soviet Union were, of course, not new but from 1970 they increased in intensity and quality. Many Soviet Jews criticized Zionism in such newspapers as *Pravda, Izvestia, Trud* and Republic papers such as *Pravda Ukraine, Sovetskaya Moldavia* and the *Zarya Vostaka* from Georgia. There was no uniformity in the reactions of either newspapers or writers. Some condemned Zionism and compared it with Nazism while others simply pointed out the benefits of living under socialism. Typical of the latter was the statement by an economist, Grigoriy Dzeventsky, on Tashkent television in March 1971. He said: "I am a Candidate of Economic Sciences; my sister is an engineer, a leading expert in one of the larger Moscow planning projects; her husband is a lieutenant colonel; my brother is an engineer and has an advanced degree in the technological sciences; his wife is a chemist; another brother is an electrician; his wife is an agronomist. My wife is a jurist. One cannot help asking what kind of defence our family is in need of?[58]

Anti-Semitism is a crime in the Soviet Union so there were no public anti-Semitic responses. The official reaction, as expressed in leading articles and editorials, was based in part on the contributions Jews had made to the development and defence of the Soviet Union and in part on a class analysis of Zionism as a form of nationalism which was no different from other nationalisms, including national socialism, in its performance as a doctrine of the bourgeoisie. A catalogue of Israeli acts from the Suez crisis in 1956 onwards showed it to practise militaristic imperialism, creating colonies out of Arab lands and carrying out racist policies with regards to Arabs. Israel was equated with South Africa.

The number of Jewish emigrants increased dramatically during the 1970s. From 1968 till 1982, 648,072 invitations to re-unite with families in Israel were received by Soviet Jews. Thus almost one-third of the total Jewish population received vyzovs and could, therefore, apply for exit visas. 381,700 of these, representing 58.9 per cent, did not use them for one reason or another. Altogether, 262,377 Jews left with visas for Israel in that period. At the beginning the movement was slow to take off even though the Jewish Agency sent out 27,301 vyzovs in 1969. It was not until 1971 when the full effects of the Zionist campaign within the Soviet Union were felt that emigration rose significantly. It remained at a high level until 1979 after which it tailed off to below the 1969 level. The signs were that the Zionist campaign had largely exhausted itself by the end of the decade. The following table shows the annual rate of emigration.

The Pattern of Emigration

The extent and pattern of Soviet Jewish emigration in the 1970s raised many questions, some of them contradictory. Why, in the first instance would so many Jews want to leave the Soviet Union? Why, on the other hand, did many Jews refuse to apply for visas after having received family invitations to go to Israel? Why were there changes in all of the indices in 1974, in particular in the refusal to settle in Israel. All of the people enumerated in the above table left the Soviet Union for Vienna with Israeli visas. Yet after 1974 the majority of them became what the Israelis called "drop-outs"; that is they changed their minds about their ultimate destination when they arrived at the Vienna reception centre. Why should Israel which started the agitation over Soviet Jewry become so unpopular with them? Each of these

TABLE II

JEWISH EMIGRATION FROM THE USSR 1968-1984[59]

YEAR	NO. OF EMIGRANTS	% WHO REFUSED TO GO TO ISRAEL	NO. OF VYZOVS	% OF VYZOVS ACTUALLY USED
(i)	(ii)	(iii)	(iv)	(v)
1968	229	0	6,786	3.4
1969	2,979	0	27,301	10.9
1970	1,027	0	4,830	21.3
1971	13,022	0.5	40,794	31.9
1972	31,681	0.8	67,895	46.7
1973	34,733	4.2	58,216	59.7
1974	20,628	18.8	42,843	48.1
1975	13,221	37.3	34.145	38.7
1976	14,261	49.1	36,104	39.5
1977	16,736	50.7	43,052	38.9
1978	28,865	58.4	107,212	26.9
1979	51,333	66.3	128,891	39.8
1980	21,471	65.6	32,335	66.4
1981	9,449	80.6	10,922	86.5
1982	2,688	–	3,159	85.1
1983	1,314	–	1,530	85.9
1984	896	–	1,140	78.6

questions is reflected in the statistics. The answers clarify the whole issue of Soviet Jewry.

The desire to emigrate varied widely between the Republics. The greatest interest was shown by the non-Ashkenazi Jews, described as Georgian Jews, Bukharans and Mountain Jews, whose Jewishness was expressed through their religion. They had lived in the Soviet Union since its creation but had retained a distinct sense of being Jewish. For them the final voyage was to Israel. Between 1968 and 1980 almost 20 per cent more Jews than were registered as such in Georgia received vyzovs and almost 60 per cent of them actually emigrated. In Azerbaidzhan and Tadzhikistan where non-Ashkenazis also lived the interest in emigration was high though the picture there is complicated by the fact that half of the Soviet Central Asian Jews were Ashkenazis who had migrated from the West during and after the

Second World War. The victory in the Six Day War and the Israeli campaign which followed it had an immediate impact on the non-Ashkenazis. They made up a substantial part of the flow from 1971 to 1974. Emigrating to Israel for them was not a rejection of the Soviet Union but a fulfilment of a prophesy.

Most of the remaining emigrants came from areas at the periphery of the Soviet Union which became part of that country during the Second World War. The areas were Lithuania, Latvia and parts of the Ukraine, Moldavia and Byelorussia. Although they did not express their Jewishness with the intensity of the non-Ashkenazis they were the least assimilated, and the most restless among Soviet Jews. Their experience of socialism had been relatively brief and they lived among a gentile population which had not been educated out of all of its racial prejudices. By the early 1970s they had been long enough away from the pre-war ghettos to forget them but not long enough under socialism to realize its benefits. The Israeli campaign provided an escape route for them.

The areas least affected by the call to emigrate were the three Slav Republics which had been in the Soviet Union since the beginning, namely the Ukraine, Byelorussia and the Russian Federation. Most of the emigrants from the Ukraine and Byelorussia came from parts annexed from Poland during the war. There was virtually no interest shown in emigration by the Ashkenazis Jews in the heartland of the Soviet Union. This is shown by the fact that only 13.8 per cent of the Jewish population of the RSFSR received vyzovs between 1968 and 1980 while only 4.4 per cent actually emigrated. The distribution of vyzovs and the extent of emigration from the various republics is shown in Table III

It is clear that anti-Semitism as a generalised form of discrimination was not responsible for this emigration. In Georgia, with the highest rate of emigration, there were not even rumours of anti-Semitism. Jews in the periphery, some still with memories of ghettos and the holocaust may have identified some aspects of socialist planning as discriminatory. The illusory freedom of ghetto life had gone. They were living in a collectivist society where the practice of nationalism in whatever form was discouraged. But none of this caused them to rank anti-Semitism as a significant factor in causing emigration.[62] The propaganda about Soviet anti-Semitism aroused Western Jews but not Soviet ones for they knew better. Moreover, if anti-Semitism was as

170

TABLE III
SOVIET JEWISH EMIGRATION BY REPUBLIC
1968-1980[60]

| REPUBLIC | VYZOVS | | EMIGRANTS | |
	NO. OF VYZOVS	% OF JEWISH POPULATION IN REPUBLIC	NUMBER	% OF JEWISH POPULATION IN REPUBLIC
Georgia	66,144	119.3[61]	32929	59.4
Lithuania	13,868	58.7	11615	49.2
Latvia	20,334	55.4	13153	35.8
Moldavia	50,926	51.9	27376	27.9
Tadzhikistan	7,760	53.1	2981	20.4
Azerbaidzhan	29,501	71.4	7244	17.5
Uzbekistan	46,773	45.5	16247	15.8
Ukraine	246,571	31.7	91656	11.8
Byelorussia	31,220	21.0	10469	7.1
RSFSR	111,821	13.8	35702	4.4

prevalent as the Western media maintained, why then did the majority of those who received family invitations from Israel refuse to emigrate? Zionist writers have claimed that this was so because the Soviet government restricted emigration by imposing quotas for each Republic but there were no quotas. 95 per cent of all visa applicants in the 1970s were successful.

The unsuccessful ones were called 'refuseniks' and their plight was widely publicized in the West. Some had waited for 10 or more years for a visa and by 1985 it was claimed that more than 8,000 names had accumulated on the 'refusenik' list. The reasons for failing to obtain a visa were because the applicants were involved in secret work, or were engaged in a major branch of the military, or were under investigation, or had failed in some way to comply with the regulations. About 25 to 30 per cent of the 'refuseniks' received visas each year but some could never qualify and bore a perpetual grudge against the Soviet authorities which was exploited by the Western advocates of free Soviet emigration.

There is a big step between receiving an invitation from Israel and taking the decision to emigrate. Some of the vyzovs were unsolicited. The Jewish agencies were keen to involve as many

Soviet Jews as possible in the emigration process and took the initiative in sending out invitations. The women's Zionist organization in the USA, Hadassa, for instance, systematically set about collecting the names and addresses of Soviet Jews. It was not difficult to find name-sakes in Israel to establish vague family relationships. Hadassa then sent vyzovs to a large number of unsuspecting Soviet Jews who had never thought of emigration and who presumably destroyed their invitations. The ones who had sought the invitations had to weigh the costs and advantages of emigration. The first flow of emigrants consisted mainly of Zionists. After that the reasons were mainly material. The advantages, therefore, had to be expressed in terms of ease of settlement, the provision of jobs, opportunities for material advancement. Even the Georgian Jews were discouraged by letters complaining of absorption difficulties. There was a growing reluctance by recent immigrants to accommodate new immigrants, a phenomenon common in American history. New immigrants engaged in mounting protests about their treatment. Israeli bureacuracy, it was alleged, was worse than that in the Soviet Union. There were house shortages, job shortages and a high rate of inflation. Then from 1973 there was the realization that Israel was a dangerous place in which to live. The euphoria following the Six Day War disappeared entirely after the fourth Arab-Israeli conflict, the Yom Kippur War, which began in October 1973. This war was expensive in lives and equipment and inconclusive in its results. Israel was shown to be vulnerable to attack. The deployment of new technology against tanks and aircraft made sure that the days of quick victories, as in the Six Day War, were over. Israel's future wars were going to be prolonged and total. It was not an attractive proposition for would-be Soviet emigrants.

The Yom Kippur War had a dramatic impact on the flow of emigrants to Israel. Its immediate effect was to divert the emigrants to the USA. All Soviet Jewish emigrants left with Israeli visas, travelled to Vienna where they entered a reception camp and became the responsibility of the Hebrew Immigrant Aid Society. HIAS provided subsistence, arranged and financed transport and handed out wages so that the emigrants could ease themselves relatively painlessly into the new society. It was a highly organised and well-endowed operation involving few of the hardships which earlier emigrants to other societies had had to endure.

From 1973 there was a notable increase in the number of people who decided in Vienna that they would prefer to travel on to the USA. HIAS, with finance from New York Jewry, was able to meet the cost of this change of plans. The US government facilitated it by granting refugee status to all Soviet Jewish emigrants. In American eyes the emigrants were emigrés. The annual rate of "drop-outs" is illustrated clearly in the following table:

TABLE IV
DESTINATION OF SOVIET JEWISH EMIGRANTS
BY PERIOD[63]

PERIOD	ISRAEL	ELSEWHERE	% GOING ELSEWHERE
1968-1973	82,211	1,765	2.1
1974-1975	25,347	8,807	25.8
1976-1979	45,433	66,410	59.4
1980-1984	10,861	25,208	69.9
1968-1984	163,852	102,190	38.4

The emigrants, on arriving in Vienna, gave a number of reasons for changing their minds. It was, they said, the climate, a fear of war, apprehension about Israel's future, general absorption difficulties and, in the later, part of the decade, a desire to re-unite with families in the USA,though it was noted that "the 'drop-outs' often attempt to 'send' their old and ailing parents to Israel, while they themselves aim for the USA, Canada, Australia or Germany."[64] The Jews who emigrated after 1974 were increasingly the highly qualified residents of the main Soviet cities, who were simply seeking to acquire the life-styles of Western intellectual society. From 63 per cent to 85 per cent of all the emigrants from Kharkov, Odessa, Kiev, Leningrad, Minsk and Moscow between 1968 and 1980 were 'drop-outs'. The essential character of the process was revealed by one of the emigrants in 1978, a 37 year old head of a scientific laboratory in Novosibirsk in Western Siberia. He went abroad to read a paper at a conference. When he returned he asked at his laboratory "When can I go abroad again?" and was told "In four or five years". He said "Suddenly I understood profoundly what Pavlov

173

meant when he spoke of their 'reflex of freedom': that craving for unrestrained movement without which humans in particular become bored and depressed. I was bored by the passport system, the impossibility of changing one's place of residence or travelling abroad, by the Soviet way of life in general. Anti-Semitism was not a factor in my decision to emigrate."[65]

From the Soviet point of view, the 'drop-outs' changed the character of the emigration process from one to facilitate repatriation and re-unite families to straight-forward emigration. Some Zionists felt that this threatened the possibility of Soviet Jews emigrating to Israel in the future and put pressure on the HIAS to stop financing 'drop-outs'. The Soviet government, however, took no action to stop the flow. Emigration dried up at its source as the figures given above show. In Lithuania, for instance, there was not one application for an exit visa in 1985.[66] In fact by then the process was beginning to reverse. It was reported from the USA that there was a "continuous upswing in the numbers of Soviet Jews leaving Israel."[67] This was part of a general movement from Israel. In 1981-82, 33,000 people entered Israel while 45,000 left it. The latest development is for Jews to return to the Soviet Union, dissatisfied with all Western options. This movement back is difficult. First, those who have received financial assistance from Jewish emigration agencies on the way out have to repay it before they are allowed to leave for the Soviet Union. Many emigrants have been unable to do this. Secondly there is no organization to facilitate the return. There is no resettlement camp in Vienna to arrange for finance and documents so the returnees live and work as best they can in a neighbourhood of Vienna. There is delay at the Soviet end for the Jews who wish to return home have to re-apply for Soviet citizenship which they renounced when they left. Nonetheless Jews are returning in small but increasing numbers.

The Dialectics of the Jewish Question

The Soviet Jewish question is both complex and contradictory. The issue as formulated in the West is that Soviet Jews, by being refused the right to leave the Soviet Union, are being prevented from escaping from unacceptable, discriminatory treatment. They are, therefore, denied an inalienable right to leave and re-enter their country freely. This is an infringement of a basic human right, founded on 'natural law'. The 'right to leave' is put

174

next in priority to the 'right to life' itself, and at the heart of all other civil, political, economic, social and cultural rights. The Western advocates of the 'right to leave' refer to the United Nations Universal Declaration of Human Rights, endorsed in the autumn of 1948, which stated "Everyone has the right to leave any country, including his own, and to return to his country". The issue was elaborated and endorsed by a United Nations Report in 1963 called "The Study of Discrimination in Respect of the Right of Everyone to Leave Any Country, Including His Own and to Return to His Country." This Report regarded the 'right to leave' as a constituent element of personal liberty. Further United Nations' declarations were made in 1965 and 1966 concerning the right of a person to leave any country. By 1970 it was clearly enshrined in international law.

The 'right to leave' as perceived by the United Nations was never absolute but subject to reasonable and necessary restrictions to protect national security, public order, public health or morals, or the rights and freedoms of others. In capitalist societies these considerations are generally theoretically subordinate to the freedom of an individual to choose. Indeed under capitalism the major moral issue is the freedom of choice. The 'right to leave' is a facet of this. The United Nations Declarations, by giving preeminence to the 'right to leave', were simply, therefore, reiterating individualism as the core value.

In socialist societies where collective considerations are paramount, individual rights are derived ones, conditional upon the protection of community interests. A United Nations of Socialist Societies would alter the format of a Declaration of Human Rights by reversing the emphasis on individual and collective rights. There would be no natural right to leave, only the facility to emigrate on compassionate grounds such as repatriation and re-uniting families. That has been the practice of the Soviet Union.

Enunciating the 'right to leave' as a principle at this period of history is not fortuitous but to support the practice of international capitalism. It has been done in defiance of the individual interests of many Soviet Jews who have been used as pawns in the Cold War struggle to preserve the hegemony of capitalism. The linch-pin in this particular struggle is the existence of the Zionist state, Israel, perpetually and virtually totally indebted to US financial interests. There is now a homeland to which Jews can be directed and which is eager to accept them. If there were no homeland

175

there would be no Jewish question, except for committed Zionists seeking a homeland. There was no Jewish question on the agendas of governments before 1945 when ghettos and the holocaust dominated Jewish lives in Europe, when anti-Semitism was real and bitter. Even after Israel had been formed there was not really a Jewish question until it felt sufficiently strong and confident to project its Zionist philosophy. The existence of Israel was a necessary condition for the Soviet Jewish question but Zionism was the catalyst.

The Soviet treatment of Jews was not a causal factor in the emigration process. In the period between 1948 and 1953 when there was some discrimination against Jewish intellectuals there was condemnation from the West but no Soviet Jewish question. The question appeared when Soviet Jews had recovered from those setbacks and were benefiting from the post-war reconstruction in the country as a whole. As figures shown earlier in this chapter indicate, Jews were a relatively privileged group at the end of the 1960s. The issue of anti-Semitism in the Soviet Union arose as a major issue in the West to meet the needs of an aggressive Israeli nationalism after 1967. Indeed anti-Semitism is a corollary of Israeli nationalism. Nation-creating tendencies amongst a scattered people require a perception of the world outside as inferior, hostile and unsatisfactory. Once the Zionist flag began to be waved by Israel there were bound to be accusations of discrimination against Jews outside otherwise the waving was without meaning.

It was equally inevitable that the accusations should be directed at the Soviet Union. There were approximately 2 million Jews there without the freedom to emigrate and subject to powerful assimilating tendencies which were the antithesis of Zionism. There could never be any compatability between socialism which unites on a class basis and a nationalism which is based on religion. This, of course, was one reason for Israel's pre-occupation with Soviet Jewry. Israel's case was taken up by the Western world, however for a different reason. It was a case which could be used to defame the Soviet Union. The Soviet Jewish question was quickly recognized as an instrument of anti-Sovietism. It turned out to be highly effective.

Once the issue became a part of Cold War politics then Soviet Jews lost their identities as people and became political pawns. They could be moved at the whim of the player. Their own personal interests disappeared from sight. Many Soviet Jews were unwittingly sucked into the emigration process by the sheer weight of propaganda and Jewish social pressure. For many of them this created personal tragedies. Although emigration allowed relatively wide kinship groups to unite it frequently shattered nuclear families. The images which many had of life in the West were illusory. Absorptive problems were difficult. From being highly qualified intellectuals in the Soviet Union they became unskilled lower middle class workers in the USA. Ninety per cent of Soviet emigrant doctors failed to obtain American qualifications to practice.[68] In comparison with urban Soviet life, Israeli society was closed and uncultured whereas America was dominated by small-town materialism. The new immigrants quickly acquired cars but lost much which gave life substance. The letters to Soviet kin from emigrants revealed much unhappiness. To that has to be added the unhappiness of deserted wives, children and husbands. None of this mattered to the purveyors of anti-Sovietism.

Unfortunately, the Western Jews who campaigned so vigorously, and often in all innocence, also treated Soviet Jews as pawns. For the ordinary participants it was the campaign which mattered whereas for the organizers in the higher echelons of World Jewry the primary issue was the survival of Israel. It was logical that organized Jewry should support the Israeli campaign. They did so by financing the emigration process, by organizing agitations against the Soviet Union and by raising the issue constantly as a major human rights violation. They nurtured Israel so carefully that any criticism against it was construed an anti-Semitic. When the Soviet Union was criticized for its human rights record, nothing was said about the Israeli treatment of Palestinian Arabs or about the methods of control used in the 'administered' territories. Yet Israel's own human rights record was infamous. It expropriated Arab land, destroyed Arab homes and property, denied them rights of citizenship and used arrests, interrogations and imprisonment as common methods of control. The Defence Committee for Palestinian Detainees claimed in the early 1980s that 500 people were arrested every month, of whom 85 per cent were released soon afterwards.[69] Demonstrations by Arabs were suppressed. "A report of the International Federation of Human Rights, drawn up after a mission carried out between 26 August and 7 September 1982 in the Occupied Territories mentions that "in a recent period 31 persons were killed by bullets, and 586 were wounded, 251 of them by bullets in the course of

177

demonstrations on the public streets."[70] The Israelis used expulsion from the country as a punishment for Palestinian Arabs. More than 30 Arabs were expelled in an 18 months period after June 1985.[71] The catalogue of human rights violations by Israel in the Lebanon is long and detailed. Constraints on the 'right to leave' seem minor and insignificant by comparison, yet the comparison is never made by Western Jewish critics of the Soviet Union.

The Western campaign for the emigration of Soviet Jewry has regenerated anti-Semitism. The failure to differentiate between Jewishness on the one hand and Zionism and Israel on the other has got the lines crossed. Whenever criticisms of Israeli foreign policy are described as anti-Semitic then non-Jews tend to identify Israeli behaviour with Jewishness rather than to see it as a consequence of bourgeois nationalism. The description of Soviet criticisms of Zionism as anti-Semitic have a similar consequence. Thus Jewishness is highlighted as a variable in situations where it plays no part. Similarly, the nation-building propaganda of Israel focusses attention on all Jews as potential adherents of Zionism so that the critics of Zionism become suspicious of the loyalties of Jews. This attracts attention to Jews not because of what they do or say but because of their nationality and this is basically racist. It is inevitable that questions will be asked of Jews in the Soviet Union after the massive campaign to persuade all Jews that their allegiance lies with Israel. Where do their loyalties lie? To what extent can trust be put in them? These questions raise no problems in capitalist societies for Zionism is consistent with capitalist philosophy. But to proclaim it in a socialist society is to challenge socialist legitimacy. For this reason Zionists have sometimes been punished for engaging in anti-state activities. In this way the Jewish question became linked to the entirely separate issue of dissent in the Soviet Union which was discussed in the previous chapter.

FOOTNOTES

1. *Soviet-Jewish Emigration and Soviet Nationality Policy* by Victor Zaslavsky and Robert J Brym, London, 1983, p. 9.
2. ibid, pp. 9-10.
3. Quoted from *The Jews and other National Minorities under the Soviets* by Avrahm Yarmolinsky, New York, 1928, p. 48.
4. Zaslavsky and Brym, op cit, pp. 11-12.
5. ibid.

6. *Soviet Communism: A New Civilization?* by S & B Webb, London, 1935, p. 152.
7. ibid, p. 153.
8. Zaslavsky and Brym, op cit, p. 17.
9. *Soviet but not Russian* by William Mandel, California, 1985, p. 320.
10. *The Destruction of the European Jews* by Raul Hilberg, Chicago, 1961, p. 187. Heydrich was assassinated in Prague in 1942 and the inhabitants of Lidice were massacred as a reprisal.
11. ibid, p. 192.
12. *Jewish Responses to Nazi Persecution* by Isaiah Trunk, a compilation of memoirs by survivors, New York, 1979, p. 40.
13. ibid.
14. ibid.
15. Hilberg, op cit, p. 197.
16. See *The Abandonment of the Jews. America and the Holocaust, 1941-1945* by David S Wyman, New York, 1984, pp. 19-30.
17. Quoted in *The Holocaust Denial* by Gill Seidel, 1986, p. xiv.
18. ibid, p. xv.
19. Wyman, op cit, p. 6.
20. Seidel, op cit, p. xv.
21. Wyman, op cit, p. 8.
22. *Britain and the Jews of Europe 1939-45* by Bernard Wasserstein, Oxford, 1979.
23. Seidel, op cit, p. xvi.
24. Wasserstein, op cit, p. 346. It was estimated that 3000 had been admitted between 1933 and 1939 (ibid p. 28).
25. ibid, p. 19.
26. ibid, p. 20.
27. ibid.
28. *Auschwitz and the Allies* by Martin Gilbert, London, 1981.
29. Wyman, op cit, pp. 8-9.
30. ibid, pp. x-xi.
31. ibid, p. 136.
32. Quoted from Cabinet Minutes, 16 May, 1945, by Wasserstein, op cit, p. 131.
33. Quoted in *Soviet Jewish Affairs,* Vol 15, No 1, p. 18.
34. Quoted in *Soviet But Not Russian* by William Mandel, p. 326.
35. Quoted in *Soviet Jewish Affairs,* Vol 15, No 1, p. 19.
36. See "Jews in the 1979 Soviet Census: Initial Data" by Mordechai Altshuler, *Soviet Jewish Affairs,* Vol 10, No 3, 1980, pp. 6-7.
37. Source: "The Jews in the 1979 Soviet Census: Initial Data" by Mordechai Altshuler, *Soviet Jewish Affairs,* Vol 10, No 3, 1980, p. 9. Data for 3 of the Republics, covering 2 per cent of the country's Jews was not published.
38. Quoted from Zaslavsky and Brym, op cit, p. 13.
39. *Soviet-Jewish Emigration and Soviet Nationality Policy,* op cit, pp. 25-26.
40. ibid, p. 15.
41. "The Silent Majority" by T Friedgut, *Soviet Jewish Affairs,* Vol 10, No 2, May 1980, p. 6.
42. Zaslavsky and Brym, op cit, p. 12.
43. ibid, pp. 13-14.
44. ibid, p. 13.

45. See "A Periodization of Soviet Policy Towards the Jews" by William Orbach, *Soviet Jewish Affairs*, Vol 12, No 3, p. 58.
46. "The Silent Majority" by T Friedgut, *Soviet Jewish Affairs*, Vol 10, No 2, pp. 14-15.
47. "A Note on Jewish Membership of the Soviet Communist Party" by Everett M Jacobs, *Soviet Jewish Affairs*, Vol 6, No 2, 1976, pp. 114-115.
48. "Jews and Emigration" by Igor Birman, *Soviet Jewish Affairs*, Vol 9, No 2, 1979, p. 49.
49. *My Russia*, p. 165.
50. *Soviet but not Russian*, op cit, p. 307.
51. "Jewish Emigration" by Z Nezer, *Soviet Jewish Affairs*, Vol 12, No 3, Nov 1982, p. 5.
52. Quoted in "Soviet Jews and Israeli Citizenship: The Nationality Amendment Law of 1971" by Leonard Schroeter, *Soviet Jewish Affairs, No 2, November 1971*.
53. *Zaslavsky and Brym*, op cit, p. 43.
54. This was how Jonathan Frankel say the situation from a Zionist perspective in "The Anti-Zionist Press Campaigns", *Soviet Jewish Affairs*, No 3, 1972.
55. Quoted by Zaslavsky and Brym, op cit, p. 38.
56. Quoted by G Ginsburg in "New Soviet Laws on Emigration", *Soviet Jewish Affairs*, Vol 6, No 2, 1976, p. 9.
57. Zaslavsky and Brym, op cit, p. 134.
58. *Soviet Jewish Affairs*, No 3, May 1972, p. 15.
59. Compiled from sources in *Soviet Jewish Affairs*, Vol 11, No 2, p. 16 and Vol 15, No 2, p. 42.
60. *Soviet Jewish Affairs*, May, 1981, pp. 11-12.
61. This figure is over 100 per cent because 19.3 per cent more than the registered number of Jews in Georgia received vyzovs.
62. In a survey of emigrants only 5.3-6.0 per cent said they had suffered directly from discrimination. See "Emigration and Identity" by B Pinkus, *Soviet Jewish Affairs*, November, 1985, p. 13.
63. *Soviet Jewish Affairs*, November, 1985, p. 20.
64. ibid, May 1981, pp. 16-17.
65. Zaslavsky and Brym, op cit, p. 56.
66. *Soviet Weekly*, 14 December, 1985, p. 10.
67. *Soviet Jewish Affairs*, November, 1985, p. 24.
68. ibid, p. 27n.
69. *Israel and Palestine. Human Rights in Israel and in the Occupied Territories*, END Papers, 9 Winter, 1984-5, p. 20.
70. ibid, p. 27.
71. *The Guardian*, 13 November, 1986.

Chapter Seven
The Human Rights Issue

Whenever Britain and the USA comment about human rights in the Soviet Union it is always with reference only to political rights. Yet whenever the issue of 'human rights' has been debated internationally a much wider and socially relevant definition has been used. The United Nations, for instance, flung the net wide and considered that human rights were infringed through internal state oppression, fascism, colonialism, racism, apartheid and genocide on the one hand and by the denial of a range of social, economic and cultural rights such as the right to work, to adequate subsistance, education, health care, protection in old age and the right to speak the indigenous language, on the other. The Universal Declaration of Human Rights, adopted by the United Nations on 10 December, 1948, covered the right to life, to work, to support when unemployed, to fair and favourable working conditions, to social security, to medical care and to education as well as to political rights. Experience in the histories of all countries and in the contemporary lives of Third World countries has shown that political rights are mere gestures if people are denied the right to work and, therefore, to subsistance. The freedom to speak her mind is little consolation to a starving woman. Economic rights are a precondition for permanent, effective political freedom. The causal link runs from the economic base to every facet of freedom for if there is not equality through the social relations of production there cannot be equality anywhere else. The primacy of economic rights, however, is not asserted in a mechanistic way but through a dialectical process so that different facets of freedom interact and influence each other. If one facet is missing then the others must be marred. There may be short-run situations when the causal process is reversed as in present day South Africa where blacks need political freedom in order to break apartheid and extend their economic rights. But in the long-run the quality of their political freedom will be determined by the extent of their

181

economic rights. If South African blacks achieve universal suffrage but remain as employees to white employers then their achievements will indeed be limited.

The Soviet Union has its own historically determined pattern of freedom. By abolishing private property it has eliminated structural economic inequality. It specifies and guarantees the rights which flow from this through a written code in its Constitution. Thus a whole series of economic, social and cultural rights are ensured by the Constitution and backed by the force of law. They fall into three categories which are symbolised by the right to work, the rights of women and ethnic equality.

The Right to Work

This has a high priority in Soviet society and is enshrined in Article 40 of the Constitution which states: "Citizens of the USSR have the right to work (that is, to guarantee employment and pay in accordance with the quantity and quality of their work, and not below the state-established minimum), including the right to choose their trade or occupation, type of job and work in accordance with their inclinations, abilities, training and education, with due account of the needs of the society." The guarantee of such an important right carries responsibilities. Soviet people have an obligation to contribute to society by working, following the precept laid down by Lenin that those who do not work shall not eat. The emphasis on the right to work arose out of the experience of instability and insecurity in capitalist labour markets. The accompanying obligation to work has its basis in the collectivist ethic of Soviet society which imposes on everyone of working age, without exception, the responsibility to contribute to the general welfare of the society.

The ability of the Soviet Union to fulfil this Constitutional obligation has been hampered by the enormity of the economic and social problems which followed the Revolution. The devastation caused by the Civil War and the Allied intervention to topple the Soviet government and the ensuing economic blockage by international capitalism, plus the internal divisions between industrial workers and the peasants and between the rich and poor peasant, created almost overwhelming difficulties for a decade and a half. In 1922 it was estimated that there were half a million registered unemployed but this figure was swollen by the movement of population from the countryside to the towns in search of work. By 1926 the registered unemployed had risen to 1 million while the actual figure was at least two million.[1] This situation continued despite the reduction of the working day to seven hours and the introduction of multiple shift working. The incidence of unemployment was only alleviated after the application of the First Five Year Plan in 1929 which generated widespread constructional work. At the end of that Plan the problem of unemployment gave way to a problem of labour scarcity and this has remained the case ever since.

The position in contemporary Soviet society is that industrial change is planned in a balanced fashion so that where redundancies occur, for whatever reason, they can be compensated for by alternative job opportunities. A factory, mill or mine cannot be closed without provisions for alternative work, nor can new technology be introduced unless the employment prospects of workers affected by it have been protected. No manager can dismiss a worker without the sanction of the local trade union committee and even with that the worker has to be provided with another job. In effect most dismissals result in workers being transferred from one job to another within the same production unit.

Conditions of employment are governed by a highly detailed Labour Code which is legally binding. Every contingency is provided for under the Code in order to protect the interests of workers. Each worker signs a labour agreement whereby "the person employed undertakes to do work in a definite trade speciality or in some other capacity in conformity with internal regulations." Article 12 adds that "The Administrative cannot demand that the factory worker or office employee do work which is not stipulated in the labour agreement." Workers cannot be transferred (Article 13) "to another job at the same enterprise, institution or organization, to another enterprise, institution or organization, or to a different locality, even if the enterprise institution or organization is moved there" without the consent of the person concerned, except under very stringent and limited cicumstances concerning breaches of labour discipline. A worker can cancel a labour agreement after giving two weeks' notice but an enterprise can only do so for reasons stipulated in the Code and with the prior agreement of the local trade union committee. If management acts outside this agreement then a worker is legally protected.

The practical application of the Labour Code produces some

183

underemployment and causes some enterprises to carry surplus labour. It may retard the pace of technological change. But these are the costs of protecting the employment rights of workers. In Soviet society the term efficiency has a social component so that before technology is applied, questions, such as for what purpose is it intended and who will benefit from it, have to be asked, and not in some indefinable long term, but in the here and now.

A direct and important consequence of maintaining full employment is that it eliminates the most important source of poverty in industrialized societies, namely unemployment. The possibility of poverty occurring is further reduced by the fact that almost 40 per cent of the living standards of everyone is met by a social wage through which esssential components are either provided free or are heavily subsidized.

Peoples' needs are met by a series of rights in addition to that guaranteeing work. There is a right to housing so that, although there may be over-crowding or inadequate accommodation, there are no homeless. Indeed, the cost of accommodation for everyone throughout the Soviet Union has been maintained at approximately 6 per cent of annual income since the 1950s. There are rights to education, health protection and social security in sickness and old age, of which all provisions are free. Workers are entitled to rest and leisure after a working week of 41 hours so that overtime working is illegal. The vast majority of workers are trade union members and for them and their families the cost of their annual holidays is subsidized by at least 60 per cent. There has been a remarkable degree of stability in the Soviet Union over the last 30 years in the prices of essential foodstuffs. There are no charges for local telephone calls; the prices of internal city transport have been maintained at their 1956 level; books and educational aids are subsidized. It may be that there are still pockets of poverty but it is becoming increasingly difficult to find them.

The Position of Women

The position of women in any society is a reliable guide to the character of its freedoms for no society can be truly free unless women have equality with men. The Soviet Union has laid the basis for equality by providing for it in its Constitution. This, of course, is only a necessary condition so that even with it equality in practice may be evasive. But it is a major step to make discrimination against women illegal.

Article 35 of the Constitution accords equality of rights between women and men. It states: "Exercise of these rights is ensured by according women equal access with men to education and vocational and professional training, equal opportunities in employment, remuneration, and promotion, and in social and political and cultural activity, and by special labour and health protection measures for women; by providing conditions enabling mothers to work; by legal protection, and material and moral support for mothers and children, including paid leave and other benefits for expectant mothers, and gradual reduction of working time for mothers with small children."

Article 53 refers to the position of women in marriage. "Marriage", it states, "is based on the free consent of the woman and the man; the spouses are completely equal in their family relations. The state helps the family by providing and developing a broad system of childcare institutions, by organizing and improving communal services and public catering, by paying grants on the birth of a child, by providing children's allowances and benefits for large families, and other forms of family allowances and assistance." The family relationship has altered and alternated since the Bolshevik Revolution. Through the Revolution marriage and divorce became matters of mutual consent; divorce could be initiated by either party; marriage became a legally egalitarian institution thus removing important restrictions on the freedom of women. Abortion was widely practised as a form of birth control in the 1920s but it was banned between 1936 and 1955 when population growth was regarded as being essential for the economy. Divorce was made more difficult. Those restrictions have now been eased. There are other indicators of equality, as Albert Szymanski stated: "Marriage is considered to be neither a means for the economic support of women, nor for the provision of household services by women. Men have no legal obligation to support their wives or ex-wives; women have no legal obligation to provide their husbands with any services. Forcible sex by husbands is legally defined as rape; women have the right to retain their maiden name, to control an equal share of the communal property and, of course, equal personal and property rights."[2]

The experience of the Soviet Union since 1917 is that further equality is dependent upon socializing men and women about sex roles and gender and that this is a slow and uncertain process.

Sexism is still practised within families. Women still combine paid employment with unpaid domestic labour. Despite the provisions in the Constitution for sex equality in occupational promotion it remains difficult for women to penetrate the upper levels of decision-making on the same scale as men. Nonetheless Soviet sex equality is qualitatively better than in the West. Women make up 51 per cent of the Soviet labour force. They comprise almost the same proportion of members of the local Soviets of People's Deputies and a third of the USSR Supreme Soviet. More women than men, 59 per cent as against 41 per cent, have higher education qualifications. Women are frequently directors of factories, mills, offices and state farms and leaders of trade unions. They are least visible in the higher reaches of the Communist Party, in the Politburo and on the Party Central Committee, though those bodies consistently pursue policies favourable to women.

Virtually all Soviet women workers are trade union members compared with less than 40 per cent of the British female labour force. Soviet women, in April 1986, comprised 67.7 per cent of the elected members of local trade union committees, 64.6 per cent of trade union bodies at Republic, Territorial and Regional level, 43.5 per cent of the membership of central trade union committees and 35.8 per cent of the AUCCTU, the supreme trade union council. In the Soviet Union women workers are spread throughout all occupations, except underground mining where it is illegal for them to work. In Britain, on the other hand, women are concentrated in what have come to be called 'women's occupations'. Between sixty-six and seventy-six per cent of all employees in education, welfare, health, clerical work, selling, catering, cleaning, hairdressing and other personal services are women. Yet in the 9 trade unions which largely organized those occupations in 1985 and had, therefore, the highest density of female membership, only 19 per cent of the central executive committee members and about 9 per cent of the full-time officers were women. These figures are a marked improvement on those of even four years previously when less than 13 per cent of central executive committee members and less than 6 per cent of full-time officers were women.

The Ethnic Minorities

A similar emphasis against discrimination is adopted in the case of ethnicity and colour. Article 36 of the Constitution states:

"Citizens of the USSR of different races and nationalities have equal rights. . . Any direct or indirect limitation of the rights of citizens or establishment of direct or indirect privileges on grounds of race or nationality, and any advocacy of racial or national exclusiveness, hostility or contempt, are punishable by law." The question of the rights of nationalities has been important since the time of Revolution when Joseph Stalin became the Commissar of Nationalities. His task was to bring former colonies in the Czar's empire into a socialist unity with the already ethnically diverse Russia. Azerbaidzhan in the Trans-caucus, and the Middle Asian Republics of Kazakhstan, Turkmenistan, Kirgizistan, Uzbekistan and Tadzhikistan before the Revolution were identical to bordering colonies in the Ottoman and British empires. They were equally exploited, deprived and subjugated. All the indices of underdevelopment were present. They were as Iran, Afghanistan, Pakistan, Tibet and Northern India have remained, namely economically underdeveloped with the majority of their population living under conditions of abject poverty.

The colonies of the Czarist empire developed in a manner familiar from the experience of British colonies in Africa and Asia. They had virtually no industrial development but served metropolitan Russia with raw materials and minerals and acted as minor but expanding markets for consumer products. For this purpose they were kept in bondage and received the minimum of education, social services and health care. Indeed, the vast majority of the people were excluded from such provisions and depended upon kinship, clan or tribal assistance. In most cases there was only local industry consisting of small artisan works. In 1911, Turkestan, for example, had 143 artisan enterprises, of which only 9 employed more than 25 workers. In 1913 there were only 204 workers in Tadzhikistan. About one per cent of the populations of Soviet Asia belonged to the industrial working class.[3] This level of development was comparable to that in Nigeria in the late 1950s.

After the Revolution each of the Republics in Soviet Asia underwent dramatic changes. Between 1913 and 1978 industrial output in Turkmenistan increased by 74 times and 11 times after 1940; in Tadzhikistan it increased by 138 times and 16 times after 1940; in Kirgizistan industrial output rose by 333 times and 34 times after 1940; in Uzbekistan it multiplied by 71 times and 15 times after 1940; in Kazarkhistan the increase was 232 times and

30 times after 1940 while in Azerbaidzhan it went up by 62 times and 11 times after 1940.[4] Agricultural output also increased but not by such spectacular proportions.

These results came about through Soviet Asia's participation in the series of national 5 Year Plans which transferred resources from the richer regions of European Russia until indigenous resources could be developed. Now Soviet Asia is rich with oil minerals, fruit and cotton. Baku, the capital of Azerbaidzhan, is the centre of the oil extractive and refining industry as well as being a major port. Its wealth is evident in its buildings, parks, leisure and cultural facilities. Uzbekistan is the country's biggest cotton producer. Its capital, Tashkent, is a major industrial and educational centre with relevance beyond Uzbekistan. Four-fifths of the area of Turkmenistan was occupied by the Kara-Kum Desert but it is now an irrigated fruit and cotton producing centre. The Republics of Soviet Russia can be identified by their specialisms but otherwise, in economic terms, there is little to distinguish them from other Soviet Republics. Each of the fifteen Soviet Republics depends upon local primary products. Kazakhistan, for example, has rich mineral deposits on which has been built a thriving heavy industry with a greater output per head of coal, iron ore, cement and sulphuric acid than the USSR average.

The continuing policy of Soviet governments has been to achieve national equality whilst encouraging cultural diversity. This has meant raising educational standards through the medium of indigenous languages. There was much scope for this. At the turn of the century only 2.6 per cent of the indigenous population of Central Asia could read or write, which was about a tenth of the rate in central Russia. There was not one higher school in Central Asia. David Lane wrote that "In 1900 only 0.5 per cent of the Kirghiz and 2 per cent of the Kazakhs were literat. In 1911, of the 20 million muslim population, only 32,000 were enrolled in Muslim religious schools and 46,000 in Russian elementary schools. In Burgat-Mongolia the number of schools rose from 48 in 1917 to 700 in 1932-33, an increase from 1,000 to 67,000 pupils. It was claimed that 99.3 per cent of children of school age were attending school in Bashkiria in 1932-33." The literacy rate in Tatania which had been 19 per cent before 1917 was over 90 per cent in 1932-33.[5] In 1917, only 2 per cent of the population of Uzbekistan could read or write yet by 1982 Tashkent was the largest publisher of books in the Soviet Union after Moscow.

In many countries language has become a medium through which political liberation activities have been pursued. This is because conquering nations impose their languages as both a symbol of their own power and the subservience of the conquered. It is used as a real instrument of power for controlling communications and imposing the dominant culture. The history of colonialism is replete with illustrations. The British, French, Spanish, Portugese, Dutch and Germans have each in their time forcibly imposed their languages on conquered nations, insisting that commerce, legal affairs and government should be conducted in them. The British even placed a legal obligation on trade unions in African colonies which organized predominantly illiterate workers to appoint officials who were literate in English. There are many anecdotes about the way in which black African servants in expatriate households became objects of fun and derision because of their inability to cope with a foreign language and an alien culture. The power which white South African mine owners have exercised over black miners has been symbolised by the humiliating way the miners have been compelled to speak through Fanagalo, a patois comprised of Arabic, English and Zulu and designed to communicate the commmands of white managements. The right to speak their own tribal language would be, for black miners, a clear sign of emancipation.

It is informative to compare the relationships between the languages of the Soviet Union with the treatment of Welsh and Gaelic in relation to English in Great Britain. The closest comparison is between the languages of the former Islamic colonies of Czarist Russia which are now Soviet Republics and Russian on the one hand and the British languages on the other hand. The English tried to destroy the indigenous languages in Wales and Scotland in the process of colonizing them. Neither Welsh nor Gaelic was ever given official recognition. They were suppressed through the educational system until the 1960s when it was really too late to save them. Through education the idea became prevalent that English was the natural language for academic studies and the professions and that the indigenous languages represented the backwardness of the poor and socially inferior. People with social pretensions, therefore, preferred the language of the colonizers. This ideological bias against Welsh and Gaelic has had an important derogatory influence but the main source of obstruction has come from government action. By forbidding their use in official transactions and preventing their development in schools the British government has largely made Welsh and Gaelic speakers into illiterates and has prevented the development of the languages. The languages have, in consequence, been spoken by a declining proportion of the population, the dramatic extent of which can be seen in the table below. A speaker at the Sixth Annual Congress of Celtic Studies in 1979 asserted that the "decline has now reached a point where people expect the language to disappear early in the 21st century unless something is done not only to stem the tide but to reverse it pretty effectively."[6] The political significance of reversing the decline was explained by Mr Saunders Lewis, a prominent Welsh nationalist in a BBC broadcast in 1962. He said "To restore the language is nothing short of revolution . . . It is by revolutionary methods that success is possible. Perhaps the language would bring self-government in its wake . . . The language is more important than self-government."[7] Saunders' challenge was taken up by members of the Welsh Nationalist Party who founded Cymdeithas yr Iaith Gymraeg, the Welsh Language Society, which spearheaded the movement for Welsh independence with civil disobedience tactics.

The Soviet Union has never had an official, *de jure* language. All the languages of the indigenous peoples have been treated as equal in administrative, judicial and official proceedings. In the Constitution, Article 45 gives people the right "to attend a school

TABLE V

CHANGES IN THE NUMBER OF WELSH SPEAKERS IN WALES, 1891-1971[8]

YEAR	TOTAL POPULATION (1)	NUMBER OF WELSH SPEAKERS (2)	WELSH SPEAKERS AS A PROPORTION OF TOTAL POPULATION IN WALES (3)
1891	1,629,630	880,000	54.00
1901	1,859,000	929,500	50.00
1911	2,273,023	977,400	43.00
1921	2,492,162	922,100	37.00
1931	2,331,026	909,100	37.00
1951	2,472,962	714,686	28.90
1961	2,523,085	656,002	26.00
1971	2,602,697	542,402	20.84

TABLE VI

CHANGES IN THE NUMBER OF GAELIC SPEAKERS IN SCOTLAND, 1891-1971[9]

YEAR	TOTAL POPULATION AGED 3 YEARS AND OVER (1)	NUMBER OF GAELIC SPEAKERS (2)	GAELIC SPEAKERS AS A PROPORTION OF (1) (3)
1891	3,721,778	254,415	6.84
1901	4,146,733	230,806	5.57
1911	4,439,802	202,398	4.56
1921	4,573,471	158,779	3.47
1931	4,588,909	136,135	2.97
1951	4,826,814	95,447	1.98
1961	4,892,822	80,978	1.66
1971	5,228,965	88,892	1.67

where teaching is in the native language" and this has been practised with over 50 languages. This emphasis on indigenous language, however, has not prevented Russian from becoming the dominant one. It was the language of the colonizers in Czarist Russia and possessed the status of the dominant power. It is the language of the largest ethnic group in post-Revolutionary Russia. It is the *lingua franca* for all the diverse language groups and, since, 1938 has been a compulsory school subject. Most of higher education is conducted in Russian. Without question Russian is encroaching on the native languages yet as recently as 1970 Russian was spoken by only 14.5 per cent of the Uzbeks, 16.6 per cent of the Azerbaidzhanis and 15 per cent of the Tadzhiks. In the following ten years these percentages rose appreciably but it was still the case that from a quarter to two-thirds of the national Muslim groups had little or no understanding of Russian. After 70 years of communist government the vast majority of the Islamic peoples in the Soviet Union still claim their own national languages as their mother tongues.

The following table which shows the preference of the Islamic peoples for their own languages also provides evidence in some cases of an increasing reliance on indigenous languages since the Revolution. When the 1926 Census was taken only about 20 out of 150 national languages had a developed literary form. For the rest, alphabets, standardised forms of grammar and vocabularies were provided. Books and newspapers were printed in each of

TABLE VII

LANGUAGES OF SOVIET ISLAMIC PEOPLES[10]

Ethnic Group	Percentage claiming own language as mother tongue		Percentage speaking Russian as second language	
	1926	1970	1970	1979
Uzbeks	99.1	98.5	14.5	49.3
Kazakhs	99.6	97.5	41.8	52.3
Tatars	98.9	85.9	62.5	68.9
Azerbaidzhanis	93.8	97.9	16.6	29.5
Tadzhiks	98.3	97.8	15.5	29.6
Turkmen	97.3	98.7	15.4	25.4
Kirghiz	99.0	97.9	19.1	29.4
Chuvash	98.7	81.7	58.4	64.8
Bashkirs	53.8	67.0	53.3	64.9
Chechens	99.7	98.6	66.7	76.0
Kabevrdians	99.3	97.9	71.4	76.7
Karakalpuks	87.5	95.9	10.4	45.1
Uighurs	52.7	86.1	35.6	52.1
Ingush	99.5	97.4	71.2	79.6
Karachais	99.5	97.7	67.6	75.5
Kurds	34.4	83.6	19.6	25.4
Balkars	99.6	96.9	71.5	77.4
Dungans	99.2	94.8	48.0	62.8
Cherkess	98.4	91.4	70.0	69.6
Persians	67.8	30.7	33.9	57.1
Abazins	94.4	95.3	69.5	75.4
Baluchis	99.9	98.1	2.9	4.9

the languages so that people could become literate in them. Indeed if the national languages had not been developed it is unlikely that there would have been such a rapid improvement in literacy after the Revolution. The experience then of the various Soviet linguistic groups has been the contrary of the Welsh and the Scots. There has been no sign of colonialism in the relationship between Russian and the other Soviet languages. Clearly, when languages and cultures are separated from economic exploitation they can grow and flourish freely without the negative features of political nationalism.

The equalising processes in Soviet society can be seen through the provision of education and medical services. The Soviet Asian Republics have educational facilities which compare favourably with the rest of the country. For example, whereas the number of students for every 10,000 populations was 187 for the Soviet Union as a whole in 1968-69, it ranged from 131 in Turkmenistan to 192 Uzbekistan. These figures were lower than that for the USA, which was 226, but they were much higher than in Britain where only 63 out of every 10,000 were students and in Iran, Pakistan and Turkey where the figures were 14, 26 and 30 respectively.[11]

The Soviet health care provisions are made through a system of hospitals, polyclinics, overnight disease prevention centres, sanitorias, rest centres and holiday homes. Shortly after the Revolution Lenin issued a decree taking over all the salubrious resorts, which hitherto had been used by the rich and royalty, for use by the workers and peasants. Now these resorts, mainly in the Caucasian mountains and on the Black Sea coast are centres for treatment, rest and holidays. Each layer of the pyramid of services is staffed by qualified medical personnel, including doctors.

The availability of doctors for the general population is a useful indicator of the spread of health care. In the middle 1960s there were 259 doctors for each 100,000 population in the Soviet Union as a whole, the ratio was lower in Azerbaidzhan where it was 243 and in Soviet Asia where it ranged from 154 in Tadzhikistan to 201 in Kazakhistan but these differences were minimal in comparison with the ratios in Third World countries. In Pakistan, for example, there were only 16 doctors for every 100,000 population; in India the comparable figure was 22 and in Iran, 35. Tadzhikistan, the Republic least provided with doctors, nonetheless had more for every 100,000 population than Britain where the figure was 152.[12] During the decade of the 1970s coinciding with the period of detente there was a large increase in the number of Soviet doctors so that in 1980 there were 375 for every 100,000 population compared with 159 in Japan, 164 in Britain, 153 in France, 198 in Italy and 225 in the USA.

The Soviet Asian Republics have differed from other Republics in some respects. They have had a faster population growth in the post-war period than the predominantly Slav areas. Between 1970 and 1979 the population growth rate for the Slav peoples in the Soviet Union was 5.8 per cent compared with 23.6 per cent for the Islamic people. The rate of growth for the Uzbeks and the Tadzhiks was more than 35 per cent. This has had the effect of showing a slower rate of per capita income growth for Soviet Asia than for other areas. In reality, however, wage rates there have been as much as 20 per cent above the average as a way of attracting labour and stimulating productivity.[13]

Whatever differences do exist between the Soviet Republics, however, they are less than those which exist between areas in Britain. There are no differences in employment levels in the USSR but in Britain in 1986 the percentage rates of unemployment ranged from 7.3 per cent in the Home Counties to 20 per cent in parts of the North East and nearly 19 per cent in the Clyde district of Scotland with concomitant variations in living standards. Indeed the visible differences between regions in Britain are much more obvious than anything found in the Soviet Union.

A similar picture is provided when comparisons are made with the USA. There are wide variations in the overall living standards of different ethnic groups in the USA. The following table shows how badly Blacks, Native Americans and Hispanics fare in relation to white Americans in all the indices.

There are also marked regional variations in the USA. Take, for example, the position of Appalachia in the USA. Appalachia consists of the coal producing regions of Kentucky, West Virginia, Tennessee and Virginia and it has a continuous history

TABLE VIII

SOCIAL INDICATORS FOR SELECTED MINORITIES IN THE USA IN 1970

MINORITY	MEAN FAMILY INCOME	POOR %	COLLEGE EDUCATED	PERCENTAGE UNEMPLOYED
White American	$11,348	8.6	11.3	4.9
Black American	$ 7,074	29.9	4.4	6.9
Native American	$ 6,857	33.3	3.8	11.1
Oriental American	$12,240	8.8	26.4	3.2
Mexican American	$ 8,192	21.2	4.5	6.4

Source: American Public Health Association, *Minority Health Chart Book*, 1974.

of poverty and deprivation in relation to the rest of the USA. Many American social analysts have commented on this fact. Cynthia Duncan from Berea in Kentucky stated that "Chronic poverty has plagued rural Kentucky since the turn of the century, especially counties in which residents depend upon small farms or coal mining for their livelihoods".[14] John Gaventa, writing from Tennessee, said "the images most often associated with Central Appalachia are those of poverty . . . Although by 1974 per capita income in Central Appalachia had risen to 65 per cent of the nation's average (up from 52 per cent in 1965) in 1970, 35 per cent of families lived below the poverty level, 72 per cent of the adult population had less than a high school education and problems of unemployment and poor health care persisted."[15] The issue for Appalachia is not simply that it portrays persistent poverty within a generally rich country but that Appalachia itself possesses tremendous wealth in the form of natural resources. It is the most important coal producing region in the USA and ranks high as a mineral producer. "Central Appalachia", Gaventa commented, "is a region of poverty amidst riches." No matter what the condition of the American economy, none of the wealth goes to the Appalachian people. This was so even during the coal boom period in the 1970s. The paradox is not explained by ethnic discrimination for the inhabitants of Appalachia are predominantly white Americans. Different explanations have been given for it, such as the personality defects of the Appalachian mountain folk and neglect by the Federal government but the one which has received greatest currency is that it is a case of colonial exploitation. Helen Lewis, one of Appalachia's most incisive sociologists, saw the paradox as a "process through which dominant outside industrial interests establish control, exploit the region, and maintain their domination and subjugation of the region."[16] She added that "Appalachia is a good example of colonial domination by outside interests . . ." The Soviet Union contains no region which could even remotely be described by such an explanation because it does not contain the contradictions which produce exploitative relations. There is no dominant Soviet Republic which exploits the resources of other Republics; nor is there a dominant class which resides in one Republic and exploits the resources of others. There is no exploitative relationship between the Russian Soviet Federal Socialist Republic which contains Moscow and Leningrad, and Uzbekistan, Azerbaidzhan or any other Republics in the Soviet Union.

The Absence of Imperialism

Human rights involve the relationships between countries as well as between individuals within a country. One country can deny human rights to the inhabitants of another. This is what the United Nations meant by including fascism, colonialism and genocide in its Declaration in 1948. It is under this heading that the Soviet Union has been accused in the West of infringing human rights in East European Socialist countries and Third World countries with whom it has relationships. The Socialist countries are generally described as Soviet satellites but specific allegations have been made about the presence of Soviet troops in Hungary in 1956, Czechoslovakia in 1968 and Afghanistan in 1979. It is also asserted that the Soviet Union is imperialist in its relations with Cuba, Vietnam, Nicaragua, Mozambique and Angola, to whom it provides aid.

There is a close parallel between the external policies of a country and how it treats its own parts, namely classes, sexes, ethnic minorities and regions. Indeed they all belong to the same processes. If a country is exploitative and discriminating in the conduct of its domestic affairs it will be imperialist in its external relations. Similarly if a nation behaves towards others in an imperialist way this is information about its structural character. On the other hand, a country which does not contain the contradictions which give rise to exploitation cannot be imperialist in the strict meaning of the term in its external relations.

Imperialism is a condition of society and not simply an explanation of inter-country relations. The classic case of imperialism is where one country seeks to solve its economic problems by exploiting others through acquiring control of their raw materials, utilizing their supplies of labour and gaining exclusive access to their markets. Colonialism is a particular form of imperialism whereby these palliatives are reached through the acquisition of land for permanent settlement on it. Africa, for example, provides an illustration of extensive imperialism with pockets of colonialism in Algeria, Kenya, Zimbabwe and South Africa.

The conclusion that Appalachia has been treated as a colony is a statement about the predatory condition of American society. It is saying that Appalachia has been exploited for its coal and minerals and its supplies of labour. And as it has no other redeeming features for American capitalism, when these have been exhausted or displaced there will be no further use for it. The exploitation of the Durham coalfield in Britain and the dereliction caused in Wales and Scotland have been similar experiences to that of Appalachia. The point is that in the struggle for private profit through the free market domestic sources of materials, labour and markets are invariably tapped first. When these are inadequate the search extends abroad. External exploitation is, therefore, an extension of internal exploitative processes. When the giant oil multinational companies which own and exploit Appalachia's coal reserves found them inadequate they sought coal in Third World countries and began to withdraw from Appalachia. Occidental Petroleum opened mammoth opencast mines in China while Exxon invested in coal production in Columbia in South America. British textile companies, unable to make profits from production in Lancashire and Yorkshire, transferred their production to South-East Asia. In other words, the substance of imperialism is the constant, unremitting struggle through competitive markets for lower costs and higher profits. In appearances, Appalachia, South Wales, South Africa, Taiwan and Scotland may appear to be different but analytically they are the same.

The point to recognize is not simply that there is a similarity between domestic and foreign relationships but that one is derived from and interacts with the other. If a society is not imperialist within itself then it cannot be imperialist with others. Thus, looking at how a society conducts its own affairs is the key to understanding its international relations. There are no class antagonisms in the Soviet Union; whilst sex equality has not been achieved it has a substantial economic foundation; there are distinct linguistic and cultural differences between the many ethnic groups but these are not reflected in national independence movements of the kind which exists in Wales or Scotland. Some ethnic groups, particularly in the Republics of the Ukraine, Lithuania, Latvia and Estonia, have a highly developed sense of nationality with fringe elements which would prefer political separation from the Soviet Union.Much of the discussion about the nationalism of those groups, however, stems from the imagination of exiles who are anti-communist, rather than from Soviet reality. There are no nationalist movements, with either indigenous or exiled bases, for the liberation of the former Czarist Asian colonies.

The Second World War was a testing ground for the unity of

the Soviet Union. If any of the large ethnic groups such as the Ukrainians had wanted political independence then the conditions of the war would have provided them with opportunities to achieve it. When the Germans invaded the Soviet Union in 1941 a few small ethnic groups were sufficiently disaffected, or misguided, to seek collaboration with them in the hope of thereby gaining independence. This was to be expected. The Revolution was only 24 years old; it had been extended to the countryside barely 11 years before. The Baltic Republics of Lithuania, Latvia and Estonia had been associated with the Soviet Union for a mere year when the Germans invaded and they contained significant groups of middle-class traders, rich peasants and government functionaries who had no sympathy for communism. In the Baltic Republics and those parts of the Ukraine and Byelorussia which had been part of Poland until September 1939 when the Red Army occupied Eastern Poland, there were nationalist organizations which collaborated with the German invaders. The Lithuanian Partisans, the Latvian Perkonkursts (Thunder-Cross) and the Organization of Ukrainian Nationalists (OUN) were pro-German, anti-Semitic and anti-Soviet. The OUN had paramilitary units, namely, the Ukrainska Powstanska Armia (UPA), led by Andrei Melnik and Stephen Bandera, which became active only after the withdrawal of the Soviet forces. It murdered large sections of the Jewish population before the arrival of the German army.[17]

The nationalist groups looked to the Germans for political independence but this was refused. They then found themselves fighting both the Germans and the partisan units attached to the Red Army. In the Ukraine they split into three groups and fought each other until 1943 when the Bandera faction came out on top. They sought influence whenever they could get it in the Nazi occupied territories and achieved some prominence and criminal notoriety as kapos in concentration camps, particularly in the notorious Treblinka camp in Poland.

In so far as the nationalist groups had any influence, however, it was a dwindling asset. They suffered increasingly from defections and were opposed by a large, growing and militarily significant Ukrainian Partisan Movement under the leadership of General Strokach. The Ukrainian partisans did not consist of unco-ordinated gangs in the forests, though doubtless many such groups existed. They operated under the auspices of the Red Army and in the winter of 1943 passed under its direct control. In

198

August, 1943, Strokach co-ordinated the activities of 20 partisan groups totalling about 17,000 members in West Ukraine alone, cutting the German lines of communication and preventing the movement of reserves to Kiev.[18] The Ukrainian partisans came under the direct control of the Communist Party committees in the partisan areas from 13 January 1944.[19] The same happened elsewhere in the Soviet Union. The initiative for preparing for the defeat of the Germans passed to the local people. So it was the Ukrainians who organized for the advance of the Red Army, containing many Ukrainian units, to recapture their own territory by the Spring of 1944.

There were a few cases of collaboration with the invading German army amongst the Moslem communities in the Crimea and Northern Caucasia. The Crimea was occupied by the Germans from 1941-1944 and shortly after it was liberated in May 1944 almost 200,000 Crimea Tatars were exiled to Central Asia and Kazakhstan as punishment for collaboration. They were officially rehabilitated in 1967 and allowed to return to their previous homes. The Chechen and Ingush peoples were similarly deported from their homeland in the Northern Caucasus to Central Asia around the same time but rehabilitated in 1957 in the wake of the Twentieth Party Congress. When the German Army entered the Karachaj Autonomous Province in August 1942 and the Kabardino-Balkar Autonomous Republic in October 1942 some of the Karachais and the Balkans collaborated. Their communities were punished in 1944 through deportation which was also rescinded in 1957.[20] It was characteristic of the Soviet war effort that no property was spared and no human effort withheld to defeat the German Army. The other side of this coin was an intolerance of those who failed to provide that degree of commitment. Temporary deportation was a minor price to pay compared with the phenomenal costs of opposition to the German army borne by the vast majority of Soviet people.

The classical Western explanation of the commitment of the former Czarist Asian colonies to the USSR is that it results from centralized state coercion, organized and managed from Moscow. This follows from the Western assumption that the Soviet Union is a totalitarian state in which there can be no voluntaristic political behaviour. There are, however, two difficulties with this explanation. First, even if the Western assumption is valid, it has to be explained why those Republics possess no national liberation movements for though struggles for political independence have been subdued they have rarely been eradicated. There should at least be language societies taking up the cause of liberation, as in Wales, or, at the most, armed struggles, as in Northern Ireland or the Basque region of Spain. If they have been coerced into national unity and they possess no visible signs of disaffection then they are clearly historical oddities. Secondly, the explanation has to clarify not simply why the Asian Republics are a part of the USSR but why they are beneficiaries from being Soviet Republics for they provide the most complete examples this century of the transformation of societies from under-developed colonial Third World states to developed status without the destruction of their indigenous languages and cultures. It is clear that in neither instance can coercion figure in the answer.

There are clearly no internal contradictions in Soviet society which could generate imperialist external relations. There are no obvious economic reasons why it should want to exercise control over other territories. It has an abundance of raw materials and a vastly under-exploited domestic market. The Soviet Union's main task is to develop its own potential and it can do this without exploiting others. But if this is the case what determines its relations with other countries.

There are two sets of explanations. The Soviet Union still has a fear of counter-revolution and a deep sensitivity about protecting its borders. It will require many generations of world peace to erase the memory of the German invasion of 1941. It requires a long-term stability on its borders to lessen its fears. This is one reason why the Soviet Union places such emphasis on maintaining the Yalta Agreement of 1945 which drew lines of demarcation between capitalist and communist spheres of interest. And it accounts for its reaction to what it perceived as counter-revolutionary pressures in Hungary, Czechoslovakia and Afghanistan. No country can ignore its own history, particularly one in which it has been ravaged twice in living memory.

A different set of non-exploitative factors accounts for the Soviet Union's relations with Vietnam, Cuba, Nicaragua, Mozambique, Angola and liberation movements in general. Communism is an ideology which expresses the aspirations of ordinary working people, whether they are wage earners or peasants. The Soviet Union symbolizes that ideology and, therefore, has an identity with working class struggles whenever they take place. Where it is possible for the Soviet Union to give

200

assistance it does so. It has been materially involved in all the major revolutionary movements since 1945, from China to Nicaragua.

This involvement is construed in the West as an international communist conspiracy to subvert and grasp power in Western democracies and their allies which is initiated and directed from Moscow. Communist activity everywhere is perceived in the same terms. The American government reacts to the presence of indigenous communists by describing them as puppets of Moscow; the British government accuses British communists of spreading an "alien ideology", meaning a Russian one, and advises them "to go back to Moscow". Western capitalism views communism as Soviet imperialism. Every act of aid, therefore, whether it takes the form of medical supplies or guns, is regarded as a subversive act in the interest of the Soviet Union. The American government is especially sensitive, therefore, when Soviet aid reaches countries, like Nicaragua, which are in the American sphere of influence. This sensitivity is not like that of the Soviet Union, about protecting its borders. The USA has never experienced war on its own soil since the Civil War nor has it ever been threatened with invasion. There is no possibility of tiny Nicaragua or any other nearby recalcitrant republic threatening the USA in any way. American sensitivity arises from the Western capitalist belief that revolutions can be exported and the main vehicle for doing this is ideology. Social theory in the West, including sociology and economics, teaches that all societies contain intrinsic consensus qualities and that change, in consequence, comes about through external pressures. This is the theoretical basis for the belief in the international communist conspiracy. The Communist Party in the Soviet Union, directed by the Politburo in Moscow, is perceived, therefore, as a conspirator par excellence, converting vulnerable Third World countries to communism.

The reality of the relationship between the Soviet Union and Third World countries is different from this. There has been no example of any country in history experiencing a revolutionary transformation for any reason except contradictions in its own social forces. Revolutions arise only out of material conditions. They cannot be packaged and posted from Moscow, or anywhere else. They are essentially domestic affairs, as the Nicaraguan Sandinistas will testify. Ideas help to clarify issues, to identify the most important causal variables and, therefore, to formulate action which relates to the needs of the situation. In no sense can the ideas have any effect except through the material conditions and for this they have to be strictly relevant. In so far, then, as Soviet propaganda has any impact it is because it is addressed to conditions which already have a revolutionary potential. If the propaganda is hand-made from specifically Soviet conditions then it can have little effect even if a revolutionary potential exists. The gist of this point is that capitalism creates its own revolutions and generates its own ideas about them. Marxism has to have rather special homespun qualities to be of any use.

There is then no possibility of the Soviet Union creating a communist revolution overseas though it can help to sustain one already undertaken. Its main contribution to liberation movements in Third World countries is encouragement firstly by symbolising a successful workers' revolution and secondly by providing comradeship backed by material succour and support. It is of great significance, for instance, for the Nicaraguan peasants to recognize that their struggle is part of a wider struggle for emancipation and that they have friends and allies in various parts of the world. It is also important that they receive material assistance. Whether or not this type of Soviet involvement extends or retards human rights depends on who answers the question. No doubt the Sandinista soldier recuperating in a Soviet rest home and the Nicaraguan peasants defending the Revolution which freed them from the tyranny of an American sponsored dictatorship will think that the Soviet Union has a positive interest in their human rights.

FOOTNOTES

1. *Soviet Economic Development Since 1917* by Maurice Dobb, 1948, pp. 189-191.
2. Szymanski, op. cit., p. 103-4. See also Gail W Lapidus, *Women in Soviet Society,* California, 1978.
3. *Socialism and Capitalism: Score and Prospects,* Progress Publishers, Moscow, 1971.
4. Szymanski, op. cit., p. 39.
5. *Politics and Society in the USSR,* by David Lane, 1970 and 1978, p. 441.
6. *Proceedings of the Sixth International Congress of Celtic Studies,* University College, Galway, 3-13 July, 1979, Dublin, 1983, p. 85.
7. ibid, p. 91.
8. Source: *Proceedings of the Sixth International Congress of Celtic Studies,* 1986, p. 85 and p. 100.
9. ibid, p. 100.

10. Abstracted from *Islamic Peoples of the Soviet Union* by Shirin Akiner, 1983, Tables 2.3 and 2.4, pp. 26-29.
11. *Socialism and Capitalism: Score and Prospects,* op. cit., p. 62.
12. ibid, p. 64.
13. Lane, op cit, p. 398.
14. *Kentucky Economy. Review and Perspective,* Summer, 1984, Vol. 8, No. 2, p. 8.
15. *Power and Powerlessness. Quiescence and Rebellion in an Appalachian Valley,* Oxford, 1980, p. 34.
16. *Colonialism in Modern America: The Appalachian Case,* by Helen Matthews Lewis, Linda Johnson and Donald Askins, North Carolina, 1978, p. 2.
17. *Jewish Responses to Nazi Persecution* by Isaiah Trunk, New York, 1979, pp. 38-39. Also *The Road to Berlin* by John Erickson, 1983. pp. 182-183.
18. Erickson, ibid, p. 124.
19. ibid, p. 147.
20. Akiner, op. cit., p. 87, p. 175, p. 198, p. 203 and p. 227.

PART III
Power in the USA

Chapter Eight
The Potsdam Conference:
A Spoiled Opportunity[1]

History is a process in which great men and women play only minor parts, affecting timing and pace but rarely direction. Occasionally, however, they may figure as a vital part in completing the jigsaw, making for success or failure. In other words, they do not by themselves have any causal significance in determining historical events but without them, events would be different. It is clear, for example, that Lenin did not create the Bolshevik Revolution but that without his leadership it might not have taken place when it did or in the same precise form. The Revolution occurred through an historically unique set of circumstances of which the quality of his leadership was one essential element. It is for this reason, and not as the architects of victory or the creators of defeat, that personalities are interesting.

The part which personalities have played in the history of anti-Sovietism should be analyzed in the same manner. Political leaders moved in and out of the events following the Bolshevik Revolution but until the Second World War started with the involvement of the Soviet Union nothing happened to the historical jigsaw to make them significant. Then, from 1941 there were dramatic changes in the conditions which had given rise to anti-Sovietism.

The two sides, capitalist and socialist, were posited in a situation in which sheer survival became more important than ideological disagreements. As enforced allies, the USA and Britain on the one side and the Soviet Union on the other, recognized the value of mutual support and co-operation. It may have been that this recognition was simply a legitimation and rationalization of the conditions enforced on them. This seemed to be the case with Winston Churchill, the British Prime Minister. He gave total support to the war effort along with the Soviet Union but it was always a matter of expediency. Churchill's mind was never free of schemes which, whilst prosecuting the war, restrained Soviet expansion at the same time. His war strategy was strongly influenced by this factor.

This did not seem to be the case with the US President, Franklin D. Roosevelt, who showed all the signs of conversion in his attitude to the Soviet Union. His wartime experience convinced him that not only should the USA and the Soviet Union collaborate in the post-war period but that they could in fact do so. He reasoned that if it was possible to collaborate in war then why not in peacetime? One consequence of Roosevelt's conversion was that he found himself in disagreement with Churchill more frequently than with Stalin.

It seems clear, therefore, that in the combination of circumstances which forged the wartime alliance the personality of Roosevelt played a significant part. He was not compelled by the force of circumstances in the same way as Churchill. There were not the same powerful dramatic pressures to support the Soviet Union in the USA as in Britain. Indeed in the USA anti-Soviet forces, such as the American Federation of Labor, maintained their stances despite the war. Roosevelt could have been much more circumspect about the Soviet Union than he was without any loss to his prestige. Churchill, on the other hand, would have faced mounting criticism if he had hedged his public support for the Soviet war effort. He was, in any event, criticized for not opening a Second Front sooner than 1944.

The issues raised in this chapter concern the immediate post-war period. President Roosevelt died on 12 April 1945, more than three years before the end of his term of office and a mere 27 days before the final capitulation of the German army. It is a legitimate question to ask whether the war settlement would have been different if Roosevelt had not died. He was succeeded by Harry S. Truman whose attitude towards the Soviet Union remained unalterably hostile during the war. Truman was present at Potsdam in July 1945 when the three heads of state held their only meeting in peacetime, when the news was received of the successful testing of the atom bomb and when the attitudes which coalesced into the 'Cold War' became apparent. There were other changes in the Conference personnel. Winston Churchill's place was taken over by Clement Attlee, the new Labour Prime Minister, but this had no dramatic implications, for the outcome of the Conference, except that Attlee was more compliant in his dealings with the Americans than Churchill would have been.

The Potsdam Conference was a unique historical opportunity. Held in the wake of the victories of the Red Army, it was the first occasion in the history of the Soviet Union in peacetime when it was treated as an equal partner in negotiations with Britain and the USA. Before then the Western capitalist states had always acted from a position of economic and military superiority and with a high degree of contempt and hostility towards the Soviet Union. It was an occasion on which the collaboration of the war years could have been continued but instead it was marked by the transformation of the pre-war Western attitude of 'confident hostility' towards the Soviet Union to one of 'fearful hostility', leading to the 'Cold War'. Lastly it could have been the occasion at which nuclear secrets were shared but instead it was the beginning of the nuclear posturing of the US government.

The previous summit meeting had been at Yalta in the Soviet Union in February, 1945. That conference had been held at a critical phase of the war. A German counter-offensive had been mounted in the middle of December, 1944 and Churchill had appealed for Soviet help to relieve the pressure on the Western Front. A month later the Soviet forces attacked along the Eastern Front for the sole purpose of helping the Western allies.[2] The need for military interdependence was glaringly obvious. The Western allies had no choice but to recognize the Soviet Union as a major power.

The victories of the Red Army, leaving the Germans defeated and demoralized, created a euphoria in Britain about the Soviet Union which pervaded the relations between the countries. Chester Wilmot, a critical observer of the Soviet Union, wrote that "in the Anglo-Saxon countries there was a tremendous upsurge of sympathy and goodwill towards the Soviet Union in recognition of the Red Army's heroic resistance."[3] But there was more to it than an admiration of military prowess. The Red Army had drawn attention to the phenomenal powers of survival and resilience shown by Soviet society in general. Virtually the whole of European Russia had been over-run by the Germans and subjected to a 'scorched earth' policy. Between 1941 and 1945, 1710 cities and over 70,000 villages were razed to the ground. Premier cities such as Leningrad, Kiev, Minsk and Stalingrad were almost totally destroyed. 40,390 miles of railway track were lost as was 60 per cent of the Soviet steel and coal industries. Yet neither the social fabric of Soviet life, nor its economic organization was destroyed. Soviet society recovered and provided the means for victory. The flickering admiration which British workers had expressed for a land without capitalists before the war turned to a glow which had political repercussions. There is no doubt that the Labour Party's unexpected momentous electoral victory in July 1945, on the eve of the Potsdam Conference, was due in part to the popularity of Soviet socialism. The Labour Party owed a debt to the Soviet people which it never repaid or even acknowledged.

The environmental context of Potsdam had other qualities. The European war had ended and with it went the military need for unity. Like countries following successful national liberation struggles, old divisions and some new ones surfaced to make life difficult. There was still some need for collaboration in the Far East but that was rapidly lessening. Roosevelt had asked Stalin for assistance in the war against Japan once the European war was over and this had been agreed at the Tehran Conference in November, 1943. By the time of Potsdam the Americans were apprehensive lest that assistance led to Soviet territorial claims in the Far East. Churchill, observing American reactions, noted to his Foreign Secretary, Anthony Eden, "It is clear that the United States do not at the present time desire Russian participation in the war against Japan."[4] But whilst military prerequisites for international collaboration had gone, economic and political ones had taken their place. The political face of Europe had been transformed by the war. The Red Army was in occupation of a substantial part of East and Central Europe, including Prussia and Berlin, and exercised influence there by protecting the social forces for change and facilitating the rise to power of working class organizations. The Western powers had to put large question marks against the political futures of Poland, Hungary, Czechoslovakia, Rumania, Bulgaria, Yugoslavia and, maybe, Germany itself, which disturbed them. The pre-war fascist regimes which had acted as bulwarks against the spread of communism no longer existed and the West could not assume that similarly compliant governments would emerge.

Virtually independently of this context, however, the British and American delegations went to the Potsdam Conference with different approaches which were partly determined by their own traditional perceptions of wartime unity with the Soviet Union. There was also an important new face at the Conference table. Harry S Truman was a bitter, calculating anti-Communist who, immediately after the Soviet Union was invaded suggested that the United States help whichever side seemed to be losing. He said that "If we see that Germany is winning we ought to help Russia and if Russia is winning we ought to help Germany and that way let them kill as many as possible."[5] One of Truman's first major acts of foreign policy after succeeding Roosevelt as President was to end Lend-Lease deliveries to the Soviet Union on 11 May 1945 without consultation and in such an abrupt fashion that ships on the high seas were recalled with their cargoes. Truman, however, was unsure of himself amidst the great leaders at Potsdam and, in any event, he was still served by aides chosen by Roosevelt. In fact most of the civilian members of the American delegation to Potsdam were career officials in the State Department and Foreign Service who had served Roosevelt.

The difference between the American and British attitudes was accurately expressed by Lord Halifax, the British Ambassador in Washington, when he wrote in a note to Winston Churchill: "I judge that American tactics with the Russians will be to display at the outset confidence in Russian willingness to co-operate. I should also expect the Americans in dealing with us to be more responsive to arguments based upon the danger of economic chaos in European countries than to the balder pleas about the risks of extreme left Governments or of the spread of Communism . . . At the back of their minds there are still lingering suspicions that we want to back Right Wing Governments or monarchies for their own sake."[6] The Americans, in their own briefing notes for Potsdam, confirmed this impression. And even though the British delegation changed during the Conference they had no need to alter their view. Churchill had called a snap election for 5 July 1945 and he had to leave the Conference for the poll result on 26 July. Churchill, whose party was resoundly defeated, did not return. Instead the British delegation comprised the new Prime Minister, Clement Attlee, and the new Foreign Secretary, Ernest Bevin. It is to the lasting shame of that Labour government that its representatives did not reflect the warmth and admiration for the Soviet Union which was being expressed by the majority of the British electorate. The British delegates produced the conventional social democratic hostility to communism which in some ways was more damaging to the Conference proceedings than that of Mr Churchill. Fortunately, Attlee and Bevin, like Truman, were inexperienced and hesitant in world politics.

The Potsdam Conference was one brief but critical moment in the history of contemporary capitalism when the stage of the world was occupied by the Soviet Union with the consent of the

USA and grudging acquiescence by Britain. It was acknowledged in its new status long enough for its imprint to be made on the post-war world. That imprint has been consolidated and enlarged over the last 40 years. If the perception of international power at Potsdam had been different, as it was for example, when Winston Churchill made his speech at Fulton, Missouri, USA on 5 March 1946 in which he stated that "an iron curtain has descended across the continent. Behind that line lies all the capitals of the ancient states of central and eastern Europe . . . subject in one form or another . . . to a very high increasing measure of control from Moscow . . ." then the peace of the world would have been in jeopardy for the third time this century. The post-war settlement expressed through the Potsdam Agreement was based on a balance of power which was not distorted by the intense anti-Soviet propaganda which both preceded and followed it. Any other settlement would have contained instabilities and contradictions which would have disrupted world relationships within a decade for it would not have been based on the reality of post-war power.

The Watershed

The Potsdam Conference was a watershed in the history of hostility shown by the Western capitalist powers towards the Soviet Union. There had been no real break in the Western capitalist desire to destroy the Soviet Union. At first the Bolshevik Revolution was regarded with contempt. Few Western politicans expected the new Bolshevik Government to last longer than six months. When it did their contempt was tinged with annoyance and they intervened. When the war of intervention failed they turned to economic and ideological pressures. But throughout the inter-war years the Soviet Union never ranked high for discussion on the agendas of the Western powers. They adopted an attitude of "confident hostility". They feared communism but did not regard the Soviet Union as a threat in itself. They had a low regard for its militancy prowess as was evidenced by the reporting by the Western press of the Soviet-Finnish War in 1939 and the forecasts by British politicians that the Germans would take from 3 to 6 weeks to conquer the Soviet Union.

The Western perception of Soviet military prowess changed during the second world war. No Western politicians expected the German advances to be reversed when Odessa, Stalingrad and Kiev were occupied, when Leningrad was under siege and German guns were in the Western suburbs of Moscow. None of them expected Soviet industry, eighty per cent of which was on wheels in the autumn of 1941, being transported to the East, to have the resilience for recovery. None of them expected Soviet society to recover from the self-inflicted "scorched earth" policy which they pursued in the fight against the German army. Yet against appalling odds the German army was turned back, Soviet industry did recover and Soviet society was re-established. This was a frightening spectacle for Western capitalists.

Once the war with Germany was over and the war with Japan was in its terminal stage the Western powers were confronted by a Soviet Union which bore no resemblance to that of the inter-war years. The world balance of power had altered inexorably. The Western powers became not simply fearful of communism but also of the Soviet Union. They became apprehensive about every move made by the Soviet Government. They adopted an attitude of "fearful hostility".

As I have indicated above there were forces at Potsdam which prevented the overt expression of fear and hostility and which extended the comradely unity from war into peace. But already tension was building up in the background over such issues as Polish boundaries, the election of governments in Bulgaria, Hungary and Rumania, the allocation of responsibilities in occupied Germany and reparations. There had been a calculated move to divide the Allied Powers even before the final defeat of Germany when the German High Command attempted to negotiate a peace treaty only on the Western Front, leaving it free to fight the Soviet Union. Governments in exile which expressed pre-war political aims and did not reflect post-war realities attempted to regain their positions and in doing so put wedges between the Soviet Union and the Western powers.

Differences over the meaning of democracy emerged in all the discussions about the occupied territories. The Western powers insisted that democracy meant the creation of a multi-party parliamentary system in the mould of their own images and the holding of free elections, while the Soviet Union insisted that democracy could only be based on the assumption of power by the majority, that is the working class. There was no compromise solution to this problem for the Soviet perception involved the removal of power from the minority bourgeoisie while the Western one entailed the continuation of their power position. This difference was the essence of the struggle between capitalism and communism. It took on a new meaning for the West after Potsdam for the influence of Soviet democracy had been extended over much of central and eastern Europe, was growing in China and emerging in South East Asia. The "cordon sanitaire" around the Soviet Union had been broken. It was now the hegemony of capitalism which was under threat. The power of the Soviet Union was not simply something remembered from battles won but could be seen in its extending influence in the world.

This new power situation had important consequences for the anti-communist strategies of Western capitalism. After the Bolshevik revolution the USA engaged in its own ideological cleansing campaign through the Red Scare. When that was over it retreated into isolationism. The British Government conducted its own internal campaign but primarily against the trade union movement, which culminated in the defeat of the General Strike in 1926. Thereafter the progressive forces were fragmented and weakened. There had not been a plague of revolutions following the Bolshevik one. It was sufficient safeguard for capitalist interests to isolate and ignore the Soviet Union.

After the Potsdam Conference the Soviet hegemony could not be ignored by the capitalist countries. It could not be attacked physically though such threats were made. So a war was launched by subversive propaganda and economic destabilization measures. The Cold War which had been unnecessary before 1941 became a necessary part of capitalist reality after 1945. It is unlikely that Roosevelt's presence at Potsdam would have altered this situation significantly. No doubt he would have been more conciliatory in his conversations with Stalin and the 'Cold War' would have been eased slowly in, following a period of political ambivalence. But Roosevelt would have been the political leader of the same combination of forces in the USA as was Truman. The United States had emerged from the war as the world's most economically powerful country. Its war losses had been minimal but its war gains had been tremendous. Capitalism there, after the crisis of the 1930s, was confident, rampant and intolerant. Its newly found assertiveness was reflected subsequently in the electoral victories of the Republican Party in 1946, in anti-labour legislative and McCarthyist political repression but already by 1945 it was beginning to realize its new identity as the messiah of private property. The Potsdam Conference, then, marked both the recognition of Soviet power and the beginning of a campaign by American capitalism to cut it down to size. Franklin D Roosevelt would have had to accommodate to these developments in much the same way as Truman and Eisenhower did though he might have pre-empted Eisenhower's speech of 1961 and warned Americans in better time of the inordinate power of the military-industrial complex.

Nuclear Posturing

The last point concerns the impact of the explosion of the first atomic bomb on 16 July 1945, one day before the Potsdam Conference opened. President Truman knew that the result would be known whilst he was at Potsdam. He was told that the test had been successful on the first day of the Conference. By 21 July, he had received a report on the explosion from General Groves in New Mexico. The following day he was told by Henry Stimson, the US Secretary for War, that a bomb would be ready for use against Japan early in August.

The question of who to inform about the bomb had occupied the minds of Roosevelt, Churchill and others who knew about its development. In 1943 President Roosevelt and Winston Churchill had agreed that "The suggestion that the world should be informed . . with a view to international agreement regarding its control and use is not accepted. The matter should continue to be regarded as of the utmost secrecy; but when a 'bomb' is finally available it might perhaps, after mature consideration, be used against the Japanese who should be warned that the bombardment will be repeated until they surrender".[7] The Interim Committee set up by Roosevelt to deal with policies concerning the production and use of the bomb reached a similar conclusion. So when Stalin attended Potsdam, he had not been told by Roosevelt or Churchill that an atomic bomb was being produced.

The issue took on a new urgency during the Conference. Should Stalin be told or should he learn through its use? If he should be told, then how? How much should he be told? Should all the information about the atomic bomb be shared with the Soviet Union and, therefore, become international property? To some extent all of these questions were pre-empted by the 1943 decision not to inform the Soviet Union about development or research phase. From the outset, the atomic bomb was regarded as the property of the USA and, through affinity, Britain. When the question of its use was raised, therefore, it was in the context of protecting the interests of those countries. From the inception of the 1943 Agreement the atomic bomb was regarded as an instrument to give the Western powers military superiority over the Soviet Union. The occasion of the Potsdam Conference, when the bomb was known to exist but before it had been used, was the last opportunity for making it international property without cumbersome complicated control mechanisms.

Two months before the Conference, Henry Stimson, who chaired the Interim Committee, reflected that the bomb would strengthen the US position if the Soviet Union developed pretensions in the Far East; that it was a "master card in our hand"; that it would enable the US to regain the diplomatic superiority which it had lost to the Soviet Union.[8] Stimson was a liberal who later changed his mind about the matter. Churchill's equivocations were of a different order. He was animated by the news of the explosion and preferred not to inform the Soviet leaders at all about it. But he soon changed his mind and revelled, in conversation with his Chief of Staff, Field-Marshall Lord Alanbrooke, in the use of the bomb to bring the Soviet Union to heel, to restore the diplomatic equilibrium which he considered had been distorted during the war.[9] President Truman was delighted by the news which gave him, he said, an entirely new feeling of confidence. His aides remarked that he showed a new gusto and firmness. Churchill confirmed this impression.[10] He too speculated about the bomb though at this stage it was about whether in exchange for information about it the Soviet leaders would offer concessions to settle the Polish, Rumanian and Yugoslav problems. Thus nuclear posturing had begun.

Nothing would have been easier, given the will, for President Truman to have approached Marshall Stalin on 18 July 1945, for a formal meeting to present him with the news of the successful test, adding that the American government wished to share its atomic information with the Soviet Union and to collaborate in developing nuclear power for peaceful purposes. In effect this is the conclusion Henry Stimson reached in September 1945, on the point of his retirement as Secretary of State for War. He stated that "unless the Soviets are voluntarily invited into the partnership upon a basis of co-operation and trust, we are going to maintain the Anglo-Saxon bloc over against the Soviets in the possession of this weapon. Such a condition will almost certainly stimulate feverish activity on the part of the Soviet towards the development of this bomb in what will in effect be a secret armament race of a rather desperate character . . . To put the matter concisely, I consider the problem of our satisfactory relations with Russia as not merely connected with but is virtually dominated by the problem of the atomic bomb . . ."[11] Stimson was accurate in his estimation but he was too late for the US had already used atomic bombs twice in Japan and had gloried in the power of sole possession.

The Americans at Potsdam did not possess the will to share their findings with their erstwhile ally in war. They did not even explain the nature of the explosion. Instead, whilst the Heads of State were waiting for their cars on 24 July at the end of a Plenary Session, President Truman sauntered over to Stalin by himself and casually mentioned to him that the US "had a new weapon of unusual destructive force". The news was dropped like a piece of gossip. Marshall Stalin said he was glad to hear about it but made no inquiries and appeared to be disinterested. Churchill asked Truman, "How did it go?" and was told "He never asked a question". Stalin's attitude to the question before the Conference remained unaltered. The news had no visible effect upon the outcome of the Conference. So what could have been an occasion of great historical significance became no more than a footnote in the gossip columns.

Once the atomic bomb had been produced, used and accumulated and the Cold War had begun in earnest there was no question of its renunciation by the USA government. At no time did the Americans wish to relinquish the military superiority they believed the bomb conferred on them. All plans and proposals to control nuclear weapons, starting with the Baruch Plan [12] in June 1946 and extending to the Soviet Peace Proposals on 15 January, 1986 to eliminate all nuclear weapons by the year 2000, have stumbled over this fact.

FOOTNOTES

1. A version of this chapter was read at the International Scientific Conference on the Fortieth Anniversary of the Potsdam Conference, at Potsdam, the German Democratic Republic, 18 and 19 July 1985.
2. *Russia is for Peace* by D N Pritt, pp. 12-13.
3. *The Struggle for Europe* by Chester Wilmot, p. 713.
4. *Churchill and the Bomb. A Study of Pragmatism*, by Ernie Troy, 1984, p. 31.
5. *The New York Times*, 24 June 1941, p. 7.
6. Quoted by Herbert Feis in *Between War and Peace*, 1960, p. 157.
7. Quoted by Feis, op cit, p. 172.
8. ibid, p. 80.

9. *Triumph in the West* by Sir Arthur Bryant.
10. Feis, op cit, p. 179.
11. *The Origins of the Cold War 1941-1947* by Walter Lafeber, New York, p. 67.
12. See *Russia is for Peace* by D N Pritt, 1951, chapter VIII for a discussion of the Baruch proposals.

Chapter Nine
The President's Electors

Political Responsibility

The President of the USA has considerable power. He is head of the American armed forces with authority he cannot delegate. He appoints his own government so that it reflects his perception of reality. With a bit of luck he can mould the Supreme Court to endorse his policies. He may have to argue with Congress though that depends upon the balance of political forces at the time. Democratic Presidents have often been able to rely on comfortable majorities in the House of Representatives and of Senate. Whatever the substance may reveal, the form shows a person at the apex of the power structure making decisions on behalf of the American people to whom he is also responsible. His power and prestige are derived from his position as a democratically elected representative of the whole of the American people.

American Presidents, at least since the end of the Second World War, have never tired of reminding the world of their democratic credentials. President Reagan has been especially active in this respect, usually in order to contrast himself with the leaders of socialist countries. They have not made distinctions between themselves and their governments on the one hand and the American people on the other. When they spoke, their voice was that of the American people. This contrasts with the critics of American foreign policy who go out of their way to distinguish between government and people. The ordinary American people are rarely blamed for the consequences of America's acts abroad. Soviet leaders have been particularly concerned to make this dichotomy, emphasizing that when they are attacking American imperialism they are not attacking ordinary Americans. The same has been done in the British Peace Movement, taking care not to generate anti-Americanism when arousing opposition to the American government.

This is not the only occasion on which citizens of a country have been absolved of responsibility for their government's actions.

Nazism, and not the German people, was usually blamed for genocide against the Jews and for the horrors of the Second World War. In some situations where regimes maintain themselves solely through the use of military power it might make sense to split the people from their governments but even there people are ultimately responsible for the form their government takes. Where governments and political leaders claim to be representative of the views of ordinary people, as in the USA, it is analytically incorrect and politically unwise to make such a distinction. It must be presumed that if a government is allowed to operate without protest it is either because its citizens do not want to change it because they agree with it or because they have withdrawn from protest through disillusionment or fear. Either way involves complicity.

It is plain that in order to understand the political processes of any country all the components must be viewed as a dialectically related totality. In the case of the USA, its Constitution, in any event, with its checks and balances, was constructed as a totality. No part makes sense without reference to the other parts. An essential element in it is the electorate for the Constitution was constructed to vest ultimate power and final responsibilities in those people with the right to vote. They were given an inalienable right to choose, to change their minds and to choose again and so on. The functioning of the Constitution depends upon the extent and manner of political involvement of ordinary American people. In order to understand the body politic of American society, therefore, it is necessary to know something about the attitudes of ordinary Americans towards politics, the government, the office of President, to foreign relations in general and the Soviet Union in particular. The Constitution distributes powers for the everyday running of American political life between the Congress, the Executive and the Courts so that each has some degree of autonomy but each is ultimately answerable to the electorate.

This matter of attributing responsibility is a complicated one. One can understand, given the context of Nazi rule, why German families closed their curtains and bolted their doors during the Week of the Broken Glass which started on 9 November 1938 when outside, in an outburst of organized spontaneity, the Nazis destroyed Jewish property, assaulted and killed Jewish people. But were they not assenting to the crimes by hiding their faces and containing their opposition? The Nuremburg Trials after the last war showed that the cut-off point for responsibility for government actions is by no means clearly defined. Are those who execute orders as culpible as those who give them? At what level in the hierarchy of administration were Germans involved in the transportation of Jews to concentration camps, innocent of the crime of genocide? Were the railway guards who facilitated their transportation or the clerks who checked the inventory of confiscated Jewish property innocent or guilty of the crime?

The issue is clearer in the case of South Africa today. White South Africans seemingly identify with the policy of apartheid but does that mean that every white South African should be treated as a pariah? Or is there a cut-off point, say at the level of children where responsibility ceases? But at what age is a person a child without responsibility? We know from the experience of Soweto how foolhardy it is to regard children as of no political consequence.

The American Attitude to Politics

There is obviously a *prima facie* case for implicating the American people in the processes which result in bellicose anti-Sovietism and the nuclear arms build-up. I am not suggesting, however, that the European Peace Movements should start blaming the American people for their complicity. So long as there is an opportunity for the US government to step back from the provocation which could lead to a nuclear war the verdict must be suspended. If the point of no return is ever reached there can be no doubt who the guilty people will be for the only effective way of altering American priorities abroad is through pressures organized by the Americans themselves. They must be reminded constantly of their obligations in the world community.

During the summer of 1984, leading up to the Presidential election in November, I travelled for three months around the coalfields of central Appalachia in Eastern Kentucky, West Virginia, Virginia and Northern Tennessee, observing and talking to ordinary folk, representatives of trade unions, employers, politicians, teachers of different sorts and research workers. The experience showed the American people as being essentially isolationist with little interest in the vast military-industrial complex which provided the impetus for military superiority. It was as if these two vital elements in American society were leading entirely separate lives.

The British, of course, do have a problem when visiting and assessing the USA for they think they know and understand it before they even get there. This sense of knowing stems from sharing a common language and literary culture and from the ideological impact of American films and television soap operas which familiarize us with the trivia of American family life, the Mafia and the police. America, for the British, does not contain variety and contrasts but simply wealthy, corrupt, sensuous jet-setting families, criminals and over-worked, self-righteous police detectives.

The problem reveals itself when the British visitor discovers that Americans are numerous, diverse and distinctly foreign. Despite the common language and the prevalance of European heritages, the USA is a foreign country with a culture which is as alien to the British as those of Central or Eastern Europe. Its customs, practices and institutions have developed out of the peculiar conditions which have comprised American history. The common language creates an illusion; the family stereotype is a con; the over-worked self-righteous detective is a creation of over-worked, self-righteous script writers.

The sharpest of these cultural shocks, however, comes from learning that Americans know relatively little about the lives of other Americans in other parts of their own country and are not particularly interested in them except insofar as they have a personal significance. Coming from a tiny, compact island I expected to find it difficult to visualize the vastness of the USA, covering thousands of miles with mountains, plains, forests and deserts, a variety of climates and a complexity of ethnicity. But my difficulty seemed to be less than that of many Americans who have only a vague conception of the totality of their country. They see and identify with tiny segments, with a state at the most, but usually with a county or a neighbourhood, a hamlet or the hollow where they live.

Americans tend not to see themselves as belonging to a vast complex society delineated by the forces of history. They are insular and parochial in the sense that they often do not even recognize a world outside their own narrowly prescribed experiences. Beyond the state borders things get rather blurred. My distinctly English accent indicated not that I was from a foreign country but came from "out of state". A foreigner was simply a stranger driving a car with an "out of state" number plate on it.

One can understand and appreciate local loyalties and commitments. I admire cultural independence and support national self-determination. It is stimulating to see people determined to preserve their language and culture. As a Welshman whose language was suppressed by English colonialism I share in that determination. It is a commonplace phenomenon in Europe, particularly in the Balkans and among the Baltic states. The Soviet Union has within it more than 100 languages which have been preserved and extended through unrestrained use.

The American variety of loyalties is something different. It does not concern language, ethnicity or culture. It is more a lack of interest in what goes on elsewhere, than a commitment to local, ethnic, community developments. Sadly, its genesis is isolationism. Its consequence is a USA in a universe with no neighbours, no international obligations. It starts with a fragmented electorate distrustful of any form of government, certainly cynical about central government, tolerant of corruption in politics because politics are separated from important subsistance activities. I frequently had conversations with coal miners in Kentucky who, unmoved, described vote buying as if it were a normal and legitimate political activity. This attitude permeates all political persuasions so that even those who describe themselves as socialists reject state intervention as a means of solving economic and social problems because they fail to see state activity as anything but corrupt and demeaning. American coal miners whose problems stem directly from exploitation by multinational coalowners never consider public ownership as even a first step towards their resolution.

The cynicism of Americans towards their political processes causes many of them to withdraw from it altogether. United States residents of voting age can only vote if they are registered voters. American blacks have traditionally been reluctant to register because they have been alienated from politics through the failure of government to tackle their basic problems. In eleven Southern States with a relatively high incidence of black people, only 29.1 per cent of the black population of voting age were registered in 1960 when Jack Kennedy was elected. This figure had risen to 58.5 per cent in the 1984 Presidential election in part because of the Presidential nomination campaign by the black candidate, Jesse Jackson. Amongst the white population of voting age in the same states, 61.1 per cent were registered in 1960 and only 66.5 per cent in 1984. In the United Stated as a whole fractionally over 70 per cent of the population of voting age

223

have been eligible to vote during the last three Presidential elections. Nowadays black and whites distance themselves from politics in almost equal proportions. The world outside of their hollows, their hamlets, their compact neighbourhood communities, goes on despite them. Indeed for many – nothing matters outside of the family struggle for subsistence.

Not all the registered voters use their votes. Indeed the percentage of people of voting age who actually vote has risen more slowly than the percentage increase in registration, signifying that an increasing number of people who are not new registrations are dropping out. The percentage of people of voting age who voted in Presidential elections has risen slowly from 43.6 per cent in 1920 to 59.1 per cent in 1940 when President Roosevelt was at the height of his popularity. In the highly contentious Presidential election of 1948 when Harry Truman was successful only 51.1 per cent of the population of voting age bothered to vote. The percentage rose to 61.4 per cent the next time round in 1952 but fell subsequently until in 1980 it was 52.6 per cent.

The point is that in most Presidential elections almost half of the electorate do not bother to vote. In the internationally critical 1984 election 81,350,000 people eligible to vote did not bother to participate. Harry S Truman, whose policies sparked off the Cold War, was endorsed by only 25.3 per of the American electorate in 1948.[1] President Reagan achieved a landslide victory with the support of only 31.3 per cent of the voting population.

This level of indifference to elections which have dramatic international implications is alarming. The USA to the outside world is not a collection of loosely related, semi-autonomous states or counties but a totality of a mighty industrial machine in the vanguard of technological progress, capable of imposing its will on less powerful countries, of bullying them, of marauding the world like a latter-day swashbuckling pirate. The Cruise missiles in Britain and the Pershing missiles in West Germany are not from Ohio or Maine but from the USA; the naval fleet which patrols the Persian Gulf and Straits of Hormuz does not belong to South Carolina; it is an American fleet. The planes which bombed Libya were American while the military advisers who operate in El Salvador and Honduras are not West Virginians or Kentuckians but Americans. The threat to Nicaragua is from the USA as a totality and not from one part of it.

How the USA holds itself together and conducts itself as a unified nation in the world is of vital concern throughout the world. It has the power to make or destroy. The political processes which produce a President, a government, a Congress can have direct survival consequences for families more than 3000 miles away across the Atlantic Ocean. They have already been decisive for so many families inVietnam, in the Middle East and Latin America.

Now if the Flemish in Belgium or the Serbs in Yugoslavia or the Welsh in Britain concentrate on studying their navels it is of their concern with only minor implications for the wider world. But if the residents of Texas or Tennessee ignore the Federal political processes which produce government decision-makers and fail to see that across the oceans there are people just like themselves who want to live and let live, then they are evading an enormous social responsibility for whether they participate or not, understand the issues or not, the US government makes decisions and deploys its frightening military power.

There is more to this matter than simply a refusal to vote. Many Americans know little about the outside world. It has become fashionable in recent years for American tourists to take sentimental journeys in search of their roots but this is more of a fetish than a concern about their original Europeon communities. When the immigrants arrived from Europe in the 19th and early 20th centuries they consciously cut their roots for themselves and their descendants. Some had an antipathy towards their original countries which has been perpetuated. Many Russian immigrants who escaped the brutality of Czarist Russia have transferred their hatred of Russia into anti-Sovietism without regard for changing circumstances. Facts have not mattered. Indeed in their circumscribed communities, served by local, parochial newspapers which are often on the level of church magazines, and dependent for world news on truncated and partial television reports, the American public is largely unaware of events, people and sensibilities beyond their borders. Except for the occasional 'on the spot' television report, which is tailored for them anyway, Americans rely on information acquired through military service but even this suffers from the influence of ethnocentricity.

There is a renewed interest in American academic circles in the Vietnam War. Questions are being raised about its consequences after more than a decade of silence but they are all about the psychology of Vietnam veterans and not about the Vietnamese people. Even after inflicting such horrendous damage on the communities of Vietnam, Americans focus their minds only on

225

the rehabilitation of their defeated army. Other, earlier wars have been distorted through lapses of memory. This is particularly the case with the Second World War. Polls have shown that many American children believe that the Soviet Union fought with the Nazis against the USA in that war. This, of course, is consistent with the present portrayal of the Soviet Union as the enemy. Some distortions are just plainly bizarre. I was present in July 1984 in a Federal Court in Pikeville, Kentucky to hear a case brought against a Local of the United Mine Workers of America under the Taft-Hartley Act. The Local had called a strike which the coal employer claimed was in contravention of the Act. The Local, on the other hand, said that the employer had provoked the strike so that it would be fined and made bankrupt. The provocation is the crucial bit of the anecdote. The mine had relatively recently been bought by Royal Dutch Shell and on the occasion of a visit to the mine by Shell directors from Holland the management flew the Dutch flag alongside the Stars and Stripes of the USA. This was offensive to the miners in two ways. First, the Dutch flag was not flown the regulation distance below the American flag and, secondly, the miners refused to work under the flag of a country which they alleged was communist and had fought against them in the Second World War. This information had been passed on to them by veterans of that War. The Judge was unable to adjudicate on such a delicate question of patriotism and passed the case on to another court.

The 1984 Presidential election did not even excite interest as a television spectacle. While the world's eyes followed the events from the primaries to Party Conventions, to the hustings and television debates the American public was plainly bored and preferred soap operas. When people do not fully and genuinely participate in the political processes they allow politics to become trivialized, distorted, even corrupted. It was sickening to think that the possibility of detente between the Soviet Union and the USA or the survival of an independent Socialist Nicaragua might depend on the publicity given to the credibility of the tax returns of Mr John Zaccaro, the husband of Geraldine Ferraro the Democratic Party's Vice-Presidential candidate or the vague, unsubstantiated Mafia connections of Mrs Ferraro's husband's father in the 1950s or President Reagan's hesitancy in a television debate or his stumble on the steps of an aircraft. Not even the very real social problems of the USA were aired. Such trivializing was an obscenity.

Consensus and Community Protests

The American language of politics expresses the overwhelming dominance of consensus politics. Communism and Socialism are not terms to be raised, even for denigration or refutation. The label nearest these forbidden categories is 'liberal', associated with the reforms of Roosevelt's New Deal period. But according to a *New York Times* and CBS News poll in November 1984 it was a political disadvantage even to carry that label. Fifteen per cent

TABLE IX[3]

POLITICAL LABELS: WHICH ONES STICK?

The New York Times/CBS News/Poll

The percentage of Americans who said a given label would make them think better or worse of a public figure. For most groups, the percentages were close to those of the entire population, but Southern whites, union members, the elderly and those with low and high family incomes differed from the average.

	Total	Southern whites	Union members	65 years and older	Income Under $12,500	$50,000 and up
Liberal						
Better	15	12	16	19	16	11
Worse	17	26	7	14	12	28
Moderate						
Better	21	23	17	37	25	23
Worse	6	9	8	6	3	8
Conservative						
Better	27	35	22	35	29	30
Worse	13	12	16	7	9	18
Populist						
Better	6	5	7	8	6	6
Worse	21	28	24	20	21	22
Progressive						
Better	37	44	30	45	37	37
Worse	7	8	8	5	7	9

Based on telephone interviews with 1,659 adults, Nov. 6-10, 1984.

of those polled thought better of politicians described as 'liberal' but seventeen per cent thought worse of them. The most popular political labels were 'moderate', 'conservative' and 'progressive'.[2] The meaning of the labels varied, depending on whether the questions were asked of southern whites, union members, pensioners or people with high or low incomes, but, except for the liberal label, the variations were not significant. The ideological dice, as the above table indicates, is loaded in support of capitalism.

The American electorate tends not only to think differently about politics compared to its British counterpart, but to express itself differently in institutional terms. Although American society is economically polarised with a rich elite of employers and a wide base of poverty in the manner of other capitalist societies this is not reflected in institutionalized politics. The working class has no formal presence in American politics. The interests of neither the poor and underprivileged in general nor the substantial minorities of blacks and hispanics in particular are represented in Congress in institutional forms. The approach to equality, poverty and deprivation is an *ad hoc,* individualistic one, dependent upon the presence of sympathetic persons in political positions. In consequence, there are no systematic, organized expressions of opposition to the capitalist system within the legitimate framework of political activity. There are no open debates about alternative forms of society and no rhetoric challenging the dominant ideology. The discussion is concentrated on the centre and right of political options within a common conceptual framework.

The American workers do not use trade unions as a forum for political opposition as do British workers. Trade unionism was extensive and influential during President Roosevelt's New Deal period but since the passage of the Taft-Hartley Act in 1947 and the enforcement in 20 States of oppressive Right to Work laws organized labour has become a declining rump. The percentage of the workforce organized by unions has fallen from about 50 in 1946 to about 18 in 1987. The distribution of organized workers is very uneven between states and industries, leaving many areas virtually untouched by unions. They are strongest in such industries as coal mining, iron and steel, docking and automobile production. They are, therefore, most significant in New York, West Virginia, Michigan, Pennsylvania, Illinois, Missouri, Ohio and Indiana which are old-established centres of industry. But these are areas of declining industry. Moreover, notwithstanding the decline, the frontiers of trade unionism are being pushed back in those industries by aggressive employers and repressive laws. Nowadays only about 65 per cent of American coal miners are organized and they account for less than 50 per cent of total coal production. American workers had a similar experience in the 1920s and they will doubtless recover as they did then. But in the meantime the combination of a serious membership decline with a commitment to the capitalist system has undermined even their role as pressure groups.

The most extensive form of oppositional politics is through community protest groups covering a range of environmental and peace issues. There has been a proliferation of 'Concerned Citizens' associations and 'Community Preservation' groups protesting about strip-mining, chemical pollution, offences against Native Americans and the unrestrained anti-social activities of multi-national companies in general. There are up to 100 national peace groups, focussing on particular aspects of the peace issue such as nuclear testing, S.D.I., or the protection of jobs. And there are many more local peace groups organizing demonstrations and marches, and linking up with protest groups over American involvement in Nicaragua and El Salvador. There is a plethora of groups agitating for a 'Hands Off Nicaragua' policy just as in the late 1960s there were many calling for peace in Vietnam. At community level in the U.S. political action is multifarious and extensive.

The main characteristics of community politics are its source of weakness. It is primarily single issue protest, fragmented and without any ideological basis. It can, therefore, be relatively easily defused. The end of the Vietnam War also signalled the end of protests about American imperialism until the campaign against the U.S. government's involvement in Nicaragua was launched. When the U.S. leaves Nicaragua to determine its own future the public interest in imperialism will again subside until such time as it hurts the American conscience. That is the manner of protest politics. A conciliatory gesture by the U.S. govenment towards the Soviet Union would calm down peace protests; a test ban or a nuclear freeze would convince many Americans to disband their groups. The Peace Movement could expire without having touched the causes of the nuclear arms build-up. The reason for this characteristic of community protest action is that it is not about causes but only their visible manifestations. The action is taken, not because of an analytical understanding of the politics of government or multi-national companies but through a dislike of some consequences of their behaviour. Community protests, therefore, have no permanence though their causes are endemic.

American society is not static or permanent in its present form despite the longevity of its two-party system and its aggressive endorsement of capitalism. The social forces which act on its electorate are continually reshaping its attitudes. Sometimes the changes re-inforce the system as did the rise of the Moral Majority Movement in the late 1970s and the longer-run decline in trade unionism. At other times the contradictions which inexorably beset the system predominate and produce new political alignments. The Civil Rights Movement in the 1960s did not remove the causes of discrimination against American blacks but it did raise their political consciousness so that they more readily identify with oppressed peoples in Third World countries. The correlation of Third World problems with the arms race has taken many of them into the Peace Movement. The rapidly growing population of hispanics provides natural allies for the people of Nicaragua and encourages a sympathetic relationship with the Soviet Union which gives material support to Nicaragua. Women, engaged in their own struggles, form the basis of the Peace Movement and seek detente with the Soviet Union. These changes are giving a wider meaning to community protest action and are encouraging the process of unification. One manifestation of the process was the formation of the Rainbow Coalition in April, 1986, under the influence of Dr Jesse Jackson. Delegates from groups in 42 states attended its inauguration and supported peace initiatives with the Soviet Union. The Rainbow Coalition is as yet merely a tendency within the Democratic Party but it is linking up with the main U.S. Peace Organizations and may eventually form the basis for a national political opposition. All-in-all, the American electorate is slowly, almost unknown to itself, being converted to a new awareness of its world responsibilities.

FOOTNOTES

1. All of the election figures are published in the yearly *Statistical Abstract of the United States* and in *America Votes. A Handbook of Contemporary American Election Statistics*, published every two years by the Elections Research Center, Congressional Quarterly, Washington.
2. *The New York Times*, 24 November, 1984.
3. ibid.

Chapter Ten
The President's Advisers

Institutional Policy-Making

Once the American electorate chooses a President how influential is he in formulating foreign policy? Who is it who dreams up the marauding, vandalizing military escapades which have so often characterized American policies since the end of the Second World War? Who is it who says crush any attempt anywhere to challenge US hegemony? Who says destabilize Chile, invade Grenada, intervene in the Lebanon, crush the Sandinistas in Nicaragua, support reaction in El Salvador, bomb Libya and assassinate Colonel Gadafi? Who, in much broader terms, sets the parameters for a policy of containment of the Soviet Union and within them decides to harbour pre-emptive strike intentions?

There is no doubt that the President of the USA is vested with sufficient formal political and military powers to make all these decisions himself. But he operates within a political context of control specified by the American Constitution. This inhibits certain acts of military aggression and imposes financial constraints on overseas military activities. The President has to carry the American Congress with him in general but in matters concerning the Soviet Union this has never been a problem. More often than not Congress has been a more willing Soviet hunter than the President. All proposals designed as responses to a Soviet threat and have sailed through Congress. A plan to give aid to a Western supported government in Greece in 1947 fell flat in Congress until the Under-Secretary, Dean Acheson, said it was in response to "an eager and ruthless opponent."[1] This scenario was repeated many times, resulting in the financing of NATO, SEATO, bilateral treaties with Japan, Korea and Taiwan at an annual cost of millions of dollars. The Federal coffers were generously open for military programmes and military allies. Congress responded most eagerly when it came to action against the Soviet Union or its allies. It supported constraints on East-West trade, the passing of the Export Control Act of 1949 to

231

regulate American exports and the Battle Act of 1951 to discourage American allies from selling strategic goods. It has always quickly endorsed military action against allies of the Soviet Union, for instance, Korea, Vietnam, Cuba and Grenada. In recent years, since the Vietnam War experience, Congress has been more guarded in its anti-Soviet reflexes but the effect has been to scale down rather than stop action.

Given the willingness of Congress to pursue anti-Soviet policies the President has been given much freedom to develop initiatives without prior Congress approval. Indeed, one political commentator noted that such "a wealth of precedent has been established, through a dozen years of successive crises, that in the world-wide confrontation with communism it was for the president to set the policy, the Congress to support it."[2] How did he, therefore, go about setting the policy? Well, firstly, he did it within the very severe constraints set by the needs of American capitalism. It was never a case of collaborating with the Soviet Union but of altering the methods of containment, of shifting emphases. These emphases, of course, were important and ranged from detente to plain military pugnacity, from the negotiation of treaties to their abrogation, through degrees of Cold War. In the age of nuclear weapons where the President is the Chief of the American armed forces and controls the trigger, a difference in emphasis can mean the difference between a nuclear war or not.

Each of the eight American Presidents since 1945 have operated within an institutional policy-making framework which they have used, adopted or altered according to their own whims. Each President takes over the procedures of his predecessor and fits them for his own use. Within the field of foreign policy there are three sets of institutional interest. There is the Central Intelligence Agency with a high degree of autonomy to pursue peripheral issues; the State and Defense Departments, staffed by career officials with their own resource materials and bureaucratic interests; and the White House itself containing the President and his entourage of advisers. These agencies sometimes project different, contradictory policies, even to the point of cancelling each other's effect. The CIA, of course, is a covert organization so that the public disagreements emanate from the State and Defense Departments and the Pentagon. The President has the last word in such cases but he may only be able to paper over the cracks. The eight Presidents have vacillated in their preferences.

In 1947 President Truman established the National Security Council, run by a National Security Assistant, in the White House. The contenders for the ear of the President have thus been the National Security Assistant, the Secretary of State and, to a lesser extent, the Secretary of Defense. The President, of course, appointed each one, but the National Security Assistant has become a pivotal position with a relatively easy access to the President, able to accumulate influence and to assume the role of the premier adviser. Henry Kissinger was the classic case of the premier adviser when he was the National Security Assistant to President Nixon. The changes in the relationships between policy-making agencies have largely involved reducing the status of the National Security Assistant in relation to the Secretary of State and then building it up again. Much then depended in this struggle upon the personalities involved and the advisers with whom each was able to surround himself.

The President chooses his Executive, or government, and all his principal advisers. Usually a new President replaces the whole upper layer of officials concerned with foreign affairs and defense, from members of the Cabinet, the National Security Assistant and his staff down to assistant secretaries and even lower in some instances. He is not constrained in his choice by political party affiliations. He can, and often does, go outside of political parties to industry, banks and universities for candidates. He may not have any particular source except his friends, as in the case of President Reagan. By and large Presidents have gone to manufacturing and finance institutions for people with executive talent and to universities for advisers. The universities, particularly the elite Ivy League ones, have served the Presidency well. The Harvard historian Arthur Schlesinger, the economic historian W W Rostow from the Massachusetts Institute of Technology, Eugene Staley the Stanford University economist, McGeorge Bundy, the Dean of Humanities at Harvard University, Henry Kissinger, the specialist in international relations at Harvard University and the Soviet specialist Zbigniew Brzezinski have all achieved notoriety as advisers.

The Classic Role of Academics

But what exactly do they contribute? Firstly, the majority of American Presidents have been virtually ignorant of foreign affairs. Only Presidents Eisenhower and Nixon had any prior experience of international affairs. Eisenhower's experience came as the Supreme Commander of the Allied Forces in Europe during the Second World War and as head of NATO in 1951-52. Nixon acquired experience during his eight years as Vice-President to Eisenhower. The rest had been either Senators or State Governors. They desperately needed advice in well-packaged briefings or, as with President Reagan, in easily understood video recordings. The nature of the advice varied with the personality of the President. Three Presidents, Truman, Eisenhower and Nixon each wanted a clearly articulated general policy towards the Soviet Union which would provide answers to ad hoc issues. Presidents Kennedy, Johnson and Carter pursued pragmatic policies and therefore required detailed assessments of issues as they arose. Kennedy, for example, modified his position after the Cuban missile crisis as Carter did after Soviet troops entered Afghanistan. President Reagan, mistaking a "rhetorical stance for strategy"[3] is more dependent upon script-writers than advisers.

But whether they provided the broad sweep policy, packaged like the Truman Doctrine, or, for example, a highly detailed assessment of Soviet influence in Mozambique, the academic advisers gave theoretical legitimation for the dominant ideas in American capitalist society. They added different glosses to the same product. The slogans and clichés which rolled off the tongues of Presidents and their Press Secretaries, the slick public relations expressions of foreign policy, the justifications for foraging into some foreign country such as 'defending the free world', 'protecting democracy' and 'preserving the American way of life', all have had their bases in the theorizing of foreign policy specialists in universities and research institutes.

The classical role of academics is to serve the status quo through formulating complex erudite theories and explanations no matter how cruel and oppressive the system might be. The killings in Chile, the mining of Nicaraguan harbours, the genocidal attacks on Vietnam, the bombing of Libya all have their theoretical justification in the theses of American academics.[4] This point was made more explicitly by André Gunder Frank in his article "The Sociology of Development and Underdevelopment of Sociology".[5] He wrote: "Roosevelt's and Kennedy's brains trusts co-opted all sorts of American social scientists. Harvard historian Arthur Schlesinger Jr's aid to the development of underdeveloped countries has so far consisted in writing the now famous White Paper on Cuba which was intended to justify the coming invasion of that country at the Bay of Pigs. He later admitted lying about the invasion in the "national interest". Stanford economist Eugene Staley wrote *The Future of Underdeveloped Countries* and then planned it in the renowned Staley – (General Maxwell) Taylor Plan to put 15 million Vietnamese in the concentration camps they euphemistically christened "strategic hamlets". Since the failure of that effort at development planning, MIT economic historian Walt Whitman Rostow has escalated the effort by writing *The Stages of Economic Growth: A Non-Communist Manifesto*. He wrote of these stages at the CIA – financed Center for International Studies on the Charles River and has been operationalizing them on the Potomac as President Johnson's chief adviser on Vietnam. It is on behalf of economic growth that Rostow has become the principal architect of escalation, from napalming the South to bombing the North and beyond . . . Meanwhile, after performing his role as Dean of Humanities at Harvard University, McGeorge Bundy becomes W W Rostow's superior in Washington, and goes on television to explain to the misguided and incredulous why this economic development theory and policy is humanitarian . . ." Gunder Frank, whose concern is with developing countries, stated that "the American social scientific way of life . . . has its own essential role in the imperialist exploitation, oppression, and underdevelopment of the majority of mankind."[6] He was, in fact, writing about academics in general. Rarely do they bite the hand that feeds them. They endorse the legitimacy of free, private enterprise and facilitate its survival. They damn as unworthy, oppressive, brutal, anything which gets in its way. And they do it all so cleverly, in moderated tones and footnoted texts. And in case their readers begin to ask disturbing questions they avoid the sticky ones, like the parts played by military-industrial complexes and the social consequences of their actions. Somewhere in the Pentagon Files there must be a memorandum explaining the effectiveness of theatre nuclear war as a means of dampening the ardour of the Soviet Union.

Detente or Containment

The President's advisers on Soviet policy base their analyses, and therefore their advice, on assumptions about the Soviet Union. They would claim, of course, that whatever they assume is derived from the behaviour of the Soviet Union and does not need to be verified. Indeed the time has long since past when statements about the Soviet Union have to be substantiated by empirical evidence. The assumptions they make are consistent with the dominant capitalist view of communism and, therefore, endorse the contention that the Soviet Union is the enemy of the USA. The policy options which follow from this are limited and obvious.

Academic advisers are invariably specialists in one aspect or other of foreign relations who have written extensively on their subjects. It is possible, therefore, to discover their attitudes and, within them, to identify their biases. But this would be an arduous and rather tedious process. Professor Joseph S Nye Jnr, professor of government at Harvard University has simplified the task by putting together the views of 13 advisers about different aspects of US relations with the Soviet Union in a single volume. In a book called *The Making of America's Soviet Policy*[7] 13 high ranking academics who have served as advisers covering the period from 1945 till 1984 explain their views succinctly and to the point. Eight of the essayists are from Harvard University. American Presidents, despite their own origins, seem to hold a common view about the source of intellectual excellence. All of the contributors deal with American-Soviet relationships from the point of view of American policy-making institutions. Each one postulates the Soviet Union as an enemy. The task of American foreign policy then has to be to disarm, contain, weaken and, maybe, as a last resort, to destroy the Soviet Union. The advice is always concerned, therefore, with deterring, destabilizing and direct confrontation.

The advisers thus limit themselves, in effect, to two options; either to seek accommodation through detente or to contain the Soviet Union through military superiority. The essays are pervaded by a suspicion of detente. One contributor, Robert R Bowie, a scholar with an illustrious record as an adviser, formerly Director of the Harvard Center for International Affairs, described the "Nixon detente" as the most costly mistake in post-war American strategy, along with the Vietnam War.[8] Another contributor, Stanley Hoffmann, chairman of the Center for European Studies at Harvard University put the issue more explicitly. "But once detente is", he wrote, "so to speak, in orbit, the issue becomes one of preventing the Soviets from, or punishing them for, doing hostile things, and the tools first used as goods must now be used as possible sanctions, the carrots must become sticks . . ."[9] Detente, Hoffmann argued, began to be seen as appeasement. He added: "What made this view fashionable way beyond the conservative and neo conservative fringes was a combination of three factors. One was the worry about the changes in the strategic balance . . . A second factor was growing indignation at Soviet human rights violations . . . A third one was the evidence of fiascos abroad: in South East Asia, in southern Africa . . ."[10] One of the lessons Hoffmann drew from an analysis of detente, and presumably this would be listed as a policy recommendation, was to "be modest in our expectation about Soviet behaviour . . . It is not in our interest to make of the Soviet Union a partner in the settlement of conflict far removed from its area of vital interests. It is not in our interest to sign vague statements of principle. It is not likely that trade can ever become a major factor in Soviet-American relations . . ."[11] And so the recommendations were handed from one adviser to another.

If this is the view about detente, then what about the alternative option: containment through strength? The logic of this option means not simply nuclear superiority but destroying every visible evidence of the spread of Soviet influence, wherever it is found – in other words, repressing progressive movements. And just as attempts to quell domestic communism spill over to become generally repressive of progressive movements because of the difficulty of identifying communism as a social force, so international anti-communism becomes general and indiscriminate repression. Any country which attempts to distance itself from the hegemony of American capitalism becomes a target. Libya has suffered largely for this reason. Nicaragua, Mozambique and Angola are other targets of US hostility. Tiny Grenada was invaded for its affront to the USA. Ordinary people suffer; they may be killed; their environments are shattered. The costs can be horrendous as the millions of dead and injured Vietnamese testify. Seen in this light the alternative to detente has no moral basis: it is plainly evil.

The academic advisers who wend their way through the leafy suburbs of bourgeois America, with their briefcases containing their precious Soviet policy memoranda, are not paid to count social costs. Their task is to provide options. It is governments which choose. They would, in any event, be abhorred by the suggestion that they were in any sense responsible for devastating ordinary people's lives, for underpinning the script of 'Rambo' as single-handedly he rampages against communists. But that is precisely what they are doing. Not, of course, on their own. The basis of American foreign policy is to protect the international rights of private capital, which, in effect, means the interests of multi-national companies. The President's advisers compound the pressures which those interests generate and which comprise the military-industrial complex. They provide respectable cover. The origin of international tyranny, however, is not wholly institutional. Many individuals, whose lives may seemingly be otherwise unblameworthy contribute to it. They, as well as vast institutions, have a moral responsibility for the consequences of their actions.

FOOTNOTES

1. *Present at the Creation: My Years at the State Department* by Dean Acheson, 1969, p. 219.
2. *The Decline and Resurgence of Congress* by James L Sundquist, 1981, p. 118.
3. "The President and the Executive Branch" by Robert R Bowie, in *The Making of America's Soviet Policy,* ed by Joseph S Nye Jr, 1984, p. 67. This is an informative if biased account.
4. I am not suggesting that only American academics engage in this practice. No matter what the society, academics generally, though not invariably, engage in it though most do not really know that they are doing it.
5. First published in the Summer, 1967 issue of *Catalyst* and reprinted numerously. It is taken here from *Latin America: Underdevelopment or Revolution* by André Gunder Frank, 1969, p. 28.
6. *Critique and Anti-Critique. Essays on Dependence and Reformism* by André Gunder Frank, 1984, p. 19.
7. *The Making of America's Soviet Policy* edited by Joseph S Nye Jr, A Council on Foreign Relations Book, Yale University Press, 1984.
8. ibid, p. 91.
9. ibid, p. 248.
10. ibid, pp. 256-7.
11. ibid, p. 260.

Chapter Eleven
The President's Masters[1]

The Valedictory Speech of President Eisenhower

When in January 1961, Dwight D Eisenhower left his office after two terms as President of the USA it was expected that the old soldier would engage in a bit of sentimental leave-taking and slip quietly away for a game of golf. Much to the surprise of political commentators in Washington he did not do this but instead launched a bitter criticism of the military leaders and arms manufacturers who had shaped his foreign policies.

Although Eisenhower was a Republican President he had been courted by the Democratic Party which would dearly have liked to have him as its presidential candidate in 1948 instead of Harry S Truman. There was, in those days, little difference at least in the foreign policies of the two parties. Eisenhower continued the Cold War policies of Truman though in a more conservative manner. His tenure, though interspersed with dramatic domestic and international events, was not characterized by intelligent, independent political decision-making. He was ranked as average by a group of historians who had been asked to rate Presidents of the USA according to their performances.[2]

President Eisenhower was sternly anti-communist and in his discussions with his successor, John F Kennedy, he listed "the continuing Communist Threat to the West" as one of the foremost problems facing him.[3] He accepted the National Security Council Document 68 produced in 1950 at Truman's request which portrayed the Soviet Union as an implacably hostile, expansionist military threat which had to be countered by an expanded Western conventional and nuclear military force. More than Truman, he played down conventional arms and treated nuclear weapons as part of the arsenal to be employed wherever they could be militarily and politically useful.[4] He had been willing to use covert means to resist the spread of communism in Third World countries. In Iran in 1953, Eisenhower directed the CIA to topple the Premier Mohammed Mossadeq and install the Shah in his place, which it did. The following year, when the CIA informed Eisenhower that the legitimate government of Guatemala was communist in its composition and policies he toppled it by military force and then went on television to tell the American people "that communism's first foothold in the hemisphere had been halted by an uprising of freedom-loving Guatamalans".[5] The CIA displayed its new found status and power under Eisenhower when it opened its vast new offices in Langley, Virginia in 1959.

The Soviet achievement in launching Sputnik 1 in October 1957 shocked the American people. "Overnight," it was reported, "there developed a widespread fear that the country lay at the mercy of the Russian military machine and that our own government and its military arm had abruptly lost the power to defend the mainland itself . . ."[6] American spending on space and missile research escalated. Already, at the beginning of Eisenhower's Presidency, following the end of the Korean war, the defence budget had been tripled. In his final budget statement it was announced that US spending on defence had reached a peacetime record.[7] He left a considerable legacy: "a substantial military and space programme that would reach fruition under later administrations, and also the foundations of a policy on outer space that would guide future U.S. presidents for many years."[8]

President Eisenhower gave little indication during his tenure of an awareness of problems in the international capitalist power structure. He refused to support Britain's imperialist venture during the Suez crisis of 1956 but given America's own role in Latin America and the Far East that was plain hypocracy. He had had several opportunities during the Congressional debates over defence programmes in his second term to express his concern about the way in which private profit-making exploited the interests of national security but had said nothing apart from an occasional cryptic remark at his news conferences that "obviously something besides the strict military needs of this country are coming to influence decisions".[9]

In a variety of ways Eisenhower consolidated the power of American capital. He refrained from publicly criticizing Senator Joseph McCarthy in his witch-hunt of communists and allowed him a free-ride. He permitted the harassment of Robert J Oppenheimer, the scientist most responsible for constructing the first atomic bomb, for his dissenting opinions and past association with communists. And he failed to respond to widespread national and international pressure to grant clemency to Ethel and Julius Rosenberg in 1953, sentenced to death for allegedly passing secret information on the production of atomic bombs to the Soviet Union. In general, President Eisenhower disliked political dissent because, he argued, it provided communists with contentious issues to exploit.

Halfway through his second-term of office, Eisenhower decided to expose the influence of the post-war complex of power-holders in the USA, but to do so in his last major speech when, of course, it was too late for him either to do anything about it or to face the repercussions. Perhaps he wanted to avoid the derogatory treatment of dissenting views by American society at that time. The sociologist, C. Wright Mills, had described the locus of power in American capitalism in 1959 when he wrote: "Within American society, major national power now resides in the economic, the political, and the military domains . . . The economy—once a scatter of small production units in autonomous balance—has become dominated by two or three hundred giant corporations, administratively and politically interrelated, which together hold the keys to economic decisions . . . The military order, once a slim establishment in a context of distrust fed by state militia, has become the largest and most expensive feature of government . . ."[10] C. Wright Mills was both distrusted by the establishment and discriminated against in his own University because of his opinions. Yet what he wrote was a mild observation compared to the televised valedictory speech made by President Eisenhower from the White House on 17 January 1961, three days before he finally relinquished office. Quite clearly Eisenhower's speechwriter, Malcolm Moss, should have been his political advisor. Eisenhower said:

"America is today the strongest, the most influential and most productive nation in the world. Undoubtedly proud of this pre-eminence, we yet realize that America's leadership and prestige depend . . . on how we use our power in the interests of world peace and human betterment. . . .

We face a hostile ideology – global in scope, atheistic in character, ruthless in purpose and insidious in method . . . . But threats, new in kind or degree, constantly arise. Of them I mention only two. A vital

241

element in keeping the peace is our military establishment . . . Until the latest of our world conflicts, the United States had no armaments industry . . . We have been compelled to create a permanent armaments industry of vast proportions. Added to this, three and a half million men and women are directly engaged in the defense establishment. We annually spend on military security alone more than the net income of all United States corporations.

Now this conjunction of an immense military establishment and a large arms industry is new in the American experience. The total influence – economic, political, even spiritual – is felt in every city, every state house, every office of the Federal Government. We recognize the imperative need for this development. Yet we must not fail to comprehend its grave implications. Our toil, resources and livelihood are all involved; so is the very structure of our society.

In the councils of Government we must guard against the acquisition of unwarranted influence, whether sought or unsought, of the military – industrial complex. The potential for the disastrous rise of misplaced power exists and will persist.

We must never let the weight of this combination endanger our liberties or democratic process. We should take nothing for granted. Only an alert and knowledgeable citizenry can compel the proper meshing of the huge industrial and military machine of defense with our peaceful methods and goals so that security and liberty may prosper together.

Akin to and largely responsible for the sweeping changes in our industrial-military fortune has been the technological revolution during recent decades.

In this revolution research has become central. It also becomes more formalized, complex and costly. A steadily increasing share is conducted for, by, or at the direction of the Federal Government . . . The prospect of domination of the nation's scholars by Federal employment, project allocations and the power of money is ever present and is gravely to be regarded.

Yet, in holding scientific research and discovering in respect . . . we must be alert to the equal and opposite danger that public policy could itself become the captive of a scientific-technological elite . ."[11]

President Eisenhower's warning went unheeded. It was in any event too late. His statement was about a special case of the power of monopoly capital which in one vital respect was a deviation from the norm. For the first time in American history, government had become the executive not merely of a bourgeois class which was motivated by personal profit-making but by one which sought profit from war. More importantly, as conventional arms were displaced as prime weapons by nuclear missiles the profits were sought from means which could lead to the annihilation of the world. This process had begun with the Manhatten Project in 1945 but was leisurely until the Soviet Union had tested its first bomb in 1949. As the Soviet Union had no means of launching an atomic bomb for another decade the pressure on the US to accumulate nuclear weapons was not great.

The Rhetoric of Presidents

The mood of America, changed by the launching of Sputnik I, was heightened by the Cuban crisis in 1962. After his inauguration in January 1961, immediately following Eisenhower's speech, John Kennedy started a rapid acceleration of nuclear arms production. The feasibility of a limited nuclear war was discussed. And although the balance of nuclear military power lay overwhelmingly with the USA in 1962, the Cuban crisis caused the President to accelerate even further the production of space and nuclear missiles. This arms building spree was in the services of a rampant imperialism. The USA, by 1959, had a total of 275 major base complexes in 31 countries and more than 1,400 foreign bases, counting all sites where Americans were then stationed and sites designed for emergency occupation. The bases were manned by approximately a million American troops.[12] The USA was a member of NATO and the South-East Asia Treaty Organization and had bilateral treaties with dozens of countries as a means of isolating and containing communism. It was increasingly implicated in trying to prevent the Vietnamese from obtaining independence. As the conflict with Vietnam unfolded the armaments manufacturers were given a real war to exploit. The rate of consumption of US ammunition during a peak month of the Vietnam War was greater than for a comparable period in the Second World War or the Korean War.[13] The 1973 Yom Kippur War in the Middle East prompted a further expansion in the US ammunition base as the Americans speeded up supplies to the Israelis. From 1970 to 1978 the army alone spent $1.8 billion on an unprecedented programme of ammunition plant modernization.

The rhetoric of the Presidents varied. President Kennedy paled Eiserhower into insignificance, describing Eisenhower's mushroomed defence expenditure as complacent, passive and inadequate. He advocated a global anti-communist role for the US which re-affirmed the image of the Soviet Union contained in Truman's National Security Document 68.[14] Kennedy exposed a "flexible response" tactic with an increase in ground forces, intercontinental ballistic missiles, Polaris and tactical nuclear weapons. However, he moderated his approach to the Soviet Union before he was assassinated. This re-appraisal continued throughout President Johnson's period of office during which time there were agreements with the Soviet Union on the 'hot line', grain sales to the Soviet Union, the Limited Test Ban Treaty, the Non-Proliferation Treaty, plans for strategic arms talks and 'bridge-building' efforts through trade and communciations with Eastern European socialist countries. Detente was counterbalanced by the Vietnam War for Presidents Johnson and Nixon. The rhetoric was placatory. Nixon reaffirmed treaty commitments and the nuclear deterrence but destabilized whenever he could, as in Chile, and sought to strengthen the position of the USA through links with China. President Ford, who filled in after President Nixon had been impeached, relied wholly on Nixon's Secretary of State, Henry Kissinger, and continued Nixon's balancing act. President Carter started his tenure in 1976 in a conciliatory mood, trying to gain the acceptance of the second Strategic Arms Limitation Agreement, SALT-2, by the US Congress. The agreement was never submitted to the US Senate for ratification and Carter asked for it to be taken off the Senate's calendar after Soviet troops had moved into Afghanistan in December, 1979. By that time US opinion had begun to harden against the Soviet Union and along with it went President Carter. The US administration, still following Trumen's NSC Document 68, saw the Soviet hand in the national liberation movements which were spreading in Africa and Latin America. President Carter, trying to match the stridently anti-Soviet rhetoric of Ronald Reagan in his Presidential campaign, signed Directive 59 in July 1980, which marked the abandonment of deterrence and gave priority to a first-strike capability. By the time of the Presidential Election in 1980 there was little to distinguish between the policies of the two main candidates. However, the winner's rhetorical belligerence, his public preference for increased expenditure on arms, his hostility towards national liberation movements, his predilection for ignoring treaties and his endeavour to take the arms race into space, marked him off from his predecessors. President Reagan reflected an accumulation of the most bellicose phases of post-war Presidents.

The background to the rhetoric, however, no matter how shrill, was similar for all the Presidents. Frequently their rhetoric was not matched by corresponding policies. The conciliatory tones did not halt the research, planning and development of nuclear, chemical and conventional weapons, nor did implacably hostile attitudes necessarily indicate that preparations were underway to wage war. Presidents were pragmatic in their responses, changing them like the wind and rarely getting their acts together. Under President Reagan, for example, there was a greatly increased arms programme but without a consistent strategy so that he opposed the Siberian oil pipeline yet promoted grain sales to the Soviet Union.

US Expenditure on Arms

The backcloth to this background was the extent to which military expenditure cut into the US gross national product. The USA consistently diverted more of its resources to military uses than any other Western capitalist country. In 1983, the US expended at least twice as much of its GNP on military production as any other capitalist country, apart from the UK, Greece and Portugal. The variations in the proportion of the GNP devoted to arms generally reflected America's imperialist activities. It was high under John F Kennedy because of the fear generated by the launching of Sputnik I, the Cuban crisis and heightening international tension. It remained high during the years of detente with the Soviet Union because of the Vietnam War and fell sharply once the Americans began to pull out. The proportion was at its lowest point in the brief period between the end of the Vietnam War in 1974 and end of detente 3 or 4 years later. Then it began to climb as more resources went for nuclear arms in general and space research in particular. Table XI shows first how the U.S. reacted to the launching of Sputnik I with a sevenfold increase in the amount devoted to space research in a period of 4 years. Quite clearly the relaxation of tension during detente enabled the Americans to soft peddle on space research and to focus their minds on Vietnam and the Middle East. During the Yom Kippur War in 1973 the USA sent considerable supplies of arms to Israel and assumed a continuing high level presence in that area. The change in emphasis came during President Carter's period of office but with little publicity. The table shows the phenomenal increase in space research and development after Ronald Reagan was elected as President.

TABLE X

ARMS EXPENDITURE IN THE USA AS A PERCENTAGE OF THE GROSS NATIONAL PRODUCT, 1963-1983[15]

(1) Year	(2) Arms expenditure as Percentage of GNP	(3) Percentage changes in col (2)	(4) Encumbent[16] President
1963	8.86		John F Kennedy
1964	8.1	−8.6	Lyndon Johnson[17]
1968	9.3	+14.8	Lyndon Johnson
1972	6.6	−29.0	Richard Nixon
1976	5.3	−19.7	Gerald Ford[18]
1980	5.5	+3.8	Jimmy Carter
1984	6.9[19]	+25.5	Ronald Reagan

The military-industrial complex, whose interests are served by the increases in defence expenditure, has been exercising greater influence over Presidential and, therefore, government, decision-making. It has set the hidden agendas of post-war US governments, establishing their priorities so that issues affecting the welfare of the people, such as jobs, education, health-care facilities and social security have been pushed to the bottom of the list. Its influence, moreover, has not been exercised through secret breakfast meetings with the President, though these undoubtedly have had some significance, but through the manner in which defence expenditure has become pivotal in the economies of local communities throughout the USA, often determining their economic survival.

TABLE XI

SPACE EXPENDITURE BY THE US GOVERNMENT, 1963-1984[20]

(1) Year	(2) Total Space Expenditure (Millions of dollars)	(3) Percentage changes in col (2)	(4) Encumbent[21] President
1959	784.7		Dwight Eisenhower
1963	5434.5	+592.6	John F Kennedy
1964	6831.4	+25.7	Lyndon Johnson
1968	6528.9	−4.4	Lyndon Johnson
1972	4574.7	−29.9	Richard Nixon
1976	5319.9	+16.3	Gerald Ford
1980	8688.8	+63.3	Jimmy Carter
1984	17477.3	+101.1	Ronald Reagan

Each President is served by a network of advisory bodies. When he has a problem or when he wants clarification of an issue, perhaps even when he wants information, there is always a study group or departmental committee ready to serve him. The advice he gets, say on the choice of weapons systems, may be important for the fortunes of particular manufacturers but it is not vital for the military-industrial complex as a whole. In general it is a ritual which gives an acceptable image to the process of private profit-making.

When the Reagan administration was formed early in 1981 it gave no indication of its policy on space issues. In August, President Reagan directed the National Security Council to review space policy. As he had no knowledge of such matters and was inexperienced in foreign affairs this seemed a sensible step to take. The NSC set up an inter-agency working group consisting of representatives of the Departments of State, Defense and Commerce, the Central Intelligence Agency, the Chiefs of Staff of the Armed Forces and of a number of government agencies like the National Aeronautics and Space Administration (NASA). The military was well represented but not the private armaments manufacturers.

The advice given to Reagan, as to his predecessors, came from the professionals in government departments and economic agencies. The different Presidential encumbents varied in the ways in which they sought this advice, by overplaying or underplaying the role of the National Security Council in relation to the Departments of State and Defence, by preferring informal meetings, as did Kennedy, or secret cabals, as did Nixon, often including only himself and Henry Kissinger. Whichever method was used there was competition between the players, private and public arguments about alternative courses of action; there were doves and hawks often negating each other but essentially playing the same game, as with Casper Weinberger the inveterate hawk and George Shultz the uncertain dove in the Reagan administration.

It was a year before Reagan received advice from the space review study group but long before then the parameters of government policy had been pronounced by Casper Weinberger, the new Secretary of Defense, when, in October 1981, he said that the USA would "continue to pursue an operational antisatellite system" in pursuit of the government's declared policy of being able to fight and prevail in a nuclear war.[22] In a step which gave a practical twist to Weinberger's statement, and in the same month as he made his speech, the government awarded contracts worth $418.8 million to the giant armaments firm, Vought and Boeing, to continue with research into an antisatellite system. This put the space review into perspective. It was to provide operational details for an already articulated policy.

SDI Contracts

The Strategic Defense Initiative provides a similar example. President Reagan made his "Star Wars" speech on 23rd March, 1983 which purported to initiate research into a major ballistic missile defence system. It was described as a speech from the top.[23] Apparently even the Secretary of State, George Schultz, and the Secretary of Defense, Casper Weinberger, knew of it only in its final states. But which top? The effect was to accelerate the transfer of US resources to defence expenditure and, within that, to gain space research priority over other defence items. From 1980 until 1984 the expenditure on space activities more than doubled. During 1983 and 1984 it rose from $12,440.7 million to $17,477.3 million an increase of 40.48 per cent. There were many beneficiaries. On the day of the summit meeting on 19th November 1985 between President Reagan and Mr. Mikhail

248

Gorbachev *The New York Times* published the following two tables:

TABLE XII

'STAR WAR' CONTRACTS AND CONTRACTORS[24]

The largest prime contractors ranked by total 1985 Strategic Defense Initiative Awards. Listed in millions of dollars, excluding government agencies.

COMPANY	CONTRACTS AWARDED	PRIMARY RESEARCH AREA
Boeing	$112.2	Airborne infra red sensor
TRW	84.3	Mirad ground based laser; Alpha space based laser
Hughes Aircraft	60.1	Airborne sensors, kinetic energy weapons
M.I.T.'s Lincoln Labs.	59.7	Processing sensor data
Avco	53.4	Laser research, optical tracking
Lockheed	45.7	Laser research, kinetic energy weapons
Rockwell	42.0	Gallium arsenide semi-conductors, space surveillance and tracking
Teledyne Brown Eng.	40.1	Systems engineering
LTV Aerospace	25.1	Radar interceptors, homing devices
Aerojet-General	22.6	Sensor experiments, space boosters

The above tables show only the most lucrative contracts. At that time the top ten SDI contractors commanded more than 60 per cent of the contract money. The firms most preferred by the government were those which were well established in the nuclear missile business and which had built Minuteman Missiles, MX missiles and military satellites. The Pentagon had already spent more than $2 billion on space defence research spread over more than 1,500 contractors. Indeed in October 1985, the

TABLE XIII

'STAR WAR' CONTRACTS AND CONTRACTORS[25]

Total awards to date to prime contractors for all projects, in millions of dollars.

COMPANY	TOTAL AWARDED TO DATE
TRW	$323.9
Boeing	217.4
Lockheed	192.0
Teledyne Brown	180.0
Rockwell	165.7
Hughes Aircraft	155.7
LTV Aerospace	98.6
McDonnel Douglas	75.9
Avco Corporation	72.7
BDM International	62.4

government had published a 28 page list of SDI related contracts, many of which had gone to small enterprises. The amount of money spent on space research was miniscule by Defense Department standards but the programme's potential was not, for the estimates for a fully deployed system varied between $400 billion and $1.5 trillion. The firms were still in the paper phase of research and the real profits were due when they engaged in technology demonstrations of specific hardware systems from laser weapons to advanced radar systems. Nonetheless an industry had already risen around SDI during the previous 18 months in California's aerospace and electronic industries centre.

President Reagan's televised speech mapped out his goal. It was to "embark on a program to counter the awesome Soviet missile threat with measures that are defensive" but he was vague about the scope of the protection to be provided and the means to achieve it. Was he, for example, contemplating a single system? Would it provide a complete population defence? Was it, in any event, feasible? Two days after the speech Reagan signed National Security Decision Directive 85, entitled "Eliminating the Threat from Ballistic Missiles" which directed the bureaucracy to conduct "an intensive effort to define a long-term research and development programme aimed at an ultimate goal of eliminating the threat posed by nuclear ballistic missiles". To facilitate this effort he ordered a study to be undertaken "to assess the roles that ballistic missile defence would play in future security strategy of the United States and our allies".[26] Casper Weinberger established study groups which were organized on the basis of subgroups to carry out these instructions. The first group reported by October with eight volumes of evidence giving a generally optimistic assessment of the long-term feasibility of achieving a ballistic missile defence system. A second report, out at the same time, was also enthusiastic. The reports were passed through the bureaucratic process which led to the President. They were combined and processed until they formed a simple set of recommendations confirming the practicability of the President's original aim.

The SDI contractors had good reason to be pleased with this intellectual exercise. Their future profits were assured, unless of course the USA and the Soviet Union reached an agreement which would cause the USA to abandon SDI. They were afraid lest the Soviet Union introduced new compelling peace initiatives. When Mr Gorbachev announced the Soviet Union's comprehensive plan for the abolition of all nuclear weapons by the year 2000 they were appalled. According to the *Washington Post* they even viewed as ominous the Soviet proposal for a quick 50 per cent reduction in the number of weapons. It reported that "many U.S. contractors fear that weapons they have researched and developed for years will become objects of superpower bargaining before entering the lucrative stage of full production".[27] This spectre arose when the summit meeting took place between President Reagan and Mr Gorbachev in November, 1985. The contractors were apprehensive lest Soviet concessions persuaded Congress to try to pare the programme down. They were unsure about committing their own capital to a programme which could be scuttled at any time. It was clear that the conventional defence budget would be relatively stable in the near future so, *The New York Times* reported, "every company is on notice that, if they want to be a long-term player, they can't let S.D.I. get away".[28]

Arms and the Community

In reality the US contractors had little cause to worry. Already, on 31 March 1984, President Reagan had assured them that "no arrangements or arguments beyond those already governing

251

military activities in outer space have been found to date that are judged to be in the overall interest of the United States and its allies".[29] They were part of the fastest growing industry in the USA. Their share value had increased almost 40-fold since the 1970s. They were in a no-risks business. The state guaranteed the credits, the outlets and profits. Whatever the amount of the bill it was always met by the tax payers. But the greatest guarantee of profitable survival was the manner in which defence contracts had permeated the whole of American society. In previous periods of military mobilization the American public was hostile to those who profited from war. Those days have long since gone. Since the first years of the Reagan administration hostility "has given way to the notion that defense industry profit is as American as new china for the First Lady".[30] Everyone wanted to share in it. The research workers from the Highlander Research and Education Centre in Tennessee, USA, who investigated the impact of military production in eight states in the upper south in the 1980s commented that "The Pentagon's state-by-state print-outs of prime contracts helped us understand that defense dollars permeate nearly every town or county in the region rather than a few centres of weapons production and that much of that money does not go for the tanks, guns and planes we imagined it did. A little bit of research revealed that the Defense Department's version of a public works program exerts an enormous influence over our region's economy – through all its well publicized ways and by propping up countless marginal institutions and enterprises from small town sheriff departments to doughnut makers to strip miners. We learned that despite all the money and influence, and despite the national mythology, the South . . . actually doesn't differ from the rest of the country in the extent of its dependence upon and its politicians' hankering for military contracts".[31]

The SDI is an issue concerning jobs as well as military strategy. *The New York Times* reported that "some in Congress argue that strategic defense, like nuclear missile and aircraft contruction programmes, will create a host of highly skilled and unskilled jobs . . ."[32] This is borne out by the way in which state governments "have elevated military construction and payroll to the most coveted form of federal aid. Defense industries are becoming the coin of the economic development realm . . ."[33] North Carolina holds, "Procurement conferences" to "offer a time-honoured opportunity for contractors and military installations to advertise themselves to prospective suppliers – and for congress people to help their corporate constituents do business with the government".[34] Tennessee's Economic and Community Development Office was prepared in 1982 to take anything from consoles for tracking systems to radar systems, laser homing devices, air-delivered clusters of mines and 155mm launching tubes for guns. What it did get in Huntsville, due to the lobbying of influential Howard Baker when he was Senator, was a contract to produce ghoulish body bags, a symbol of the Vietnam War, in preparation for the nuclear holocaust, making it one of the highest per capita recipients of defence contracts in Southern USA.[35] The contract office of Robins AFB, a large industrial complex in Georgia, boasted that 1,229 firms had signed up for sub-contracting work there during 1981.[36] All eight states in the Highlander study tried to interest small businesses in the advantages of sub-contracting with the prime defence contractors, many with illustrious names such as Hercules, Inc. which produced agent orange during the Vietnam War; J. P. Stevens, manufacturers of army uniforms and a notorious anti-union firm; Dupont, the original American armaments manufacturer, and Union Carbide, infamous for the Bhopal tragedy in India but also the sole private contractor in the manufacture of the first atom bomb by the Manhattan Project and the private corporation synonymous with the nuclear complex at Oak Ridge, Tenessee from where US nuclear weapons production is controlled. Oak Ridge produces parts for every major nuclear weapons system.

The intricate system of subcontracting linked the prosperity of a multiplicity of local communities to the concerns of the multinational arms manufacturers. The survival of the prime contractors depended upon the US pursuit of world military superiority and so, therefore, did that of the local communities. It was not simply Union Carbide, General Dynamics or IBM which considered the possibility of detente as ominous. Pentagon dollars shored up sweat-shops in the South's textile industry and small-time suppliers of everything needed to maintain the expansion of a military production system. A reduction in the Defence Budget would ripple ruin through American society like a wave. This is the meaning of the militarization of American society. It does not necessarily entail jackbooted black or brown shirts pounding in local town squares. It comes about through a national economic dependency on war. The authors of the Highlander study gave their version of militarization when they stated:

"We think that the U.S. military production system is . . . a maddeningly unimaginative, not to mention dangerous, way to offer public works jobs and conduct centralized economic planning through the back door. Making body bags in Scott County, Tennessee, may help shore up corporate power or establish consensus among the nation's haves, but it has very little to do with militarily defending places, people or ideas . . .

"The hall-mark of the military production system, at least in our region, is choicelessness. In communities all around the South, military production is one of the few – if not the only – games in town. Various social programmes and civilian industries may create more jobs than capital-intensive airframe assembly . . . but the actual choice many people face is: work in a plant making military boots or military beans or don't work at all. Their families and neighbours feel the ripples of that choicelessness. Multiply all those folks by their counterparts around the U.S. and you have a profoundly dependent economic constituency. Unless it has the freedom to change, chances for any arms race changing are slight."[37]

As so many industrial workers know, sub-contracting can involve a repressive authoritarian relationship. British trade unions have consistently fought against it in the lives of their members, in coal mining, iron and steel and building in particular. It creates a state of dependence and stifles dissent. People become grateful for small mercies and refrain from complaining about low pay and oppressive conditions. This is characteristic of all sub-contracting relationships. Small businesses and local communities become equally subservient to the wishes of the contractors as do individual work-people. In order to maintain their precarious stakes they support and protect the system which oppresses them. When given a free election they vote for it. They endorse its ideology believing that it acts in their own interests. At no point are the intentions of the prime contractors questioned for they are embodied in that same ideology. In this way a consensus is achieved.

Long and Short War Scenarios

In the USA the consensus is about accepting the legitimacy of arms production, even though this exposes them to the possibility of genocide and only in the most macabre way serves the interests of the dominant contractors. It is another of those intriguing contradictions in American society. Those people who are tied up in the militarization of American society and are, therefore, dependant upon the extension of America imperialism, are essentially isolationist in their political practice. They want to be left alone but their ability to do this is dependant upon the destruction of the lives of others, in societies and cultures they seemingly care little about.

The questions to be asked about these contradictions do not concern individuals but are about the structural conditions which give rise to them and the ideology which re-inforces them. The same applies to those contradictions which envelope the executives of the major American corporations and multinational companies. In a society where private capital dominates these executives have the greatest power. Their primary concern is to maintain the hegemony of private capital. They maraud the world in pursuit of this concern. Herein lies the genesis of their anti-Sovietism. They can never accept a social organization in which private capital is non-existent and which, through its successes, shows that private capital is both dispensible and a transient phenomenon. Yet their very acts to protect private capital lead to its possible destruction.

The Highlander Report relates an incident which occurred two days after Ronald Reagan was elected as President in 1980 but which had been planned by President Carter and his National Security Adviser, Zbigniew Brzezinski, two years before. It illustrates the contradiction of private capital and it reads like a sick game:

> "Two days after Ronald Reagan swamped Jimmy Carter in the 1980 presidential election, Washington went to war. Between November 6-26, the military and Carter's civilian agencies conducted the biggest government-wide mobilization exercise since World War II, battening down various governmental hatches and pretending that the balloon was about to go up in western Europe.
>
> "Called Operation Proud Spirit, that exercise was part of an effort kicked off nearly two years earlier by National Security Advisor, Zbigniew Brzezinski. In the

Spring of 1979, before Iran and before Afghanistan, Brzezinski directed 21 government agencies to review their mobilization plans, an effort that culminated in Carter's 1980 Presidential Directive 57 – a broad blue print for mobilizing the military, the civilian population and American industry. Proud Spirit itself emerged as something less than a smashing success. While bureaucrats hunkered in imaginary fox holes, the Pentagon's Worldwide Military Command and Control System (WMCCS), said to be the world's largest and most expensive computer system, "fell flat on its ass", according to one Pentagon player for twelve crucial hours, the system failed to sift and relay reports on unit readiness and transportation and to issue deployment orders.

"But there was more going on during Proud Spirit than electronic failures and electoral post mortems. Between November 12 and 19, a few dozen men gathered at the Pentagon and the National Defense University at Fort McNair. Called together by Army Chief of Staff Edward C. Meyer, the men represented some of the weightiest corporations in military contracting; RCA, ITT, Raytheon, Boeing, Hughes, General Dynamics, Honeywell, Martin Marietta, and seventeen others. Military-industrial get-togethers happen every day in Washington but the men who attended this meeting were not the high-powered lobbyists who represent the defense primes in the capital. Instead they were the companies' chief executive officers (CEO). And not all of them represented corporations with obvious or long-standing ties to the military. General Foods, Caterpillar, the Associated General Contractors, and Republic Steel mixed with DoD's leading beneficiaries.

"General Meyer's Partners in Prepondence were in Washington to talk about the guts of the Carter-Brzezinski initiative – industrial mobilization. Earlier in the year, *Business Week* had published a landmark article, "Why the U.S. Can't Rearm Fast", alleging breakdowns and bottlenecks throughout the nation's military production system. Within weeks after the CEOs concluded their business at Proud Spirit, the House Arms Service Committee and DoD's Defense

Science Board released reports echoing and embellishing *Business Week's* cry of alarm. The reports painted a picture of a dangerously deteriorating defense industrial base abandoned by contractors, frustrated by long lead times and capacity shortages, saddled by regulatory red tape and inconsistent buying patterns, perilously over-reliant on foreign sources of hard goods and nonfuel minerals and facing a critical shortage of skilled engineers, technicians and blue-collar workers.

"Meyer's invitees were presented a stunningly solicitous list of Army questions about fixing their alleged problems. "What kind of financial or legislative incentives are required to motivate indirectly to invest in new facilities and to generally expand the industrial base? . . . Given the eventual shortage of technically skilled workers to what extent should defense producers change over to equipment-intensive, computer-driven plants? . . . Should the federal government be responsible for construction to expand facilities to satisfy mobilization needs, to fund it, and to perform the engineering and construction."[38]

The question which followed inevitably from these questions was 'what kind of war are we mobilizing for?' Is it for a short war or a long war? For a short war scenario mobilization would be irrelevant because it could come too late. On this point the Director of the Defense Advanced Research Projects Agency explained that "Modern weapons make the first battle the last. The manufacturing base that was critical to the U.S. in the past wars will be of little use to us in future conflicts that are likely to be short, violent and dominated by advanced technology. There simply won't be any time to mobilize an entire nation and its manufacturing base." This vision dominated US military thinking until the end of the 1970s and, therefore, determined the nature and extent of their industrial demands. It came in part from a belief that the Soviet Union, even during the period of detente, would embark on a nuclear attack without warning, thus provoking an almost instantaneous nuclear war; and in part from the US's actual involvement in wars since 1945. The Vietnam War was defined as a 'short' war, as were the Arab-Israeli conflicts. Whilst this view prevailed the role of industry was largely

257

confined to the supply and maintenance of weapons of war. This, of course, was highly profitable for the small exclusive set of armaments manufacturers. "Short war" thinking was challenged in the late 1970s and eventually demolished during President Reagan's first year in office. It was supplanted by the belief that both the USA and the Soviet Union would engage in conventional war similar to World War II and would hold back from using nuclear weapons even when one side was clearly winning. The Highlander Report commented that "The Pentagon's 1970s preparations to fight one and a half wars turned to a 1980s vision of unparalleled, long-term destruction in any number of theaters. Advocates claim that altering the defence industrial base to cope with a long war's demands deters conflict by sending adversaries signals that the US has every contingency covered, including a replay of World War II . . . Long war many be a dubious strategic construct. But one thing it does undeniably well is shake the Pentagon's money tree. It makes almost any industrial base look inadequate for the job ahead."[39]

Once 'long-war' planning became the cornerstone of industrial policy both the military and industrial sections of the complex moved in with claims of lack of preparedness, of industrial deterioration, of shortages of almost anything, of over-reliance on either foreign-based multinationals or US multinationals which operate abroad, such as Texas Instruments and other firms which produce 85 per cent of all US military semi-conductors in south-east Asia. Thus the 'long-war' strategy coincided with the isolationist attitudes of Americans in general. It involved reversing the trend and bringing jobs back to the US, moving towards a state of autarky by eliminating what is described as "over-reliance on off-shore sourcing". It became patriotic and seemingly good economic sense to engage in preparations of war in peacetime. With this policy the military-industrial complex was having all of its own way: there was a consensus about the economics of militarizing American society; most people believed they were benefiting from it and the complex retained its hold on the system, reaping in fat guaranteed profits at the same time.

The Responsibility of the President

Where does the President stand in relation to the military industrial complex? If Eisenhower thought in 1961 that it had "unwarranted influence" what is Reagan's position? Anthony

Lewis, the *New York Times'* columnist, for instance believes that influence has grown beyond Eisenhower's worst nightmares.[40] What kind of accomplice is Reagan then in bringing about the militarisation of American society? Does he lead or is he led?

The President signs the Directives which initiate or confirm policies. He stipulates the formulas with which the study groups have to grapple. His is the main public voice uttering policies on behalf of the government. It was President Reagan who campaigned on the need to rebuild US military power and who equated military power with national pride and international status. Whenever he has had the opportunity he has glorified the actions of American armed forces in the Lebanon, in invading Grenada and in bombing Libya. He has provided the ideological trappings for the militarization of American society. His signature had authorized the transfer of federal funds from social to military uses. Without his active involvement and full commitment the process could not take place. What kind of responsibility does this confer on him?

There is no question that the actions of the President serve the interests of the military-industrial complex but he is not their servant in the sense that he takes orders from them. On the contrary, in personal relations both the military chiefs and the leaders of industry are solicitous of him, acknowledging his superior status. There is, in fact, no need for him or them to examine the nature of their relationship. They all share the same ideology. It is inconceivable to imagine an American President being elected through the existing system who did not toll the virtues of individualism, of private profit and the accumulation of capital. They pursue the same aims. The President as a political leader has to mediate between competing interest groups but his primary aim must coincide with that of the dominant economic group in the society, otherwise the system would lack cohesion and become destabilized. Even during the New Deal period of President Frankin D Roosevelt when he introduced legislation to encourage trade unionism and assist the poor, the prime government intention was to protect the institutions of capitalism. The existing political processes in the USA do not allow for major dissent against capitalism.

The main question to be asked about the President of the USA is not whether he is the master or servant of this or that particular group but what is the nature of the system of which his position is an integral part for it is that which confers a behaviour pattern on him irrespective of his political party. There has been no President since 1945 who has not been anti-communist and anti-Soviet, who has not been vitally concerned with securing military superiority for the USA, who has been unwilling to overthrow by subversion or force if necessary those states within the hemisphere of the US and sometimes without, who have challenged its hegemony. It has not mattered that during that period four Presidents have been from the Democratic Party and four from the Republican Party.

Capitalism comprises sets and layers of exploitative relations derived from the antagonistic class relationship between the owners and non-owners of property. Exploiters are pitted against the exploited and rival exploiters are pitted against each other. This system operates with a ruthless disregard of personalities and of compassion for people. This characteristic is present within a single capitalist country and in its relations with others.[41] On an international level there is a hierarchy of nations, exploiting and being exploited. This is what makes up the capitalist system.

Each of the nations, have need for armed forces both to protect themselves and to encroach on others. The country at the top of the hierarchy uses military power to drive off challengers and to extend its influence. Thus militarism and imperialism are two sides of the same coin. Precisely how militaristic a country needs to be, however, depends on circumstances. Imperialism does not necessarily involve a high level of militarism. Positions in the hierarchy can be secured by ideology as well as force. The British in the 19th Century were imperialist without being overtly militaristic. The USA in the years leading up to the Second World War had similar qualities.

What accounts then for the growth of militarism in present-day USA? The USA, as the leading capitalist nation since 1945 is in a unique historical position. It is jostled by Germany and Japan for the leading position but although this in the past has led to wars it is not now the main threat. The insecurity of the USA stems from the existence of a large and increasing segment of socialism in the world which is the antithesis of capitalism. Its position as the leading nation is threatened because the system itself is threatened. This has never happened before. In the inter-war years the Soviet Union existed but it was not feared. The Americans, victims of their own propaganda, believed that the new Soviet state was perpetually on the verge of disintegration and would if attacked topple like a pack of cards. The resilience of the Soviet people in the Second World War, the economic achievements of its system and the tremendous victories of the Red Army shattered those delusions. The spread of socialism has prevented the pieces being put together. The American defeat in Vietnam confirmed the vulnerability of capitalism and the potential of socialism.

So it is the socialist challenge to private property rights which is the real threat to the USA and all the Presidential talk about Soviet aggressiveness is a smokescreen to cover this fact. The threat, therefore, is global. It is not one, moreover, which can be met by economic and ideological methods which had failed in the interwar years when socialism was a fragile thing. The crude use of military power is the only option left. This was made clear when President Truman announced his Doctrine of Containment on 12 March 1947.[42] "No pronouncement", D F Fleming commented, "could have been more sweeping. Wherever a Communist rebellion developed the United States would suppress it. Wherever the Soviet Union attempted to push outward, at any point around its vast circumference, the United States would resist. The United States would become the world's anti-Communist, anti-Russian policeman".[43] Thus was created the need for a huge sprawling, marauding military machine.

The decision to start this process rather than to seek accommodation with the Soviet Union was a Presidential one but he made it as the custodian of the private enterprise system, reflecting the needs of that system. Once it was made then the Pentagon began priming the pump of military production which quickly developed its own dynamism, grew under its own momentum and made its own demands on the political leaders. The role of Presidents and lesser political leaders thereafter has been to facilitate the transfer of the nation's resources to the custody of arms manufacturers and to legitimize it as a patriotic act. This all the Presidents have done though with varying degrees of public commitment.

If the US President has masters then the apparent culprits are the leading executives of the largest conglomerates of private capital involved in arms production, namely the multinational companies. The military chiefs undoubtedly comprise an influential pressure group but they are formally subordinate to the President and owe their appointments to him. The executives of the multinational companies, on the other hand, are largely autonomous and have vital economic power bases. They control budgets greater than those of many states. On their own they can destabilize governments and topple political leaders. It is not impossible to conceive that the US President could be a casualty.

If we reason on the basis of appearances in this case we conclude by condemning multinational companies. That was the way President Eisenhower proceeded. If he had remained in office after his valedictory address presumably he would have proposed constraints on the core elements of the military-industrial complex such as a code of conduct similar to that drawn up by the UN or a Senate investigation with much publicity about chicanery over arms contracts. No such actions would, of course, have resolved the problem which, as I have already pointed out, is no less than the militarization of American society.

Appearances, as all social analysts should know, can be misleading. Multinational companies are the latest expressions of the tendency under capitalism for the degree of monopoly to increase. Their behaviour is not unethical according to the values of capitalism nor is it different from that of any other monopolies in similar circumstances. It is difficult to distinguish between the activities of Krupp and Thyssen during the rise of Nazism and Union Carbide and General Dynamics in contemporary USA. The multinationals, like their minnions, respond to their situations. They could not do otherwise and survive. Those situations are set by the capitalist mode of production. If a President wants to alter the behaviour of multinational companies and destroy the influence of the military-industrial complex there is only one course; it is to abolish that mode and replace it with a socialist one. The difficulty is that he is as much a puppet in the system as the leading arms manufacturers, a servant of the hidden hands of the market which are trying to maximize private profit for those who already have most.

The conclusion of this chapter taken by itself is pessimistic for it seems that the only effective constraint on the multinational beneficiaries of nuclear arms production is the abolition of the system which spawns them. But multinationals and Presidents are but parts of the jigsaw which make up international society. The desire of the Soviet Union for peace, the peace initiatives of the non-aligned nations and the campaigns of Peace Movements in Europe together generate a world opinion in favour of peace which American society cannot ignore and which reinforce those in the US who favour the elimination of nuclear weapons. It is clear, however, that the problem which American arms production creates for the world can only be resolved within and by American society.

Arms production has become the engineer of the US economy. To displace it would cause severe dislocation. On the other hand the possible consequences of continuing with it could be the annihilation of the society which feeds from it. It is this choice which will force a solution involving the elimination of nuclear weapons. The electorate of American society is a vital part of the jigsaw. The choice it faces must compel it to silence the advisers and cut off the funds on which nuclear arms production depends. When there is no profit in arms production the multinationals will be forced to do other less damaging things.

FOOTNOTES

1. The Presidents of the USA since 1948 have been:
    1948 – Harry S Truman
    1952 – Dwight D Eisenhower
    1960 – John F Kennedy (succeeded by Lyndon Johnson on his assassination in 1963 until 1964)
    1964 – Lyndon Johnson
    1968 – Richard Nixon (succeeded by Gerald Ford on his impeachment in 1974 until 1976)
    1976 – Jimmy Carter
    1980 – Ronald Reagan
    1984 – Ronald Reagan
2. *The Presidency of Dwight D Eisenhower* by Elmo Richardson, 1979, p. 192.
3. *The New York Times*, 18 January 1961.
4. "The President and the Executive Branch" by Robert R. Bowie in *The Making of America's Soviet Policy*, edited by Joseph S. Nye, Jr., p. 69.
5. Elmo Richardson, op. cit., pp. 74-75.
6. Stated by James Killian, Special Assistant to the President for Science and Technology; quoted by Paul B Stares in *Space Weapons and U.S. Strategy. Origins and Development*, p. 39.
7. *The New York Times*, 18 January 1961.
8. Stares, op. cit., p. 58.
9. Richardson, op. cit., p. 185.
10. *The Power Elite*, 1958, pp. 6-7. Mills was the Professor of Sociology at Columbia University.
11. Reported in full in *The New York Times*, 18 January 1961.
12. *Monopoly Capital* by Paul A Baran and Paul M Sweezy, 1966, p. 190.
13. *Our Own Worst Enemy* by Highlander Research and Education Centre, Tennessee, USA, 1983, p. 229. This book is a valuable, highly detailed account of the militarization of the US economy.
14. Robert R Bowie, op. cit., p. 71.
15. Source: *World Military Expenditure and Arms Transfer;* published annually by the US Arms Control and Disarmament Agency.

16. This column indicates the President who was in office at the time of the election and, therefore, concerned with the arms expenditure for the previous 4 years.

17. Lyndon Johnson became President for one year on the assassination of John F Kennedy in 1963, before being elected in his own right.

18. Gerald Ford assumed office on the impeachment of Richard Nixon in August 1974. He was therefore President for only 2 years and bore little responsibility for their events.

19. This figure has been obtained from the 1985 Year Book of the Stockholm International Peace Research Institute.

20. Source: *Space Weapons and U.S. Strategy, Origins and Development* by Paul B Stares, p. 255.

21. Explanations concerning Presidents are as in the previous table, except that the 1959 figures, the year before the Presidential election, are intended to show the level of space expenditure before the full effect of the launching of Sputnik I was felt, compared with 1963 when it was in full swing.

22. Stares, op. cit., p. 217.

23. ibid, p. 225

24. *New York Times,* 19 November 1985.

25. Source: Federation of American Scientists (*New York Times,* 19 November 1985).

26. Paul B Stares, op. cit., pp. 225-229

27. *The Washington Post,* 19 November 1985.

28. *The New York Times,* 19 November 1985.

29. Quoted by Paul B Stares, op. cit., p. 216.

30. *Our Own Worst Enemy,* op. cit., p. 6.

31. ibid, p. 6.

32. *The New York Times,* 19 November 1985.

33. *Our Own Worst Enemy,* op cit, p. 12.

34. ibid, p. 13.

35. ibid, p. 55.

36. ibid, pp. 13-14.

37. ibid, p. 191.

38. ibid, pp. 1-2.

39. ibid, pp. 3-4.

40. *Lexington Herald – Leader,* Lexington, Kentucky 23 November 1985.

41. See *Monopoly Capital* by Paul A Baran and Paul M Sweezy 1968, Penguin Edition, chapter 7, for a further and penetrating analysis of this question.

42. See *The Origins of the Cold War* by Martin McCauley, 1983, pp. 65-69.

43. *The Cold War and its Origins* by D F Fleming 1960, volume 1, p. 446.

PART IV
Anti-Sovietism in Practice

Chapter Twelve
Trade Unions And Anti-Sovietism

The Contradictions

The general effect of the continual projection of the Soviet Union as the evil antithesis of Western democratic values is to convince electors in capitalist countries to give political endorsement to the anti-Soviet policies of their governments. This is crucially important for governments for none could sustain such policies for long unless they had some credibility with ordinary people. But that is not the end of the matter. Nor is it necessarily the most important factor in the long-run. Electors endorse or reject policies; they do not determine or apply them. Political practice is the work of institutions not of individuals. The really important factor, therefore, is the extent to which institutions reflect in their practice the ideology which portrays the Soviet Union as a contamination.

The institutions which comprise the state, in that they uniformly project and endorse the dominant ideology, have no problem with anti-Sovietism. It is an integral part of their value system. It would be unrealistic to expect them to be different. The mass media, the established churches, private industry, the judiciary and Parliament itself protect, nurture and extend the interests of private property. If they, or any significant part of them, were otherwise then the system would be destabilized.

It is a different matter where institutions which reflect the contradictions of capitalism are concerned for they are agents of change in society. Their values differ from the dominant values of the society; in some cases they are the antithesis of them so conformity for them means deserting their principles and becoming integrated into the system. The main type of institutions which can be affected in this way are trade unions. Their histories show vividly how anti-Sovietism in practice negates their primary objectives.

Trade unionism all over the world, even where it tends to conform to capitalist ethics, stands for collectivist values which are the antithesis of the individualism of capitalism. Unions are based on solidarity; in their unadulterated form they practise democracy and they aim for various types of equality. These values arise out of the day-to-day experiences of wage and salary earners. A logical consequence of the preference for collectivism between workers in their own organizations is an extension of it to the wider society involving a belief in socialism entailing public ownership of the means of production, the use of centralized planning mechanisms to distribute resources and government provided health services, education and social services.

This has been recognized by many British trade unions, some of which have written socialist objectives into their constitutions. For example, paragraph 3(s) in the rule book of the National Union of Mineworkers states that it is an object of the union "to join in with other organizations for the purpose of and with the view to complete abolition of Capitalism." The Amalgamated Union of Building Trade Workers which has now amalgamated with other building trade unions to form UCCAT, aimed for "the establishment of the Co-operative Commonwealth the world over." An aim of the United Society of Boilermakers, which was established in 1834, was "the extension of co-operative production to assist in altering the competitive system of industry for a co-operative system of ownership and control by the workers . . ." The Transport and General Workers' Union sets out to extend "co-operative production and distribution." There are many similar examples. These aims have consistently been represented in policies about nationalization, centralized planning and government services. The Trades Union Congress has regularly advocated socialist policies over the last 70 years, even though it has practised social engineering in its day-to-day activities. There is no doubt that the socialist transformation of Britain is an issue for British trade unions. It impinges on the question of anti-Sovietism in two ways.

First it is in the interest of the private owners of the means of production to frustrate the socialist objectives of unions and to prevent those unions which have not reached that stage from doing so. The ideological means of doing this involves praising capitalism and denigrating socialism. In domestic politics this is done by linking nationalization with bureaucracy and government planning with subsidies and the profligate spending of 'taxpayers' money'. Government interference is correlated with inefficiency and wastefulness. Conservative governments have had considerable

268

success in imprinting these correlations on the minds of British electors. Even in the USA where the limits of socialism are confined to discussions about the introduction of a state organized health service the same arguments are pungently made.

The ideologists of capitalism emphasize the defects of various socialist measures introduced in Britain since 1945 but they would find it considerably more difficult to make their point if they were not able to substantiate their arguments by referring to the practice of socialism in the Soviet Union. There was considerably more discussion in the British Labour Movement about socialist alternatives to capitalism before the 1917 Revolution than afterwards. There was then more popular and imaginative literature about socialism. Some of the aims of unions quoted above were framed before 1917 and give some indication of the visions of trade unionists before the Western propaganda machine got to work on the image of the Soviet Union. The effect of anti-Sovietism was eventually to close the most viable and important option in the socialist debate. In its most intense periods it effectively killed off the debate altogether. The Western designation of the Soviet Union became the linchpin in the protective mechanism of capitalism.

Secondly, in so far as trade unions which have socialist objectives themselves practise anti-Soviet propaganda they are engaged in a self-defeating operation for how can they convince their members of the value of socialism if they denigrate the main country which practises it? In this sense anti-Sovietism is like a deathwish. Put differently, the projection of the Soviet Union as a successful socialist experiment would facilitate the spread of socialist ideas everywhere but particularly in those labour movements where the debate about socialism has already started. The attitude of trade unions to the Soviet Union is then a measure of their political consciousness.

The British trade union movement's view of the Soviet Union is complicated by the issue of communism as opposed to social democracy and by communist activities within unions. But it starts with its own particular contradiction which marks it off from most other trade union movements. The effect of these different strands has been to create an attitude of ambivalence.

British trade unions have always been pragmatic and economistic in their approach to their own daily tasks despite whatever they may have written into their constitutions. Although this is in effect a theoretical position it has been articulated as anti-theory, expressed through a disdain of intellectuals and a preference for practical, down-to-earth matters. Indeed it reflects the false division between theory and practice which characterizes British social science.

The consequences have been important in British political life. In the first place the pragmatic, empirical approach of trade unions determined the nature of the Labour Party and set the tone for political discussions in the Labour Movement as a whole. The Labour Party took its terms of reference about political theory from the unions which formed it. Theory was never important; it did not bind or divide or differentiate between political positions as it did in many Continental countries where political parties preceded the growth of trade unions. Where political action against the capitalist system was initially by political groups rather than unions it was usually formulated by intellectuals concerned about the finesse of analysis, with a tendency to argue with each other and to split into factions. The Social Democratic Labour Party in Czarist Russia had these characteristics from its formation and implanted them on the trade unions they formed. The German Social Democratic party was a Marxist party before the First World War which was deeply concerned about theoretical heresies. It was over Marxist revisionism in that Party that the major debate between Karl Kautsky, Rosa Luxemburg, Lenin and Eduard Bernstein occurred in the 1890s. Whenever political parties within the Labour Movement have come before trade unions then ideological divisions have split the unions into rival, competitive groups with contrary views of socialism and dogmatic positions in relation to the Soviet Union. Thus in Germany during the Weimar Republic there were national trade union centres representing Marxists, Christians and employer-supported organizations; in France since 1949 there have been central bodies representing communists, socialist anti-communist and Christian unions.

The British trade union attitude which scorned, even trivialized, theory, meant that dogma was never so important as to divide the movement. Alone amongst the major trade union movements of the world, the Trades Union Congress has remained unchallenged since its formation in 1868. Because, however, it regarded theory as irrelevant it tolerated different political perspectives. Trade unionists who were communists were not generally disqualified from participating; indeed many were elected to offices at all levels of the union hierarchies. Unions frequently publicly adopted anti-communist policies yet still tolerated communists in their councils. In the same way they have pronounced support for anti-Soviet policies through the TUC whilst enjoying positive relations with individual Soviet trade unions. This ambivalence was reflected in the attitudes of individual trade union leaders. W M Citrine, for example, was a committed anti-communist when he was the general secretary of the TUC from 1926 until 1946, yet he, more than any other European trade union leader, pressed to establish relations between Western and Soviet trade unions.

The Impact of the Bolshevik Revolution

The attitude of British trade unions towards the Soviet Union went through distinct phases. At the outset, from the October Revolution until the General Strike in 1926, British unions endorsed and supported Bolshevik Russia. They welcomed the October Revolution and opposed British intervention to topple the Bolshevik government from 1918 to 1920. The Parliamentary Committee of the TUC demanded the withdrawal of British troops from Russia shortly after the snap general election in 1918. It repeated its demand the following year. Then, on 10 May, 1920, London dockers translated words into action and refused to load the *Jolly George,* bound for Poland, because they suspected it of carrying munitions for use against the Bolsheviks. A Special Trades Union Congress in July 1920 threatened to call a strike unless the government ceased its production of arms against the Bolsheviks. The TUC then joined forces with the Executive Committee of the Labour Party and the Parliamentary Labour Party and in an historically unique act threatened a general strike and formed a Council of Action to implement it. Many local initiatives were taken and 350 local councils of action were formed to mobilize workers in support of the Bolshevik Revolution. The Council of Action called a National Conference in London on 13 August, 1920, where previously inveterate opponents of direct action, such as J H Thomas and J R Clynes, pledged their support for a resolution authorizing the Council of Action to call "for any and every form of withdrawal of labour which circum-stances may require to give effect to . . . [its] policy . . . [and] in order to sweep away secret bargaining and diplomacy and to assure that the foreign policy of Great Britain may be in accord with the well-known desires of the people for an end to war and the interminable threats of war".[1] No strike was called. The occasion was the war between Poland and Bolshevik Russia. When the British threatened to intervene it was to prevent the Bolsheviks from occupying Warsaw but from August 1920 the Polish army under French leadership repelled the Red Army, making intervention unnecessary. The British government was able to project its innocence.

The Council of Action's campaign tapped the underlying sympathy which British workers had for their Russian counterparts in their attempt to establish a Workers' State. That feeling was never entirely eroded by anti-Soviet propaganda. There has always been a sufficient recognition of the importance of class amongst British trade unionists for them to identify in some way with a working class which had acquired state power, no matter what mistakes it was alleged they were making. This recognition was enhanced by the sacrifices of the Soviet people and the victories of the Red Army during the Second World War and it continued to be a factor which unions had to contend with even at the height of the Cold War. There was never a total capitulation to anti-Soviet propaganda with the consequence that British unions played an exceptional role through to 1949 in maintaining relations with Soviet trade unions.

Three trade union delegations went from Britain to Soviet Russia between 1917 and 1926. The first in 1920 was a joint TUC and Labour Party delegation led by Ben Turner, the leader of the Textile Workers' Union, and included the dockers' leader Ben Tillett, and Margaret Bondfield from the National Union of General Workers. It went on a fact-finding mission and returned to accuse the British press of perverting the facts about Russia. They had seen no one dying of starvation in the streets, no interference with religious observation, no evidence that the Commissars were living in luxury and, they added, neither women nor children had been nationalized. Turner was convinced that the Bolshevik government was supported by the mass of the people.[2]

The tenor of the second delegation's Report in 1924 was similar to that of 1920. It made two important points. First, it stated that "there can be no peace and progress in European civilization until the Union of Socialist Soviet Republics is admitted on a basis of general agreement to a free and friendly footing in the community of peoples . . ."[3] This opinion was sadly confirmed in the late 1930s when the ostracism of the Soviet Union by the West stopped the formation of an anti-Nazi alliance effective enough to prevent war. Secondly, the delegation this time was wholly organized by the TUC and led by A A Purcell of the Furnishing Trades Union and a consistent advocate of close relations between Britain and Soviet Russia, who recognized the consequences for the Labour Movement of anti-Sovietism. Its Report stated that "misrepresentations as to the results of the Russian Revolution have been used as a "red herring" to divert and distract the British people from the pursuit of reforms and reconstructions essential to their own peace and prosperity."[4] This, too, was sadly confirmed by subsequent experiences, particularly when in the Cold War period the TUC itself engaged in anti-Soviet propaganda. These premonitions, including most of the Report itself were condemned by the press, except for the *Daily Herald*. The third delegation went in the autumn of 1925 simply to discuss establishing formal relationships between the TUC and the Soviet AUCCTU.

Both Fred Bramley, the general secretary of the TUC from 1923 till 1926[5], and A A Purcell favoured the establishment of a formal Anglo-Soviet Committee and while in Moscow they had discussions with the leaders of the All-Russian Central Council of Trade Unions on that question. The international trade union movement was divided into two conflicting organizations. Western, but mainly European, trade union centres were represented by the International Federation of Trade Union which had been founded in 1901 but reconstituted in 1919. A Soviet initiated Red International of Labour Unions held its inaugural conference in July 1921. Britain was represented on its Provisional Committee by J T Murphy, the convenor of the Sheffield Shop Stewards' Committee. From then there was bitter wrangling between the two organizations with the British TUC attempting to act as a broker. The disagreements were deeply ideological but the argument was over the technicalities of affiliation. The IFTU was prepared to consider applications for membership from RTUI affiliates in accordance with its own statutes whereas the All-Russian Central Council of Trade Unions, for its part, wanted a preliminary conference without pre-conditions to examine the possibility of forming a united world organization. The British TUC though affiliated to the IFTU favoured the Soviet proposal. The TUC was defeated at the IFTU General Council in February, 1925 and thereafter formal communications between the two centres ceased until after the Soviet Union was admitted to membership of the League of Nations in September 1934. The

TUC again made a proposal to admit the AUCCTU to membership of the IFTU in 1935 and in 1939 but the majority of the European trade union centres rejected the idea. Walter Citrine reported that if the TUC had pressed the matter the IFTU would have split. The TUC had communicated with the affiliates of the IFTU prior to the VIIIth IFTU Congress in July 1939, stating that

"it is absolutely essential that Russia should join with the democratic Powers in resisting Nazi and Fascist aggression. Our General Council feel it encumbent upon them to do their utmost with a view to inducing other National Centres to recognize this point of view, and to get them to realize that, just as it is important that Russia should stand with the democratic Powers for the preservation of peace, so it is equally essential that the Russian Trade Unions should take their place in the IFTU and thus strengthen the solidarity of the International Trade Union Movement."

"It is far from the intention of the TUC General Council to do anything which might tend to widen any divisions that now exist, but they think that present circumstances fully justify them in approaching, in the most fraternal spirit, the other National Centres which have hitherto opposed the Russian affiliation. We earnestly appeal to them to re-examine the matter and consider whether they can change their views, so that when the British Resolution comes up for discussion at the Congress, their delegates will have been instructed to give it their support."[6]

The resolution was defeated. Only France, Mexico and Norway supported the British position. The majority insisted, as it had done in 1925, that Soviet trade unions had to accept the statutes of the IFTU to qualify for affiliation. The objections to meeting the Soviet trade unions were not overcome until the Red Army began its memorable series of victories against the Nazis. In 1943 the Trades Union Congress took the initiative again and decided to convene a world trade union conference in London in 1944 along lines agreed by the Soviet AUCCTU. It issued invitations to 71 trade union organizations in 31 countries. The Conference was eventually held in February, 1945 and, for the first time, drew together unions from all areas of the world irrespective of their ideological positions. The only major trade union centre which refused to participate was the American Federation of Labour. The outcome of the Conference was the formation of the World Federation of Trade Unions.

The Anglo-Russian Trade Union Committee

The Labour government in 1924 gave diplomatic recognition to the Soviet Union. The Russian delegation which came to Britian to negotiate the terms of the treaty contained four prominent trade unionists, including Mikhail Tomsky, the chairman of the AUCCTU, who met with members of the TUC General Council for the first time in a formal session. They discussed trade union unity. Tomsky was invited to the Trades Union Congress in September 1924 where he raised the issue. Hardly had the invitation been sent than the AUCCTU requested the TUC to send a delegation to the Soviet Union "in order to establish permanent regular connections between the two Movements". This was the delegation which reported extensively on labour conditions early in 1925 but it also discussed the creation of an Anglo-Russian Committee with Tomsky. Then in April 1925, an Anglo-Russian Trade Union Conference was held in London, organized by the TUC, at which an Anglo-Russian Committee was formed. Fred Bramley, the TUC secretary who had been consistently in favour of unity, proposed an annex to the Conference declaration which suggested exchanging documents of mutual interest and memoranda on special topics; developing the closest possible mutual aid; establishing an Anglo-Russian joint advisory council comprising a chairman, secretary and three additional representatives from each organization. The declaration, plus its annex were endorsed by the TUC in September 1925 and the new Committee held its first meeting shortly afterwards. Fred Bramley was at this stage critically ill and W M Citrine became the Committee's secretary. Citrine, with George Hicks, the general secretary of the Amalgamated Union of Building Trade Workers, went to the Soviet Union in the autumn to discuss the future activities of the Committee.[7]

The Committee, however, had no future. It became a casualty of the 1926 General Strike like so much else in industrial relations in Britain, though not before it was castigated in Britain and abroad. The only foreign trade union centre to regard it as a positive step towards world trade union unity was the Norwegian Arbeidernes Faglige Landsorganisasjon. They wanted to join it. The Germans denounced it, as did the IFTU. The American Federation of Labour regarded the Committee as an "attempt to destroy from ambush the freedom of workers in democratic countries." The AFL, however, did not even affiliate to the IFTU until 1937 after which it led the opposition to unity with the Soviet trade unions. The British Labour Party was critical of the TUC's step and, to emphasize its point, started a serious campaign against domestic communists at its Annual Conference in 1925. The incipient anti-Sovietism of the British media began to mature with such a prize target as the Anglo-Russian Committee.

It is possible that the Committee would not have survived the ideological attacks on it even if the General Strike had not occurred. The General Council of the TUC had significantly changed its composition between 1924 and 1926. Two influential right-wing leaders J H Thomas and Margaret Bondfield had returned after serving in the short-lived Labour government. It had new members, including Ernest Bevin, the powerful leader of the Transport and General Workers' Union. Walter Citrine had taken over the secretaryship of the Council from Bramley. This General Council had different priorities compared with the 1924 one. Anglo-Soviet relations which had been important for Bramley were displaced from the TUC agenda by acute domestic issues in the pre and post General Strike situation. But more importantly the perspectives of the TUC about the Soviet Union had begun to change. Bolshevism to the mid-twenties generation of union leaders was not about a glorious workers' Revolution but a communist state which was here to stay, which had inspired the creation of communist parties bent on revolution in numerous countries and had attracted the most militant of their members to challenge official union orthodoxy and stimulate class confrontational politics on an international level through the Third Communist International (Comintern) and the Red International of Labour Unions. It was quite easy to view the established Soviet State in the international conspiracy terms conjured by the mass media. The actions of the Soviet trade unions during the General Strike tended to confirm that view in the councils of the TUC. The pattern of anti-Sovietism which was consolidated after 1949 began to take shape.

The Soviet AUCCTU offered material assistance to the TUC General Council as soon as the General Strike was called. It suggested that every Soviet trade unionist should contribute one quarter of one day's wages to support the strikers. The total amounted to about 2 million rubles of which 250,000 rubles were sent immediately. The General Council refused the money, however, and returned the cheque to Moscow. The AUCCTU responded by turning the money over to the Miners' Federation of Great Britain during the nine months' lock-out after the

General Strike had been terminated. The MFGB had appealed for international support and received almost £1,250,000 from Soviet trade unionists, amounting to over two-thirds of all funds collected and more than 90 per cent of the receipts from outside Britain.[8] There is no doubt that this money enabled the MFGB to survive the lock-out. In the view of Herbert Smith, the President of the MFGB, the Russian workers understood the meaning of solidarity.[9] The money was sent without conditions but in the hope that relations between Soviet and British miners would be strengthened and formalized.

When the General Strike was called off some Soviet leaders reacted by criticizing the TUC General Council and proffering advice to the unions affiliated to it. Zinoviev, the secretary of Comintern, accused the General Council of being a "stinking corpse" while Tomsky complained that it had isolated the British workers from the international proletariat. All of this, according to Citrine, was gross interference in the affairs of British unions in violation of the first principle agreed to by the Anglo-Russian Committee. Citrine wrote that "The Russians could not keep their bargain . . . They definitely interfered in the Strike of 1926, abusing the General Council of the TUC and appealing to the members of Trade Unions over their heads . . . Because of this the Committee was dissolved."[10] Only two meetings of the Committee were held after the Strike, in Paris on 30 July 1926 and in Berlin on 23 August in the same year. Mikhail Tomsky was refused a visa to enter Britain so he was unable to address the 1927 Trades Union Congress in Bournemouth where the TUC made the final break with the Anglo-Russian Committee. There were no further formal contacts between the British TUC and the Soviet AUCCTU until after the Germans had invaded the Soviet Union in 1941.

The Campaign Against Communists

The year 1927 marked the visible beginning of a different phase in the attitude of British trade unions towards the Soviet Union which, with varying degrees of intensity and an interruption during the Second World War, has continued till today. It is one in which the policy of the TUC is determined less by class identity and solidarity and more by political expediency. The TUC became increasingly concerned about its own survival as an institution. Under Walter Citrine's direction it sought status and political acceptability and this involved taking rough edges off protest and pursuing only the realizable. For example, during the 1930s, it ceased trying to reduce unemployment and concentrated on administering it to lessen its impact. It wanted consultations with governments and counted its success in this respect in terms of the number of government committees TUC nominees attended. The TUC directory of committees listed only one government committee on which the General Council was represented in 1931 but twelve in 1938-39.[11] A small but indicative sign of the change was the willingness of union leaders to accept State honours. Six trade union leaders had received knighthoods prior to 1935 but mainly for their political work. In 1935 both the general secretary of the TUC and a prominent member of the General Council received knighthoods from a conservative government. *The Times,* reporting on the 1935 Birthday Honours List, stated that "As for our national affairs, the great part played in them by the Trade Unions is recognized by the fact that two members at the next meeting of the TUC will be Sir Arthur Pugh and Sir Walter Citrine."[12] This was a mere nine years since the TUC was denounced as an agent of international communism.

The TUC turned in on itself in its endeavour to gain respectability; its focus was communist trade unionists. The General Council had ended the General Strike without a 'no victimization' clause. In consequence large numbers of militant trade unionists were dismissed and blacklisted by employers without union protection. Then the TUC began its own campaign. In 1928 Walter Citrine published a 29 page booklet called *Democracy or Disruption* which examined the influence of communists in unions. From 1923 communists put pressure on unions through their own involvement but also through the National Minority Movement, an organization with individual membership which aimed to form factory committees, to lessen inter-union rivalry and strengthen local Trades Councils. The members of the National Minority Movement, however, were vulnerable to trade union discipline for it was a body which lay outside unions and could be proscribed by them. This weakness was lessened from 1932 by the formation of the Rank-and-File Movement which was based on the affiliation of union branches and shop stewards' committees and which had no individual membership. Rank-and-File Movements were established in different industries and regions where they organized militant action. For example, the London Busman's Rank-and-File Movement was organized in 1932 and had a considerable influence in the Coronation Strike of London Busmen in 1937. Working alongside these unofficial movements was the National Unemployed Workers' Movement, formed in 1921 and led by the influential communist Wal Hannington. After the General Strike these organizations became the prime targets of TUC hostility.[13]

The high point of the TUC's anti-communist campaign was the publication in October 1934 of Circulars 16 and 17, subsequently described as the Black Circulars, advising unions about the influence of communists and instructing trades councils not to allow communists to be delegates. Circular 17 to Unions, signed by Citrine, stated: "I have to ask that your Executive Committee will give consideration to the possibility of drawing up regulations or amending the rules of your organization so as to empower them to reject the nominations of members of disruptive bodies for any official position within your organization . . ."[14] Circular 16 to trades councils, more strongly worded, contained the General Council ruling "that any Trades Council which admits delegates who are associated with Communist or Fascist organizations, or their ancillary bodies shall be removed from the list of Trades Councils recognized by Congress . . ." A new set of model rules was formulated for trades councils which embodied the General Council decision. Both circulars received mixed receptions. Of the 211 unions affiliated to the TUC in 1935 only 41 replied that they were in general agreement with the policy. There was a greater degree of consensus among trade councils for 283 replied that they accepted the policy of political proscription; 18 expressed their dissent and 80 did not reply at all.[15]

The TUC policy had a limited effect in practice at local level for the period was marked by a growing militancy among workers as unions recouped the membership losses incurred during the depression in the early 1930s. Workers were politicized by the intensified political campaign against fascism and by the impact of the Spanish Civil War. The dilemma which unions faced was characterized by the Transport and General Workers' Union during the 1937 London bus strike. The strike was organized by the Rank-and-File Movement which, despite the Black Circular, claimed the affiliation of thirty-one out of fifty London busmen's branches and the allegiance of all except one of the members of the Union's Central Area Bus Committee. The leaders of the strike were Bert Papworth and Bill Jones, both communists, each of whom was expelled for his strike activities but re-admitted and then promptly elected to the General Executive Council of the Union.[16]

This paradox of union members electing communists to official union positions contrary to the anti-communist policies of their unions was a common phenomenon even during the Cold War period for it reflected the reality of industrial relations. At shop-floor level it was the class antagonisms not ideological perspectives which determined the behaviour of workers while the further the analysis was from point of production pressures the more ideology exercised influence. This paradox influenced the behaviour of the TUC and had its counterpart in its approach to international communism. The TUC supported the Western stereotype of the Soviet Union yet was compelled by the exigencies of practical political situations to seek unity with Soviet trade unions. This was best illustrated by the formation of the Anglo-Soviet Trade Union Committee in 1941.

The Creation of World Trade Union Unity

The indifference shown by the British government to the Soviet Union during its attempts to create a united anti-fascist front from the mid-1930s, turned to hostility after the Soviet-German Non-Aggression Pact was signed in August 1939 and Britain had declared war on Germany on 3 September. There were some in Britain who defined the Soviet Union as an ally of Germany but others who regarded it, and not Nazi Germany, as the main enemy. This hostility intensified after the Red Army occupied Eastern Poland on 17 September, 1939 and engaged in war with Finland during December. This was the period of the "phoney" war between Britain, France and Germany so the media had little to divert it from an anti-Soviet agitation. The situation created havoc with allegiances in the Labour Movement. The British Communist Party itself was divided over whether or not to support the war with Germany in the light of the Soviet position. The Soviet Union was accused of imperialism. There was talk of waging war against it, which prompted Labour leaders to advise caution. Mr Herbert Morrison, for instance, whilst wholeheartedly condemning the Soviet Union, said on 4 December that "If British reactionaries and Herr Hitler made any move towards a Nazi-British alliance against Russia, Labour would oppose it."[17]

The President of the Miners' Federation of Great Britain, Will

Lawther, distanced his union from the more extreme denunciations being made. He said that "while we agree that this action (against Finland) is wrong, the Mineworkers' Federation does not associate itself with the general anti-Soviet or Fascist declarations."[18] In a rather futile practical gesture Britain activated the defunct League of Nations so that the Soviet Union could be expelled from it on 14 December, 1939.

The trade unions participated in all this with varying degrees of complicity. The Annual Congress of the TUC was not held in September 1939 so there was not a collective view of the situation for the Trade Union Movement as a whole. The TUC General Council had pressed the IFTU to consider the affiliation of Soviet trade unions earlier in the year but it acquiesced when it was turned down. The question could hardly have been raised anyway while the Soviet pact with Germany was intact. When Walter Citrine visited the Annual Convention of the American Federation of Labour in November 1940 he did not mention the Soviet situation though he did talk with William Green, the AF of L President, about the sad plight of the IFTU which by then was a tiny rump, having lost Norway, Denmark, Holland, Belgium and France through the German occupation of Europe that year.[19]

The invasion of the Soviet Union by German armies on Sunday 22 June 1941 had an instantaneous impact in Britain. Mr Churchill speaking on the day of the invasion, said: "No one has been a more persistent opponent of Communism than I have been for the last 25 years. I will unsay no word that I have spoken about it, but all this fades away before the spectacle which is now unfolding . . . We have offered to the Government of Soviet Russia any technical or economic assistance which is in our power and which is likely to be of service to them . . . The Russian danger is therefore our danger . . . just as the cause of any Russian fighting for his hearth and home is the cause of free men and free peoples in every quarter of the globe . . ."[20] On 12 July, 1941, as the Russian armies were retreating, an Anglo-Soviet Agreement was signed in which both sides agreed, that "during this war they will neither negotiate nor conclude an armistice or treaty of peace except by mutual agreement." Announcing the Treaty, Mr Churchill said: "It is, of course, an alliance, and the Russian people are now our allies".

Perceptions of the alliance were bound to be influenced by the years of constant anti-Soviet propaganda. Some of those who had perpetuated the propaganda became victims of it. W P and Zelda

Coates commented that "There was nothing to choose between the views published in the press on June 23, and those expressed privately in the corridors of the House of Commons when the members reassembled on June 24. One member in conversation with the authors summed up the judgement of the majority of his colleagues thus: "The Red Army at most will last three months". It is perfectly true that there were men and women in Whitehall, Fleet Street and in all parties in the House of Commons who had accurate ideas of the prowess of the Soviet Forces, but they were in a minority. The majority were blinded by prejudice, political and social . . ."[21]

Military prowess, however, was not a criterion which concerned the mass of trade unionists in Britain. The important fact was that they and the Soviet Workers were fighting on the same side. The reality of this exposed the fraudulent character of anti-Sovietism. This point was made by a miners' delegate at the TUC in September 1941 when he said: "The workers of Britain anxiously want the closest association with the workers of Russia. The workers of this country are beginning to see that all they have read abut the wickedness of the Russian Government is not true. They are beginning to see that they have been tricked, duped and doped by unscrupulous liars inspired by class prejudice and class interests . . ."[22] All in all the immediate and widespread identity of British workers with the Soviet people indicated how superficially anti-Soviet propaganda had penetrated the consciousness of many ordinary workers. No one at that time was inspired by Red Army victories for there were none. There were only retreats and defeats, devastation and killing. When Europe had been over-run there had not been comparable expressions of identity with the workers of France, Belgium, Denmark and Holland; nor had there been one when the Germany Army ploughed through Poland.

When the Annual Congress of the TUC met in September, 1941, in Edinburgh the position on all war fronts was critical. On the second day the TUC debated an emergency motion, moved by Citrine, which, amongst other things, stated:

"The Congress, mindful of the pledge given by the Trade Union and Labour Movement to support Soviet Russia in every possibly way, offers organized collaboration with the Russian Trade Union Movement. Congress therefore cordially endorsed the proposal of the General Council for the establishment of an Anglo-Russian Trade Union Council, composed of an equal number of representatives of the All-Union Central Council of Trade Unions of the USSR and of the British TUC General Council and providing for regular meetings alternatively in Russia and Great Britain for the exchange of views and information upon the problems with which the Trade Union movement in each country is called upon to deal, and affording opportunity for joint counsel and co-operation on matters of common concern, on the definite understanding that there shall be no interference on questions of internal policy and organization which must remain the exclusive responsibility of each body."

In the subsequent debate the only criticisms of the motion were that it should have been more forthright in welcoming co-operation with the Soviet Union and should have been less prescriptive until the Soviet trade unions had made their views known. It was acclaimed. The day following the debate Stalin informed Churchill of the desperate situation of the Red Army. Without a Second Front this year, he stated, in the Balkans or France and without substantial supplies of arms and aluminium "the Soviet Union will either be defeated or weakened to the extent that it will lose for a long time the ability to help its Allies by active operations at the front against Hitlerism."[23] Virtually the whole of European Russia had fallen to the German army. Kiev was lost 17 days later; Odessa was evacuated on 1 October; the Germans were approaching Stalingrad on the Volga River; an offensive on Moscow was expected at any time. None of this tragic news was received by British unions in a defeatist manner. All the divisions in the Trade Union Movement had disappeared, as had the doubts about the character of the war. British communists became catalysts in raising the war effort in industry.

Within a month of the Congress, Citrine and a General Council delegation of four travelled to Moscow. The AUCCTU had suggested only one alteration in the TUC terms, namely that the word Soviet should be used in the title instead of Russian, so there was no delay in setting up the Committee. A formal meeting between the two sides was held in Moscow on 15 October at which an Eight Point Declaration was agreed, listing the achievements and aims of the meeting.[24] The Committee functioned effectively until February, 1945 when the first preliminary World Trade Union Conference was held. After the USA entered the war in December, 1941 the TUC tried to persuade the American Federation of Labour to join an All-Allied Trade Union Committee but it would not, even then, sit on a Committee with Russians; nor would it share American representation with its rival central organization, the Congress of Industrial Organizations.[25] The collaboration between the governments of the Allied Powers, involving meetings between Stalin, Roosevelt and Churchill, was never matched at trade union level.

Long before the end of the war, but after the Battle of Stalingrad at the end of November, 1942 when the balance of war was finally tipped in favour of the Red Army, there were discussions in Britain about world trade union unity. This was one of many topics raised in connection with post-war structures. The needs of the war had altered the focus of the dominant ideology from class antagonism, in which socialism and communism were denigrated, to class collaboration, in which socialists and communists were praised for fighting the Germans. British workers, therefore, did not have to contend with a conflict of ideas about their industrial experiences. Their feelings of oneness with the Soviet workers were stimulated by communist shop stewards, and, in the interest of enhancing the war effort, encouraged by media and politicans alike. In this unique historical situation it seemed almost natural to talk about future post-war collaboration between unions in all the allied countries.

Such talk led to a resolution at the 1943 Trades Union Congress calling for a World Conference of representatives of the organized workers of all countries as soon as war conditions permitted with the intention of promoting the widest possible unity in the international trade union movement. Following consultations with a Soviet delegation at the Congress the General Council invited representatives from 71 trade union organizations in 31 countries to a Conference in London on 5 June 1944. The date of the Conference, however, was changed, because of the opening of the Second Front in France, to 6-17 February 1945. The outcome was the formation of an Administration Committee with the task of drafting a constitution for a World Federation of Trade Unions. The only dissenting voice was that of the American Federation of Labour which refused to participate in the preparatory committee and in the Conference itself. The Congress of Industrial Organizations, however, was present and represented American labour interests. A reconvened World Trade Union Conference in October 1945 formally established the World Federation of Trade Unions. Sir Walter Citrine was elected as President, with seven Vice-Presidents including Mr V V Kuznetsov from the AUCCTU and Mr Sidney Hillman from the CIO. The general secretary was Mr Louis Saillant from France, with two assistant secretaries, one from the Soviet Union and one from the USA.[26] Thus, for the first time since the Bolshevik Revolution, there existed a single body embracing unions from capitalist countries and the Soviet Union. Its scope extended over 56 countries with 66½ million organized workers.

Trade Unions and the Cold War

1945, the year of the formation of the World Federation of Trade Unions, was a watershed year in international relations. A catalogue of events reveals its significance. The Yalta Conference between the heads of state of the three Great Powers was held in February when decisions were reached which largely determined the political shape of the post-war world. On 12 April, Franklin D Roosevelt died. Roosevelt, as President of the USA, exercised a powerful moderating influence between Churchill and Stalin. The war in Europe ended on 8 May. The Charter of the United Nations was signed at San Fransisco on 26 June. The first post-European War Conference between the heads of the three Great Powers was held in Potsdam in July. Also in July the USA successfully tested its first atomic bomb which, in August, was dropped on Hiroshima and Nagasaki in Japan without the involvement or even knowledge of the Soviet Union. The war with Japan ended on 15 August.

The processes which these events communicated were twofold. First the emergence of the Soviet Union as a major world power and second the end of wartime detente and the re-emergence of pre-war anti-Sovietism but in a new, intense and potentially explosive form. The two processes were inter-related in that the form of anti-Sovietism was determined by the Soviet Union's newly recognized world power status. It was no longer possible for the West to treat the Soviet Union in a contemptuous, dismissive manner as in the interwar years. The method the West chose was to make military threats backed by arms superiority. This was the 'Cold War' phase.

The post-war intentions of the Western powers towards the Soviet Union were indicated by a succession of acts by the US after Roosevelt's death, such as the abrupt ending of the Lease Lend after 8 May, the decision to keep the knowledge of the atomic bomb from the Soviet Union at the Potsdam Conference, the Truman Declaration and the Marshall Plan. These were accompanied by intense anti-communist campaigns throughout the West. By 1949 the armoury of the 'Cold War' had been fully displayed.

The British Trade Union Movement participated fully in the processes hostile to communism and the Soviet Union. Its activities had two related aspects. The first was that it identified with the policies of the government concerning the Soviet Union. The second one was it displayed its commitment to anti-communism by purging itself of communist influences. Given the development of the TÚC since 1926 as a conformist institution within the framework of capitalism it was unlikely that it would analyze foreign allegiances in class rather than nationalistic terms. Once the British government had taken its position in the 'Cold War', with the media in full support, the TUC had neither the capacity nor the courage to step back and question the wisdom of what was being done. An added complication, of course, was that it was a Labour government which was pursuing 'Cold War' policies with a Foreign Secretary, Ernest Bevin, who had been a leading member of the TUC General Council, taking the initiatives. The primary foreign policy question after 1945 was not why the TUC turned on its erstwhile trade union ally in the Soviet Union so quickly and abruptly but why the Labour Government sided with American imperialism against Britain's most crucial ally in the war, as soon as it was sworn into office. This was a major political turnabout, taken without discussion in the Labour Movement or consultation with the electorate and evidenced as early as the Potsdam Conference during which the British General Election result was announced and the Labour leaders Clement Attlee and Ernest Bevin attended as replacement members for Winston Churchill and Anthony Eden.

The attitude of the TUC after 1946 might, to a slight extent, have been influenced by changes in its personnel. Sir Walter Citrine left the general secretaryship of the TUC in 1946 and was succeeded by an innocuous and uninspiring Vincent Tewson. Citrine had always claimed that his dislike of British communists had not influenced his view that Soviet trade unions should be part of the international trade union movement and to some extent the history of the 1930s bears that out. The leadership of the General Council was taken over by Arthur Deakin, Bevin's successor as general secretary of the Transport and General Workers' Union. Deakin unhesitatingly and enthusiastically pursued Bevin's policies. But he and Tewson, unlike Citrine, were unable to differentiate between domestic and international communism. They turned against both the Soviet Union and communists in Unions. Under Deakin's influence, the Transport and General Workers' Union proscribed communists from taking office in the union from 1949. The TUC under Tewson became an instrument for proscribing pro-communist organizations. The TUC General Council was dominated by a group of union leaders who were anti-communist and fervently loyal to Labour Government's foreign policies.

A prominent feature of the 'Cold War' was its totality and its pervasiveness. It penetrated all aspects of life and all manner of institutions. The government's foreign policy was no longer a matter confined to the corridors of Whitehall and Parliament. The change occurred because of the West's belief in the international communist conspiracy theory. The Soviet Union was perceived not simply as an enemy power but as one which was at the centre of a world conspiracy to destroy Western values and institutions. According to this theory the hand of Moscow could be seen directing every communist shop steward. The TUC itself made the point in a statement issued on 27 October 1948 when it stated that the General Council urged the executives of all affiliated unions, their district and branch committees, their responsible officer and loyal members "to counteract every manifestation of Communist influences within their unions; and to open the eyes of all workpeople to the dangerous subversive activities which are being engineered in opposition to the declared policy of the Trade Union Movement. In the considered view of the General Council, energetic steps must be taken to stop these evil machinations which threaten the economic recovery of the country. Steady progress is being made in the economic rehabilitation of this country and towards the restoration of a stable economy in Europe. Attempts to wreck economic recovery in the interests of a foreign power whose policy is to keep the world divided, impoverished, and in constant dread of a third world war, must be condemned and repudiated by all trade unionists."[27] This statement was reprinted in a TUC document about communism in 1955 which made the conspiracy point more explicit. The Communist Party, it stated, "is not a political party in the normal sense. It must never get out of step with other Communist parties of the world. If it does, it gets into trouble with its masters in Moscow . . . ."[28] The conspiracy network, the TUC alleged, operated in five main ways in that "they have attacked trade union support for defence in the West, they have plugged the phoney "Peace Campaign" all round the globe, they have cultivated unofficial groups and invited them to Russia and other satellite countries, they have tried to woo some unions with offers of trips and they have pressed for the setting up of bogus trade union unity committees."[29] It would be difficult to find a more uncritical commitment to anti-Sovietism than that.

The ideological climate in the West after 1945 inevitably influenced ordinary trade unionists towards anti-Sovietism even though many of them had been impressed during the war by Red Army victories. 'Cold War' policies began to be endorsed by individual unions. Unions affiliated to the TUC began to be differentiated according to their reactions to the TUC policy. For the first time ideological divisions became pronounced in the British trade union movement. Even the British miners who still remembered the vital help Soviet miners gave them in 1926 veered towards anti-communism. Will Lawther, the President of the National Union of Mineworkers from 1944 till 1954 belonged to the cabel of right wing union leaders on the General Council around Arthur Deakin. And when Arthur Horner, the communist General Secretary of the NUM publicly supported a French miners' strike in 1948 which was led by their communist oriented union he was admonished by the NUM executive for speaking 'contrary to union policy'.[30]

Most British trade unions endorsed the policy of anti-communism though very few implemented it through their rules. The National Union of Blastfurnacemen had practised political discrimination since 1936. Indeed its rules read like a 1930s recital of political agitation, stating: "Members or Supporters of the Communist Party, the National Minority Movement, the International Class War Prisoners' Aid Society, the National Unemployed Workers' Committee Movement, or the Fascist Party, or any allied or similar organizations, shall not be eligible to hold any office or to represent the Union at any Congress or Conference." The Transport and General Workers' Union, the National Union of Operative Heating Engineers and the Clerical and Administrative Workers' Union had rules forbidding communists (and fascists, to give the rules credibility) from holding office.

The practice of anti-communism, however, was most effective at an informal level where communist trade unionists were competing for posts and influence with non-communists. There

288

were anti-communist influences quite apart from the media in general. Both Catholic Action and Moral Re-Armament organized well-endowed campaigns for their own candidates and against communists. A special journal for trade unionists called *IRIS News* sponsored by Jack Tanner, a former left-wing President of the Amalgamated Engineering Union, was concerned entirely with anti-communism. Anti-communist pamphlets were published, such as *The Communist Solar System* by IRIS, and *The Peril in our Midst* by Woodrow Wyatt, to highlight the international implications of supporting communists at work. It was at the level of work, however, that the contradiction in the anti-communist campaign appeared. Communists generally were active trade unionists; they gave effective local leadership and consequently were frequently elected to local union posts. Even at the height of the 'Cold War', communist workers were elected to responsible union posts at the branch level of the union hierarchies. They were most successful at that level because media influences there were weakest. Anti-communism was strongest in regional and national union elections but it was never wholly effective. In the early 1950s, there were communist full-time officials in the majority of areas of the NUM, while in the T&GWU before 1949, nine of the 34 members of its Executive Council were communists and in some industries such as the docks, road passenger transport and engineering they were the dominant leaders. In the Midlands car industry communists were constantly elected as convenors of shop stewards. This patchy picture is simply intended to show that the ideological pressures against communism were frequently resisted. Moreover, because workers tended to trust communists to represent them at work, their view of the Soviet Union was softened. There was a considerable gap between the media presentation of the Soviet Union and the views of it held by ordinary workers.

The intensity of 'Cold War' pressures inevitably penetrated the World Federation of Trade Unions. The Executive Board was weakened by the loss of two of the triumverate which had formed the WFTU. Sir Walter Citrine resigned in 1946 and Sidney Hillman, Vice-President of the CIO died in July 1946, leaving only the Soviet delegate, V V Kuznetsov, from the original group. Their successors had much less commitment to the idea of world trade union unity. Each side began to be suspicious of the other. Whenever the communist members made a proposal, such as meeting in Havana or attending a mass rally in Czechoslovakia, it was perceived as part of a communist conspiracy. Similarly the Soviet representatives believed that Arthur Deakin, who had succeeded Citrine as the President of the WFTU, was acting in the interests of the Western powers.[31] The Marshall Plan, announced in June 1947, became the factor which intensified the growing divisions in the WFTU. James Carey wanted to raise the issue at the Executive Board but the Soviet representatives said it was a matter for a more representative gathering. Whilst this procedural discussion was going on the General Council of the TUC, claiming the matter had to be discussed promptly convened a conference of trade union central organizations in March, 1948 which approved of the Marshall Plan. The genesis of a breakaway had been formed. Western union leaders began denouncing the WFTU as a tool of Soviet propaganda. Its publications were attacked for political bias. Sir Vincent Tewson, Citrine's successor from the TUC, speaking for the Western delegates, criticised the WFTU administration for incompetence and wastage. The differences widened after the British Trades Union Congress rejected a motion in 1948 which stated that "This Congress re-affirms its support of the WFTU and urges its representatives to resist attempts to destroy unity inside this body . . ." Deakin, for the General Council, spoke against the motion and made public his criticisms of the WFTU. The final break came on 19 January 1949 when Deakin and Carey, followed by other members of the British, American and Dutch delegations left a meeting of the Executive Bureau and resigned from their positions. The decision to secede was endorsed by the TUC in September, 1949 by 6,250,000 votes to 1,017,000. In December, 1949, a new organization, the International Confederation of Free Trade Unions was formed in London. That act institutionalized the division in world trade union unity. In effect, it resurrected the International Federation of Trade Unions, which had been formally dissolved on 14 December 1945, but with a more intense and bitter anti-Sovietism.

The AFL-CIO

The attitude of American trade unions towards the Soviet Union has always been less ambivalent than that of the British unions. The American Federation of Labour has been consistently anti-Soviet since 1917. The contradiction which has beset British unions, whereby they have endeavoured to combine an underlying sympathy with Soviet workers with an institutional hostility to domestic communists, has no presence in the USA. The American trade unions displayed no admiration for the Bolshevik Revolution and except for the New Deal period, they have tried to purge themselved of communist influences. When the International Federation of Trade Unions was reconstituted in 1919 it offended the American Federation of Labour by opposing the Western blockade of Bolshevik Russia and by supporting the socialization of industry. The AFL refused to affiliate and practised the isolationism which characterised the whole of American society. The first delegation of American trade unionists to visit the Soviet Union did not go until 1927 following which the contacts were largely individualistic and desultory. The interest of American unions in foreign affairs began to increase from the mid-1930s as the international concern about the rise of Fascism began to spread. In consequence the AFL affiliated to the IFTU in 1937 but it was immediately confronted with the unacceptable British proposition that the Soviet AUCCTU should affiliate to the IFTU. William Green, the President of the AFL, reported with the comment that the affiliation of the Soviet unions would create disunity and, perhaps, the destruction of the IFTU. He said that the "Council of Trade Unions of the Soviet Government of Russia does not represent a democratic trade union movement free from government domination and control. In this respect, we cannot distinguish any difference between the Central Council of Trade Unions of the Soviet Government of Russia and the Nazi and Fascist – controlled labour front movement of Germany and Italy."[32] This view was maintained even during the Second World War. Indeed, in its report to the AFL Convention in San Francisco in 1947, the AFL Executive went so far as to criticize the US government for co-operating with the Soviet Union during the war. That same Convention gave full endorsement of the Marshall Plan and US foreign policy. The 'Cold War' was merely an opportunity for the AFL to indulge more freely and expensively in its political prejudice.

The AFL co-operated with the American government in its anti-communist scare campaign following the First World War and maintained a consistent hostility towards domestic communists throughout the inter-war years. US trade unions were encouraged to legislate against communist members, as the United Mine Workers of America did at its Convention in 1927. But they expressed their anti-communist sentiments mostly through internal union campaigns against all kinds of dissenters. John L Lewis for example, assumed financial control of recalcitrant locals and districts of the UMWA. This enabled him to suspend elected officials and to appoint his own trustees or receivers to run them. Increasingly in the inter-war years the districts of the UMWA came under Lewis's control. Dissent was often suppressed by physical means. The International Brotherhood of Teamsters made membership of the Communist Party illegal in 1935 but its main factional struggles involved members of Trotskyist organisations. One of Jimmy Hoffa's first organizing jobs was to wrest control of a Teamsters' local in Minneapolis from members of the Socialist Workers' Party. Hoffa said "I went there to Minneapolis . . . took over the office, brought in a hundred crack guys, had the war. We won every battle. And we finally took the union over and then Farrell left and went with the Socialist Party".[33] Hoffa, who became a notorious President of the Teamsters, was allegedly aided in his 'anti-Communist' campaign by "the Minneapolis Police Department, the courts of the city, the country, and the state . . . the mayor, the governor and an anti-labor law that had been . . . put through by the Republican governor of the State . . ."[34] That was but one small illustration of the methods which became common in the Teamsters' union.

The major progressive force in the American trade union movement from 1935 was the Committee of Industrial Organizations which was formed as a breakaway from the AFL in 1935 with the purpose of organizing the mass production industries by using the facilities provided by the National Labor Relations Act of that year. The initiative for forming the CIO came from John L Lewis, the President of the United Mine Workers' of America. The UMWA largely financed the CIO. Lewis appointed the organizers to lead the recruitment campaigns in the major industries. Many of them came from the UMWA. He appointed many communists who had been excluded from office in AFL unions and some of whom he had discriminated against in his own union, to spearhead the campaigns. The CIO started, therefore, with a strong faction of progressive trade unionists. By the outbreak of the Second World War there were, thus, two trade union centres in the USA representing different political perspectives. The AFL was the larger one but the CIO was more dynamic and politically progressive.

The CIO represented the left wing of the American labour movement. It was not, however, politically homogeneous. Some CIO unions, the most prominent of which were the United Electrical, Radio and Machine Workers of America, the International Union of Mine Mill and Smelting Workers and the International Longshoremen's and Warehousemen's Union had progressive leaderships. Others such as the United Automobile Workers were the scene of much faction fighting. Walter Reuther had worked in a motor car plant in Gorki in the Soviet Union for 16 months in 1933 and 1934. He returned full of praise for the Soviet system but by the outbreak of the Second World War he had became a supporter of the Democratic Party.[35] When he contested the Presidency of the UAW in 1946, which he narrowly won, Reuther was then acknowledged leader of the anti-communist faction in the union. He subsequently used the same organizational techniques as John L Lewis to suppress dissent in the UAW and he swung his union behind the government in the Cold War period. Other CIO leaders, such as Michael Quill, President of the Transport Workers' Union of America, made dramatic transitions to political conformity. There were some CIO leaders who were anti-communist from the outset but until the end of the war they were in a minority. The outcome of the bitter factional struggles extended their influence and accounted, in part, for the switch in the approach of the CIO towards the Soviet Union after the war.

The CIO had supported moves to establish international trade union unity before the USA entered the war. When the Anglo-Soviet Trade Union Committee was formed it urged the AFL and other American unions to join it. Individual affiliates, such as the National Maritime Union, sought to establish their own ties with similarly organized Soviet trade unions. The example set by the CIO caused dissension among AFL Unions. In New York a group of 150 officials in AFL unions formed a Committee to Promote the Unity of the Trade Union Movements of the United Nations. "Hundreds of local AFL unions, more than a dozen State Federations and a number of international unions favoured full cooperation by all sections of the American labor movement with the Anglo-Soviet Trade Union Committee and AFL membership in it."[36] Then when the AFL refused to take part in the discussions which led to the formation of the World Federation of Trade Unions in 1943 and 1944 the CIO enthusiastically took its place. Shortly after the end of the war the CIO suggested to the Soviet AUCCTU that they exchange delegations and in consequence in July and August, 1945, a Soviet Trade Union delegation visited major cities in the USA followed by an American delegation to the Soviet Union in October. The climax in the relations between the CIO and the Soviet Trade Union ˙ came when an American-Soviet Trade Union Committee was established at the end of 1945. The CIO nominated five of its most prestigious officials to sit on it. The warmth of feeling which the CIO expressed towards the Soviet Union was revealed by the report of the American delegation in October, 1945. It stated: "We were horrified by the wholesale destruction wrought by the Nazis; but we were filled with the greatest admiration for the determination and united effort of the people, which has already brought about substantial reconstruction and promise great things for future elevation of living standards."[37] Philip Murray the President of the CIO, commented that the Report was important for all those American workers who wanted to know the truth about the Soviet trade unions. Then, as in Britain, without any visible warning the truth gave way to the stereotype.

The view of the AFL all along was that any dealings with the Soviet trade unions would give recognition to American communists and they intended to avoid that possibility. The CIO, with an already significant communist influence, could not make that correlation. It was reported that after the war the CIO had eighteen affiliates which were allegedly run by communists.[38] There were influential communist factions in many other unions so that the CIO's route to political conformity had to be different. Once chosen, its task was to withdraw recognition from its communist organizers and members.

The CIO gave way to the intense domestic pressures after the war for a consensus in international affairs. Within 18 months of the end of the war it joined some of its affiliates in the hunt for communist trade unionists. The first step was a decision by its Executive Board in November 1946 to authorize its President to take over the funds and property of those sections of its organization which refused to accept CIO policy. This was followed fairly quickly by a denunciation of US communists for interfering in the affairs of the CIO. The CIO, however, maintained its foreign alliances until 1947 when it reiterated its support for the WFTU. From then, however, it deserted radical politics and placed itself firmly behind the Cold War policies of the US government. It moved in support of the Truman Doctrine of 12 March, 1947 which initiated overt US material support for the right-wing forces in Greece and Turkey and wherever they appeared. It endorsed the Marshall Plan in June of the same year and then, in the 1948 Presidential Election campaign, backed the

Democratic Party candidate, Harry S Truman rather than Henry Wallace from the newly established Progressive Party who favoured close, friendly relations with the Soviet Union. These were the policy issues which became the subject of CIO hegemony over its affiliates. They constituted a loyalty test for all American unions.

At this stage the CIO became an adherent of the international communist conspiracy theory and identified a stooge, a fellow-traveller or an agent in every communist supporter. It used various methods to uncover and expurgate them. The CIO lifted its prohibition on membership raiding between affiliates. The Electrical, Radio and Machine Workers' Union, for instance, was raided by the United Automobile Workers. In April 1948, Walter Reuther announced that the UAW would admit rank and file members who wanted to escape from progressive unions. Secessions were encouraged. For example, forty-two locals representing about 26,000 workers with bargaining rights in Connecticut left the International Union of Mine Mill and Smelter Workers.[39] Factional struggles were intensified and communist officials either recanted, as did Michael Quill, the leader of the Transport Workers' of America, or were deposed, as in the case of the officials of the Industrial Union of Marine and Shipbuilding Workers' Association. The CIO then turned on the unions which refused to compromise their positions in any way. The United Electrical Workers, the largest of the progressive unions, was expelled by the 1949 CIO Convention through a resolution which accused it of betraying "the economic, political and social welfare of the CIO, its affiliates and general membership". The union was described in the debate as being "virtually padded by and through the employment of many Communist agents (who) . . . are inbred with a feeling of hatred against democratic institutions and democratic countries . . ."[40] The same Convention added a new section to the CIO Constitution which stated: "No individual shall be eligible to serve either as an officer or as a member of the Executive Board who is a member of the Communist Party . . ." Walter Reuther had unsuccessfully tried to persuade the CIO to discriminate against communists the year before. In 1949, however, there was a national paranoia about communist subversion and unions took up the hunt with enthusiasm. Informing against communists was encouraged as being in the national interest. The President of the American Radio Association gave a lead and reported ten unions for having communist officials. The CIO appointed a committee to hear the charges and found them proved. Nine of the unions were expelled. In the tenth union, the United Furniture Workers of America, its policy was overturned during the course of the proceedings after a campaign led by its President, Morris Pizer, so no action was taken against it.

In most cases, the expelled unions, which represented government workers, office employees, food and tobacco workers and workers in fisheries and the farm equipment industry were destroyed. In order to undermine the United Electrical Workers the CIO established the International Union of Electrical, Radio and Machine Workers under the leadership of James Carey, the former member of the Executive Board of the WFTU. The United Electrical Workers survived but in a truncated form. The Union of Mine, Mill and Smelter Workers also survived with a loss of members. The International Longshoremen's and Ware-housemens's Union under the leadership of Harry Bridges maintained its membership and control of dock workers on the US West coast after it was expelled but it was the only union to do so. There was little need for the Congressional Committee on Un-American Activities to be concerned about communist subversion in unions for the unions themselves relentlessly pursued communists,. By 1954, according to the US Bureau of Labor Statistics, "fifty-nine of a hundred unions had amended their constitutions to bar Communists from holding office. Forty-one of them discriminated not only against Party members but also against advocates and supporters. Forty unions barred Communists not only from office but also from membership. Nor were such provisions mere window dressing; expulsions were numerous and almost always upheld by the courts".[41] Because it was often difficult to identify communists the unions acted against dissenters in general. The classic role which unions have performed in history of giving collective protection to unpopular, dissenting causes ceased in the US. Instead unions began to use systematic institutional means to curb dissent. In the United Mine Workers of America, for instance, 19 of the 23 Districts had officials appointed by the Union President by 1972 in order to maintain political conformity. Every District which dared to defy the President was placed in 'trusteeship'. Defiant officials lost their jobs. But the consequence was more serious than that. The general climate in the US was such that political non-conformity everywhere was penalized. The few people who stood against the erosion of civil rights were invariably penalised themselves. Few workers were prepared to risk their jobs and livelihoods through opposing the government's foreign policies or protesting about the arrests and trials of communists for subversion. American workers in general, as individuals and collectively, took the lessons of the Cold War period to heart and retreated either into orthodoxy or apathy.[42] Thereafter, the government was able to undertake virtually any foreign adventure without united protests from organized labour.

The CIO leaders made it clear that their primary concern was what they described as the international communist conspiracy. The communists they hunted were regarded as Soviet agents. The American trade union historian, Philip Taft, expressed in his own work the reasoning which underlay this paranoia "The attacks on Socialists and other dissidents", he stated, "ended at the conventions and were never in the entire history of the AFL carried beyond that point. Nor was the loyalty of Socialists to the labor movement ever questioned. The Communists . . . presented a different issue. Following the dictates of an international conspiratorial apparatus in the service of a foreign power, the communists had been shown to be ready to sacrifice the interests of their own members and the country and its people when it suited the ends of the Soviet Union."[43] Somewhere in the speeches of the union officials who spearheaded the anti-communist campaign this point was invariably made. When Philip Murray, President of the CIO, attacked the leaders of the United Electrical Workers, he spoke of their programme as "an echo of the Comintern" and added that their allegiances were "pledged to a foreign government."[44] Walter Reuther described members of the Communist Party as "colonial agents using the trade-union movement as a base of operations for serving the needs of the Soviet Union".[45] The unions had become the purveyors of anti-Sovietism.

The sign that the CIO had completed its transition from radical politics was its merger with the ALF in 1955. From then it became part of the most conservative advocate of consensus politics in the Western hemisphere. The AFL-CIO operated outside the USA in effect as a government agency and depended upon government funds to finance its operations. The focus of those activities was always anti-Sovietism. Frequent allegations were made that its two main post-war directors of international affairs, Jay Lovestone and Irving Brown, were CIA employees. In 1964 a House of

297

Representatives Banking Committee report revealed that several US unions had taken CIA money, while former CIA agents declared that they had worked for institutes in Third World countries which were funded through the AFL-CIO. This last allegation was the main theme of an article in *Business Week* on 4 November, 1985. In describing the link between the AFL-CIO and the US government in the conduct of international affairs, the article stated that: "Through a group of little known institutes, the AFL-CIO spends $43 million a year in 83 countries – often for anti-communist projects that tend to merge with the Administration's foreign policy themes". The allegation focussed on four operating units for the AFL-CIO International Affairs Department located in different areas of the world. They were the American Institute for Free Labor Development, operating in 22 Latin American countries in opposition to indigenous liberation movements, the African-American Labor Centre with bases in 25 African countries, the Asian-American Free Labor Institute which worked in 31 Asian and Middle East countries, especially in the Philippines in an attempt to create an anti-Marcos trade union movement which was acceptable to the American government, and the Free Trade Union Institute which channelled funds to unions in Europe. Ninety per cent of the 1985 AFL-CIO budget for these institutes came from US government sources, namely the Agency for International Development, the National Endowment for Democracy and the US Information Agency. The combined cost of the four institutes was almost as great as the total budget for all the AFL-CIO activities in the US. With such an institutionalized financial tie-up between the AFL-CIO and the US government it was virtually impossible for unions to be used as platforms for attacks on government foreign policies. This situation, however, began to show signs of change in the early 1980s.

American unions are now experiencing contradictions which are beginning to crack the 'Cold War' moulds into which most of them were set so that the post-war consensus on US foreign policy is being undermined. In recent years the membership composition of US unions has been dramatically altered due to an influx of women, blacks and hispanics. Coincident with this, the old guard of the AFL-CIO leadership has been dying away to be replaced by a much more politically heterogeneous and progressive leadership. This change has been reflected in trade union action. In 1983 the presidents of 22 AFL-CIO affiliated unions formed the National Labor Committee in Support of Democracy and Human Rights in El Salvador and Nicaragua. A number of unions, including the normally politically conservative United Mine Workers of America, have united in opposition to the US government's policy on South Africa and are campaigning against apartheid. By 1987 fifteen large unions had passed peace resolutions, seeking an arms accord with the Soviet Union. Some unions now send delegations to the Soviet Union though the US State Department consistently prevents them from receiving trade union delegations from the Soviet Union. These changes represent small but significant steps towards rejecting anti-Sovietism as the primary aim of US trade union policy abroad. It still remains the case, however, that, except for a brief period in 1977-8, no Soviet trade union delegation has been allowed into the USA since 1949. Moreover, both the AFL and the AFL-CIO have never in their history had any formal contacts with the Soviet AUCCTU. The AFL-CIO has indeed been more extreme on this issue than the ICFTU which it has consistently accused of being too soft on communism. It was partly for this reason that the AFL-CIO disaffiliated from the ICFTU in 1969.[46]

Bilateral Trade Union Unity

The Western secession from the World Federation of Trade Unions had a number of important consequences for trade union unity. First, it removed the regular, automatic procedures which brought union leaders together from capitalist and socialist countries. So long as the WFTU existed as the single world central body then trade unionists met from all over the world no matter what the politicians and governments were doing and saying about each other. That facility was important because it enabled some differences to be clarified and cleared up before they intensified. After the split, communist and non-communist trade unionists only met in an ad hoc fashion, following special initiatives. Such meetings were vulnerable to changes in the world political climate and to altering political moods. Those contacts, without the institutional backing provided by the WFTU, were fragile and uncertain.

Secondly, once the split was institutionalized by the formation of the International Confederation of Free Trade Unions, then it took on a form which was difficult to eliminate. Two institutions faced each other which were motivated by desires for self-survival as much, if not more, than the principle of trade union unity. The ICFTU had functions which were created by the split; the positions which its officials held were dependent upon its perpetuation; the status which they acquired was derived from it. There were vested institutional interests which flourished in anti-communism and which, therefore, operated to develop, extend and intensify it. Success for the ICFTU was measured, therefore, in terms of the spread of anti-communist and anti-Soviet beliefs and attitudes rather than in the spread of trade unionism throughout the world.

This brought with it a third consequence, namely an intensificia-tion of anti-Sovietism within and between trade unions. Member-ship of the World Federation of Trade Unions had a moderating effect upon the involvement of British unions in the early stages of the 'Cold War'. There was a measure of institutional loyalty even when the practice of unity began to fracture. The split, however, not only removed the constraints but acted as a catalyst for competitive, hostile propaganda. A constant stream of publications confirming and elaborating the conventional Western stereotype of the Soviet Union flowed from the Brussels' headquarters of the ICFTU to all the world's non-communist trade union centres. Western countries were defined as democratic while socialist ones were described as totalitarian. Westen trade unions were 'free' while socialist ones were tools of the state or appendages of the Communist Party. This distinction was illustrated by the comments on the activities of the International Confederation of Free Trade Unions in the TUC General Council's Report for 1957. There, under the heading "Relations of Free Trade Unions with Dictatorship Countries", it stated, without explanation or supporting data, that "The principles and functions of free trade unions and those of communist organizations are fundamentally different. Representatives of a free Trade Union Movement can initiate and determine policy within their own ranks, irrespective of Government or Party. Communist unions, on the other hand, are merely agents or instruments of their Government . . ."[47] Western trade union centres began stipulating that they could not have relations with unions in socialist countries unless they were "free", "independent" or bona fide, meaning like themselves.

Immediately after the breach the World Federation of Trade Unions attempted to overcome it by appealing directly to individual unions in Britain. It continued to invite unions to

300

meetings and conferences. The TUC reacted by advising unions to have no contact of any kind with the WFTU or its affiliates. This advice was given regularly thereafter. At first the unions complied. The National Executive Committee of the National Union of Mineworkers, for instance, which had always been positive in its attitude to international unity, began to reject WFTU invitations after 1949. Virtually all TUC affiliated unions did likewise at the outset. But pressure was quickly generated to heal the breach. As early as 1954 the Annual Conference of the NUM voted to establish "international trade union unity as the best means of protecting the interests of workers of all countries". Then in 1956 it called for the re-establishment of the Anglo-Soviet Trade Union Committee. These moves for unity with Soviet trade unions, however, had little effect on the TUC for more than a decade, for just when the relationship began to improve a crisis would occur which would cause it to regress.

The first major crisis was when Soviet troops moved into Hungary at the end of October in 1956. The TUC General Council reacted swiftly. It reported: "The Hungarian uprising was at first successful. For a few days it seemed that the Hungarian people might be able to shake off the regime imposed on them, and to choose their own way of life. Their Soviet overlords thought otherwise and moved in armed forces to crush ruthlessly the Hungarian Revolution."[48] The General Council set up a "Help for Hungarian Workers' Fund", distributed a million copies of a leaflet condemning the action of the Soviet government, protested to the Soviet Ambassador in London and then, on 30 November, "considered ways in which the British Trade Union Movement could give further expression to its condemnation ·of the action of the Soviet Government in Hungary". It decided "that there was a case for the cessation of all trade union exchange visits with the USSR" and circularized all affiliated unions, trades councils and trade council federations advising them to abandon plans to visit the USSR. A number of unions, including the Transport and General Workers' Union, the National Union of General and Municipal Workers, the Amalgamated Union of Building Trade Workers and the Iron and Steel Trades Confederation, cancelled their proposed trips.

Despite the events in 1956, however, bilateral arrangements were continued between British and Soviet trade unions in defiance of repeated TUC advice to the contrary and despite intensive anti-Soviet propaganda. During the 1957 Congress of the TUC which was dominated by anti-Soviet emotion, Dave Bowman, from the National Union of Railwaymen, criticized the General Council and stated that his union intended to send a delegation to the Soviet Union in a couple of weeks. He added: "In conversations with a number of delegates here I learn that a number of trade unions have either accepted or are in the process of considering invitations from the East European countries . . ."[49]

Individual trade unions, though they participated in the formulation of TUC policy, were affected only indirectly by the split which produced the International Confederation of Free Trade Unions, for only trade union centres were affiliated to the WFTU and the ICFTU. Their main international relationships were conducted through the long-established International Trade Secretariats which were autonomous bodies with jurisdiction in specific industries. There were, for instance, ITS's for transport, mining, printing and public employment. The Soviet trade unions had never belonged to them. And they had never affiliated to the International Federation of Trade Unions in the interwar years because they had refused to sacrifice their autonomy. A condition of the success of the WFTU in 1945 was that the Soviet trade unions should join the International Trade Secretariats which should then become Trade Departments of the WFTU. This fusion was not achieved in the short life of the WFTU.[50]

The British unions were in a dilemma. They were important affiliates of the International Trade Secretariats both before the split in world trade unity and afterwards and they played an influential role in determining their policy. Yet they generally resented the situation in which they could not establish contacts with trade unions in socialist countries. The International Trade Secretariats had close organizational and even closer ideological links with the International Confederation of Free Trade Unions. They identified with its anti-communism. The British unions resolved their dilemma by ignoring the existence of the ICFTU and not allowing the commitment to the ITSs to hamper the development of relationships with socialist trade unions. Within five years of the formation of the ICFTU there was a regular exchange of union delegations between Britain and the socialist countries. This was especially the case in Scotland where the Scottish Trades Union Congress, acting independently of its counterpart over the border, encouraged a consistently sympathetic approach to the socialist countries.

This patchwork unity with socialist trade unions inevitably generated pressures for a more systematic, centralized and formal unity. Once the 1956 crisis had receded in the collective memory of the unions they began to resolve to mend the breach. The question of world trade union unity was raised but not voted on at the 1965 TUC but in 1967 the Congress of the TUC adopted a resolution regretting the divisions in the world trade union movement and urging the General Council "to explore all possible means of achieving friendly contacts and consultations with all *bona fide* trade union organizations with the minimum objectives of hastening the social advance of workers in all countries and preserving world peace."[51] The impact of this resolution was destroyed because it was referred to the ICFTU "Committee on Relations with Communist Controlled Trade Union Organizations" and shelved. But before any union could query the General Council's action another crisis broke out in Czechoslovakia and the process of severing relationships with socialist unions began all over again.

The General Council of the TUC met on 21 August 1968 and issued a statement condemning the movement of troops from Warsaw Pact countries into Czechoslovakia. It stated that "In the light of this invasion the General Council have come to the conclusion that it would no longer be useful to pursue current contacts with the Trade Union Movement of the Soviet Union, or with those of the countries associated in the attack. These contacts were resumed in recent years in the expectation, now shown to be completely unjustified, that the Soviet Government was moving towards an attitude of greater independence for the satellite countries, greater freedom for its own citizens and in particular greater freedom for the trade unions of those countries to reflect the experience and working class interests of their members . . . the General Council suggest to all their affiliated unions that they also should reconsider their attitude towards visits of delegations to or from any of those countries whose troops have invaded Czechoslovakia."

It had become a feature of TUC responses to crises involving the Soviet Union to condemn the whole society for the actions of its government. This stemmed from its perception of a communist society as a totality in which everything and everyone was subjected to the control of the Communist Party. It had no such perception of the USA which it defined as a pluralistic society with many interest groups acting independently and without responsibility to each other. This anomalous behaviour was described by Ken Gill, representing the Draughtsmen's and Allied Technicians' Association at the 1968 TUC, when he said that the movement of Soviet troops into Czechoslovakia had been described as Soviet imperialism but "have we, as the British Trade Union Movement, always opposed every aspect of British imperialism, and when we have failed to oppose those aspects have we been boycotted by the rest of the world trade union Movement?" He added that the British trade union movement "has very firmly declared itself against the action of the United States in Vietnam and whatever one may say about the situation in Czechoslovakia it cannot be compared with the carnage that goes on daily in that unhappy country. However . . . DATA, and many other trade unionists here would never suggest that we break our traditional bonds with the American trade union movement . . ."[52]

It was only unions in socialist countries that were held responsible for the actions of their governments and penalized for them. But, as after 1956, the penalties were short-lived and the pressures for unity re-emerged. By 1975 the TUC had agreed that "the time is ripe for an initiative to be taken to bring the two world trade union centres, ie the WFTU and the ICFTU, more closely together". The issue was raised again in 1979 but the General Council declined to alter its policy of pursuing parallel relationships for fear of being expelled from the ICFTU.[53] In the meantime the ICFTU entrusted with the task of healing the breach between itself and the WFTU was complaining to the International Labour Organization that there was no freedom of association in the Soviet Union.

By now the behaviour of the TUC was predictable. In a crisis involving a conflict of ideologies the TUC would respond as if it were seeking the seal of approval from the Foreign Office and would advocate boycotts, sanctions or reprisals of one kind or another against socialist trade unions. The events in Poland from 1980 confirmed this prediction. In 1980 following a strike in the Gdansk shipyard, the trade union organization called Solidarity was formed. It grew rapidly and displaced all of the existing unions. The TUC General Council recognized it and the ICFTU urged that it should be given full support. Assistance was provided in money and kind. Both the European TUC and the International Metalworkers' Federation shared in this gesture. Virtually all of the Western trade union movements identified with the new Polish development. Then, arising out of the political crisis which the actions of Solidarity created, the Polish government imposed martial law on 13 December 1981. All trade union activity was suspended and many union officials were arrested. Solidarity was disbanded.

No foreign troops were engaged in Poland yet stories circulated about the involvement of the Soviet Union. The Soviet hand was seen everywhere, inevitably, from the Western point of view, with sinister implications. The General Council considered severing all contacts with Eastern European national trade union centres but decided on this occasion to circulate them with a request for their views about the Polish crisis and asking if they would use their influence "to encourage an end to repression" in Poland. They were to be judged by their replies. Affiliated unions were asked to do likewise.

Replies were received from the German Democratic Republic, Czechoslovkia, the Soviet Union, Hungary, Bulgaria and Yugoslavia. That from the GDR caused consternation in the TUC General Council for it accused the British of arrogance and double standards, stating that their approach to problems in socialist countries was inconsistent with their attitude to the denial of trade union rights in El Salvador and South Africa.[54] The General Council reacted by severing relations with the GDR Free Trade Union Council, causing a rupture which has still not been healed. There was a similar reaction to the answer from the Central Council of Czechoslovakia Trade Unions which blamed the "destructive activity of Solidarity" for the crisis. The General Council, however, decided not to break relations but to communicate with the CCCTU only for the purpose of restoring Solidarity. The Soviet AUCCTU replied in more measured terms but insisted that the Polish government was justified in its actions by the political character and intentions of Solidarity. The relationship with the AUCCTU was cooled by the reply but not broken off. The TUC attitude to Solidarity has remained unchanged even though it no longer exists. On 8 October 1982, a new law was passed enabling trade union activity to be resumed. As a result, enterprise unions were formed by former Solidarity members which were linked through 134 different federations. In November 1984 a new central union organization was established, called the National Trade Union Alliance. The TUC has no relations with this body. Bilateral relations between individual unions in Britain and Poland have been slow to develop in the wake of the crisis.

In general, with the exception of Poland and the German Democratic Republic, the attitude of the TUC towards union centres in the socialist countries nowadays is distant but friendly. The TUC is handicapped by its own affiliation to the ICFTU but within this constraint it is willing to make informal contacts. The TUC has continued with the mediating role it has played since 1917 though on a lower key and with less commitment than in the interwar years. It has pressed, for instance, for the inclusion of socialist trade unions in the European Trades Union Congress but without success. But it has done nothing at any level to foster relations between them. Yet the TUC is repeating its earlier experiences. As the last crisis involving the Soviet Union is receding in the memory of the TUC its attitude towards the Soviet AUCCTU is mellowing. In a surprise move the TUC General Council sent an official delegation headed by the General Secretary to the Eighteenth Congress of Soviet Trade Unions in March 1987. The last equivalent delegation to a Congress of Soviet Trade Unions had been in November, 1924 when the TUC attended the Sixth Congress. After the break up of the WFTU in 1949 there was no official contact between the TUC and the AUCCTU until 1966 when a British delegation visited Moscow. Then in 1972, Vic Feather, the TUC General Secretary led a delegation of General Council members to the Soviet Union. A Soviet delegation came to Britain in 1975, led by A N Shelepin, the president of the AUCCTU, and discussed an expansion of various forms of bilateral contacts "in the spirit of co-operation which had existed between them during the war". But before anything further was done the crises in Poland and Afghanistan occurred and relations deteriorated. The next official contact was the March 1987 one. This was followed within a few weeks by another official TUC delegation, again led by the TUC General Secretary, Norman Willis, to inspect the site of the nuclear power disaster at Chernobyl. Clearly, unless another international incident intervenes, there will be demands from British trade unions for the TUC to re-establish formal links with the Soviet AUCCTU.

Pressures for a formal institutional relationship with Soviet trade unions have been re-inforced by re-alignments in the field of international trade unionism. The ideological division created in 1949 has been overcome by two important groups of workers. There are signs that their example will be followed by others in, for example, the occupations dealing with medical work. The first significant and permanent removal of the 'Cold War' barrier was in 1974 when 25 entertainment and communications unions from 19 socialist and capitalist countries, founded the International Federation of Audio-Visual Workers' Union (FISTAV). Their purpose was to enable unions to meet over common issues irrespective of whether they were affiliated to the ICFTU or the WFTU or to neither. By 1984 the number of affiliates had increased to 58, of whom 38 were affiliated to the ICFTU and 11 to the WFTU. Only unions in two major countries, namely the USA and West Germany, have refused to affiliate to the International. FISTAV was opposed by the ICFTU and refused affiliation to the European Trades Union Congress. It survived the Polish crisis. It refused to recognize Solidarity as a bona fide trade union which qualified for affiliation but otherwise adopted a neutral position to preserve its own unity. A new Polish Cultural and Art Workers' Union was accepted into membership in 1987. FISTAV, with its headquarters in Paris, holds its meetings alternately in a capitalist or socialist country and provides much opportunity for representatives from capitalist countries to mix with their socialist counterparts. Its experience confirms that from a trade union point of view this is wholly advantageous.

The second and probably the strongest pressure has come from the formation in September 1985 of a new miners' international trade secretariat which encompasses miners from communist and non-communist countries. The NUM had consistently expressed its dissatisfaction with the ideological division which split the world trade union movement. It believed that the interests of miners transcended political differences. This belief prompted it to convene a world miners' peace conference in 1981 which was attended by all the major miners' unions except those from West Germany and the USA. Then in 1982 the NUM initiated talks with the French Miners' Union, the CGT and the Soviet Miners Union to explore the possibility of forming an entirely new international organization which united all miners from all countries, without any discrimination. The outcome was the formation three years after the initial talks, of the International Miners' Organization. The NUM withdrew from the ICFTU affiliate, the Miners' International Federation, which the British miners had been instrumental in forming in 1893. The miners' trade secretariat belonging to the WFTU was dissolved. Miners from socialist, Third World and capitalist countries were brought together in a single organization for the first time. Now miners from capitalist countries meet with Soviet miners on a regular formal and normal basis rather than fortuitously as previously.

Anti-Sovietism and Class Consciousness

The history of the attitudes of Western trade unions towards the Soviet Union varies between countries. It shows a marked distinction between Britain and the USA which has its basis in the class character of trade unionism in the two countries at the time of the Bolshevik Revolution. In Britain there was a sharp class conflict between 1917 and 1926 with unions relying on industrial action to achieve political ends, especially in the immediate aftermath of the war. In this milieu some British unions envied the Russian workers while others sympathised with them. The result was a sense of identity with the aims of the Bolshevik Revolution which was never entirely eradicated. It was reinforced by the Soviet victories in World War Two. The American trade unions were in an entirely different situation after 1917 for through their pursuit of business unionism they were mostly propagators of the US capitalist ideology. Moreover from 1918 to 1923 they lived through and collaborated with the state oppression of political non-conformity and acquiesced in the state destruction of the International Workers of the World, the main union to challenge American political orthodoxy. They had little class understanding of their own situation and, therefore, no insights into the nature of the Bolshevik Revolution. In the main, US trade unions welcomed the overthrow of the Czar in March 1917 but were out of sympathy with the Bolsheviks in October. Once the anti-Soviet propaganda machine went into operation the US trade unions went along with it and reinforced its impact. That remained the position of the AFL even during the Second World War. The CIO adopted a more sympathetic stance during the war but its friendliness towards the Soviet Union was dissipated during the 'Cold War'. Thereafter the AFL-CIO was an advocate of anti-Sovietism without any rank and file membership constraints.

Anti-Sovietism is an essential element of capitalist ideology with a specific objective, namely to undermine class analysis and discredit socialism. Its purpose is not to clarify and illuminate the internal conditions and external aspirations of the Soviet Union but to distort them in every way possible to protect capitalist power relations. In so far as trade unions are anti-Soviet therefore, they are collaborating with capitalism and weakening their own positions in the class struggle. Events since 1917 have shown that British unions, however, have never been fully or consistently collaborative. Their anti-Sovietism has vacillated. In simplistic terms it can be portrayed as a gut feeling of class identity struggling for expression through a pervasive hostile ideology. Sometimes the gut feeling is dominant, as between 1917 and 1926 and during the Second World War. At other times it is subdued or overwhelmed as during the crises in 1956, 1968 and 1980-82. But it has never been destroyed. Almost as soon as the crises are over the feeling of identity re-emerges.

The impact of the dominant ideology has varied over time, between unions and at different levels of union organization. In general its greatest impact has been at the level of the Trades Union Congress because it is most amenable to pressures for conformity due to its relations with governments, with national employers' bodies and with the International Confederation of Free Trade Unions. Official TUC advice to unions during international crises involving the Soviet Union has consistently conformed to Government policy and, therefore, to the Western stereotype of the Soviet Union. The responses of the delegates at the Annual Trades Union Congress have, without exception, emotionally and intolerantly conformed to the same standard. It has been as if the widely publicized details of the Soviet tank and troop movements have been perceived as conclusive evidence that the Soviet Union is the enemy, stopping off at Budapest and Prague en route for the Channel ports. The results have been baseless outbursts of sickening patriotism exposing the effects of the constant drip of anti-Soviet propaganda. They have always been short-lived departures from otherwise rational deliberations but they have had influential consequences.

When trade unions, either singly or collectively in the TUC re-inforce the dominant ideology they make dissent difficult by making it a matter for individual action. It is hazardous for individuals to attempt to break through emotionally-sustained national consensuses of the kind generated during the Hungarian, Czechoslovakian and Polish crises. They are accused of treachery, of following instructions from Moscow, of advocating an alien creed. Counter-arguments, therefore, are either not put or are received with closed minds. Such occasions show how easily the trade union movement can be persuaded to work against its own best interests. When it condemns Soviet socialism it is undermining socialism itself and, therefore, its own aspirations.

FOOTNOTES

1. *Trade Unions and the Government* by V L Allen, p. 162.
2. *British Labour Delegation to Russia, 1920, Report*, London 1920. Also *Britain and the Bolshevik Revolution* by Stephen White, London, 1979, p. 14.
3. *Russia* The Official Report of the British Trades Union delegation to Russia in November and December 1924.
4. ibid, p. 1.
5. Bramley died of cancer on 14 October 1925 and was succeeded by W M Citrine in 1926.
6. *In Russia Now* by Sir Walter Citrine, 1942, p. 12.
7. The only detailed history of the formation, life and ending of the Committee is *The United Front* by Daniel F Calhoun, Cambridge, 1976 where there is much information hidden behind a barrier of prejudice. See also TUC Annual Reports, 1924, 25 and 26. Also *I Search for Truth in Russia* by W M Citrine, 1936; *In Russia Now* by Sir Walter Citrine, 1942; *Men and Work: An Autobiography*, by W M Citrine, 1964; and *Forty-Five Years. International Federation of Trade Unions* by Walter Schevenels, 1956.
8. Calhoun, op cit, p. 250 and *A History of Anglo-Soviet Relations* by W P and Zelda K Coates, 1943, pp. 228-232.
9. *Labour Monthly*, June 1926, pp. 375-8.
10. *I Search for Truth in Russia*, p. 300
11. Allen, op cit., pp. 32-3.
12. ibid.
13. See *The Post-War History of the British Working Class* by Allen Hutt, 1938, for details of the activities of the three organizations.
14. TUC Report, 1935, p. 111.
15. ibid, p. 112.
16. See Allen, op cit, pp. 63-73.
17. *History of Anglo-Soviet Relations* by W P and Zelda K Coates, p. 632.
18. ibid.
19. *My American Diary* by Sir Walter Citrine, 1941, p. 241.
20. W P and Zelda K Coates, op cit, pp. 677-678.
21. ibid, p. 680. It was said that the German Military Command expected victory in six weeks.
22. TUC Report, 1941, p. 253.
23. *The Road to Stalingrad* by John Erickson, London, 1975, p. 212.
24. The Eight Point Declaration is published in *Russia Now* by Sir Walter Citrine, pp. 118-119.
25. *Forty-Five Years. International Federation of Trade Unions* by Walter Schevenels, pp. 295-296.
26. For details of the formation of the WFTU from the 1943 Trades Union Congress onwards see TUC Reports for 1943, 1944, 1945 and 1946.

27. Reprinted in *The TUC and Communism,* published by the TUC, March, 1955.
28. ibid, p. 3.
29. ibid, p. 5.
30. *The Militancy of British Miners,* by V L Allen, pp. 121-124.
31. See *Trade Union Leadership* by V L Allen, pp. 289-312 for an examination of the WFTU Executive Board Minutes.
32. *Organized Labor in American History* by Philip Taft, New York, 1964, p. 597.
33. *The Hoffa Wars* by Dan E Moldea, New York, 1978, p. 32.
34. ibid, pp. 32-33.
35. *The UAW and Walter Reuther* by Irving Howe and B J Widick, New York, 1949, pp. 194-197.
36. *Recent History of the Labor Movement in the United States, 1939-1965,* Progressive Publishers, Moscow, 1979, pp. 121-122.
37. ibid, pp. 196-197.
38. Taft, op cit, p. 623.
39. ibid, p. 624.
40. ibid, p. 628.
41. *The Great Fear. The Anti-Communist Purge under Truman and Eisenhower,* by David Caute, p. 353.
42. ibid, pp. 353-4.
43. Taft, op cit, p. 624.
44. ibid, p. 627-628.
45. Howe and Widick, op cit, p. 267.
46. The public explanation for its disaffiliation concerned domestic US trade union politics. The United Automobile Workers had withdrawn from the AFL-CIO and had affiliated separately to the ICFTU. This, claimed the AFL-CIO, was an offence to its integrity so it withdrew from the ICFTU.
47. TUC Report, 1956, p. 194.
48. TUC Report, 1957, p. 195.
49. TUC Report, 1957, p. 413.
50. *Trade Union Leadership,* op cit, pp. 301-306
51. TUC Report, 1967, p. 291.
52. TUC Report, 1968, p. 485.
53. See TUC Report 1980, p. 213.
54. See TUC Report, 1982, pp. 220-221.

Chapter Thirteen
The Peace Movement and the Enemy

Peace Activity During War

There were various forms of peace action in Britain this century before the formation of the Campaign for Nuclear Disarmament though none was sustained and national in scope. By and large the anti-war protests were directed at particular wars whilst they were in progress and this gave rise to difficulties for they had to contend with populist expressions of patriotism and jingoism. They tended to be marginalized and projected not as anti-war but as acts of treason. For example, all the obstacles encountered by peace activists were present during the Boer War which started in the autumn of 1899 and lasted for 32 months. The main opposition to the war came from a section of the opposition Liberal Party, supported by the two main socialist organizations, the Independent Labour Party and the Social Democratic Federation. The war, however, was generally popular. Even the conduct of the war did not evoke opposition. There was some criticism of, but no general revulsion against, the British Army policy of burning Boer farms and of establishing concentration camps in which some thousands of Boer women and children died. The widespread pro-war sentiment was expressed at times through violence against those opposed to the war. Two meetings of the young Member of Parliament, David Lloyd-George, were broken up because he was opposed to the war. The Liberals were divided into the Liberal Imperialists and the pro-Boer or Little Englander factions. Members of this latter group were accused of a lack of patriotism, defeatism and treason. It was reasoned that if they were in favour of peace they would compromise with the enemy and, in effect support the Boers. A League of Liberals Against Aggression and Militarism was formed, to which David Lloyd-George belonged, but it had little consequence.

After the Boer War had ended the issue of war loomed large in discussions at international Labour and Socialist gatherings. It was the Socialists and not the Liberals who prescribed how to avoid war. The International Socialist Congress in 1907 spelled out the prescription. It emphasized that imperialism was the prime cause of war and that, therefore, the working class had a common interest in all countries to unite and oppose it. The prescription was based on international working class solidarity. Every Socialist or Labour Party should use all of its power to prevent war and then, if war broke out nonetheless, they should pursue militant anti-war policies and "use the political and economic crises created by the war to rouse the populace from its slumbers, and . . . hasten the fall of capitalist society".[1] The implication was that the working class should call general strikes in the affected countries. This seemed a real possibility when the discussion was about war threats. But when war actually broke out in August 1914 the working classes in Germany, Britain and France became enveloped in patriotism and war opposition crumbled. G D H Cole described the events in Britain. He stated that "the Labour Party and the Trades Union Congress, after taking part in peace demonstrations up to August 4th, 1914, speedily rallied to the national cause, leaving the ILP and a majority of the British Socialist Party to form a small minority in opposition . . . The Labour Party, which began by urging the working-class movements to concentrate on measures for the relief of distress, was soon involved, jointly with the other political parties, in a recruiting campaign. The Trades Union Congress issued a strongly worded appeal for soldiers . . . Undoubtedly at this stage, and throughout the earlier part of the War, the overwhelming mass of working-class, as of other opinion in Great Britain, was strongly "pro-war", just as it was in France, or Germany, or even Austria-Hungary. Everywhere in Western Europe, the declared Socialist policy of opposition had dramatically collapsed; and the small minorities which opposed the War were for the time driven almost to silence."[2] The experience of the Boer War was thus repeated though the lesson was more bitter and unpalatable. Fine phrases about international solidarity had come to nothing. Even individuals who did not display their commitment to war by volunteering for military service were sought were sought out for ridicule and social ostracism. Those who refused to serve were imprisoned. It was illegal to profess a conscientious objection to war.

Whilst the patriotism unleashed by the declaration of war overwhelmed opposition to it, it did not eliminate it. Small socialist groups survived and slowly as the material conditions of the war changed they gained strength. The sheer length of the war and the horrendous, senseless slaughter undermined the commitment to it. A Peace Conference, attended by militant shop stewards and socialists, was held in Leeds in June 1917 and called for the end of the war and the formation of Workers' and Soldiers' Councils of the kind formed by Russian workers. But it had no formal identity nor did any of the peace activities. Then in 1917 the Russian workers showed British workers a way out when they seized power in November and immediately issued a peace decree. The signing of the Treaty of Brest-Litovsk in March 1918 reminded British workers of their war weariness. An anti-war movement began to emerge and to gain momentum but it remained marginal to the war effort.

Peace Activity in Peacetime

The bloody and exhausting First World War gave rise to cries of "Never Again". For almost a decade and a half the British people were sickened by the thought of war. And as no Western government could actually afford to wage war no pressure was put on people to change their views. A peace industry flourished through the League of Nations. The Oxford University Union held a debate in February, 1933 which resolved that "this House will in no circumstances fight for its King and Country." It was given world-wide prominence as an indicator of pacifist sentiments in Britain. The Peace Pledge Union was formed in October, 1934 when Canon 'Dick' Sheppard of St Martin-in-the-Fields appealed to men to sign a pledge stating "I renounce War and never again will I suport or sanction another, and I will do all in my power to persuade others to do the same". By the middle of 1936 the Peace Pledge Union had 100,000 male members and it was seeking a similar number of women members. Peace societies flourished in universities. Much literature was published which declaimed war.[3] There were massive majorities against a range of war options in the Peace Ballot which was organized by the League of Nations in 1935. Both the TUC and the Labour Party assisted with the Ballot in which more than 11,600,000 votes were cast. War, it was felt, had become too terrible to happen with the invention of aeroplanes, poison gas and high explosives. Five main questions were asked starting with 'Should Britain remain a member of the League of Nations?' and progressing to whether military measures should be used to stop one nation attacking

314

another. Almost as many people, 90.13 per cent, favoured prohibiting the manufacture and sale of arms for private profit as wanted an all-round reduction of armaments. 87 per cent supported economic sanctions to prevent one nation from attacking another.[4]

The opinion in Britain which favoured peace and reconciliation was not harnessed into a movement. It did not have an institutional expression commensurate with its importance. It was reflected in the policies of the Communist and Labour Parties but the former was tiny and the Labour Party, between 1931 and 1935, had only a rump of 60 Members of Parliament compared with 517 who supported the 'National' government. It reflected, in effect, a revulsion to war in general. It was based on a fear of a future world war and was not directed at any particular potential aggressor. The anti-war feeling was at its climax when the government was persuaded to support a policy of economic sanctions against Italy for its wanton aggression against Abyssinia. But public opinion was not enough to compel the government to use sanctions as a serious and sustained attempt to destroy Italy's war effort. Italy conquered Abyssinia in defiance of the League of Nations in general and of Britain in particular. It was an ominous sign.

The British concern about peace was expressed against an increasingly unstable and threatening international background. The menace of European fascism was growing though there was no common agreement about its danger. The threat to world peace was the imperialism of Nazi Germany but there were divided opinions about whether or not it was the main enemy. There were influential sections in the British Government and media which were sympathetic towards Nazi Germany. But increasingly during the 1930s the desire for peace became an anxiety about fascism. This created class divisions for it was the Labour Movement which showed greatest concern. The class nature of peace activity was exacerbated by the admission of the Soviet Union to membership of the League of Nations, making a popular front against war possible. The Western countries, however, not only refused to accept the Soviet Union as an ally but were not sure that it was not the principal enemy. The British government showed its ambivalence by accommodating to the wishes of Nazi Germany until 1939, when it was too late to take preventative collective action. Under such circumstances it was impossible to mobilize mass support for a peace movement in

Britain. Moreover, as the possibility of war increased through the Nazi annexation of territories, so the discussion about avoiding war grew less and a campaign to rearm gained momentum. The Labour Movement was torn by conflicting priorities. It wanted to stand for peace and disarmament on the one hand and yet rearm against the aggressiveness of the fascist powers on the other. The class character of the Spanish Civil War gave a further twist to Labour's contradiction for it became clear there that Germany and Italy could only be checked by superior military power. The peace activists of the early 1930s became the advocates of re-armament in the late 1930s. The transformation was completed for most when the Second World War started. After the German invasion of the Soviet Union the pacifist argument against war was the only one to retain any legitimacy. The experience of the First World War was not repeated for the Labour Movement. There was a greater tolerance of individuals who conscientiously objected to war but there was no movement from any quarter for a peace settlement. Because the war was defined as a fight for freedom and not as a result of imperialism there were no demands from the Labour Movement to end it without victory. Indeed, on the contrary, for the activists who in 1917 would have been attending the Peace Conference in Leeds, were pressing for the opening of a Second Front in 1942 to relieve the pressure on the Soviet Union.

The Changed Character of War

War throughout history has had many causes but in capitalist history its predominant structural cause has been the unequal, antagonistic relations between countries. Capitalist countries, like individual enterprises, can only thrive by being successful in competition, and this entails seeking dominance in their markets. They have to seek greater market shares at the expense of others and gain market superiority by actually controlling markets and sources of raw materials. The capitalist countries are always in degrees of conflict with each other and war is one of the means used to resolve it. In the past, moreover, war has had therapeutic qualities for some countries. It has been used to overcome domestic government problems by diverting attention to external issues and by generating national unity in divisive circumstances. It has acted as a release valve for countries trapped by the contradiction which creates over-production and thereby rescues them from the political and social consequences of economic depression. Armaments production is not dependent upon market forces and though it generously generates profit it does not take place simply because profit can be made. It occurs because of the need for war but in the process it consumes unused resources, particularly labour, and by increasing the level of incomes it raises the level of effective demand for goods and services and, thereby, stimulates further economic activity. It is not the only route out of a depression but it has been a sure one, readily available when other options, such as imperialist exploitation and the discovery of new, untapped markets, have been closed. For these reasons waging war has been a legitimate part of capitalist morality.

The functions of war have been transformed, however, by the invention and acquisition of nuclear weapons by the USA since 1945 and the Soviet Union since 1949. War with nuclear weapons can resolve no difficulties for it can have no other consequences than the annihilation of all the societies involved, even the universe itself. Its function as a means of aiding survival, even at the painful destructive expense of others, has thus ended abruptly. With nuclear weapons the perpetrators of war suffer equally with the victims. This has transformed the character of peace activities for whereas in the past it was possible to stigmatize anti-war sentiments as unpatriotic now it is those who favour war who threaten the cohesion and existence of nation states. In a nuclear age the peace activists are the true patriots. Moreover, because the consequences of a nuclear war cannot be confined to the direct participants or borne by one class rather than another the interest in peace transcends national boundaries and cuts across social class lines. There are no havens where the rich and powerful can hide themselves. The fruits of war becomes a hideous joke. For the first time in history there is a universal reason for peace.

The Peace Movement

A few scientists became apprehensive about nuclear weapons as soon as their horrific, awesome impact on Hiroshima and Nagasaki became known and when they realized that a new, frightening chapter in the history of war had been opened. Robert J Oppenheimer who led the team which produced the first atomic bomb was quick to realize the significance of the page in history he had written but this led him only to advise caution, to oppose the development of the Hydrogen Bomb and to work to maintain the US monopoly of the weapon. Oppenheimer was one of the authors of the Acheson-Lilienthal Report of March 1946 which formed the basis of the Baruch Plan. On 24th January 1946 the General Assembly of the United Nations Organization set up an Atomic Energy Commission with instructions to make proposals for "the control of atomic energy to the extent necessary to ensure its use only for peaceful purposes" and for "the elimination from national armaments of atomic weapons and of all other major weapons adaptable to mass destruction." The Americans used the idea of an international control commission on which to base their own proposals to prevent the spread of nuclear technology without interfering with their own monopoly. This was the essence of the Baruch Plan.[5] It was vetoed by the Soviet Union. Oppenheimer changed his attitude towards the Hydrogen Bomb after Edward Teller had made the practical breakthrough in 1951. He said that the H Bomb was "technically so sweet that you could not argue."[6] It was exploded for the first time at Eniwetok in November 1952. Oppenheimer's voice was muted on all questions, however, by the US administration's efforts to declare him a subversive for his 'association' with communists. It required great courage and self-sacrifice for an American scientist to associate with peace initiatives at that time. The freedom of assembly was not extended to those who desired peace with the Soviet Union. Facilities for meetings were denied them and when demonstrations were organized on the streets they were physically attacked. For example the New York Mayor O'Dwyer sent one thousand police to suppress a peace demonstration in Union Square in August 1950.[7] No truly international peace conferences could be held in the USA because the government consistently refused to issue visas to suspected Soviet sympathisers.

The Baruch Plan was a plausible alternative to the suggestion of a preventative war with which some politicians and military leaders on both sides of the Atlantic toyed, believing that the USA should use its overwhelming military superiority to subdue the Soviet Union before it acquired a nuclear capability sufficient to counter that of the USA. This view was expressed by Bertrand Russell in 1948 when he said:

"The question is whether there is to be war or whether

318

there is not; and there is only one course of action open to us. That is to strengthen the Western Alliance morally and physically as much and as quickly as possible and hope it may become obvious to the Russians that they can't make war successfully. If there is war, it should be won as quickly as possible. That is the line of policy which the Western nations are now pursuing. They are preparing for whatever the Russians may have in store. The time is not unlimited. Sooner or later the Russians will have atomic bombs and when they have them, it will be a much tougher proposition. Everything must be done in a hurry . . ."[8]

Russell had an intense hatred of communism. He believed that the Soviet Union wanted to over-run Western Europe. He painted a grotesque picture of the consequences if they were allowed to do so.

"The destruction", he stated, "will be such as no subsequent re-conquest can be used. Practically the whole educated population will be sent to labour camps in NE Siberia or on the shores of the White Sea where most will die of hardships and the survivors will be turned into animals . . . Atomic bombs, if used, will at first have to be dropped on W Europe since Russia will be out of reach . . . I have no doubt that America would win in the end, but unless W Europe can be preserved from invasion, it will be lost to civilization for centuries. Even at such a price, I think war would be worth while. Communism must be wiped out, and, world government established."[9]

This gross distortion of the character of the Soviet Union was largely shared by the American Presidents Truman and Eisenhower, who held office from 1945 till the end of the 1950s. Both of them held the view that nuclear weapons, like conventional ones, were to be used if necessary. On various occasions they threatened to use the bomb and presumably believed, like Bertrand Russell, that "you can't threaten unless you're prepared to have your bluff called."[10] But it was one thing to engage in a game of bluff when the Soviet Union did not possess nuclear weapons and quite something different to do so after 1949 when the Soviet Union began to stockpile its own bombs, even though

319

on a minimal scale compared to the USA. The game, too, was changed by the invention of the Hydrogen Bomb, many times more powerful than those bombs which devastated Hiroshima and Nagasaki. The Soviet Union tested its own Hydrogen Bomb in August 1953. This change in the balance of nuclear power altered the awareness of many people to the dangers of nuclear weapons because nuclear war, rather than a one-sided bombardment, became a possibility. Bertrand Russell responded promptly to the new circumstances. "The situation now," he said, "is that we cannot defeat Russia except by defeating ourselves. Those who still advocate war seem to me to be living in a fool's paradise."[11] Russell made an analogy with duelling. "Duelling" he said "was a recognized method of settling quarrels between men of high social standing so long as the duellists stood 20 paces apart and fired at each other with pistols of a primitive type. If the rule had been that they should stand a yard apart with pistols at each other's hearts we doubt whether it would long have remained a recognized method of settling affairs of honour."[12]

The first articulate opposition in the West to nuclear weapons came from scientists in Britain and France, led by J D Bernal, the eminent physicist from Birkbeck College, and Frédéric Joliot-Curie, equally eminent and the High Commissioner of the French Atomic Energy Commission. Bernal was close to the British Communist Party while Joliot-Curie was a card-carrying member in France. Neither of these scientists was quietened by 'Cold War' pressures. Each of them expressed his friendship towards the Soviet Union frequently and openly and in the same breath condemned the capitalist system. The British Association for the Advancement of Science expelled Bernal from its Council in 1949 for stating that peace and capitalism were incompatible conditions because in the capitalist world science is in the hands of those who hated peace and wanted war.[13] Joliot-Curie, within a year, was dismissed by the French Prime Minister from his post as head of the French Atomic Energy Commission. Both Bernal and Joliot-Curie were link-persons between Western and Soviet scientists and helped to create a basis for international understanding. Bernal defined the paramount need of the world as the establishment of peace and joined with others in forming a new organization, Science for Peace, in 1952 on this basis. For five years this group was the principal anti-war platform for British scientists.[14]

The first major attempt to create an international movement

for peace was the Soviet sponsored World Congress of Intellectuals in Breslau in August 1948 which launched an International Liaison Committee of Intellectuals for Peace. This body became the World Peace Council in April 1949 with Joliot-Curie as its President. One of the catalysts for an international peace forum was the World Federation of Scientific Workers which was established in 1946 from an idea by Bernal and with Joliot-Curie as its chairperson. The WFSW was not a trade union but a broad association of unions and associations of scientific workers with the aim of utilizing science for the promotion of peace and welfare. The World Peace Council became the umbrella organization for a number of national peace committees of which the British Peace Committee was one. At this time 'peace' was a word denuded of its real meaning by the 'Cold War' hysteria. A 'peace committee' was regarded as a communist front, as an instrument of Soviet foreign policy. Every peace initiative with which the Soviet Union was connected such as the Stockholm Peace Appeal in 1950, which 14 million people signed and called for the complete elimination of nuclear weapons, the succession of World Peace Congresses in Paris in 1949, Warsaw 1950, Vienna 1954 and Helsinki in 1955 were all derided in the West as Soviet propaganda stunts. When Professor Bernal and Ivor Montague attempted to convene the World Peace Congress in Sheffield in 1950 the Labour government destroyed it by refusing to issue visas to Soviet delegates. Despite the hostility a number of peace groups were formed between 1950 and 1952 by members of different professions in Britain. There were 'Artists for Peace', 'the Medical Association for the Prevention of War', 'the Musicians' Organization for Peace', 'Science for Peace' and 'Teachers for Peace' and each one was labelled as a communist front organization and dismissed as irrelevant except as possible espionage units.

After the USA and the Soviet Union had acquired Hydrogen Bombs by the mid-1950s the worst nuclear war scenario was possible. The background was the 'Cold War' of which the logic seemed to be war itself. The years were marked by events, any of which could have triggered off a conflict. In 1949 there was the blockade of Berlin following the decision of the British and Americans to breach the Potsdam Agreement and establish a West German state. Two years later the Korean War started and the US administration debated whether or not to use atomic bombs against the Chinese. The enormity of the gravity of this

321

situation was slow to dawn on non-communist intellectuals in the West. Then quite suddenly they became aware of the cataclysmic possibilities. Scientists began to recognize the social consequences of their research. Bertrand Russell was at the centre of the new realization. In 1955 he and Einstein issued a declaration about the dangers of nuclear war, signed by Einstein during the week of his death, and endorsed by nearly a dozen eminent scientists, including a number of Nobel Prize winners. Its signatories spanned East and West, communists and non-communists. The Declaration, which emphasized that neither side could hope for victory in a nuclear war and that there was a real possibility of the extermination of the human race by dust and rain from radio-active clouds, asserted that it was only through an avoidance of war, and not just a prohibition of nuclear weapons, that such a catastrophe could be avoided. This belief was based on the assumption that a straightforward prohibition would be breached if a war with conventional arms broke out.[15]

All this time the communist scientists campaigned for peace in the background. The difference was that what they were saying and doing were being repeated by hitherto indifferent or even, like Russell, hostile scientists. Russell followed the Declaration by convening the Pugwash Conference on Science and World Affairs in 1957. This brought together highly placed scientists from East and West on a regular basis. [16] Four years earlier, J D Bernal had started a similar venture when he organised "a world-wide meeting of scientists of such repute that governments would pay attention to their conclusions on nuclear warfare and other subjects."[17] The Pugwash Conference was an imitation of Bernal's. Through it and the meetings of scientists it stimulated, discussions about peace and nuclear war ceased to be the prerogative of communist scientists such as Bernal and Joliot-Curie. Nonetheless peace conferences continued to be regarded by Western governments as communist inspired.

The years following 1956 were propitious for debate in Britain. The British Communist Party had suffered a severe rupture through the disaffection of many of those members who regarded themselves as intellectuals, following Mr Khrushchev's revelations about Stalin at the 20th Congress of the CPSU and because of the use of Soviet troops in the Hungarian uprising in 1956. Ex-communists became the organizers of New Left groups which dominated left-wing intellectual circles. Different strands of the New Left took up the issue of nuclear weapons. Then, on 4th

October 1957, the Soviet Union launched the world's first earth satellite. A month later another Soviet satellite, better equipped than the first was sent into space. With space travel possible, nuclear weapons took on a new disturbing dimension. No country was safe from them. No people could hide from them. Peace discussions spread beyond the narrow circle of communists, Nobel Prize winners and pacifists. A fear of nuclear war entered the consciousness of many people and, for the first time in British history, a mass Peace Movement began to form.

The various groups adopted distinctive positions in relation to nuclear weapons. One of them advocated multilateral disarmament, another proposed a ban on tests, while a third was in favour of unilateral nuclear disarmament by Britain. The strands began to merge in 1957 and 1958 to demand a general renunciation of nuclear weapons by Britain. The organizational basis of this new Peace Movement was the Peace Pledge Union which had organized protests against US nuclear weapons in Britain since 1952, the Friends Peace Movement and the Council for the Abolition of Nuclear Weapons Tests, formed mainly by women members of the Hampstead Labour Party. This last group sought eminent names in support of its aim and when it had J B Priestley, Sir Julian Huxley, Canon Collins and Bertrand Russell on its list it described itself as a national 'Campaign Committee for Nuclear Disarmament'. The genesis of the Campaign for Nuclear Disarmament was thus formed.[18] Mrs Peggy Duff became its organizing secretary and Bertrand Russell its president. Mass support for the Campaign was provided by the Easter March in 1958 from Trafalgar Square to the Weapon Research Establishment in Aldermaston, Berkshire. The idea for the march did not originate with CND but from a Direct Action group. CND, however, took it over and benefited from its tremendous mobilizing effects. It transformed CND from a Hampstead clique into a national protest movement. Hundreds of local groups were formed, public meetings were held and Parliament was lobbied. Some trade unions took up the issue and voted with constituency Labour Parties in October, 1960 to make unilateral nuclear disarmament the policy of the Labour Party. This particular achievement was short-lived for the opponents of unilateralism within the Labour Party regrouped and reversed the policy the following year. The reversal however, was more an indication of the depth of the opposition the consciousness about peace had aroused in the establishment than a sign of weakness. The new

Peace Movement cut across social class lines and brought together disparate and previously uncooperative political groups. Its strength was its spontaneity about a single issue which was paramount over ideological divisions.

Peace as an Antithesis of Capitalism

As capitalism traverses its historical path, exploiting workers, perpetuating inequalities and deprivation, pitting individuals, institutions and nations against each other in a struggle for survival, legitimizing the use of force as a solution to their disagreements and utilizing war as a means of resolving its problems, all in order to maximise private profits, then it turns people's attitudes against it until they see it as the source of their problems and desire to change it. In this way capitalism carries the seeds of its own transformation. This process is historically inexorable but it has many fluctuations, moves along an indeterminate time scale and is manifested in a variety of ways which counter the values of capitalism, undermine its legitimacy and force it to act contrary to its own best interests. The process is expressed through the growth of trade unionism, the rise of revolutionary political parties, the extension of public as against private enterprise and by the growth of the Peace Movement.

The Peace Movement represents the antithesis of the values of capitalism as much as collectivism does. Nuclear weapons highlight this contradiction, for capitalism, which thrives on wars by using them for therapeutic purposes, can have no use for a war which threatens its own destruction by causing universal annihilation. Yet nuclear weapons are nonetheless manufactured. Why should they be produced if they not only do not possess any socially useful qualities but have such a universally harmful potential? And why, moreover, should the Peace Movement be reviled so much by the organs of capitalism simply for protesting about weapons which, in effect, threaten the very existence of capitalism? This does seem to be a rather sick paradox.

The answer lies in understanding the structural implications of a universal prohibition of nuclear weapons. The Peace Movement, by insisting that there should be no production or use of nuclear weapon, challenges the right of the nuclear weapons producing countries in the West to operate according to their own capitalist criteria. Production in these countries is determined by the exchange-value of goods and services and not by their socially-useful qualities. It may add to the profitability of a good for it to be socially useful but it is not necessary. If a good cannot make a profit then no matter what its qualities it will not be produced within the market. In the same way, a good will be produced if it is profitable even though it may have no socially useful qualities. This is the case, for instance, with the production of drugs such as heroin. The point is that the criminal futility of using nuclear weapons has no bearing on whether or not they are produced in the West.

Nuclear weapons are not, however, produced through a free market. They are produced through government decisions and purchased with public money. There is a limited amount of competition between privately owned armaments manufacturers to whom the profits of production go. Nuclear weapons are, therefore, produced for profit just as cornflakes are. The profits from cornflakes, however, are derived from a consumer demand over which the producers through trade names and advertising exercise only a limited form of control. In the case of nuclear weapons there is no consumer influence, only consumer sanction. The decision to produce is made by politicians largely in response to pressures from the users, that is the military, and the producers, that is industry. The military-industrial complex, therefore, through its vast influence over government, makes the decisions about the production of nuclear weapons. They are engaged in a self-perpetuating creation of financial profits. The consumers, who are those deemed to be protected by nuclear weapons, only enter the decision-making stage at times of presidential and general elections and only then when they are faced with alternative options. At no time are they consulted about decisions. Instead they are subjected to perpetual propaganda about the threatening nature of the enemy to ensure that they freely give their sanction to production. A movement to stop the production of nuclear weapons entirely would both end a lucrative source of profit and would challenge the power of the military – industrial complex to determine government decisions. But to do this it is necessary to be able to control multinational companies for they are the chief profit beneficiaries. They, at the tail end of the Twentieth Century, are the bulwarks of capitalism. The Peace Movement, in effect then, poses the power of peaceful popular protest against the institutional power of vast international corporations. It also, by implication, questions the definition of the Soviet Union as the enemy and challenges the right of capitalism to protect its hegemony by force. It is in this sense that peace activities are the antithesis of capitalism.

As it is generally recognized that nuclear weapons possess no socially useful qualities and constitute a danger to the mass of the people in all countries both by the political instability they create and though the risk of use through accident, their elimination would be generally beneficial to people. The irony in this situation is that in the USA, where the dangers are less apparent than in Europe, there are likely to be no immediate social advantages from ending the misappropriation of resources for nuclear weapons production. In this respect, there is a marked distinction between the USA and the Soviet Union. In the Soviet Union a ban on production would release resources for socially useful activities because the distribution of resources is planned and a rational decision would ensure that the transition took place. In the USA, on the other hand, where nuclear weapons production has begun to figure as a core element for much economic activity, a ban on production would close an avenue of immense financial profit for a small number of powerful multinational companies without creating any immediate tangible social and economic benefits for ordinary people because there is no mechanism in the market for transferring resources from negative to positive uses. The only market criterion is profitability. The likely immediate effect of banning nuclear weapons in the USA would be increased unemployment and social deprivation.

The Campaign for Nuclear Disarmament

This organization has become the predominant element in the British Peace Movement. Other sections are significant for their special qualities. For instance, the Friends Peace Committee has played a consistently remarkable role through its understanding of the Soviet Union while the British Peace Assembly, the successor to the British Peace Committee, has special relations both with British trade unions and Peace Movements in socialist countries. Political parties, trade unions in general and peace action groups of various kinds have mainly used the umbrella organisation, CND, for peace purposes, which has also been the medium through which ordinary people in towns and villages throughout Britain have channelled their protests against nuclear weapons.

In its early days CND was comprised of people who had

recently lived through the ideological pressures of the 'Cold War' so that inevitably they possessed some feelings of anti-Sovietism. Yet anti-Sovietism did not appear to play an important part of the early affairs of CND. It derived its momentum from the fears of ordinary people about the British atomic bomb. Its unifying slogan was 'Ban the Bomb'. There were, on the other hand, some anti-communist feelings amongst its members. A number of the prominent ones had recently left the Communist Party while others, like Bertrand Russell, were implacably anti-communist. Dora Russell, whose peace activities preceded the formation of CND, explained her experience with it. "The new CND in Britain," she wrote, "campaigning only for nuclear disarmament, soon made it clear that they did not want any association with pacifists who sought understanding or had any connection with communist organizations or countries. Those who had been doing the most work for peace were now required to 'keep away' to avoid CND being smeared."[19]

Despite this political cautiousness CND marshalled an impressive display of protest by 1960 through attracting people on to the streets and gaining the official support of the Transport and General Workers' Union and other unions. Its early climax came when it shattered the bi-partisan policy on defence at the Labour Party Conference in 1960. This period of euphoria was brief for in the month of its first major success a split occurred in its ranks through the classic method of forming a splinter group to push CND further than it was capable of going without damage to itself. The question of direct action had plagued CND from the outset but it came to a head when the "Committee of 100" was formed by Bertrand Russell in October 1960 from an initiative provided by an American, Ralph Schoenman, to pursue a policy of mass civil disobedience. Many activists were siphoned off while others became disillusioned. The consequence could hardly have been better planned for the government. The Labour Party rejected unilateralism in October 1961. From that time CND activity declined and so did that of the "Committee of 100" which was disbanded in 1968. The damage had been done. As Frank Allaun commented, "The Sixties were a bad decade for CND. They came in with a bang and went out with almost nothing."[20]

Many people thought that CND was finished during the period of detente but the consciousness which had been aroused between 1957 and 1962 did not disappear entirely. Many of its activists became involved in the Peace in Vietnam campaign from

327

about 1968 till 1972 thus maintaining and extending the practice of anti-war protests. Its organization was maintained by a skeleton group of activists during difficult years so that when NATO decided to locate American cruise missiles in Britain in December, 1979 it was able to mobilize public protests. CND's growth after 1979 was phenomenal in terms of its national membership and the proliferation of local groups. In 1983, before the cruise missiles had arrived in Britain, CND's membership was almost 80,000 with more than 2000 local groups and organizations affiliated to it. There was hardly a hamlet in Britain without its CND group. Its post 1979 demonstrations dwarfed earlier ones. It became a major peace organization with a cohesion unequalled anywhere in the Western world. It contained none of the fractures which afflicted the unity of the West German Peace Movement nor did it have the inhibitions about its aims which hampered the development of peace organizations in France or the limited aims of the multitude of small and politically ineffective groups in the USA. CND's influence spread quickly. The Labour Party entered the 1983 general election with the policy of unilateral nuclear disarmament and has continued to endorse it. By 1987, 29 national trade unions, with a total membership of 6.8 million, were affiliated to CND. It fostered numerous direct action organizations by its existence and example. It has risen to far greater prominence than it reached in 1960. Although CND failed in its major aim to prevent the location of Cruise missiles at Greenham Common in England it has remained as an influential organization with the facility, which it lacked in 1960, of persisting in its policy of harnessing public opinion against the war drive activities of NATO countries.

CND has undoubtedly been the prize target for the anti-peace movement forces in the West. This was certainly the view of the British government which, in its early anxiety about the phenomenal growth of CND reacted with gimmickry. It tried to meet the CND head on by discrediting it in public through provoking a Red Scare, claiming it was under the control of communists and was receiving Russian money. When this failed CND was depicted as a fringe organization comprising weird people. When this also failed to stop CND's growth, wiser counsels prevailed and more subtle divisive and subversive policies were contrived which fed on existing doubts and prejudices in CND.

There was the attempt to distract the attention of CND from NATO by suggesting that NATO was disintegrating anyway through US impatience with the mealy-mouthed approach of Europe to the Soviet Union on the one hand and Europe's dislike of US belligerency on the other. There was talk of the emergence of a European bloc which would stand between the Soviet Union and the US. Such comments were made during the year the West European Union was celebrating the 30th Anniversary of its still birth. But NATO did not disintegrate through its own contradictions and the West European Union remained moribund. CND has not been persuaded to alter its demand that Britain should leave the NATO Alliance.

Coincident with this attempted distraction the NATO high command discussed the need to switch its emphasis from nuclear to conventional weapons, suggesting that CND's main aim was being largely fulfilled. Conventional and nuclear weapons were described as alternative forms by pointing to the capacity of Emerging Technology to prevent nuclear strikes. But this was a trap, for the NATO policy was to build up both types of weapons. NATO did not reduce its nuclear capacity. The West experienced the worst of all possible worlds.

The third device was to encourage anti-Sovietism in CND thus disabling it in its endeavour to reject nuclear weapons. In so far as CND members endorsed the Western stereotype of the Soviet Union they confirmed it as an enemy. Anti-Sovietism was genuinely subversive of CND and the most successful of the establishment anti-Peace Movement devices. Its basis was the constant stream of propaganda discrediting every aspect of Soviet life but its mechanism came from within the Peace Movement itself.

Coincident with the new growth of CND, also following the NATO decision in December 1979 to locate American medium range nuclear missiles in Western Europe, was the creation of the organization called European Nuclear Disarmament. This was formed in the spring of 1980 around an appeal initiated by Ken Coates of the Russell Peace Foundation in Nottingham, which called for the withdrawal of all nuclear weapons from European territory. It stated: "In particular, we ask the Soviet Union to halt production of the SS.20 medium range missile and we ask the United States not to implement the decision to develop cruise missiles and Pershing II missiles for deployment in Europe . . ." The essence of the appeal, however, lay in two other paragraphs. It stated "We do not wish to apportion guilt between the political and military leaders of East and West. Guilt lies squarely upon both parties. Both parties have adopted menacing postures and committed aggressive actions in different parts of the world." Then, in a seemingly innocuous statement it added "At the same time, we must defend and extend the right of all citizens, East or West, to take part in this common movement and to engage in every kind of exchange." Thus one paragraph apportioned equal blame for the nuclear arms race between the USA and the USSR while the other enabled END to make co-operation with the Soviet Peace Committee conditional upon the settlement of the "dissident" question in socialist countries.

The Russell Appeal, as it became known, was signed by many people, including leading officials of CND such as Bruce Kent, CND's new general secretary and Dan Smith its former secretary. It was drafted by E P Thompson who contributed its political emphasis and who became the principal advocate of END's aims in the Peace Movement.

The Appeal led to the formation of a number of laterally connected committees, for example an Inter-Party Parliamentary Committee and an Inter-Party Trade Union Committee, the activities of which were co-ordinated by a small central committee consisting of E P Thompson, Bruce Kent, Dan Smith, Peggy Duff who had been CND's first general secretary, and Mary Kaldor of the Armament and Disarmament Information Unit at Sussex University. Thus the basis for the END organization was laid. It renounced any intention of building a mass membership and of thus competing with CND. It concentrated on publication and on communication with European Peace Movements which sympathized with the Appeal.[21]

END, its sponsors stated, is "a resource centre serving the British Peace Movement, and in close association with CND. The immense swell of European opinion for peace poses great problems of communication: monitoring, exchanges, translations . . . Only a multi-national campaign, however loosely coordinated, will be powerful enough; and sooner or later this campaign must extend across to "the other side" also, in independent forms critical of the militarist measures of their own states . . ."[22] Its practical effect was to encumber CND with the plausible but historically inaccurate thesis of equality of blame between the superpowers, campaigning under the slogan 'dissolve the blocs'. It thus fed on anti-Soviet sentiment and drew support from those in and around the broad labour movement who were anti-communist. But its most crucial and critical role was to introduce into CND what is described as the human rights issue. In doing this END continued the practice of its main sponsor, the Russell Peace Foundation, whose "monitoring, exchanges, translations . . ." were mainly about dissident activities in socialist countries, focussing attention on individual acts of discrimination for whatever reason as a means of discrediting socialist systems. END became, in effect, the vehicle for anti-Sovietism in CND.

CND, under the influence of European Nuclear Disarmament, established contacts with 'unofficial' peace organizations in socialist countries, such as 'Charter 77' in Czechoslovakia, the Moscow Group of Trust, the Hungarian Peace Group for Dialogue, Solidarnose in Poland and the East German Christians, irrespective of their size or significance or of the consequences for their relations with the principal Peace Movements in those countries. Whenever CND delegations went to socialist countries they insisted on having parallel itinaries with the 'unofficial' groups. CND became reluctant to attend international peace conferences unless 'unofficial' peace groups were invited, even when these conferences were held within socialist countries.

The influence of END was shown through CND's selection of foreign peace groups for collaborative action. It has refused to have any contact with the old established World Peace Council. It formed alliances with anti-communist and anti-Soviet groups, such as the small French peace group, Codine, rather than with the much larger communist supported Movement de la Paix. It identified with the West German Green Party rather than the communist supported Deutsche Friedensunion which sponsored the Krefeld Appeal in November, 1980, with 6 million signatures, pledging resistance to the location of American Pershing II and Cruise missiles in Western Europe. CND also expressed its political preferences through its membership of the International Peace Co-ordination Centre which was formed by the Dutch equivalent of END, the Inter-Church Peace Council (IKV) in September, 1981. The IKV is funded by Dutch churches of all denominations to concentrate on research and communication. The International Peace Co-ordination Centre became the nerve centre for relations between Western and Socialist Peace Movements and circulated guidelines to deal with official invitations from Socialist countries which ensured that Western Peace groups would always impose conditions which made communications hazardous, relations fragile and confrontation likely.

Nuclear Parity

The insistence of the Soviet Union on maintaining military parity with the USA, that is, until Mr Gorbachev announced a unilateral moratorium on nuclear tests in August 1985, tormented the British Peace Movement. It was used by the CND leadership to give expression to anti-Sovietism but to many ordinary members it created a genuine dilemma. Whenever the Soviet Union took steps to keep pace with the USA it was blamed for accelerating the arms race. In 1983, for instance, CND leadership successfully moved a resolution at the CND Annual Conference opposing the location of Cruise missiles at Greenham Common but also condemning "the Soviet announcement of new weapons deployments in Europe and the Western Atlantic, since Soviet efforts for 'military parity' will inevitably result in another round of weapons deployment by the USA and NATO under the guise of further negotiation through strength". CND subsequently organized campaigns which implicated the Soviet Union as being jointly responsible with the USA for the nuclear arms race.

The ordinary CND member is guided by the CND Constitution which states that "it is opposed to the manufacture, stockpiling, testing, use and threatened use of nuclear, chemical and biological weapons by any country . . ." This reflects an abhorrence of all nuclear missiles anywhere, held by any country. Given the destructive powers of nuclear weapons this is a wholly justifiable sentiment but, rather like being totally opposed to sin, it is a meaningless guide to action to eliminate nuclear weapons.

Nuclear weapons carry innate dangers because they contain substances which are dangerous to health in themselves. But in this respect they are similar to nuclear power plants or dumps of nuclear waste. By their very existence they are all potential hazards to people's health. Apart from that, nuclear bombs are inanimate substances which, like guns, are harmless in themselves. They become weapons and a threat to people only in the hands of people. They get their horrific meaning from social relationships. In order to identify, therefore, the real threat which emanates from the possession of nuclear missiles it is necessary to understand the relationships of people who control them.

In context, this means analyzing the relationship between the USA and its allies on the one hand and the Soviet Union on the other. What are the dialectics of their relationship? What is the catalyst which creates it? Who is reacting to whom? Until such

332

questions as these are answered it is not possible to frame an anti-nuclear policy which bears any connection with reality. Policies based on sentiment, gut reactions or derived from false assumptions about the enemy are bound not simply to be inadequate but to compound the problem. There is no alternative to a serious, logically consistent analysis of international relations.

What does such an analysis reveal? It shows that socialism arises out of the contradictions of capitalism with capitalism standing in implacable opposition to it. The Soviet Union, which represents socialism, stands, by its very existence, as a threat to capitalism. It has, therefore, been attacked, economically desta-bilized, ideologically undermined and militarily insulated. It has been subjected to abuse, distortion and lies about its society. Yet the Soviet Union has grown stronger; its own hegemony has spread. In the inter-war it stood completely alone. Now it is at the hub of a widening circle of allies. By the same process the sphere of international capitalism is shrinking; its power is declining and, with it, its ability to make private profit and to accumulate capital is lessened. The visible appearance is a struggle between two superpowers but it is in substance a new form of social organization rising out of the contradictions of the old.

There is not, nor can there be, any equality of responsibility between the USA and the Soviet Union in the arms race. The catalyst lies in the Western struggle to preserve capitalist hegemony against the encroaching forces of socialist forms. The visible evidence is the Western struggle for markets and sources of cheap raw materials. In doing this the West is compelled to seek military superiority because that, in the last resort, is its only legitimacy. Capitalism, despite the fine words of its political leaders, has no moral superiority. It operates through stages of exploitation of regions and countries but always of workers. For every capitalist success there is on the reverse side a defeat for workers, for the poor and the deprived. This process gives rise to the contradictions which are transforming capitalist countries in their own unique historical ways. The threat to capitalism, therefore, is not exported from Moscow but arises from its own condition.

The history of the relationship between the USA and the Soviet Union since 1945 confirms the assertion that the West continually seeks and depends on military superiority. From the moment the victories of the Red Army over the Nazis put in doubt Western military superiority the USA has been pre-occupied with it. For a brief period after 1945 the USA believed it possessed superiority. Then from the first Soviet test of an atomic bomb in 1949 it pushed forward with increasing urgency to intensify the destructive capabilities of its missiles. Every change in killing power, in elusiveness, in speed, came from the USA. The Presidential advisers advised superiority; the military-industrial complex demanded it; America's NATO allies applauded it. The only visible respite was during the period of detente in the 1970s, but even detente went on against a background of forward missile planning. In the governmental scientific advisory committees, the board rooms of armaments manufacturers and in their scientific laboratories, the search for an intensified and more destructive nuclear potential which had started with the Manhattan Project continued.

At the end of detente, with the election of President Reagan, military superiority was again acclaimed as the US goal. A characteristic NATO response was published in *The Times* on Monday 26 November, 1984. Its leading article, 58½ column inches long, unashamedly bared the hawkish breast of the military-industrial complex. It enunciated "the hard simple principles of Mr Reagan's leadership for which he received such decisive confirmation in the election . . . This principle is the reassertion of American power and self-confidence and an end to appeasement . . ." Reagan's second term of office, it stated, liberated the United States "from the incubus of a period of detente and appeasement". *The Times* was undoubtedly still smarting from its own appeasement of Hitler in 1938. It presented the Western stereotype of the Soviet Union with razor sharpened lines. "Soviet society", it stated, "is mobilized for war, both a shooting war and a class war. Since the Geneva Conference of 1922 Soviet officials have been currying Western economic assistance to make up for their strategic weaknesses while their leaders have used double-talk to conceal their aggressive intentions against the free world." It quoted Zbigniew Brzezinski to add that the Soviet Union is "'a global power only in the military dimension but in no other. It is neither a genuine economic rival to the US nor – as once was the case – even a source of a globally interesting ideological experiment'. The Soviet society, *The Times* contended is "a system which operates on an inherently outmoded, malevolent, discredited and dishonourable ideology: an evil empire indeed." *The Times* gave President Reagan clear advice: cut back and control the flow of information and commodities to the Soviet Union; follow a policy of economic discipline; create dissension in the Soviet Union between the people and political leaders, and between Warsaw Pact countries. On the question of nuclear weapons it stated: "It has to be made clear to the Soviet Union that their persistent struggle in these peripheral areas makes it necessary for the United States to maintain and improve its strategic nuclear superiority over Soviet capabilities."

The Times article was not a prescription for President Reagan but an enunciation of the policies he was trying to follow. Its purpose was to advise him not to deviate from them and to show its approval of them. It revealed how the NATO mind works. With this very clear statement of intentions before it, how should the Soviet Union have reacted?

The Soviet Union reacted from the beginning by seeking nuclear parity with USA, by attempting to emulate or neutralize every advance made by the Americans. When the US improved the range or the speed of missiles, so did the Soviet Union; when it located medium range missiles in Europe so did the Soviet Union. The Soviet response, however, was never immediate and spontaneous. At each vital stage there has been a pause and a campaign to stop the escalation. The Soviet Union engaged in a Europe-wide protest to stop the location of Cruise and Pershing missiles in Western Europe; it initiated a world-wide campaign against the latest escalation, the American Strategic Defence Initiative. When the protests failed the Soviet Union then tried to retrieve the balance. It states publicly that it will never consciously allow itself to be put in a position of military inferiority and unpreparedness, as it was when the Nazis invaded its country on 22 June, 1941.

The Campaign for Nuclear Disarmament has judged these reactions in different ways. Some have argued that 'two wrongs do not make a right'. In other words, the Soviet Union should ignore the actions of the USA and pursue its own principled course. Others have said why allow an aggressive capitalist country to determine the defence priorities of a socialist country; or, more particularly, why should the Soviet Union allow the Pentagon to choose even its weapons? This is a highly plausible argument, especially for those who believe that socialism is morally superior to capitalism. But it ignores the political realities of the Soviet Union, both of its past and its present.

The Soviet Union's perception of its external relations is

335

determined in large part by its history which has distinct strands, some of which are still familiar and influential. The collective memory of the Soviet Union recalls the Western capitalist attempts to isolate, invade and destabilize it when it had not one ally in the inter-war years. It recalls its unpreparedness when the German army invaded on 22 June 1941 and the costs to the Soviet people. It remembers an Allied war-time strategy which continually sought to restrain and isolate Soviet influence. It remembers too the nuclear posturing of successive American Presidents after 1945 with the often publicly avowed aim of liberating the Soviet people from communism. For its own survival it had to be alert and sensitive and suspicious about activities around its borders.

This collective memory is enlivened by the realization that the USA is the only country possessing nuclear weapons which has used them and through their use has been exhilerated by their destructive powers. It has threatened to use them on at least eleven occasions. The Soviet people, virtually surrounded by American missile silos, would be unnatural if they were not apprehensive about the US intentions towards them. The Soviet people sensed danger when Cruise and Pershing missiles moved into Western Europe and when the US resumed nuclear testing in the Nevada Desert in March, 1986. The Soviet Union can make, and has made, unilateral concessions, but it can never for long neglect its defences without arousing the nightmares of its past and fears about its future.

Some critics grant that the Soviet Union has to respond in some way to the American war-drives but feel it is an unnecessary acceleration of the arms race for it to do so by copying American advances. The implication is that the Soviet Union is entitled to defend itself but what does this entail? If the development of weapons was stabilized then what would matter would be the sheer weight of 'fire-power'. With conventional arms this would be counted in terms of men and women, guns, tanks, ships, airplanes and the like. Parity in real terms would involve organization and quality but these would not figure prominently in any public discussion. Parity in terms of nuclear weapons is different in that given the enormous impact of individual weapons the level has long since been reached at which either side could completely devastate the other and the rest of the world as well. After that parity in numbers is superfluous. A policy which had been intended to deter has developed into one which is capable of mutually assured destruction.

Nonetheless calculations about superiority are still made in terms of numbers of nuclear warheads or missiles. The US and NATO both make calculations usually showing Soviet superiority to justify increased defence expenditure. Other calculations are made elsewhere, for example the Stockholm Institute for Peace Research, which gives different results.[23] But by and large the warhead count is now a diversion from those developments which really determine military superiority. What matters in discussing parity is whether the missiles are land, sea or air-based, whether they are comparable in speed and range, what their relative powers of elusiveness are, for these are the factors which determine first-strike capability. The discussion about parity is not about equality in numbers and types but about comparable abilities to survive and retaliate a first strike attack.[24] Obviously in making this assessment the speed with which missiles reach their targets, their range, their ability to avoid detection are of prime importance. A technological innovation in any one of these qualities could seriously adversely affect a survival response. Parity therefore involves responding to such changes. This point was made clear by Marshall Sokolorskiy in 1963 when he stated: "The rapid development of spacecraft and specifically of artificial earth satellites, which can be launched for the most diverse purposes, even as vehicles for nuclear weapons, has put a new problem on the agenda, that of defence against space devices— PKO. It is still too early to predict what line will be taken in the solution of this problem but as surely as an offensive one is created, a defensive one will be too."[25] The Soviet Union has responded similarly to subsequent developments. A failure to do so could make retaliatory defensive action outmoded and ineffectual. It could leave the Soviet Union defenceless. Given the record of Western belligerence that indeed would be an unwise thing to do.

The dilemma for the Peace Movement is that if it reacts positively to the Soviet case for parity it will be damned with the pro-Soviet label and will suffer in consequence, from the general effects of anti-Sovietism. CND has always sought to avoid doing anything which could be interpreted as pro-Soviet in the belief that this would destroy its non-aligned status. There is a mistaken belief in CND that non-alignment means never identifying with either side in the arms struggle, irrespective of the merits of their respective cases. It should mean that CND simply remains organizationally autonomous with the freedom to decide its own course and establish its own political priorities on the basis of an analysis of the situation. If this means siding with the Soviet Union CND should have the courage to say so and face any consequences which might follow from it.

The Soviet Peace Initiatives

The issue of anti-Sovietism is not being tackled by the British Peace Movement. This is partly because of the fear by the Campaign for Nuclear Disarmament that it would be accused of being pro-Soviet and partly because of its ambivalence towards the Soviet Union in any case. The public leadership attitude of CND is set by the theory that the world is dominated by two super-powers which have almost equal responsibility for the arms race. This results in it making at least moderated accusations against the Soviet Union no matter how it behaves. But in the details of its relations with socialist Peace Movements the International Committee of CND maintains a policy of camouflaged hostility.

Yet at the same time the perceptions of many ordinary people towards the Soviet Union, both within and out of the Peace Movement, are changing in a positive way. The Western image of the Soviet Union is undergoing serious revisions due to the series of Soviet peace proposals made since August 1985 and the changes under the headings of *perestroika* and *glasnost* which are taking place within the Soviet Union. Although news about the Soviet Union is still filtered through a generally hostile media, the seriousness of the Soviet desire for peace is getting through. Many people who hitherto unquestioningly accepted the Western stereotype are now recognizing its distorting qualities. Misinformation is becoming counter-productive in the West for it is being seen as such. So in the dialectical interaction between Western ideology and reality through which the perception of Soviet reality is determined, Western ideology is slowly being discredited. The Western governments are assisting in this process. As successive concessions have been made by the Soviet leadership, Western governments have found reasons for failing to respond to them. Increasingly the reasons have been recognized as excuses to evade signing an agreement. In the case of France and Britain the excuses have been exhausted and it is plain that they do not want an arms agreement which would involve destroying the missiles which they regard as their own.

The catalyst for the changes in consciousness was the Reykjavik summit meeting between Mr Gorbachev and President Reagan in October 1986. That meeting, scheduled as a mini-summit to arrange an agenda for a subsequent meeting in Washington, suddenly and unexpectedly became the venue for serious detailed negotiations about an arms control package which hitherto had been described as either a Soviet fantasy or subterfuge. There were in the region of 2000 representatives of the world's press observing the meeting, sensing an agreement, and engaging in hour by hour speculation. They were caught off their guard. Without foresight and wholly unprepared they communicated their own excitement to their readers. For a brief moment in contemporary history the facts about Soviet policies were reported without first being filtered through an anti-Soviet sieve. Readers were able to make their own judgements about the outcome of the meeting. They were assisted in doing this by the events which had preceded the meeting.

The first tangible peace initiative by the Soviet Union which broke the deadlock caused by the Americans' quest for superiority and the Soviet chase for parity was the nuclear test moratorium applied by the Soviet government unilaterally on 6 August 1985. The Soviet nuclear testing programme was suspended in the first instance until 1 January 1986. The US administration was invited to join the moratorium and to resume the negotiations, which had been ended by President Reagan, for a comprehensive test ban treaty. It refused. The British government endorsed the refusal because, it claimed, the Soviet Union would not accept an on-site system of verification. The Soviet government extended the moratorium unilaterally on three occasions. It lasted until January 1987 and was, therefore, in force at the time of the Reykjavik meeting.

When the first extension of the test ban was announced, Mr Gorbachev proposed a step-by-step plan to eliminate all nuclear weapons on both sides by the year 2000. These were the proposals of 15 January 1986. There were three stages: stage one required the Soviet Union and the USA within the period of 5 to 8 years to reduce by one-half the stock of nuclear weapons which could reach each other's territory; this stage entailed the ending of nuclear tests and of the deployment of space weapons. Stage two, which was to last for 5 to 7 years, extended nuclear disarmament to all other countries and included the elimination of tactical nuclear arms, namely those with a range of up to 1000km. Stage three completed the process of elimination until no nuclear weapons were left. The scheme was given widespread publicity in the socialist countries and evoked considerable excitement there but in the West, after an initial sceptical response, it was treated as a Soviet propaganda ploy and damned with ridicule. It was rejected out of hand by the Western governments. Even the Campaign for Nuclear Disarmament made only a token response to it. In general, the response confirmed the belief that once a country is defined as the enemy then everything it does or proposes to do has to be regarded with the deepest suspicion, as a tactic, a maneouvre, a ploy with a subversive intent.

The 15th January proposals were virtually forgotten by the late Spring when two events occurred which made indents in the consciousness of people generally in Britain and Western Europe, though not so much in the USA. The first was the bombing of Libya by US planes from British bases in April 1986. This act evoked widespread protests in Britain which cut across social class and party political lines. Large sections of the British public were suspicious of American motives and were offended that the British government should have given its support. The Peace Movement was involved in organizing protests against the American act and in doing so correlated the irresponsibility of it with questions about the competence of the US President to make decisions involving nuclear weapons. British people were becoming more fearful of the US President than they were of the projected enemy.

The second conscience changing event was the disaster at the Chernobyl nuclear power plant in the USSR on 26 April 1986. On that day explosions occurred in the fourth unit of the Chernobyl power station. The explosions caused fire which extensively damaged the reactor building, the equipment in it and the reactor core, causing radioactive releases into the atmosphere. The first indication in the West that the disaster had occurred was a cloud of radioactivity drifting across Scandinavia. The staff at the nuclear power plant at Forsmark in Sweden at first thought that their own reactor was leaking but as reports of high radioactivity came in from Stockholm, Helsinki and Oslo the Swedes suspected a radioactivity leak in the Soviet Union. The Soviet authorities then issued a statement that there had been an accident in the Ukraine causing casualties. No details were given at that stage.

It was immediately assumed in the West that the disaster was a major one because of the scale of the increase in radioactivity in Sweden in relation to the distance between Sweden and the Ukraine, which was about 800 miles. The assumption became the basis for projections about the extent of the damage to the environment and the number of casualties. In the absence of detailed information from the Soviet Union it was reasonable to expect such assessments to be made, as had been the case when an accident occurred at the Three Mile Island nuclear power station in the USA in 1979 when the US Senate was informed about it ten days after it had occurred. In the Soviet case 3 days elapsed before the extent of the damage was known but by that time the disaster had become the focus for an anti-Soviet campaign. The dilemma which Western governments faced between adopting a humanitarian attitude and exploiting the occasion for their own political ends was short-lived. The casualties became pawns as the West sought to exaggerate the accident and then portray it as a result of Soviet communism, despite the fact that between 1971 and 1984 there were 151 recorded accidents at nuclear power stations in 14 different countries, including major ones in Britain in 1957 and the USA in 1973.

The Western media did not recognize any dilemma. The United Press International quoted an unidentified resident of Kiev as the source for a report that the death toll could exceed 2000.[26] The main US television networks, ABC News, CBS News, NBC News and CNN, each repeated the UPI figure, adding that it was an unconfirmed report. In Britain, the main foreign news agency Reuters simply stated that "a reported 2000 deaths" had occurred. Additional information was allegedly provided by a Dutch amateur radio operator who claimed to have overheard a conversation between a Japanese operator and an English speaking man with a heavy Russian accent who said that there had been many hundreds of dead and wounded at Chernobyl and two meltdowns instead of one.[27] The US Pentagon combined the details of both sources in its own reports but claimed credibility by stating that it possessed information from satellite reconnaissance. *The Guardian* published the Pentagon claim, "that a second Chernobyl reactor appeared to have suffered a meltdown – or was now suffering one – and that uncontrolled fires 'spewing radiation' were still raging in the stricken Soviet plant. Estimates of the dead and injured within 10 miles of the huge radiation cloud . . . were put at 2000 to 3000 with the situation possibly deteriorating."[28] *The Guardian* had a front-page headline which stated: "US estimates up to 3000 victims from satellite information".[29] Earlier it had repeated a report that Minsk, the capital city of Byelorussia, about 300 miles to the north, had been evacuated; that Soviet medical teams trained in nuclear decontamination had been flown in from Poland, Czechoslovakia and East Germany and that nuclear technicians were being summoned to Chernobyl from all parts of the Soviet Union.

The picture of alarm was accompanied by open hostility towards the Soviet Union. For example, the US Senator Steven Symms from Idaho stated that his only regret was that the accident had not occured in the Kremlin.[30] *The New York Times,* commenting on European press reports, stated that "French and German papers see the disaster as the result of the secretive, authoritarian system of making decisions without involving the people whose lives it rules and failing to allow open debate on nuclear issues. They point out that it was the militaristic urge to disregard civilian needs that led to negligence in setting nuclear standards".[31] Most Western governments declaimed against the alleged "habitual secrecy" of the Soviet Union. President Reagan said that the attitude of the Soviet Union "manifests a disregard for the legitimate concerns of people everywhere" and contrasted the openness of the West with the Soviet Union's "secrecy and stubborn refusal to inform the international community of the common danger" from the nuclear accident.[32]

Within a day of the Western claims that there were 2000 to 3000 casualties, the Soviet authorities announced that 2 people had died and 197 had been admitted to hospital of whom 49 were released almost immediately and 18 were in a serious condition. The Soviet announcement was received with disbelief and did not stem the exaggerations. This prompted the chief of the press department of the Soviet Foreign Ministry to say: "I get the feeling that the American Press is not happy there are so few victims".[33] The claim that there had been two meltdowns, however, was retracted by the US White House task force which was monitoring the disaster. Mr Lee Thomas, the chief of the task force and the head of the Environment Protection Agency said "There has been a good bit of conjecture about that but the information I have . . . is that we don't have any indication of a problem at that (second) reactor . . ."[34] The US officials who had said there was a second meltdown refused to explain the reason for their claim. As the days went by it became clear that the

Soviet version of the causes and impact of the disaster was correct. Officials of the International Atomic Energy Agency visited Chernobyl and confirmed that version. From the day following the disaster about 48,000 people were evacuated from a 30 kilometre radius around Chernobyl. The fires were extinguished. The affected unit was encased in concrete. The number of deaths increased. By 12 May, eight people had died and 35 remained in a critical condition. Altogether 31 people died as a direct consequence of the disaster.

The Soviet government was clear about the purpose of the misinformation campaign. When Mr Gromyko nominated Mr Gorbachev to be the General Secretary of the CPSU in March 1985, he said: "We live in a world in which figuratively speaking various telescopes are aimed at the Soviet Union. They watch, just waiting for some sort of crack to appear in the Soviet leadership"[35] Mr Boris Yeltsin, the Secretary of the Moscow Communist Party, was convinced that the Western media believed they had detected such a crack and were determined to expose it. He said "Our ideological opponents do not miss a single opportunity to launch yet one more campaign against the USSR. The bourgeois propaganda media are concocting many hoaxes around the accident". There was, however, an immediate practical reason for maligning the Soviet Union. The West was under pressure from the non-aligned states to respond to the Soviet proposal for a moratorium on nuclear tests. The principle argument against it was about the difficulty of verification, with the implicit underlying assumption that the Soviet Union would cheat if permitted to do so. The Chernobyl disaster was used to buttress this objection for it was argued that if the Soviet Union was so secretive about the details of a nuclear disaster which had international effects then how could the West have confidence in any agreement that it would allow on-site verification of arms control regulations. If, it was alleged, the Soviet Union is secretive about its nuclear power stations how much more cautious will it be with respect to military installations?

This use of the Chernobyl disaster was undermined for the West by two repercussions. The first was the boomerang effect. Each of the Western countries had nuclear power plants over which there was some public disquiet. The exaggerations of the Chernobyl disaster magnified the possibilities of disasters elsewhere. Though people in Western Europe were worried about nuclear fall-out after the Chernobyl explosion they become much more anxious about fall-out from their own disasters. The anti-nuclear power movement grew in the face of government opposition.

The second repercussion was the heightened consciousness about the dangers of nuclear war. The radioactive cloud drifted from Chernobyl across Austria, to Switzerland and Italy. It reached Britain by 3 May and was carried by south-easterly winds over much of England and Wales. Every country in mainland Europe had experienced higher than normal radiation levels by the time the cloud reached Britain. Wherever it went on its unpredictable course, the cloud caused anxiety, in some instances verging on panic. People searched for iodine tablets, they ceased buying fresh milk and fresh vegetables; travellers were checked for radiation. They inundated government departments for safety advice. It became clear that the uncontrollable character of nuclear fall-out, even on the relatively small scale of Chernobyl, had exposed the psychological inability of people in general to cope with it. The lesson was that a nuclear war, apart from its physically destructive powers, would generate such hysteria that there could be no organised response to it.

The people in Western Europe were thus receptive to the news from Reykjavic that a nuclear arms control agreement was possible. And they were dismayed when the meeting ended without an agreement. But it was only in this narrowest of senses that the meeting was a failure. It had three main positive aspects. First, nuclear disarmament was brought quickly and dramatically on to the world stage after years of seemingly mundane, endless negotiations between the USA and the USSR. Secondly, it clarified issues and positions which had been clouded and confused by propaganda. 1986, the International Year of Peace, indeed became the year of clarification about peace as a result of the Reykjavic meeting. Lastly the negotiations at Reykjavic highlighted changes in the Soviet approach both to world and domestic politics and significantly modified the Western image of the Soviet Union.

The process of clarification occured as the negotiations unfolded. Mr Gorbechev submitted a package of proposals to President Reagan which involved a 50 per cent reduction in Soviet and American strategic offensive weapons over the next five years to be followed by their complete elimination, the removal of all intermediate range missiles from Europe, a substantial reduction of those in Asia and a strict verification of the nuclear weapons elimination process. Thus a significant portion of the Soviet 15 January Peace Initiatives became the subject of negotiations within reach of agreement. The proposals which had been damned by silence suddenly became negotiable issues.

On the other hand the Strategic Defence Initiative which had been portrayed in the West as a defensive shield, a peaceful protection against a pre-emptive nuclear strike, was seen as an obstacle to peace. Mr Gorbachev made it quite clear that his proposals comprised a package. On this, he said in his televised speech to the Soviet people two days after the meeting had ended:

"the third question I raised during my first conversation with the President and that formed an integral part of the package of our proposals, was the existing anti-ballistic-missile (ABM) treaty and the nuclear test ban treaty. Our approach is as follows: since we are entering an entirely new situation, when a substantial reduction of nuclear weapons and their elimination in the foreseeable future will be started, it is necessary to protect oneself from any unexpected developments. We are speaking about weapons which to this day make up the core of this country's defences. Therefore it is necessary to exclude everything that could undermine equality in the process of disarmament, to preclude any possibility of developing weapons of the new type ensuring military superiority. We regard this stance as perfectly legitimate and logical. And since that is so, we firmly stated the need for the strict observance of the 1972 ABM treaty of unlimited duration. Moreover, in order to consolidate its regime, we proposed to the President adopting a mutual pledge by the US and the Soviet Union not to use the right to pull out of the treaty for at least ten years while abolishing strategic weapons within this period.

Taking into account the particular difficulties which the Administration created for itself on this problem, when the President personally committed himself to space weapons, to the so-called SDI, we did not demand the termination of work in this area. The implication was, however, that all provisions of the ABM treaty will be fully honoured – that is, research and testing in this sphere will not go beyond laboratories. This restriction applies equally to the US and the USSR."

The negotiations agreed on the elimination of all Cruise, Pershing Ia and SS20 missiles from Europe and on scaling down the number of SS20s in Asia. They could not agree, however, over the scope of the ABM treaty. Mr Gorbachev, supported by the American officials who drafted the treaty,[36] insisted that it did not permit the testing and deployment of space weapons. President Reagan took the opposite view. No agreement was signed. The general reaction in Britain was that President Reagan's support for the Strategic Defence Initiative prevented an historic step being taken to eliminate nuclear weapons. Thereafter, SDI was seen in a much more critical way than hitherto.

The Western media attention during the Reykjavic meeting was concentrated on the person of Mr Gorbachev. It protrayed the character of the Soviet Union through his personality. Mr Gorbachev's ability to use the media, his so-called Western style of public relations, his emphasis on technology and his concern about democracy had already been noted with approval in the West. He resembled, it was claimed, Western style political leaders and was contrasted with the dour, secretive, authoritarian and bureaucratic qualities attributed to his predecessors. In this way the media image of Soviet society in general underwent perceptible changes.

Mr Gorbachev made a sucession of concessions at the Reykjavic meeting in order to reach agreement. He accepted an earlier American 'zero option' proposal to eliminate all medium range missiles in Europe and set aside the demand that British and French missiles should be included in the agreement. He agreed to more stringent measures of verification and discussed a graduated approach to a comprehensive test ban treaty in preference to the Soviet demand for an immediate ban. There were contrasting interpretations of these compromises. The Western political leaders claimed that their possession of nuclear weapons had forced the Soviet Union into a negotiating position. With twisted logic they argued that it was necessary for the West to retain nuclear weapons in order to secure their elimination. The wider public had a different view of Mr Gorbachev's behaviour for by visibly struggling for an agreement he was seen to be proving the sincerity of the Soviet Union. This impression was reinforced by the concessions which were made to the US position after the Reykjavic meeting. The Soviet Union put aside its opposition to the Star Wars programme in a statement on 22 February 1987 in order to enable negotiations on an Intermediate Range Nuclear Weapons treaty to proceed and when, in the month of July, 1987, there was stalemate in the negotiations, the Soviet leader again intervened to expedite an agreement.

The package of proposals under consideration by the arms negotiators in Geneva included the retension of 100 missiles by the Soviet Union in Asia while the USA retained a similar number on its territory. There was some disagreement about the location of the missiles because the US wanted to put its own in Alaska, within striking distance of the Soviet Union, while the Soviet Union had no means of locating its missiles within striking distance of the USA. But this was not the sticking point. The Soviet missiles were mobile and the US negotiators, forever distrustful of the enemy, contended that this made the verification of an agreement difficult for they could be transferred between Europe and Asia as the Soviet authorities thought fit. This argument was used to justify retaining missiles in West Germany though in a covert way. West Germany possesses 72 Pershing 1a missiles with US nuclear warheads and with a range of 750 kilometres. It claimed them as its own and insisted that they should not be included in an agreement between the USA and the USSR. The Soviet Union protested on the grounds that the nuclear war-heads belonged to the USA and could not be transferred to West Germany under the Non-Proliferation Treaty of 1968. The Soviet leaders had no objection to the Pershing 1a missiles remaining in West Germany without their nuclear war-heads. This was the first sticking point. The second one was the attempt by the USA to avoid destroying its European missiles by relocating them to submarines. On both counts the West wanted an agreement without seriously weakening its nuclear capability. The Soviet Union could not accept that. But it did understand that the fears of the West might stem from the mobile character of the 100 missiles in Soviet Asia. Therefore, on 22 July 1987, Mr Gorbachev stated in an interview with an Indonesian newspaper that the Soviet Union would accept a "double-zero option" involving the destruction of the 100 missiles in Soviet Asia. It was hoped that it would also remove doubts about verification. This was a genuine concession because it was not tied to equivalent disarmament moves by the US in Korea, the Philippines and the

Indian Ocean base of Diego Garcia where it has a nuclear presence. Mr Gorbachev simply hoped that that presence would not grow.[37] The first sticking point was removed when in August the West German Chancellor, Helmut Kohl, stated that his government would destroy its Pershing 1a missiles once an agreement between the US and the Soviet Union had been reached. Then on 18 September, 1987, President Reagan announced that agreement had been reached in principle to eliminate all medium-range land-based nuclear missiles and to start fresh negotiations on nuclear testing. Thus the basis was laid for signing an Intermediate Nuclear Force Agreement late in 1987.

Mr Gorbachev proved the sincerity of the Soviet Union as he removed each of the obstacles put by the West in the way of a nuclear arms agreement. It was becoming patently clear that the Soviet Union had decided that nuclear weapons had no military significance and existed solely as a hazard to the world. Mr Gorbachev's patiently presented series of concessions indicated, moreover, the mood of the constituency he represented. The Soviet people who know the horrors of war more than most, want none of it. Those who have experienced war and those who have grown up in its memory exert the pressures for an arms settlement. They are not coerced into making concessions by the possession of nuclear weapons by Britain and the USA but by the nature of war itself. The Soviet people do not have an enemy except war as a real, frightening destructive phenomenon. This fact is now entering the consciousness of people in the West.

President Reagan's constituency, on the other hand, has raised doubts in the minds of many people in the West. Mr Gorbachev commented after the Reykjavic meeting that President Reagan did not seem to be fully in command. "I saw what happened," he said, "when he consulted with his officials . . . he is not free to take his own decisions". He was flanked by a trio of advisers, Mr Richard Perle, Mr Ken Adelman and General Rowny, who were hawks in his administration and who spoke for those opposed to an agreement. President Reagan's constituency contains millions of ordinary people who want peace but it is dominated by the arms manufacturers who profit from war. President Reagan's advisers represented the interests of the latter. They sighed with relief as the prospects of a settlement were set back and applauded as each obstacle was raised. This too has begun to enter the consciousness of people in the West.

The Soviet peace initiatives, the behaviour of Mr Gorbachev

and the democratising policies of the new Soviet government are profoundly influencing international relations. They are not simply altering the contours of the stereotype but are questioning its existence. An enemy has to be perceived as unreliable and devious otherwise it does not constitute a continuous threat. The Soviet Union is seen not to behave like that any more. It is going to be increasingly difficult to maintain the fiction that the Soviet Union is the enemy.

The new influences impose equally new tasks on Western Peace Movements. From 1979 till 1985 Peace Movements were able to set policy aims which were beyond the demands of all countries engaged in the arms race. At the same time they were able to rail at the Soviet Union for not taking unilateral action or initiating positive policies. The Peace Movements grew in that period. The Soviet peace proposals combined with the events of 1986 and 1987 should have acted as an added stimulus through clarifying the issues and widening the interest in disarmament but this has not happened. Instead, Western Peace Movements have declined in significance. Although the period is a critical one for nuclear disarmament there is, in 1987, little popular agitation in support of it. The reason lies in the dilemma the Soviet proposals have created for the Western Peace Movements.

In the first place the Soviet Union has taken the initiative from the Peace Movements in the struggle for disarmament. There is nothing they can say which is in advance of what the Soviet Union is prepared to do. Their most advanced policies are less than the Soviet proposals. The main aim of CND, namely the removal of Cruise missiles from Britain, and the primary goal of END and the Western European Peace Groups, namely a nuclear-free Europe are being fulfilled through the Soviet initiatives.

In the areas where the Western Peace Movements still have a relevance they have failed to make an impact. The British and French governments are determined to retain their nuclear weapons whether or not an agreement is reached between the Soviet Union and the USA. The various Peace Movements have made no impressions on this determination. CND has not been able to persuade the British government to cancel the Trident missiles even though there is apprehension within the ruling Conservative Party about their cost. Ironically it could be the failure of the British and French Peace Movements to tame the nuclear aspirations of their own governments which stands in the way of an effective agreement between the Soviet Union and the

USA. When Mr Gorbachev offered to exclude the British and French missiles from the negotiations he assumed that world opinion would force them into line. It is unlikely, however, that the Soviet people will accept an agreement in the long-run which removes Soviet missiles from Europe whilst permitting the British and the French to keep theirs.

The Western Peace Movements still then have vital and immediate tasks to perform even if the agreement at present being negotiated is signed. Those nuclear weapons transported by air and sea remain untouched. Many thousands of nuclear warheads of all manner of types, less powerful and more powerful than the Intermediate Range, must eventually be destroyed. No Western Peace Movements have yet aspired to tackle that problem. In order to do so they must agitate in support of the Soviet proposals of 15 January 1986 for there is as yet no preferable alternative policy. If they equivocate because they are afraid of being described as pro-Soviet or refuse because they in essence still see the Soviet Union as the enemy then they will be missing, maybe spoiling, an historic opportunity to achieve real universal nuclear disarmament.

FOOTNOTES

1. *A Short History of the British Working Class Movement 1789-1947* by G D H Cole, London, 1948, p. 352.
2. ibid, p. 353.
3. *Britain Between the Wars* by C L Mowat, London, 1955, p. 537.
4. See TUC Report, 1935, p. 175.
5. See *The Origins of the Cold War* by Martin McCauley, p. 60 and pp. 111-112; also *Russia is for Peace* by D N Pritt, 1951, Chapter VIII.
6. David Caute, op cit, p. 475.
7. ibid, p. 162.
8. *The Life of Bertrand Russell* by R W Clark, 1975, p. 525.
9. ibid, p. 524.
10. ibid, p. 529.
11. ibid, p. 536.
12. ibid, p. 523.
13. *Sage: A Life of J D Bernal* by Maurice Goldsmith, 1980, pp. 184-186.
14. *The Visible College* by Gary Werskey, London, 1978, p. 307.
15. *The Autobiography of Bertrand Russell 1944-67*, p. 98, 1969, London.
16. Clark, op cit, pp. 543-547.
17. Werskey, op cit, p. 308.
18. see *The Tamarisk Tree*, Vol. 3, 1985, by Dora Russell.
19. ibid, p. 219.
20. *The CND Story: the first 25 years of CND in the words of the people involved*, edited by John Minnion and Philip Bolsover, London, 1983.

21. See *Eleventh Hour for Europe*, papers by Ken Coates . . et al, edited by Ken Coates, Nottingham, 1981.
22. Stated by E P Thompson in *The CND Story*, op cit.
23. In its Yearbook. See *Not by Numbers Alone. Assessing the Military Balance* by Andrew Kelly, Peace Studies Paper, Bradford University, Number 11.
24. This point was emphasised by Jonathan Steele in *The Limits of Soviet Power*, 1985, p.39.
25. Space Weapons and US Strategy. Origins and Development, by Paul B Stares, p. 135.
26. *The New York Times*, 1 May 1986.
27. ibid.
28. *The Guardian*, 1 May, 1986.
29. ibid.
30. *Soviet Weekly*, 17 May, 1986, p. 4.
31. *The New York Times*, 1 May 1986.
32. ibid, 4 May 1986.
33. ibid, 1 May 1986.
34. *The Guardian*, 2 May 1986.
35. Quoted in *The New York Times*, 1 May 1986.
36. *The Guardian*, 14 October 1986.
37. As reported in, *The Guardian*, 23 July 1987.

Index of Names

Duncan, Cynthia, 195
Dzevensky, Grigoriy, 167

E

Eden, Anthony, 9, 210, 286
Einstein, Albert, 322
Eisenhower, President Ike, 37, 39, 41,
    215, 233, 234, 239-243, 244, 247,
    258, 259, 262, 263n, 319
Erickson, John, 27, 203n, 310n
Ezhov, N I, 77, 93, 94, 99, 119

F

Fainsod, Merle, 82, 83, 84, 123, 137n,
    139n
Feather, Vic, 306
Feis, Herbert, 217n, 218n
Ferraro, Geraldine, 226
Fieldhouse, Roger T, 42n
Fleming, D F, 261, 264n
Ford, Gerald, 105, 244, 246, 247, 263n,
    264n
Frank, André Gunder, 234, 235, 238n
Frankel, Jonathan, 180n
Friedgut, Theodore, 110, 113, 179n,
    180n
Friedman, Milton, 34

G

Galenskov, Yuri, 102
Gaventa, John, 195
Getty, J Arch, 84, 85, 94, 98, 99, 136n,
    138n, 139n
Gilbert, Martin, 179n
Gill, Ken, xx, 304
Gillman, Peter and Leni, 63n
Ginsburg, Alexander, 102
Ginsburg, G, 180n
Goldsmith, Maurice, 350n
Gorbachev, Mikhael, 52, 74, 126, 127,
    128, 132, 139n, 249, 251, 332, 339,
    344-346, 347, 348, 350
Green, William, 281, 291
Gromyko, Andrei, 151, 343

H

Halifax, Lord, 211
Hannington, Wal, 279
Harriman, Averill, 16, 80, 81
Harris, Jonathan, 139n

Hayek, F A von, 34, 42n, 52, 63n
Haynes, Viktor, 139n
Healey, Denis, 8
Heydrich, Reinhardt, 144
Hicks, George, 275
Hicks, Mike, 102
Hilberg, Raul, 144, 179n
Hillman, Sidney, 284, 289
Hitler, 4, 61, 65, 82, 280, 334
Hoffa, Jimmy, 292
Hoffmann, Stanley, 236-237
Hook, Sidney, 39
Horner, A, 288
Howe, Irving, 311n
Hutt, Allen, 310n

I

Iagoda, G G, 94, 99

J

Jacobs, Everett M, 180n
Jackson, Jesse, 223, 230
Jasny, N, 80, 81
Johnson, Hewlett, xvii
Johnson, Lyndon, 234, 235, 244, 246,
    247, 263n, 264n
Joliot-Curie, Frédéric, 320, 321, 322
Jones, Bill, 279

K

Kaganovitch, L M, 93, 121, 122, 152,
    157
Kahn, Albert A, 10n, 23n
Kaldor, Mary, 330
Kamenev, Lev, 76, 77, 92, 157
Kaplan, Dora, 67, 76
Kaser, Michael, 138n
Kautsky, Karl, xvii, 64, 270
Kelly, Andrew, 351n
Kennan, George F, 16, 17, 23n
Kennedy, John F, 37, 223, 234, 239,
    243, 244, 245, 246, 247, 248, 263n,
    264n
Kent, Bruce, 330
Keynes, John Maynard, 14, 23n
Khaustov, Victor, 102
Khrushchev, N, 93, 120, 121, 122, 123,
    124, 125, 129, 152, 322
Killian, James, 263
Kirov, S M, 76, 77, 88, 91, 92

Index of subjects

Fascism; 34, 62, 279, 291, 315
"Final Solution"; 146
First Five Year Plan; 76, 86, 90, 118, 129, 141, 183
Forced Labour and Economic Development: an enquiry into the experience of Soviet industrialization (Swianiewicz); 80
Forced Labour in Soviet Russia (Dallin and Nicolaevsky); 78
Forty-Five Years. International Federation of Trade Unions (Schevenels); 310n
Free Trade Union Association; 111, 112
Free Trade Union Institute; 298
French Revolution; 54
Friends Peace Committee; 323, 326
From Napoleon to Stalin (Carr); xviii

G

Gaelic; 189, 191
General Strike; 271, 275, 278, 279
German Democratic Republic; 305, 306
German invasion of Soviet Union; 82-83, 101, 116, 143, 148, 160, 198, 200, 209-210, 281, 336
German Social Democratic Party; 270
Glasnost; 126, 128, 129
"Great Purge"; 77
"Great Terror"; 77
Green Party; 109, 331
Guardian, The; xix, 9, 10n, 22n, 180n, 341, 342, 351n
Gulag Archipeligo (Solzhenitsyn); 79, 136n
Gulag, the; 78

H

Hadassa; 172
Harvard University; 236
Hebrew; 163
Hebrew Immigrant Aid Society; 166, 172, 173, 174
Helsinki Declaration; 105-107
Higher Trade Union School, Moscow; xii
Hiroshima; 317, 320
History of Anglo-Soviet Relations

(Coates); 10n, 23n, 310n
History of Soviet Russia (Carr); 42n
History of the USSR (Rothstein); 42n, 136n, 138n
Holocaust; American response to, 149-150; news of, 148, 150
How Russia is ruled (Fainsod); 83, 139n
How to Secure Peace in Europe (Roberts); 138n
Human rights; 102, 105, 107, 108, 135, 136, 140, 151, 164, 177, 181-202, 237; and imperialism, 196-202; definition of, 181
Human Rights in the Soviet Union (Szymanski); 23n, 27, 42n, 43n
Hungary; xix, 31, 301, 309, 322
Hydrogen Bomb; 318, 320, 321

I

I Search for Truth in Russia (Citrine); 310n
Images and Reality in the Soviet Union (Allen); xiii, xviii
Immigration Control Procedures: Report of a Formal Investigation (CRE); 63n
Imperialism; 196-202, 260; definition of, 196
In Russia Now (Citrine); 310n
Individual freedom; 75
Individualism; 53, 57
Intellectuals; as dissidents, 113, 114, 115, 134; in Russian society, 116-117; Western Jewish, 163
Inter-Church Peace Council (IKV); 331
Intermediate Nuclear Forces Treaty (INF); 347, 348
International communism; 11-12, 17-18, 56, 201, 280, 287, 295, 297
International Confederation of Free Trade Unions; 111, 112, 290, 299-300, 302, 304, 307, 309
International Federation of Audio-Visual Workers' Union (FISTAV); 307
International Federation of Trade Unions; 273, 274, 281, 290, 291, 302
International Labour Organization; 111, 304

362

International Longshoremen's and Warehousemen's Union; 293, 296

International Miners' Organization; 307-308

International Peace Co-ordination Centre; 331

International Rescue Committee; 166

International Socialist Congress, 1907; 313

International Trade Secretariats; 302, 307

International Union of Mine Mill and Smelting Workers; 293, 295, 296

International Workers of the World; 308

Irish Catholics; 102, 136

Is the Red Flag Flying? (Szymanski); 27, 42n

Islamic Peoples of the Soviet Union (Akiner); 62n, 203n

Israel; 103, 151, 159, 161, 162, 165, 166, 168, 169, 170, 172, 173, 176, 177

Israel and Palestine. Human Rights in Israel and in the Occupied Territories (END); 180n

Italy; 315

Izvestia; 133, 167

J

Japan; war against; 210, 213, 215, 285

Jewish Agency; 166, 168

Jewish Responses to Nazi Persecution (Trunk); 179n, 203n

Jewishness and anti-Semitism; 178

Jews; 100, 103, 104, 107 112, 135, 140-180; and Jewishness, 153; and the Bolshevik Revolution, 141-142; and US immigration quotas, 147-148; as Soviet partisans, 145; assimilation of, 142, 152-158; distribution in the Soviet Union, 153, 154; education of, 155-156; emigrants as pawns, 177; emigration from the USSR, 158-161, 162-163, 168-174; hypocrisy of the British towards immigration of, 146-148; in Czarist Russia, 140-141; in the Soviet Union during war, 143-146; mass killing of by Germans, 144-145, 220;

membership of Communist Party, 157; Non-Ashkenazi, 154, 169-170; population in the Soviet Union, 143, 153-154; "Refuseniks", 171; social mobility of, 155; Soviet safe areas for, 144; violence against, 142

Jolly George; 271

Journal of the Academic Proceedings of Soviet Jewry; 164

Journal of the Royal United Services Institute for Defence Studies; 23n

K

Kentucky Economy. Review and Perspective; 203n

KGB; 22, 74, 124

Khrushchev, The Years in Power (Medvedev); 139n

Khrushchev and the Soviet Leadership (Linden); 139n

Khrushchev (Medvedev); 139n

Krefeld Appeal; 331

L

Labour Code; 130, 183

Labour Government; 7-8; 15, 211, 286, 287, 321

Labour Monthly; 310n

Labour Movement; 28, 280, 315, 316

Labour Party; 111, 210, 270, 271, 276, 313, 315, 323, 328

Language; as symbol of power, 189-192; in Scotland, 189-191; in the Soviet Union, 190-192, 200; in Wales, 189-190

Latin America: Underdevelopment or Revolution (Frank); 238n

Law of Return (Israel); 162

Leadership; in the Soviet Union, 122-123

League of Liberals Against Aggression and Militarism; 312

League of Nations; 314, 315

Left Social Revolutionaries; 67, 70

Lenin Collected Works; 136n, 139n

Let History Judge (Medvedev); 82, 136n, 137n, 138n

Letter-writing; as criticism, 132-133

Lexington Herald-Leader; 264n

Liberal Party; 312

365

281; human rights in, 181-202; intimidation of Jewish intellectuals in, 152-153; languages in, 47, 190-192; living standards in, 184; misrepresentation of, xi, xii, xv-xvi, 16-17, 24, 40, 50, 51-52, 272, 273, 319, 338; problem with dissent, 115-116; relationship with US since 1945, 333-334; size of, 48-50; support for Israel, 151; takes peace initiative, 349-350; under siege, 70

T

United Nations; 181, 196, 285, 318

United Nations Declaration of Human Rights; 175

United States; and Jewish immigrants, 147-148; anti-communist role of, 244; Battle Act of 1951, 232; community politics in, 229-230; Congress House Committee on Un-American activities, 38; Constitution, 220, 231; expenditure on arms, 245, 248; Export Control Act, 231; immigrants to, 225; immigration laws, 59; intervention in Vietnam, 135; in the immediate post-Second World War, 214; Laws on Internal Security, 11-12; McCarron Act of 1950, 38, 58-59; nuclear posturing by, 215-217; political language of, 227-228; Presidential elections, 224; Presidents of, 219, 231, 232; registration of black and white voters, 223-224; relationship with USSR since 1945, 333-334; repression of academic dissent in, 37-41; Senate Internal Security Sub-Committee, 38; Senate Permanent Sub-Committee on Investigations, 38; Smith Act of 1940, 38; Trade Reform Act of 1972, 104

Universal Declaration of Human Rights, 1948; 181, 196

V

Vietnam War; 135, 225, 229, 234, 236, 243, 244, 245, 253, 257, 304

Voice of America; 164-165

Voice of Israel; 165

Vyzov; 166, 168, 169, 170, 171, 172

W

Wage Labour and Capital (Marx); 42n

Wansee Conference; 146

War casualties; 6, 7, 314

War of Intervention; 4, 5, 15, 67, 114, 182

Wars; 3, 6; and capitalism, 316-317; mobilization for, 254-258; nuclear, 25, 152, 232, 235, 248, 257, 317; peace activity during, 312-314

Washington Post; 264n

Week of the Broken Glass; 220

Welsh; 189-190

Welsh Language Society; 190

We Shall Be All: A History of the Industrial Workers of the World (Dubofsky); 23n

West Germany; 347, 348

Western democracies; 56, 57, 58, 59, 60, 61, 62, 67, 213

White Russian Terror; 71, 142

Women in Soviet Society (Lapidus); 202n

Women; involvement in trade unions, 186; position in Soviet Union, 184-186

Working class; 65, 66, 67, 72, 73, 74, 75, 116, 213, 228, 313

World Congress of Intellectuals, 1948; 321

World Federation of Scientific Workers; 321

World Federation of Trade Unions; 274, 293, 294, 300, 301, 302, 304, 306; demise of, 289-290, 299-301; formation of, 284-285

World Jewish Congress; 166

World Military Expenditure and Arms Transfer (US); 263n

World Peace Council; 321, 331

X Y Z

Yalta Agreement; 200

Yalta Conference; 209, 285

Yiddish; 143, 152, 153, 158

Yom Kippur War; 151, 172, 244, 246

Young Communist League; 131

"Zinoviev" letter; 15

Zionism; 100, 142-143, 151, 152, 161-163, 178; attacked by USSR, 167-168, 176; propaganda of, 164-165